Lecture Notes in Computer Science 12777

More information about this subseries at http://www.springer.com/series/7409

Vincent G. Duffy (Ed.)

Digital Human Modeling and Applications in Health, Safety, Ergonomics and Risk Management

Human Body, Motion and Behavior

12th International Conference, DHM 2021
Held as Part of the 23rd HCI International Conference, HCII 2021
Virtual Event, July 24–29, 2021
Proceedings, Part I

 Springer

Editor
Vincent G. Duffy
Purdue University
West Lafayette, IN, USA

ISSN 0302-9743   ISSN 1611-3349 (electronic)
Lecture Notes in Computer Science
ISBN 978-3-030-77816-3   ISBN 978-3-030-77817-0 (eBook)
https://doi.org/10.1007/978-3-030-77817-0

LNCS Sublibrary: SL3 – Information Systems and Applications, incl. Internet/Web, and HCI

This Springer imprint is published by the registered company Springer Nature Switzerland AG
The registered company address is: Gewerbestrasse 11, 6330 Cham, Switzerland

Foreword

Human-Computer Interaction (HCI) is acquiring an ever-increasing scientific and industrial importance, and having more impact on people's everyday life, as an ever-growing number of human activities are progressively moving from the physical to the digital world. This process, which has been ongoing for some time now, has been dramatically accelerated by the COVID-19 pandemic. The HCI International (HCII) conference series, held yearly, aims to respond to the compelling need to advance the exchange of knowledge and research and development efforts on the human aspects of design and use of computing systems.

The 23rd International Conference on Human-Computer Interaction, HCI International 2021 (HCII 2021), was planned to be held at the Washington Hilton Hotel, Washington DC, USA, during July 24–29, 2021. Due to the COVID-19 pandemic and with everyone's health and safety in mind, HCII 2021 was organized and run as a virtual conference. It incorporated the 21 thematic areas and affiliated conferences listed on the following page.

A total of 5222 individuals from academia, research institutes, industry, and governmental agencies from 81 countries submitted contributions, and 1276 papers and 241 posters were included in the proceedings to appear just before the start of the conference. The contributions thoroughly cover the entire field of HCI, addressing major advances in knowledge and effective use of computers in a variety of application areas. These papers provide academics, researchers, engineers, scientists, practitioners, and students with state-of-the-art information on the most recent advances in HCI. The volumes constituting the set of proceedings to appear before the start of the conference are listed in the following pages.

The HCI International (HCII) conference also offers the option of 'Late Breaking Work' which applies both for papers and posters, and the corresponding volume(s) of the proceedings will appear after the conference. Full papers will be included in the 'HCII 2021 - Late Breaking Papers' volumes of the proceedings to be published in the Springer LNCS series, while 'Poster Extended Abstracts' will be included as short research papers in the 'HCII 2021 - Late Breaking Posters' volumes to be published in the Springer CCIS series.

The present volume contains papers submitted and presented in the context of the 12th International Conference on Digital Human Modeling and Applications in Health, Safety, Ergonomics and Risk Management (DHM 2021), an affiliated conference to HCII 2021. I would like to thank the Chair, Vincent G. Duffy, for his invaluable contribution to its organization and the preparation of the proceedings, as well as the members of the Program Board for their contributions and support. This year, the DHM affiliated conference has focused on topics related to ergonomics, human factors and occupational health, human body and motion modeling, language, communication and behavior modeling, healthcare applications, and digital human models in product and service design, as well as AI applications.

I would also like to thank the Program Board Chairs and the members of the Program Boards of all thematic areas and affiliated conferences for their contribution towards the highest scientific quality and overall success of the HCI International 2021 conference.

This conference would not have been possible without the continuous and unwavering support and advice of Gavriel Salvendy, founder, General Chair Emeritus, and Scientific Advisor. For his outstanding efforts, I would like to express my appreciation to Abbas Moallem, Communications Chair and Editor of HCI International News.

July 2021   Constantine Stephanidis

HCI International 2021 Thematic Areas and Affiliated Conferences

Thematic Areas

- HCI: Human-Computer Interaction
- HIMI: Human Interface and the Management of Information

Affiliated Conferences

- EPCE: 18th International Conference on Engineering Psychology and Cognitive Ergonomics
- UAHCI: 15th International Conference on Universal Access in Human-Computer Interaction
- VAMR: 13th International Conference on Virtual, Augmented and Mixed Reality
- CCD: 13th International Conference on Cross-Cultural Design
- SCSM: 13th International Conference on Social Computing and Social Media
- AC: 15th International Conference on Augmented Cognition
- DHM: 12th International Conference on Digital Human Modeling and Applications in Health, Safety, Ergonomics and Risk Management
- DUXU: 10th International Conference on Design, User Experience, and Usability
- DAPI: 9th International Conference on Distributed, Ambient and Pervasive Interactions
- HCIBGO: 8th International Conference on HCI in Business, Government and Organizations
- LCT: 8th International Conference on Learning and Collaboration Technologies
- ITAP: 7th International Conference on Human Aspects of IT for the Aged Population
- HCI-CPT: 3rd International Conference on HCI for Cybersecurity, Privacy and Trust
- HCI-Games: 3rd International Conference on HCI in Games
- MobiTAS: 3rd International Conference on HCI in Mobility, Transport and Automotive Systems
- AIS: 3rd International Conference on Adaptive Instructional Systems
- C&C: 9th International Conference on Culture and Computing
- MOBILE: 2nd International Conference on Design, Operation and Evaluation of Mobile Communications
- AI-HCI: 2nd International Conference on Artificial Intelligence in HCI

List of Conference Proceedings Volumes Appearing Before the Conference

http://2021.hci.international/proceedings

12th International Conference on Digital Human Modeling and Applications in Health, Safety, Ergonomics and Risk Management (DHM 2021)

Program Board Chair: **Vincent G. Duffy,** *Purdue University, USA*

- Giuseppe Andreoni, Italy
- Mária Babicsné Horváth, Hungary
- Stephen Baek, USA
- Joan Cahill, Ireland
- André Calero Valdez, Germany
- Yaqin Cao, China
- Damien Chablat, France
- H. Onan Demirel, USA
- Martin Fleischer, Germany
- Martin Fränzle, Germany
- Fu Guo, China
- Afzal Godil, USA
- Akihiko Goto, Japan
- Michael Harry, UK
- Sogand Hasanzadeh, USA
- Dan Högberg, Sweden
- Csilla Herendy, Hungary
- Mingcai Hu, China
- Genett Jimenez, Colombia
- Mohamed Fateh Karoui, USA
- Sashidharan Komandur, Norway
- Sebastian Korfmacher, Germany
- Theoni Koukoulaki, Greece
- Noriaki Kuwahara, Japan
- Byung Cheol Lee, USA
- Yi Lu, China
- Alexander Mehler, Germany
- Peter Nickel, Germany
- Thaneswer Patel, India
- Giovanni Pignoni, Norway
- Manikam Pillay, Australia
- Qing-Xing Qu, China
- Fabián R. Narváez, Ecuador
- Caterina Rizzi, Italy
- Joni Salminen, Qatar
- Juan A. Sánchez-Margallo, Spain
- Sebastian Schlund, Austria
- Deep Seth, India
- Meng-Dar Shieh, Taiwan
- Beatriz Sousa Santos, Portugal
- Leonor Teixeira, Portugal
- Renran Tian, USA
- Alexander Trende, Germany
- Dustin Van der Haar, South Africa
- Dakuo Wang, USA
- Anita Woll, Norway
- Kuan Yew Wong, Malaysia
- Shuping Xiong, South Korea
- James Yang, USA

The full list with the Program Board Chairs and the members of the Program Boards of all thematic areas and affiliated conferences is available online at:

http://www.hci.international/board-members-2021.php

HCI International 2022

The 24th International Conference on Human-Computer Interaction, HCI International 2022, will be held jointly with the affiliated conferences at the Gothia Towers Hotel and Swedish Exhibition & Congress Centre, Gothenburg, Sweden, June 26 – July 1, 2022. It will cover a broad spectrum of themes related to Human-Computer Interaction, including theoretical issues, methods, tools, processes, and case studies in HCI design, as well as novel interaction techniques, interfaces, and applications. The proceedings will be published by Springer. More information will be available on the conference website: http://2022.hci.international/:

General Chair
Prof. Constantine Stephanidis
University of Crete and ICS-FORTH
Heraklion, Crete, Greece
Email: general_chair@hcii2022.org

http://2022.hci.international/

Contents – Part I

Language, Communication and Behavior Modeling

Contents – Part II

Rethinking Healthcare

Digital Human Modeling in Product and Service Design

Ergonomics, Human Factors and Occupational Health

Addressing Human Factors and Ethics in the Design of 'Future Work' and Intelligent Systems for Use in Financial Services - Person Centered Operations, Intelligent Work & the Triple Bottom Line

Joan Cahill[1]([✉]) [iD], Vivienne Howard[1], Yufei Huang[2], Junchi Ye[1,2,3], Stephen Ralph[3], and Aidan Dillon[3]

[1] School of Psychology, Trinity College Dublin, Dublin, Ireland
cahilljo@tcd.ie
[2] Trinity School of Business, Trinity College Dublin, Dublin, Ireland
[3] Zarion Ltd., Dublin, Ireland

Abstract. New technologies are being introduced to support the future of work in Financial Services. Such technologies should enable work that is smart, healthy, and ethical. This paper presents an innovative and blended methodology for supporting the specification of these future 'intelligent work' technologies from a human factors and ethics perspective. The methodology involves the participation of a community of practice and combines traditional stakeholder evaluation methods (i.e., interviews, workshops), with participatory foresight activities, participatory co-design, and data assessment.

Keywords: Human factors · Ethics · Emerging methods · The future of work · Intelligent work · Healthy work · Triple bottom line · Operations management

1 Introduction

Work represents for an enterprise a significant cost in resource. Operational efficiencies are critical to the business model and a fundamental key performance indicator (KPI) for all stakeholders. However, as stated by Elkington (2019), in the 'Triple bottom line' accounting framework, human activity should not compromise the long-term balance between the economic, environmental, and social pillars [1]. Further, as defined by the tripartite labor collaboration work (and work activity) should be designed to benefit all stakeholders – including employers, employees, and society [2].

Financial institutions are utilizing new technologies (including machine learning and artificial intelligence) which enables them to manage their business processes, their workforce, and customer relationships. The technologies can be classified into four overall types – Robotic Process Automation (RPA) technologies, Business process management (BPM) technologies, Digital Process Automation (DPA) technologies and Dynamic case

© Springer Nature Switzerland AG 2021
V. G. Duffy (Ed.): HCII 2021, LNCS 12777, pp. 3–13, 2021.
https://doi.org/10.1007/978-3-030-77817-0_1

management (DCM) technologies. Overall, the focus is on streamlining business processes, optimizing resources, and enhancing productivity and efficiency. Although the benefits in relation to productivity/efficiency have been demonstrated, the adoption of these new technologies has been slow. In many cases, the barriers to adoption are not well researched/understood. Further, these technologies have not been considered from the perspective of the human role in the workplace and worker wellbeing. Workers have concerns about how these technologies will transform their job (including how work is assigned and assessed) and the experience of work (i.e., location of work, social interaction, workload, monitoring). The COVID 19 Pandemic and largescale transition to remote work/operations, has underscored the human and ethical issues surrounding work and workforce surveillance, issues pertaining to social isolation, and the impact on team interactions (including activities such as mentoring and formal and informal teamwork).

The 'Intelligent Work' project investigates how automation, artificial intelligence technologies and workers can work together in a more efficient, intelligent, and humane way – to improve worker wellbeing along with the company's long-term revenue. This research is part of an academic and industry collaboration between researchers at Trinity College Dublin Ireland and Zarion Ltd. The research is funded by Enterprise Ireland (Irish government agency), as part of the Innovation Partnership Program (IPP).

This paper reports on the innovative methodology used in this project to support the specification 'intelligent work' and allied technologies from a human factors and ethics perspective. First, a background to relevant concepts and methodologies is provided. The methodological approach is then introduced. A short overview of the emerging intelligent work concept is presented. The methodology is then discussed, and some conclusions drawn.

2 Background

2.1 Operations Management, Healthy Work & Workplace Wellbeing

Operational management refers to the ways in which a business manages the resources responsible for delivering work. Typically, operations management focuses on the business processes and technologies required to achieve the economic goals for the company. Often the 'human factor' and the relationship between worker wellbeing and system design is not considered. The business case for investing in worker wellbeing is well documented [3]. Poor worker wellbeing has a cost implication. For example, costs associated with reduced productivity/delays, reduced worker motivation and poor-quality work, staff retention, sick leave, errors, and poor customer service/customer retention.

New human centered business practices/operations practices are now being introduced. Such practices focus on fostering and maintaining a healthy workforce. Underpinning these approaches is the recognition that work is part of our wellbeing and a key driver of health. To this end, new work management systems and technologies are addressing how work is managed, the experience of work and the management of the home/work interface. This is particularly evidenced in healthcare and aviation [4].

Workers are not immune from common mental health problems such as anxiety and depression. At any given time, up to 18 per cent of the working age population has a mental health problem [5]. The level of control that an individual has over their work is a key factor for psychological health. As proposed in the 'Job Design Model' (JCM) job features such as skill variety, task identity, task significance, feedback, and task autonomy are enriching and thereby motivating, characteristics of work [6].

The World Health Organisation (WHO) proposes a model of the healthy workplace in which both physical and psychosocial risks are managed [7]. Stress Management Initiatives' (SMI) and 'Workplace Wellbeing Programs' (WWP) address workplace stress and overall health and wellbeing in the workplace [8]. Some wellness programs deploy corporate wellness self-tracking technologies (CWST) [9]. Workers are invited to measure and manage their own health, to improve their wellbeing, while also enhancing productivity, engagement, and performance. This approach is not uncontroversial. Some argue that CWST conflates work and health [10] and has the potential to increase worker anxiety levels [11].

2.2 Stakeholder Evaluation & Human Factors Methods

As defined in ISO 6385 [12], the discipline of human factors (HF) refers to 'the practice of designing products, systems, or processes to take proper account of the interaction between them and the people who use them' (2016). Human factors approach follows a 'socio-technical systems design' perspective. Central to this is the recognition of the interaction between people/behavior, technology/tools, work processes, workplace environments and work culture [13]. 'Stakeholder evaluation' is the gold standard for human factors action research pertaining to new technology development. The objective is to elicit the perspectives of those who have a "stake" in implementation/change. Stakeholder evaluation methods seek to involve the participation of both internal and external stakeholders. Internal stakeholders (IS) include the project team. This composition of the internal team can vary but typically includes product owners/managers, designers, software developers and business analysts. In some cases, it can also include human factors researchers and ethicists. External stakeholders (ES) refer to those stakeholders who either who are users of the technology either directly or indirectly (i.e., financial services employees working in team members, team supervisor, operations management and leadership roles, and customers of the financial services company) and those who procure the technology (i.e., financial services company). As outlined by Cousins (2013) and Wenger (1999) [14, 15], the 'Community of Practice' is the shared space in which both IS and ES come together to ideate, define, develop and evaluation the proposed solution. Human Factors action research methods are commonly used to support this process. Typically, this involves the use of Ethnographic approaches [16] such as user interviews and stakeholder workshops. Both personae-based design [17] and scenario-based design [18] methodologies are also used. The concept of 'stakeholder participation' is a critical feature of stakeholder evaluation research. As defined by Bødker (1995), design happens 'with' stakeholders, and not simply 'for' stakeholders [19]. Participatory activities can include roleplay, stakeholder ideation workshops and participatory co-design and evaluation [19].

2.3 Ethics & New Technology Development

New technologies have the potential to deliver benefits. However, such technologies are inherently uncertain. As part of new product development, researchers must consider and evaluate the human and ethical implications of things which may not yet exist and/or things have potential impacts which may be hard to predict [20]. Reijers et al. (2017) provide an overview of the different formats in which ethics analysis in technology development take many forms [21]. Brey (2017) classifies five sets of ethical impact assessment approaches. This includes generic approaches, anticipatory/foresight approaches, risk assessment approaches, experimental approaches, and participatory/deliberative ethics approaches [22]. Some researchers have combined different approaches. Cotton (2014) combines participatory/deliberative ethics approaches and stakeholder approaches [23]. Cahill (2020) argues that human factors and ethical issues must be explored in an integrated way [24]. The 'Human Factors & Ethics Canvas' introduced by Cahill combines ethics and HF methods, particularly around the collection of evidence using stakeholder evaluation methods [24].

3 Research Project & Methodology

3.1 Introduction

As indicated in Fig. 1 below, the collection of evidence follows from a socio-technical framework – involving eliciting and analyzing data about the relationships between certain structuring elements of the 'socio-technical system'. Key elements include the work itself (both transactional work and knowledge work), the individuals/people and teams performing the work, the organization, and the customer. So conceived, future automation and AI/ML intelligence will change these relationships, leading to different outcomes at an economic, ecological, and societal level (i.e., triple bottom line). Critically, this automation/technology has meaning in the context of organization specific business process and associated task workflows, organizational culture, the working environment, and regulation.

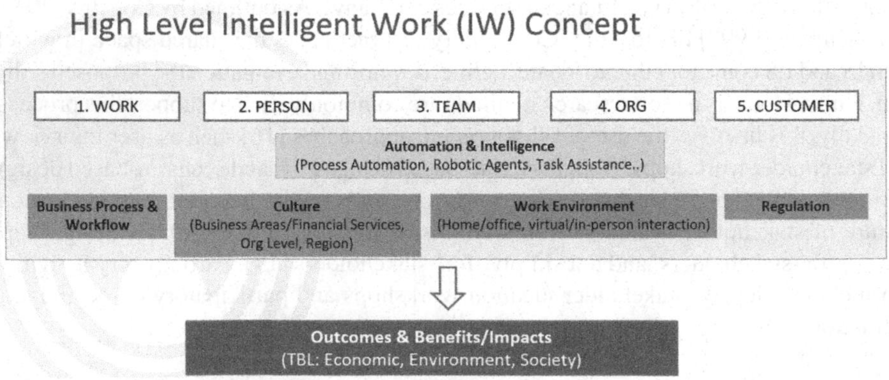

Fig. 1. Socio-technical picture

The human factors approach adopted involves building an evidence map [25] in relation to requirements for the proposed technologies, the human factors and ethical issues pertaining to the introduction of these technologies, and the business case for these technologies. In relation to the business case, this involved investigating outcomes at an (1) organizational level (i.e., profit, productivity, employee retention), a (2) work/business process level (i.e., productivity and teamwork), (3) a worker level (i.e., job satisfaction, job engagement, wellbeing in work, trust, workload, burnout etc.) and (4) a customer level (i.e., customer satisfaction, perception of brand and customer retention).

The specific methodology combined traditional human factors action research methods (i.e., interviews, workshops), with participatory foresight activities, participatory co-design and evaluation activities, and data assessment. Table 1 below provides an overview of the different human factors action research and business analysis methods used.

Table 1. Overview of research methods used

#	Method	Details
1	Interviews	Product team interviews/IS (N = 2) Interviews with Zarion staff/IS (N = 6) Interview with ends users/ES (N = 3)
2	Workshops	Product demonstration and review workshop (workshop 1/IS, N = 4) Modelling the proposed IW concept workshop (workshop 2/IS, N = 7) Evaluating the proposed IW concept workshop (workshop 3/IS, N = 7) Using data workshop (workshop 4/IS, N = 10) Business case workshop (workshop 5/IS (N = 10) Implementation, ethics & acceptability workshop (workshop 6/IS, N = 10) Final specification & implementation workshop (workshop 7/IS, N = 10)
3	Survey	Survey with end users (N = 50)
4	Data analysis	Data analysis (deidentified data)
5	Combined interview/codesign & evaluation	Co-design/evaluation/ES (N = 15)

Overall, eight phases of research involving the participation of both internal stakeholders (IS) and external stakeholders (ES) was undertaken. The details of these are as defined in Table 2 below. As the research progressed, the findings of each phase were triangulated, to further develop and validate the evidence map. The study was conducted in accordance with the Declaration of Helsinki, and the protocol was approved by the Ethics Committee of the School of Psychology, Trinity College Dublin. All field research conducted online in accordance with COVID 19 health and safety guidelines – as defined by the Health & Safety Authority, Ireland), and the definition of safe data collection, as defined by the School of Psychology, Trinity College Dublin.

Table 2. Overview of research stages, methods & outputs

#	Stage	Methods & participants	Output
1	Existing product review	Product team interviews/IS (N = 2) Product demonstration and review workshop (workshop 1/IS, N = 4):	Product description and model
2	Preliminary human factors and ethics assessment	HFEC Evaluation/IS (N = 2) Personae & scenarios specification/IS (N = 2)	Product review Personae and scenarios
3	New product ideation	N/A	Preliminary IW concept specification Definition of states
4	Mapping the problem space & further specification/validation of Concept & Requirements	Interviews/IS (N = 6) Interview/ES(N = 3) Modelling the proposed IW concept workshop (workshop 2/IS, N = 7) Survey/ES (N = 50)	Field research findings/evidence map Preliminary IW concept specification
5	Prototype Development & Interviews/codesign	Evaluating the proposed IW concept workshop (workshop 3/IS, N = 7) Interviews & codesign with external stakeholders (N = 15)	Prototype development 1
6	Operations management – data analysis	Analysis of anonymous data set	Requirements Analysis
7	Implementation & business analysis. final ethics assessment	Using data workshop (workshop 4/IS, N = 10) Business case workshop (workshop 5/IS (N = 10) Implementation, ethics & acceptability workshop (workshop 6/IS, N = 10)	Requirements Analysis Implementation plan Final human factors and ethics canvas
8	Final design & specification	Final specification & Implementation workshop (workshop 7/IS, N = 10)	Final prototype Final specification of requirement

4 Overview of Emerging Concept

The vision is to advance technology which functions as a 'balance score card' [25] linked to the 'Triple Bottom Line' [1]. The focus is on enabling/augmenting people as opposed to health monitoring. Corporate wellness approaches such as the provision of healthy food and free/subsidized access to wellness activities (i.e., yoga, mindfulness, exercise, and stress management classes) are not enough. Healthy work concepts need to be embedded in how work is planned/allocated, carried out, monitored, and evaluated/assessed. As such, healthy work underpins intelligent work. The proposed technology will enable 'intelligent work' through the application of AI/ML, which enables healthy work allocation and monitoring – balancing different perspectives and needs – the work, the person, the team, the customer, and business value. Intelligent assistants function as supportive team members – augmenting and transforming all roles, including team members, team supervisors, operations managers, and the customer. Critically, the system supports 'coaching' of team members and worker self-regulation and self-management of work.

5 Discussion: Emerging Methods & Innovation

The methodologies adopted in this project emerged out of the diverse and multidisciplinary skillset of the 'internal team'/IS. The IS comprised two organizational groups – (1) a product development team from a software development company advancing future work technologies (Zarion Ltd.), and (2) a multi-disciplinary research team from Trinity College Dublin – comprising human factors, health psychology and ethics researchers from Trinity School of Psychology, and operations management and data scientists from Trinity School of Business. As such, the composition of the IS enabled a blending of different methodological approaches and allied technology ideation, development, and evaluation methodologies to the identification of user requirements for the proposed intelligent work system.

The research methodology blends several established and innovative human factors and ethics design and assessment methods. The emerging evidence map reflected the iterative set of requirements which emerged from these different activities.

In terms of established methods, several qualitative human machine interaction (HMI) design methods were combined to supports needs analysis and requirements specification. This includes 'personae-based design', 'scenario-based design' and 'participatory design'. Survey methods were also used to elicit requirements. The survey analysis provided a complementary picture to the interview and co-design/evaluation activities.

In terms of more innovative methods – this includes the integration and application of the 'Human Factors & Ethics Canvas' (HFEC) [24], into the high-level methodology. Each of the seven stages of the HFEC was populated, with the emerging evidence picture. In relation to stage 3 (personae and scenarios), each personae and scenario was defined in relation to specific IW states. This included states to be achieved (i.e., wellness, flow, engagement), states to be managed/mitigated (i.e., stress, overwork, poor teamwork) and states to be avoided (i.e., burnout, poor interaction with team or customer, errors, and objectification of worker/over monitoring). Personae and scenarios were defined for both workers and customers. In addition, states were defined in relation to the process, the organizational culture, and the business/organization (i.e., profit, customer retention, growth etc.). This enabled an integration of both human factors and business objectives, linking to the underpinning value/benefits assessment approach (i.e., triple bottom line). This was further progressed in Stage 4 of the HFEC - the assessment of benefits, outcomes, and impact. This focus on stakeholders and assessing needs/benefits is central to participatory foresight activities.

In addition, the data points associated with evaluating states at different levels (actors, process, organization etc.) were defined. This enabled a bridge between human factors/ethics research, and the advancement of the product technical architecture. Further, it set a high-level remit for the role of this future IW system in terms of collecting and evaluating data and allied automation, artificial intelligence and machine learning functions.

A further innovation was the identification of future system requirements based on an analysis of operations management data at an insurance company. The anonymous data set (total of 117,452 records) was interrogated to understand and identify strategies for better work allocation and management and associated requirements for 'intelligent work' system. The data set pertained to operational performance at an insurance company over a fixed time-period. The data was analyzed at three levels – (1) activity/claims level, (2) individual level, and (3) team level. In relation to (1), this resulted in insight pertaining to the relationship between activity complexity and claims productivity (no of claims processed) with specific insights pertaining to the relationship between activity complexity and individual and team workloads. In relation to (2) this resulted in insights in relation to activity complexity and individual productivity, with specific insights in relation to the relationship between activity complexity and workload, work diversity, and teamwork rate. Lastly, in relation to (3), this resulted in insights pertaining to the relationship between individual productivity and team productivity, with specific insights pertaining to the relationship between productivity and individual/team location, team size, days worked and work diversity.

A key strand of this research activity involved understanding the motivations, enablers, and barriers to implementation. This links to the sixth stage in the Human Factors & Ethics Canvas (Cahill, 2020). Issues pertaining to implementation were addressed during interviews with E/S, co-design/evaluation sessions with E/S and implementation workshops with I/S. As part of this, storytelling and narrative techniques were used to capture the future 'story' and/or 'implementation' of the technology. The future 'implementation story' had a high-level tagline, a plot, a context/setting, key characters, and an ending. Participants were invited to consider two taglines and associated plots, which reflected a summary of the research findings. These were: (1) "Move from task to people centric", and (2) "The organization gets the right balance, the customer get the right balance and the people get the right balance". Storytelling was considered an accessible and user-friendly approach to product ideation, requirements specification and requirements evaluation. Overall, this storytelling approach enabled a synthesis and integration of different types of requirements (i.e., need, acceptability, ethics, software role, busines value and implementation), from different perspectives (i.e., human factors, ethics, operations management, and business case/benefits).

Some limitations should be noted. Observational research at financial services companies was planned, but not possible during the COVID 19 pandemic. Such research might have substantiated some of the issues around work practices, use of technology and work culture which arose in user interviews. Although three phases of combined interviews and co-design/evaluations were undertaken, the numbers in each phase were small (N = 5 in each phase, total number: N = 15). Further a small number of participant's completed the survey (N = 50). The operations management dataset reflected work activity that was managed without formal work allocation/process management software. Further research might involve the analysis of operations management activity where a basic and/or intelligent work allocation software platform is used.

Further research is planned. This research has resulted in a proof of concept for the future work system. To date, research is mostly conceptual. The next phases of research will involve simulation of a small set-of scenarios with accompanying intelligent work software, to demonstrate and evaluate the human factors and business benefits of embedding healthy, smart, and ethical work concepts in new 'intelligent work' technologies.

6 Conclusion

New intelligent work technologies should support enable work that is smart, healthy, and ethical. This involves moving beyond simply process automation and robotic team members. Technologies should augment all human actors, promote teamwork behaviors, and ensure that human actors can self-manage and monitor their own performance. In so doing future 'intelligent work' systems should deploy artificial intelligence (AI) and Machine Learning (ML) technologies in a human centered and ethical manner.

Disorganized, fragmented, imbalanced, and unfair workloads can impact on worker productivity, engagement, and 'the flow state'. Technology may not be the barrier here - when there is insufficient information and poor teamwork, productivity significantly decreases.

The methodologies used in this project enable the active translation of human factors and ethical principles along with stakeholder needs, into the product concept and design execution. Personae/scenarios are useful in relation to considering and documenting the needs/perspectives of different stakeholders and adjudicating between conflicting human factors and ethical goals/principles. Co-design methods are useful for product ideation and eliciting feedback about ethical issues along with implementation barriers. The use of a 'Community of Practice' has proven very beneficial. It is critical to engage both internal and external stakeholders in the human factors and ethics specification and validation of the proposed technologies, and analysis of implementation requirements, barriers, and enablers.

References

1. John, E.: Cannibals with Forks: The Triple Bottom Line of 21st Century Business. Capstone, Oxford (1999). ISBN: 9780865713925. OCLC 963459936

2. Sengenberger, W.: The International Labour Organization: Goals, Functions and Political Impact, Friedrich Ebert Stiftung, Berlin (2013)
3. Bevan, S.: The business case for employee health and wellbeing: a report prepared for investors in people UK (2010). http://workfoundation.org/assets/docs/publications/245_iip270410.pdf
4. Cahill, J., Cullen, P., Anwer, S., Gaynor, K., Wilson, S.: The requirements for new tools for use by pilots and the aviation industry to manage risks pertaining to work-related stress (WRS) and wellbeing, and the ensuing impact on performance and safety. Technologies **8**, 40 (2020). https://www.mdpi.com/2227-7080/8/3/40. https://doi.org/10.3390/technologies8030040
5. National Institute for Health & Care Excellence (NICE, 2011). Mental Wellbeing at Work. https://www.nice.org.uk/guidance/ph22
6. Hackman, J.R., Oldham, G.R.: Motivation through the design of work: test of a theory. Organ. Behav. Hum. Perform. **16**(2), 250–279 (1976)
7. The World Health Organisation (WHO): Healthy workplace model. https://www.who.int/occ upational_health/healthy_workplace_framework.pdf
8. Lois, T., Carolyn, W.: Workplace stress management interventions and health promotion. Ann. Rev. Organ. Psychol. Organ. Behav. **2**(1), 583–603 (2015). https://doi.org/10.1146/ann urev-orgpsych-032414-111341
9. Till, C., Petersen, A., Tanner, C., Munsie, M.: Creating "automatic subjects": corporate wellness and self-tracking. Health Interdis. J. Soc. Stud. Health Illness Med. **23**(4), 418 (2019)
10. Hull, G., Pasquale, F.: Toward a critical theory of corporate wellness. BioSocieties **13**(1), 190–212 (2018)
11. Moore, P., Robinson, A.: The quantified self: what counts in the neoliberal workplace. New Media Soc. **18**(11), 2774–2792 (2016)
12. International Standards Organisation (ISO): Standard 6385 (2020). https://www.iso.org/sta ndard/63785.html
13. Baxter, G., Sommerville, I.: Socio-technical systems: from design methods to systems engineering. Interact. Comput. **23**(1), 4–17 (2011). https://doi.org/10.1016/j.intcom.2010. 07.003
14. Cousins, J.B., Whitmore, E., Shulha, L.: Arguments for a common set of principles for collaborative inquiry in evaluation. Am. J. Eval. **34**, 7–22 (2013)
15. Wenger, E.: Communities of Practice: Learning, Meaning, and Identity. Cambridge University Press, Cambridge (1998)
16. Hammersley, M., Atkinson, P.: Ethnography: Principles in Practice, 3rd edn. Routledge, London (2007)
17. Pruitt, J., Grudin, J.: Personas: practice and theory. In: Proceedings of the 2003 Conference on Designing for User Experiences (DUX 2003), pp. 1–15. ACM, New York, NY, USA (2003). https://doi.org/10.1145/997078.997089
18. Carroll, J.M.: Scenario-Based Design: Envisioning Work and Technology in System Development. John Wiley and Sons, New York (1995)
19. Bødker, S.: Creating conditions for participation: conflicts and resources in systems design. Hum. Comput. Interact. **11**(3), 215–236 (1996). https://doi.org/10.1207/s15327051hci1103_2
20. Capurro, R.: Digital ethics. In: The Academy of Korean Studies (ed.) Civilization and Peace, pp. 203–214. Academy of Korean Studies 2010, Korea (2009)
21. Reijers, W., et al.: Methods for practising ethics in research and innovation: a literature review, critical analysis and recommendations. Sci. Eng. Ethics **24**, 1437 (2017)
22. Brey, P. Ethics of Emerging Technologies. In: Hansson, S.O. (ed.) Methods for the Ethics of Technology. Rowman and Littlefield International, New York (2017)
23. Cotton, M.: Ethics and Technology Assessment: A Participatory Approach. Springer, Heidelberg (2014). https://doi.org/10.1007/978-3-642-45088-4

24. Cahill, J.: Embedding ethics in human factors design and evaluation methodologies. In: Duffy, V.G. (ed.) HCII 2020. LNCS, vol. 12199, pp. 217–227. Springer, Cham (2020). https://doi. org/10.1007/978-3-030-49907-5_15
25. Miake-Lye, I.M., Hempel, S., Shanman, R.W., et al.: A systematic review of published evidence maps and their definitions, methods, and products. Syst. Rev. **5**, 28 (2016). https://doi. org/10.1186/s13643-016-0204-x

Digital Human-in-the-Loop Methodology for Early Design Computational Human Factors

H. Onan Demirel[✉], Lukman Irshad, Salman Ahmed, and Irem Y. Tumer

Oregon State University, Corvallis, OR 97331, USA
{onan.demirel,mohammoh,ahmedsal,irem.tumer}@oregonstate.edu

Abstract. Numerous computational strategies were introduced in the past decades to integrate human aspects into the design process; perhaps, none provided a broader product design capacity equal to Digital Human Modeling (DHM) research. The popularity of DHM usage in product development is increasing, and many companies take advantage of DHM in their virtual prototyping studies. However, DHM is usually interpreted as a post-conceptualization check gate methodology and is often applied to correct ergonomics assumptions. Although this approach provides some insight into product performance, designers often miss more widespread opportunities in terms of utilizing DHM as an early design stage design tool. This research presents our ongoing efforts in developing DHM-based early design computational Human Factors Engineering (HFE) support tools. We engage this reflection by summarizing two early design frameworks emerging from our recent work: (1) Prototyping Toolbox and (2) Human Error and Functional Failure Reasoning (HEFFR). These frameworks are originated from the Digital Human-in-the-loop (DHIL) methodology. DHIL proposes a simulation-based computational design methodology that builds a bridge between existing Computer-Aided Engineering (CAE) software packages and computational HFE tools to address safety, comfort, and performance-related issues early in design. Our primary focus in this paper is to demonstrate the frameworks emerging from our recent D-HIL research to promote better early design decision-making for human-centered product design.

Keywords: Digital Human Modeling · Engineering design · Human-centered design · Human Factors Engineering · Ergonomics · Fault modeling

1   Introduction

Design activities determine around 80% of the lifetime cost of a product [8]. Therefore, providing performance insight earlier, when changes are less expensive to make, saves significant time and finances. Moreover, there is better room for understanding a product earlier in the design phase since most of the product

© Springer Nature Switzerland AG 2021
V. G. Duffy (Ed.): HCII 2021, LNCS 12777, pp. 14–31, 2021.
https://doi.org/10.1007/978-3-030-77817-0_2

performance is unknown at the earlier stages of product development [5,8]. The typical design-build-test (DBT) cycle associated with the conventional design process is particularly burdensome since the fabrication of prototypes requires tooling, planning, resource allocation, experimentation, and sometimes field-tests. In the case of designing large-scale and complex products, the DBT cycle becomes impractical since assessing reliability or structural integrity on functional physical prototypes becomes infeasible. One potential solution for the DBT approach is concurrent engineering practices via computational or virtual models [12]. Discovering essential aspects of the product form, functionality, and usability through simulation and optimization workflow via computational or virtual prototypes provides a better design strategy by reducing redundant physical tests, including fabrication needed for functional prototypes [2,11].

Designing with the support of Computer-Aided Engineering (CAE) tools, as part of the concurrent design approach, has been regarded as one of the most influential technologies in modern product development. Compared to the conventional engineering design approach, which heavily relies on physical prototyping and sequential implementation, the concurrent engineering strategies utilize a CAE-based design workflow that uses software platforms to speed up the design process by running multiple design activities simultaneously [15,37]. Within the context of CAE, broad usage of physics- and math-based computer software provides advanced visualization and simulation capabilities to predict product performance before production starts. Some of the well-known software tools include Computer-Aided Design (CAD), Finite Element Analysis (FEA), Computational Fluid Dynamics (CFD), and Multi-body Dynamics (MBD). Together, the integrated CAE data and workflow form the backbone of the modern Product Life-Cycle Management (PLM) platforms.

The concurrent design workflow, through the integration of CAE visualization, simulation, and optimization tools, helps companies maintain or improve product design by reducing the resources, time, and effort needed during product development [8,13,14]. Although this is a significant improvement over the conventional approach, a substantial number of CAE work focus primarily on the products' or systems' structural elements and treat the human element in isolation [34].

The human element is one of the most critical characteristics that affect product success and final cost. However, the human element often does not receive equal attention compared to the rest of the system components (e.g., materials, machines) [15,41]. The same is true for Human Factors Engineering (HFE) practices in product development activities. For example, within the design process, HFE is less emphasized when compared to software programming or manufacturing planning [15,41]. In contrast, research shows that product development strategies should consider humans as users, operators, designers, and maintainers at the core of design activities. Improved safety, reliability, and usability are immediately related to designers' efforts in enhancing the quality of human-product interactions and are leading factors that define market share and overall success of a product. Overall, injecting HFE design principles and guidelines into the design process earlier can contribute to overall product success.

Numerous computational HFE strategies were introduced in the past decades; perhaps, none provided a broader product design capacity equal to Digital Human Modeling (DHM) research. DHM includes software representations of human musculoskeletal models, and a broad range of engineering graphics and analysis tools to visualize the human body and facilitate safety, comfort, and performance [12,15,18]. DHM software enables designers to create manikins based on anthropometric libraries that represent actual population parameters (e.g., 5th percentile Japanese male), assign realistic postures through predefined posture databases (e.g., lift-lower) or direct manipulation (e.g., inverse kinematics), import CAD models to represent products, and create HFE analysis based on ergonomics (e.g., comfort assessment) and biomechanics (e.g., joint moments) assumptions.

The popularity of DHM usage in product development is increasing, and many companies have taken advantage of DHM in their virtual prototyping studies [22]. However, DHM is usually interpreted as a post-conceptualization check gate methodology and is often applied to correct ergonomics assumptions. Although this approach provides opportunities to understand some aspects of product performance, designers often miss the opportunity of using DHM as an early design stage design tool to develop a more holistic understanding of the human elements early on.

This research presents our ongoing efforts in developing DHM-based early design computational HFE support tools. We have summarized two early design frameworks emerging from our recent work: (1) Prototyping Toolbox [2–4] and (2) Human Error and Functional Failure Reasoning (HEFFR) Framework [26,28,29]. These frameworks originated from the Digital Human-in-the-loop (D-HIL) methodology [11,15]. D-HIL is a simulation-based computational design methodology created to build a bridge between existing CAE software packages and computational HFE tools to address human well-being and performance-related issues early in design. Our primary focus in this paper is to demonstrate the D-HIL methodology and the frameworks emerging from it in the context of concurrent design to support better early design decision-making.

2   Literature Review

This section provides background information about the two computational frameworks that originated from the D-HIL methodology. Each method concentrates on different aspects of the early design HFE decision-making. While the Prototyping Toolbox framework focuses on the challenges of prototyping human-centered products early in design, the HEFFR framework provides a computational human-product interaction analysis tool to assess system-level effects of component failures and human errors acting in combination. The background information provided in this section outlines the motivation, objectives, and building blocks of each framework.

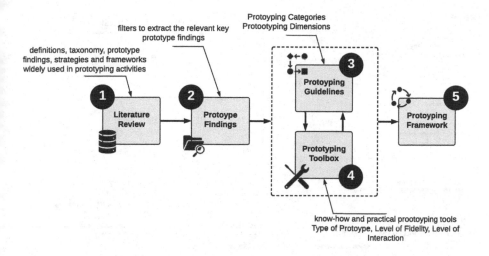

Fig. 1. Methodology to build prototyping framework

2.1   Early Design Human-Centered Prototyping Framework

Prototyping is the centerpiece in developing successful products [39], and a very costly process that can be the largest sunk cost if it is not performed properly [9,10]. Even though utmost attention is paid to prototyping activities, there is a lack of a comprehensive and widely accepted prototyping framework [6,32]. The existing prototyping frameworks rarely provide systematic guidelines or best practices to build prototypes. Rather, the focus is mainly on prototyping activities or hands-on prototyping experiences that rely on designers' intuition and experience to build the prototype [31,32]. Another shortcoming of the existing prototyping frameworks is that Human Factor Engineering (HFE) guidelines are not adequately considered [32]. The absence or partial consideration of HFE guidelines results in products or workspaces that do not address human needs and limitations adequately. The inadequacy of the current prototyping frameworks is further exacerbated by the lack of fabrication guidelines. The lack of fabrication guidelines regarding what tools and technologies to use when building a prototype causes the designers to rely on their intuition; thus, generating poor prototyping strategies and creating wide variations in prototype qualities that do not meet their intended purpose [32]. These limitations in the prototyping literature motivated the development of the human-centered product design prototyping framework discussed in this paper. The objective of the Prototyping Toolbox is to create a framework that aids designers in developing prototyping strategies during the conceptual design of products by integrating IIFE principles.

Figure 1 shows the flowchart of the methodology used to create the prototyping framework discussed in this research. Step 1 consists of a comprehensive literature review on the definitions, taxonomy, prototype findings, strategies, and frameworks that are widely used in prototyping activities. The findings from the

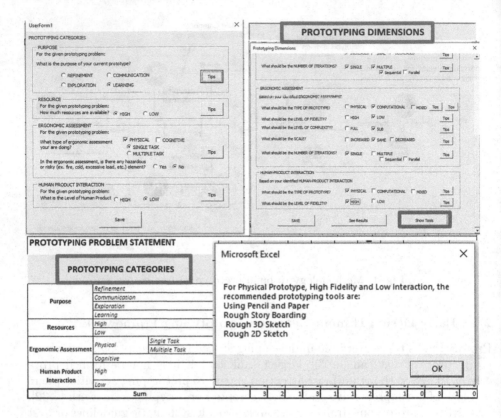

Fig. 2. Elements of the prototyping framework

literature review is used to gather information about types of prototypes (i.e., physical, computational and mixed prototype, prototype fidelity, number of iterations, etc.), human-centered design, usability testing, Digital Human Modeling, Human-Product interaction, and Performance Shaping Factors. Overall, Step 1 serves as the foundational prototyping database to capture insights and prototyping findings. Step 2 filters findings from Step 1 and extracts the relevant key prototype findings. Steps 1 and 2 provide the technical and practical literature about prototyping findings and play an instrumental role in developing the prototyping guidelines and prototyping toolboxes shown in Steps 3 and 4. In Step 3, the House of Prototyping Guidelines (HOPG) is formulated based on the prototyping theories, HFE principles, and best practices identified in Steps 1 and 2. HOPG is loosely structured based on House of Quality (HOQ) [23]. Similar to customer requirements and engineering specifications of HOQ, HOPG has Prototyping Categories (PC) and Prototyping Dimensions (PD). The PC and PD are proposed as methods to understand what the prototype is supposed to achieve and how to achieve it. PC is composed of (1) the purpose of prototyping, (2) available resources, (3) required ergonomic assessments, and (4) required human-product interaction. Likewise, PD is composed of (1) Type of Prototype,

(2) Level of Fidelity, (3) Complexity, (4) Scale, and (5) Number of Iterations. Step 4 provides generic prototyping tools that are commonly used in fabricating prototypes. Step 4 contains the know-how and toolboxes that provide practical knowledge to engineers when building prototypes. The toolbox has three axes, Type of Prototype, Level of Fidelity, and Level of Interaction. The prototyping tools are organized in this toolbox using the three axes system. Step 4 provides an inventory of tools that can be navigated using the theoretical knowledge gained from Step 3. Step 3 and Step 4 provide theoretical and practical knowledge to engineers about prototyping strategies for human-centered products and workplaces during the conceptual design process. Finally, in Step 5, the prototyping framework is presented where all the previous steps are integrated and represented via a Graphical User Interface (GUI). The GUI is developed using Excel Userform. As shown in Fig. 2, the HOPG and the Toolbox are integrated into the GUI. The prototyping and HFE guidelines can be accessed via the Tips button, which will guide the designers to identify the correct PC and PD. Once the PC and PD are identified, the recommended tools to fabricate the prototype can be accessed via the Show Tools button.

2.2 The Human Error and Functional Failure Reasoning Framework

Human errors are cited as the root cause of most accidents and performance losses in complex engineered systems [16,24]. However, a closer assessment would reveal that such mishaps often result from complex interactions between factors such as poor design, human fallibilities, and component vulnerabilities [15,20,33]. In contrast to traditional approaches of studying component and human elements in isolation, we believe that it is important to analyze the co-evolution of such factors during the design process to minimize adverse events and malfunctions in complex engineered systems. Because late design stage design changes are expensive and time-consuming, designers resort to retrofitting or finding workarounds when making design changes during later design stages [37]. As changes are made, each change will increase the potential for introducing new unforeseen vulnerabilities into the system [40], increasing the risk of potential failures. Hence, it is beneficial to conduct risk assessments early in the design process to minimize late design stage design changes and reduce cost and time-to-market.

Traditional risk assessment methods either analyze component failure or human errors in isolation or are only applicable during later design stages. For example, Failure Modes and Effects Analysis [1], Fault Tree Analysis [38], or Event Tree Analysis [21] are used to assess component failure or human errors depending on the application. However, they do not analyze the combined effects of human errors and component failures. Also, these methods are only applicable later in the design stages. Methods like Functional Failure Design Method [35], Functional Failure Identification and Propagation [30], Conceptual Stress and Conceptual Strength Interference Theory [25] were developed to move risk assessment to early design stages. These methods fall short when it comes to assessing human errors. On the other hand, human reliability assessment methods [42] such as Systematic Human Error Reduction and Prediction Approach [19], Technique for Human Error Rate Prediction [36], and Human Error Assessment and Reduction Technique analyze human errors alone and are applicable during later design stages.

Recent research has introduced the Human Error and Functional Failure Reasoning (HEFFR) framework [26] to overcome the above limitations and enable designers to assess the interaction effects of human errors and component failures during early design stages. HEFFR extends the Functional Failure Identification and Propagation framework by representing the human-system interactions in the system model and introducing human error simulation to the fault model. Overall, HEFFR takes fault scenarios that involve components and humans as inputs and produces the resulting functional failures, human errors, and their propagation paths as outputs. A depth-first search-based algorithm is used to generate potential input (fault) scenarios by considering all possible combinations of human actions and component behaviors [28]. The framework uses component failure rates and human error probabilities to estimate the likelihood of occurrence and expected cost for the resulting failures [28]. With automated scenario generation and probability calculation, designers can use the HEFFR framework to analyze a large number of potential fault scenarios involving both components and humans and prioritize them based on the severity and adopt mitigation strategies.

The HEFFR framework analyzes the effects of human errors on the system performance when acting alone or in combination with component failures. It is not capable of analyzing human performance or ergonomic vulnerabilities. Also, HEFFR is a computational framework that does not allow any human-machine interaction visualizations. The HEFFR framework can be coupled with DHM to analyze ergonomics and human performance and visualize human-machine interactions [27]. A large number of human-machine interaction points may exist in complex engineered systems, creating the need for a large number of potential DHM simulations. When coupled with HEFFR, the results from HEFFR can be used to identify and prioritize simulations relating to interactions that can have the worst severity on the system. In summary, the HEFFR framework and DHM can complement each other. DHM complements HEFFR by enabling the assessment of human performance and ergonomics and visualization of human-machine interactions. HEFFR complements DHM by allowing the prioritization and organization of simulations based on potential risk.

3   Methodology

Many DHM-based ergonomics design and analysis workflows often focus on working with manikins representing users or workers and CAD models rendering the product or work environment [7]. Typically, these manikins are built via anthropometric libraries, and simplified CAD models are imported to DHM software to create representative human-product interactions or work conditions [11]. Later, the designer selects appropriate ergonomics of simple biomechanics analysis to evaluate product interaction or work posture. Advanced versions of the DHM-based methodologies also capture standard worker anthropometry and dynamic posture changes via data collection systems such as motion capture (MoCap). Variations of these systems also allow the integration with virtual reality (VR) and augmented reality (AR) systems to enhance visualization, interaction, and immersiveness [17]. Overall, DHM-based early design methodologies are helpful in product development to capture product or system performance insight. However, most of the methodologies and workflows are limited by the availability of ergonomics or simple biomechanics toolkits supplied within the DHM software packages. The ergonomics or simple biomechanics toolkits are computational versions of standard HFE evaluation methods such as Rapid Upper Limb Assessment (RULA), joint-angle-based comfort assessments, and the National Institute for Occupational Safety and Health (NIOSH) lifting index [12]. Most of the DHM software are still standalone packages that either have no or minimal capabilities to provide integration to other important early design product visualization and evaluation techniques. Thus, many DHM users, particularly beginners and non-experts, found DHM-based early design tools to be limited, especially in early design activities.

Motivated by the above pressing needs, D-HIL is a DHM-based early design methodology that forms a more holistic workflow by integrating different visualization and evaluation tools available in CAE platforms [11,15]. More importantly, D-HIL creates opportunities for designers to devise design workflows that are unorthodox to the traditional DHM-based early design studies. Overall, it motivates designers to adopt a DHM-based early design practice by connecting with other computational tools to expand the product visualization and assessment capabilities beyond simple ergonomics or biomechanics analysis. One should note that D-HIL is not a third-party software or an automation plug-in. In a nutshell, it's a product design methodology that integrates theoretical models from core design disciplines (e.g., mechanical engineering, industrial design) and formal design techniques (e.g., optimization, structural analysis) to promote a more holistic design via DHM.

In Fig. 3, a D-HIL methodology based design timeline of a medical code cart is demonstrated. The timeline shows the evolution of the product (through the D-HIL methodology) from a rough CAD model to a photo-realistic render. One of the HFE elements evaluated with the support of DHM is the binocular vision assessment, which provides a computational binocular field-of-view of a representative nurse (e.g., 50th percentile U.S. female manikin). In this scenario, the binocular vision tool assists designers in verifying whether equipment located on the top storage area obscures the nurse's field-of-view. Medical equipment, such as defibrillators and ambulatory bags, overcrowd the upper storage and reduces visibility. Obscuration-free field-of-view is critical when rushing to emergencies. Likewise, the designer can select manikins with different anthropometric characteristics to represent nurses with different stature to broaden the solution spectrum. Meanwhile, a FEA-based approach can be used to evaluate the structural integrity of the upper storage with varying conditions of loading. For example, many "what-if" scenarios can be simulated to verify whether current design specifications meet worst-case loading scenarios. At this stage, structural analysis decisions, such as using different materials and sheet-metal wall thicknesses, can be determined. Figure 3 shows how the proposed D-HIL methodology applies to the concept development of a code cart by keeping the HFE decision-making in the loop. As a summary, insight regarding the overall system's performance can be assessed while injecting HFE early in design. Design ideas can be iterated through D-HIL methodology, and better concept models can be selected by refining infeasible or undesired models.

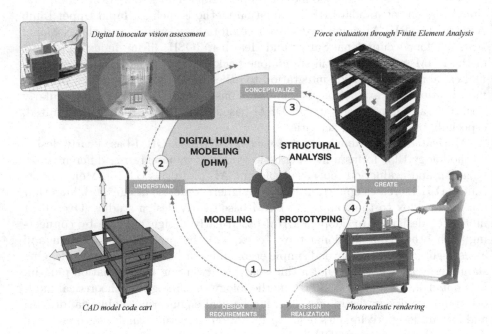

Fig. 3. The product development approach described in D-HIL methodology is applied to a concept medical code cart design

Overall, the D-HIL methodology discussed in this paper provides opportunities for better-informed decision-making through refining concepts early in design via using data capture and analysis theories and technologies. In the context of product and process development, we want to inspire the human-centered design community by demonstrating how the D-HIL approach motivates the development of computational frameworks to cope with the design challenges and early design needs. In this context, we present case studies based on two frameworks originating from our recent work in D-HIL research in the following section.

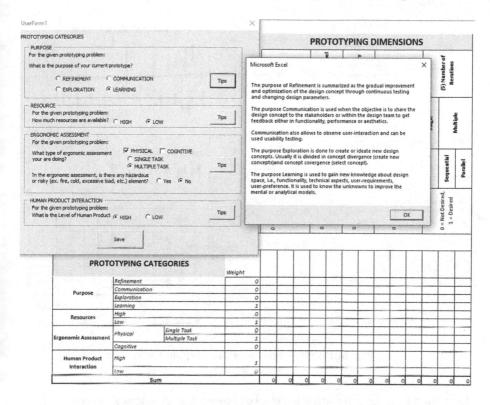

Fig. 4. Selecting prototyping categories

4 Case Studies

4.1 Case Study: Prototyping Framework

In this section, a case study is presented to demonstrate the efficacy of the prototyping framework. A prototyping problem adapted from our previous work [2] is used for the case study. The prototyping problem is as follow:

"You are to create a conceptual prototyping strategy that can be used to design a rectangle-shaped cabinet in a household setting. The objective is to create a cabinet that has the maximum storing area possible but also the user has an adequate reach and vision on every four corners. You are given low resources" [2].

The first step after reading the problem statement is to identify the Prototyping Categories. The Prototyping Categories window can be launched by clicking the Prototyping Categories button shown in Fig. 4. The designer should start with identifying the purpose of the prototype. In this case, the activity focuses on exploring design concepts and extract information about the cabinet geometry and the ergonomics (reachability and vision). So, choosing either Exploration or Learning as the Purpose of the prototype will be appropriate in this case. Next, the problem definition suggests that the resource availability

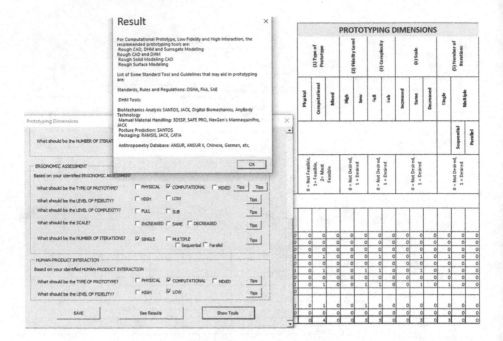

Fig. 5. Results suggesting prototyping tools

is low; therefore, Low resource is selected. Since the problem involves working on reach- and vision-related tasks, one way to interpret this information is that there is more than one task involved, and they require physical activity. Thus, Physical and Multiple options are selected. Likewise, the interaction between the human and product can be regarded as High since it involves a combination of Reaching- and Vision-related activities.

Next, the designer can launch the Prototyping Dimension window by clicking the Prototyping Dimension button, as shown in Fig. 5. The designer needs to identify appropriate prototyping dimensions (Type of Prototype, Level of Fidelity, Level of Complexity, Scale, and Number of Iterations) corresponding to each prototyping category (Purpose, Resources, Ergonomics Assessment, and Human Product Interaction). Since the prototyping problem has a relatively simple ergonomics assessment (reach and vision) and constrained with low resource availability, the default options for Prototyping Type and Level of Fidelity categories are selected as Computational and Low, respectively. In the Complexity option, the designer needs to choose whether to build the whole product or only a part. The problem states that the user should reach all four corners; thus, creating a prototype representing the entire cabinet geometry is selected. However, if the designer identifies that the cabinet geometry is symmetrical, only creating half of the cabinet will be sufficient. So, in this case, choosing either the Full or Sub prototyping option is acceptable. Let's assume Sub is selected here since the resource availability is Low. The Scale option Same (1:1 ratio) is selected.

Fig. 6. Prototype created using CAD and DHM to assess reach and vision aspects of the manikin

Any high- or low-scaling ratio will otherwise not provide the correct ergonomic assessments since reach and vision analysis requires actual dimensions of the product. The Number of Iteration could be Single as the prototyping problem is considerably simple. Perhaps, in one iteration, a solution can be achieved. However, if there is enough resource available and a satisfactory resolution is not attainable in one iteration, then the designer can choose Multiple Iteration option.

Next, the designer clicks on Save to finalize their input and use the See Results and See Tools buttons, as shown in Fig. 5, to see the list of recommended tools to fabricate the prototype. In this case, the results show low fidelity CAD and DHM as tools to consider in prototyping. These recommendations are used to create the prototype as shown in Fig. 6. Using CAD and DHM, the designer can easily and quickly design the required cabinet while fulfilling the ergonomic objectives of reaching and vision without building physical prototypes.

4.2 Case Study: The Human Error and Functional Failure Reasoning Framework

We explore an aircraft design case study to demonstrate the application of the HEFFR framework with DHM. The problem is about designing the aircraft throttle, yoke, and flap systems. The first step is to build the system model, consisting of a functional model, configuration flow graph, and action sequence graphs. The functional model represents the decomposition of the system functions as a flow, while the configuration flow graph represents the components that fulfill each function in the functional model. The arcs in the functional model and the configuration flow graph represent the flow of material, energy, and signal. The action sequence graphs represent the actions that the human needs to perform to interact with a specific component as a sequence. An action sequence

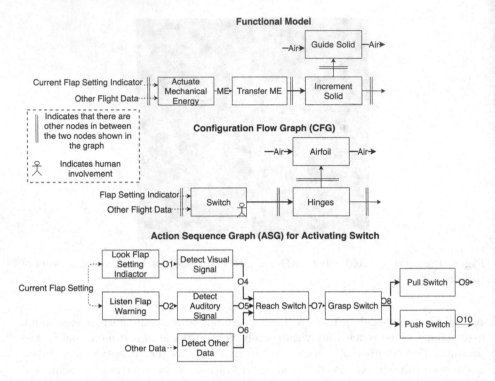

Fig. 7. Partial HEFFR system model of the flap system in an aircraft

graph is created for each component with human interactions (e.g., for the aircraft design problem, one each for the yoke, throttle lever, and flap). Figure 7 shows an example of a functional model, configuration flow graph, and the action sequence graphs for the flap system in an aircraft.

Next, the behavior modes for each component are defined. For example, the component Throttle Lever has three behavior modes: "Nominal" - the throttle is in the expected position, "Failed" - the throttle is in an unexpected position (e.g., the throttle is set to take off and go around - "toga" position when the aircraft is cruising), and "Stuck" - the throttle is stuck at the current position and it cannot be moved. Here, the behaviors "Nominal" and "Failed" are human-induced, whereas "Broken" is non-human-induced. After the behavior modes are defined, action classifications (states an action can take) for each action in the action sequence graph is defined. For example, the action "Grasp" has three classifications (Nominal Grasp, Cannot Grasp, and No Action). The next step is to set up the behavior simulation and action simulation. The action simulation takes inputs relating to humans and tracks the action classifications of each action using the action sequence graph to analyze the evolution of human-induced behavior states of the system. The behavior simulation uses inputs relating to components to track the evolution of non-human-induced behavior states of the system using the configuration flow graph. Both simulations are set up using

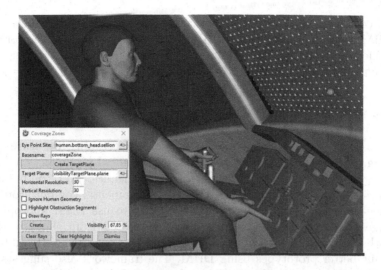

Fig. 8. DHM vision coverage analysis while reaching the flap switch in an aircraft cockpit

basic what-if scenarios. For example, what is the flow state for the component throttle lever if the behavior mode is "Failed".

Finally, the functional failure logic is defined. The functional failure logic tracks the functional health of the system using the configuration flow graph and the functional model based on the outputs of the behavior simulation and action simulation. For each function, their state is assigned as "Operating," "Degraded," or "Lost" based on the input and output flow states. For example, for the function Transfer ME, if the energy input and output are equal, it is designated as "Operating." If the energy output is less than the input, it is in a "Degraded" state. If the energy output is zero when the input is greater than zero, it is designated as "Lost." More details on how to build the system model and set up the simulation can be found in Ref. [26] Next, using the automated scenario generation algorithm [28] and the risk quantification model [29], fault scenarios involving human and components are evaluated and prioritized based on severity.

Once the failures with the most severe outcomes are identified, the human actions that contribute to them are found and prioritized. For instance, let us assume that the HEFFR analysis found that the fault scenarios relating to flap and yoke systems had the most severe outcomes. Specifically, some of the human-induced behaviors were identified as the behaviors with the highest expected cost of failure. These behaviors can be further analyzed to pinpoint action combinations that are highly likely to result in the specific behaviors. DHM simulations and ergonomic studies relating to these action combinations are given priority instead of having to focus on all probable action combinations and subsystems. In the aircraft design case study, let us assume that the analysis of the HEFFR data of the flap and yoke found that actions relating to reach and vision had the worst outcomes. As shown in Fig. 8, these actions are prioritized and analyzed using DHM rather than performing DHM simulations for every action (or steps) in the different subsystems. As design changes are made, this process can be iterated until a satisfactory design is finalized.

5   Discussions

The proposed prototyping framework bridges the prototyping literature gap by developing a prototyping framework for human-centered products. The framework integrates prototyping guidelines, HFE principles, and computational ergonomics assessment tools. Using DHM as a fundamental computational tool within the prototyping framework helps designers to use DHM appropriately. The suggestions and prototyping strategies generated from the prototyping framework can guide designers, who might not be experts in HFE, to correctly built better prototypes using DHM. The framework also suggests what ergonomic assessment should be performed using DHM and which one to avoid. Also, the prototyping framework provides suggestions on whether to build a physical, computational, or mixed prototype based on the prototyping problem, type of ergonomics assessment, and available resources. Thus knowing the correct prototyping strategies during the early design process phase allows designers to rapidly ideate, explore and test several concepts before selecting the final design. Avoiding the trial and error method of prototyping saves resources and improves product quality.

The HEFFR framework allows engineers to assess the risk of component failures and human errors acting in combination during early design stages. When applied solely, it only can identify the effects of human errors on the system. However, when used with DHM, under the D-HIL framework, it can turn into a more detailed risk assessment tool, allowing the assessment of human performance and ergonomics in the early design stages. Under the D-HIL framework, HEFFR can also complement DHM simulations by enabling designers to identify the human action combinations with the highest failure severity and prioritize them. This way, designers can give importance to human-machine interactions that can cause the worst failures rather than analyzing every possible human-machine interaction. One limitation of this approach is that it lacks fidelity compared to later design stage more detailed risk and ergonomic assessment methods. Hence, it may not fully capture potential risk when compared to the late design stage methods. Thus, the goal of this approach is not to replace the late design stage detailed studies. Rather, it is to complement them by minimizing the need for design changes at later design stages. Overall, this approach improves system and human performance and safety while reducing design cost and time.

Overall, the D-HIL methodology represented in this paper provides a viable platform to expand the coverage of HFE-based computational design methodologies by injecting DHM early in design. In contrast to many HFE methodologies, the D-HIL approach focuses on both the form and functional aspects of human-product interaction and offers opportunities to extend the DHM applications. Moreover, it provides a systematic approach on how to integrate different computational design techniques for product development research. The Prototyping Toolbox and the HEFFR framework are some of the methods that were derived to supplement the D-HIL framework as human factors based early design stage design tools. This study shows how the Prototyping Toolbox and HFEER framework can be used within the D-HIL framework to garner insight into product performance and human well-being (safety and comfort) early in design. Although the two frameworks discussed in this paper represent only a snippet of our ongoing efforts to build a more holistic HFE workflow, they show great promise in terms of finding potential human-product discrepancies and reducing the cost associated with the DBT cycle. We believe that these methods and other emerging methodologies can inspire future DHM researchers toward solving multidisciplinary early design problems using the D-HIL design workflow.

References

1. MIL-STD-1629A. Technical report, Department of Defense, Washington DC (1980)
2. Ahmed, S., Irshad, L., Demirel, H.O.: Computational prototyping methods to design human centered products of high and low level human interactions. In: International Design Engineering Technical Conferences and Computers and Information in Engineering Conference, vol. 59278, p. V007T06A047. American Society of Mechanical Engineers (2019)
3. Ahmed, S., Irshad, L., Demirel, H.O., Tumer, I.Y.: A comparison between virtual reality and digital human modeling for proactive ergonomic design. In: Duffy, V.G. (ed.) HCII 2019. LNCS, vol. 11581, pp. 3–21. Springer, Cham (2019). https://doi. org/10.1007/978-3-030-22216-1_1
4. Ahmed, S., Onan Demirel, H.: A framework to assess human performance in normal and emergency situations. ASCE-ASME J. Risk Uncertain. Eng. Syst. Part B Mech. Eng. 6(1), 011009 (2020)
5. Anderson, D.M.: Design for Manufacturability: Optimizing Cost, Quality, and Time to Market. CIM Press (2001)
6. Camburn, B., et al.: A systematic method for design prototyping. J. Mech. Des. 137(8), 081102 (2015)
7. Chaffin, D.B., Nelson, C., et al.: Digital Human Modeling for Vehicle and Workplace Design. Society of Automotive Engineers, Warrendale (2001)
8. Chang, K.H.: Design Theory and Methods Using CAD/CAE. The Computer Aided Engineering Design Series. Academic Press, Cambridge (2014)
9. Christie, E.J., et al.: Prototyping strategies: literature review and identification of critical variables. In: American Society for Engineering Education Conference (2012)
10. Cooper, R.G.: Product Leadership: Creating and Launching Superior New Products. Basic Books (1999)
11. Demirel, H.O.: Digital human-in-the-loop framework. In: Duffy, V.G. (ed.) HCII 2020. LNCS, vol. 12198, pp. 18–32. Springer, Cham (2020). https://doi.org/10. 1007/978-3-030-49904-4_2
12. Demirel, H.O., Duffy, V.G.: Applications of digital human modeling in industry. In: Duffy, V.G. (ed.) ICDHM 2007. LNCS, vol. 4561, pp. 824–832. Springer, Heidelberg (2007). https://doi.org/10.1007/978-3-540-73321-8_93

13. Demirel, H.O., Duffy, V.G.: A sustainable human centered design framework based on human factors. In: Duffy, V.G. (ed.) DHM 2013. LNCS, vol. 8025, pp. 307–315. Springer, Heidelberg (2013). https://doi.org/10.1007/978-3-642-39173-6_36
14. Demirel, H.O., Zhang, L., Duffy, V.G.: Opportunities for meeting sustainability objectives. Int. J. Ind. Ergon. **51**, 73–81 (2016)
15. Demirel, H.O.: Modular human-in-the-loop design framework based on human factors. Ph.D. thesis, Purdue University (2015)
16. Donaldson, M.S., Corrigan, J.M., Kohn, L.T., et al.: To Err is Human: Building a Safer Health System, vol. 6. National Academies Press, Washington (DC) (2000)
17. Duffy, V.G.: Modified virtual build methodology for computer-aided ergonomics and safety. Hum. Factors Ergon. Manuf. Ser. Ind. **17**(5), 413–422 (2007)
18. Duffy, V.G.: Human digital modeling in design. In: Handbook of Human Factors and Ergonomics, pp. 1016–1030 (2012)
19. Embrey, D.: SHERPA: a systematic human error reduction and prediction approach. In: Proceedings of the International Topical Meeting on Advances in Human Factors in Nuclear Power Systems (1986)
20. Endsley, M.R.: Designing for situation awareness in complex systems. In: Proceedings of the Second International Workshop on Symbiosis of Humans, Artifacts and Environment, pp. 1–14 (2001)
21. Ericson, C.A.: Event tree analysis. In: Hazard Analysis Techniques for System Safety, pp. 223–234 (2005)
22. Gawand, M.S., Demirel, H.O.: A design framework to automate task simulation and ergonomic analysis in digital human modeling. In: Duffy, V.G. (ed.) HCII 2020. LNCS, vol. 12198, pp. 50–66. Springer, Cham (2020). https://doi.org/10.1007/978-3-030-49904-4_4
23. Hauser, J.R., Clausing, D., et al.: The house of quality (1988)
24. Högberg, L.: Root causes and impacts of severe accidents at large nuclear power plants. Ambio **42**(3), 267–284 (2013). https://doi.org/10.1007/s13280-013-0382-x
25. Huang, Z., Jin, Y.: Conceptual stress and conceptual strength for functional design-for-reliability. In: ASME 2008 International Design Engineering Technical Conferences and Computers and Information in Engineering Conference, pp. 437–447. American Society of Mechanical Engineers (2008)
26. Irshad, L., Ahmed, S., Demirel, H.O., Tumer, I.: Computational functional failure analysis to identify human errors during early design stages. J. Comput. Inf. Sci. Eng. **19**(3), 031005 (2019)
27. Irshad, L., Ahmed, S., Demirel, O., Tumer, I.Y.: Coupling digital human modeling with early design stage human error analysis to assess ergonomic vulnerabilities. In: AIAA Scitech 2019 Forum, p. 2349 (2019)
28. Irshad, L., Demirel, H.O., Tumer, I.Y.: Automated generation of fault scenarios to assess potential human errors and functional failures in early design stages. J. Comput. Inf. Sci. Eng. **20**(5), 051009 (2020)
29. Irshad, L., Hulse, D., Demirel, H.O., Tumer, I.Y., Jensen, D.C.: Introducing likelihood of occurrence and expected cost to human error and functional failure reasoning framework. In: International Design Engineering Technical Conferences and Computers and Information in Engineering Conference, vol. 83976, p. V008T08A031. American Society of Mechanical Engineers (2020)
30. Kurtoglu, T., Tumer, I.Y.: A graph-based fault identification and propagation framework for functional design of complex systems. J. Mech. Des. **130**(5), 051401 (2008)

31. Lauff, C., Menold, J., Wood, K.L.: Prototyping canvas: design tool for planning purposeful prototypes. In: Proceedings of the Design Society: International Conference on Engineering Design, vol. 1, pp. 1563–1572. Cambridge University Press (2019)
32. Menold, J., Jablokow, K., Simpson, T.: Prototype for X (PFX): a holistic framework for structuring prototyping methods to support engineering design. Des. Stud. **50**, 70–112 (2017)
33. Norman, D.: The design of everyday things: revised and expanded edition. Constellation (2013)
34. Soria Zurita, N.F., Stone, R.B., Onan Demirel, H., Tumer, I.Y.: Identification of human-system interaction errors during early design stages using afunctional basis framework. ASCE-ASME J. Risk Uncertain. Eng. Syst. Part B Mech. Eng. **6**(1), 011005 (2020)
35. Stone, R.B., Tumer, I.Y., Van Wie, M.: The function-failure design method. J. Mech. Des. **127**(3), 397–407 (2005)
36. Swain, A.: Therp technique for human error rate prediction. In: Proceedings of the Symposium on Quantification of Human Performance, Albuquerque (1964)
37. Ullman, D.G.: The Mechanical Design Process, vol. 2. McGraw-Hill, New York (1992)
38. Vesely, W.E., Goldberg, F.F., Roberts, N.H., Haasl, D.F.: Fault tree handbook. Technical report, Nuclear Regulatory Commission, Washington, DC (1981)
39. Wall, M.B., Ulrich, K.T., Flowers, W.C.: Evaluating prototyping technologies for product design. Res. Eng. Des. **3**(3), 163–177 (1992). https://doi.org/10.1007/BF01580518
40. Walsh, H., Dong, A., Tumer, I.: Towards a theory for unintended consequences in engineering design. In: Proceedings of the Design Society: International Conference on Engineering Design, vol. 1, pp. 3411–3420. Cambridge University Press (2019)
41. Ward, J., Clarkson, P.: Human factors engineering and the design of medical devices (2006)
42. Williams, J.: A data-based method for assessing and reducing human error to improve operational performance. In: Conference Record for 1988 IEEE Fourth Conference on Human Factors and Power Plants, pp. 436–450. IEEE (1988)

Well-Being at Work: Applying a Novel Approach to Comfort Elicitation

Sandy Ingram[✉], Uchendu Nwachukwu, Nicole Jan, Jean-Philippe Bacher, and Florinel Radu

School of Engineering and Architecture, University of Applied Sciences and Arts Western Switzerland, Fribourg, Switzerland
sandy.ingram@hefr.ch

Abstract. This paper presents a novel approach for assessing comfort at the workplace, resulting from an interdisciplinary work between researchers in human-computer interaction, architecture, social sciences, smart buildings and energy management. A systemic comfort elicitation model including but not limited to thermal comfort, is suggested. A proof-of-concept prototype application developed based on the proposed model is also presented. The results of a first evaluation of the application's acceptability in a real working environment are discussed.

Keywords: Human-computer interaction · Human-building interaction · Interaction design · Comfort at work

1 Introduction

This paper presents a novel approach for systemic comfort elicitation at the office workplace, resulting from an interdisciplinary work between researchers in human-computer interaction, architecture, social sciences, smart buildings and energy management. While most existing studies focus on thermal comfort analysis and adaptation, the work presented in this paper adopt a holistic approach to understanding comfort. The model builds on literature findings to identify multiple comfort influence factors classified under three main dimensions (social, physical environment, and work-specific). The model considers comfort as an integral part of workflow, inviting the employer, employee group, and employers, to mindfully conscientize their emotions towards each comfort dimension as part of work habits, and take individual and collective actions to optimize comfort. The model considers comfort optimization as an iterative cycle with four main phases: 1) elicitation of how comfort is experienced, 2) automatic analysis to find correlations and causality patterns, 3) real-time reporting to inform and raise group awareness and 4) taking adaptive measures through negotiations. Awareness triggers behavioral changes at the individual, group, and organization level. Continuous comfort inquiry or elicitation enables tracking how the different comfort dimensions are experienced over time, following adaptive measures and behavioral changes. The model provides direct guidelines to the development of a digital tool facilitating ubiquitous comfort elicitation, automatic

© Springer Nature Switzerland AG 2021
V. G. Duffy (Ed.): HCII 2021, LNCS 12777, pp. 32–42, 2021.
https://doi.org/10.1007/978-3-030-77817-0_3

pattern detection, and dynamic reporting. The proposed model is implemented in a proof-of-concept application designed in a mobile-first approach. The application enables its users to express their "emotions" and identify critical influence factors affecting their comfort. In the context of a preliminary empirical evaluation of the application's accept-ability, the application is deployed in a real work environment over a period of three weeks.

The rest of the paper is organized as follows: related work is first discussed, then the proposed comfort elicitation model is described, followed by a presentation of its implemented proof-of-concept application. Finally, the application evaluation outcomes are discussed.

2 Related Work

According to existing studies, an individual's general well-being is highly correlated with his comfort at work [1]. While the notion of comfort is largely studied, there is a strong focus in the literature on "thermal comfort" [2, 3]. Such studies have led to the development of norms related to ambient temperature, humidity relative to air, and light quality and intensity. Other studies advocate more holistic and integrative approaches to understanding comfort taking into account factors, such as the interaction between the individual and the organization [4]. De Looze et al. [5] propose a systemic approach to understanding the notion of comfort with a tripartite definition: comfort is a personnel and subjective concept, it is influenced by others factors (physiological, psychological, and behavioral), and it is a reactor to an environment. Other studies, mainly focused on thermal comfort, also stress on the dynamic and adaptive nature of comfort [6–9]. Vischer [6] considers adaptive models as the ones with the biggest potential for empirical research. Humphreys et Nicol adopt an adaptive approach where a human being reacts to a situation producing discomfort [7]. The proposed adaptive approach which focuses on thermal comfort, is also applicable to all other areas present in the environment (physical, social, work-related).

According to Ortiz' adaptive model [8] on comfort dynamics, one can accept or com-pensate for a partial discomfort if he/she gets "rewards" on other aspects. Compensation for partial discomfort can also be a result of what is referred to as a negotiated collective comfort [10, 11]. Several studies in the domain of human-computer interaction focused on conscientization and awareness. A previous study reported in [12] showed how a persuasive interface [13] that provides information awareness can induce a change of behavior among users of workspace. Another HCI study also suggests [14] that group awareness helps drive the group towards a negotiation and co-construction process.

Even if models considering the global and/or dynamic nature of comfort exist, there is still a lack in the development and implementation of models that simultaneously tackle both aspects. Typically, most comfort assessment models rely on long time-consuming surveys [15, 16] that do not facilitate the implementation of an adaptive comfort model. Providing efficient, frequent, and ubiquitous means for expressing felt (dis)comfort, can present several advantages including detecting early signs of discomfort and facilitating crisis prevention and management.

The conceptual model presented in this paper combines features of the adaptive model developed for thermal comfort [9] with features from holistic models developed in [5, 8]. Last but not least, the particularity of the proposed model lies in adopting a pragmatic modeling approach with a technological facet, explicitly integrating digital system components and facilitating the model's implementation in a real working environment.

3 Conceptual Model

The conceptual comfort model proposed in this paper takes a systemic approach in understanding how comfort at office work is experienced (emotion and meaning) and provides direct implications for the model's implementation. The model entities consist of individual and group employees, comfort influence factors, in addition to three digital components: subjective and objective data collectors, data analyzers, and dynamic reporters. The model's main characteristics are described hereafter, along with their implications on the model's digital components.

- Comfort is modeled in a global multi-dimensional approach: Three main dimensions for comfort assessment are considered: physical environmental, social, and work related. Following a literature review, major influence factors are identified for every dimension (see Table 1). The model acknowledges the interaction between inter-dimension influence factors over time. As a direct implication, the analyzer should attempt to detect correlation and causality patterns between influence factors over time. For example, it can be noticed that work tasks are always perceived as difficult when work is conducted in a specific social or physical environment.

Table 1. Comfort dimensions and associated influencing factors

Comfort dimension	Factor
Work	Task challenge compared to your skills
	Result compared to expectation
Social	Support of your leader
	Feedback of your leader
	Degree of autonomy
	Exchange with your colleagues
	Exchange with your subordinates
Physical environment	Temperature
	Light
	Noise
	Air quality

- Comfort is understood as an individual negotiation process, between favorable and unfavorable influence factors. Facilitating conscientization (through feeling expression) and raising awareness are considered as fundamental in the negotiation process. The following two characteristics are derived from this one.

  - Comfort is understood as essentially subjective: the focus is put on identifying employees' felt comfort. In this view, the model recommends nudging [17] employees to conscientize his/her emotions along every comfort dimension of the proposed model. In this respect, the digital data collector enables ubiquitous expression (anytime, anywhere). The analyzer components can detect potential gaps in the same physical environment, between objectively measured comfort metrics and subjectively perceived and reported ones. The reporter's role is raising awareness related to gaps in subjective and objective data.
  - Comfort elicitation is driven by dominant emotion associated to an influence factor. The model recommends adopting a depth-first approach in subjective comfort elicitation, whereby a single dominant influence factor can be chosen per comfort dimension. The chosen factor could either consist of the one dominantly driving a positive well-being at the time of a vote. Alternatively, it could consist of the factor that is predominantly perceived as causing discomfort; it has not been compensated by other positive factors during the conscious or unconscious negotiation process. This characteristic of restricting comfort elicitation to one dominant emotion and influence factor per dimension, can be considered as the core specificity and contribution of the proposed model. First, it is consistent with the view of comfort as an individual negotiation process. Second, as a limited "questionnaire", its outcomes are still valid compared to exhaustive and long questionnaires [18]. Third, comfort elicitation by dominant emotion and factor reduces cognitive load and renders emotion expression more efficient. This model's choice directly impacts the subjective data collector design, as more efficiency yields better usability (as defined in the ISO standard[1]) and enables frequent usage.

- Comfort is understood as a collective negotiation process: the notion of collective comfort is a crucial challenge in the office work environment. Collective comfort can be addressed through a negotiation process between the employees occupying the same space and/or sharing tasks. In this view, the model recommends group awareness as a first step towards the negotiation process. Adopting a privacy-by-design paradigm, users have to accept to share their votes with a group.
- Comfort is understood as an evolving process, intrinsically integrated in workflow management. The subjective data collector must track comfort on a regular and frequent basis. With frequent comfort elicitation, the analyzer can detect whether reported emotions have evolved following (individual and collective) adaptive measures (Fig. 1).

---

[1] https://www.iso.org/obp/ui/#iso:std:iso:9241:-11:ed-2:v1:en.

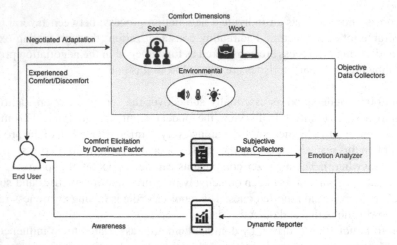

Fig. 1. Cyclic process and component relationships of the conceptual model

4   Proof-of-Concept Application

A proof-of-concept application prototype is developed based on the conceptual model proposed. The application enables users to express, follow, and understand the evolution of their emotions and their underlying factors. It is worth noting that the current application's analyzer does not yet provide advanced analysis including automatic pattern detection useful for crisis prevention and management. The analyzer is currently limited to scenarios relying on descriptive statistics. This section describes the remaining application's components recommended by the conceptual model: the subjective and objective data collectors as well as the reporters.

4.1   Objective Data Collector

In contrast with prevalent energy consumption systems relying on standard scales, this adaptive approach relies on effective usage and contextual data [19]. The objective data collector retrieves measured data from the Big Building Data (BBDATA) storage infrastructure of the Smart Living Lab [20]. BBDATA exposes sensor data via Restful Web APIs[2] provided the sensor unique identifier is known.

4.2   Subjective Data Collector

The subjective data collector proposes two different styles of comfort elicitation by dominant emotion and factor. The first style consists of a short step-by-step progressive questionnaire, where users are asked a single question at a time. Each question is answered using the traditional point-and-click interaction style as illustrated in Fig. 2 below. First, users are invited to rate their general well-being on a 4-point scale. Second, they are invited to choose a comfort dimension that is impacting their general well-being.

---

[2] https://www.amazon.com/RESTful-Web-APIs-Services-Changing/dp/1449358063.

Third, they can express in which way the chosen dimension is affecting them. Fourth, they choose one dominant impact factor among several possible options.

Fig. 2. Snapshots of the step-by-step form to retrieve dominant influential factor of a user

The alternative comfort elicitation approach consists of a grid where tabs can be used to navigate through comfort dimensions. A snapshot of the single-page view is presented in Fig. 3. The voting by dominant emotion and factor is maintained in this view. While the step-by-step questionnaire style helps new users discover the application's purpose and use it, the second should enable frequent users to express their emotions in a faster way.

Ta journée en bref

| Période | | | Salle | | |
| après-midi | | ▼ | C0019 | | ▼ |

| TRAVAIL | SOCIAL | ENVIRONNEMENT PHYSIQUE |

Température

| ❄ | 🌡 | 🌡 | 🌡 | ☀ |

Ambiance sonore

| 🔇 | 🔈 | 🔉 | 🔊 | 🕪 |

Luminosité

| ☽ | 💡 | 💡 | 💡 | ⭘ |

Fig. 3. The single-page form to retrieve the influential factor corresponding to the dominant user emotion

4.3 Configurable Reporter

The application's reporter consists of interactive dashboard that contributes to personal and group awareness. The proposed dashboard can be configured based on the period, room, theme and influence factor of interest. The dashboard proposes two complementary user interface components: 1) a heatmap showing (positive or negative) emotion trends over the selected period of time and 2) a radar chart comparing a target user's feeling to a selected group's feeling during the chosen period, and with respect to the selected influence factors.

The heatmap shows voting tendencies over selected periods of time, as illustrated in Fig. 4 below. The period can consist of days, weeks, months of seasons. When a week is chosen, the value corresponds to the most voted response for this week. By default, the target user's expressed emotions are shown over the chosen period. When the target user selects a specific group, the heatmap shows most frequency response options, discounted by the number of votes per member. When "temperature" is chosen as the influence factor, subjective answers are confronted with the objective temperature reported by physical sensors during the same time period.

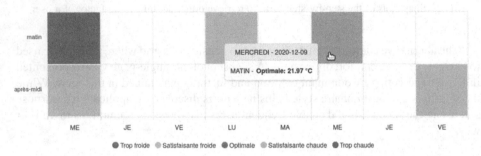

Fig. 4. A heatmap (from the reporter module) displaying user's perceived thermal comfort along with the temperature measured

While the heatmap highlights individual or group emotion polarity over a period of time for the chosen influence factor, the radar chart displays individual and group emotions simultaneously. The simultaneous superposition of individual and group the distribution along the possible voting options, helps the user realize to what extent his/her own emotions concur with emotions of other users sharing the same working environment (be it social, physical, or structural) (Fig. 5).

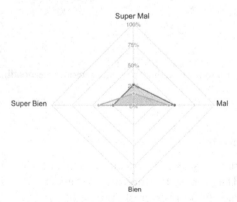

Fig. 5. A radar chart (from the reporter module) comparing a member's felt comfort (in blue) for the chosen influence factor to that of other group members (in green) (Color figure online)

5 Empirical Evaluation

A small-scale 3-week study was conducted with seven pilot users in order to assess the acceptability of the proposed proof-of-concept in a real working context. For this specific study, four indoor Multisensor[3] sensors were installed in offices occupied by one or two participants. Every deployed sensor takes measures of humidity, noise, temperature, and luminosity at regular intervals (every fifteen minutes). Sensor data were sent to BBDATA (Big Building Data) servers developed and maintained by the Smart Living Lab [20]. The application was very briefly presented to pilot users and they were encouraged to use it for a period of three weeks, to report their feelings at work. Evaluation metrics and results are discussed hereafter.

5.1 Evaluation Metrics

The User Experience Experience (UEQ) is chosen for this first experiment. Empirical studies indicate the validity of this questionnaire in capturing the perceived user experience in a comprehensive way [21]. The long version of this questionnaire contains twenty-six items, that belong to six categories allowing to evaluate the pragmatic, hedonic, and attractiveness qualities of the prototype being evaluated. Each item proposes two bipolar adjectives (e.g. impractical/practical) five options to choose from: a midway neutral point and two points on each side indicating the user's bias towards one of the proposed adjective.

5.2 Results

User answers were analyzed using the UEQ Data Analysis Tool. According to the tool guidelines, values larger than 0.8 should be interpreted as positive, and values less than -0.8 as negative. Furthermore, the analysis tool guidelines indicate that it is extremely unprobeable to observe values less or above than 2 using the questionnaire. Figure 6 shows the mean response value per category of questions. Looking at the results, the prototype's pragmatic quality (Perspicuity, Efficiency, and Dependability) as well as its attractiveness were positively perceived by participants. As far as the hedonic quality (stimulation, novelty) is concerned, participants did not perceive the application as stimulating. As indicated in Fig. 7, no question belonging to the stimulation sub-category was positively evaluated.

5.3 Discussion

Previous empirical studies indicate that up to 75% of usability issues can be detected with as little as three to five users [22]. Nevertheless, assessing the perceived usefulness and hedonic qualities of an application requires long-term studies and depends on the usage context. Other factors can explain why the application was perceived as easy to use and efficient. Dynamic reporting is not sufficiently emphasized in the current interface. In the next prototype version, alerts through visual awareness cues, push-based notifications

---

[3] https://aeotec.com/z-wave-sensor/.

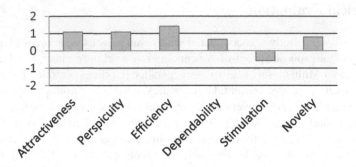

Fig. 6. Mean votes per UEQ sub-categories

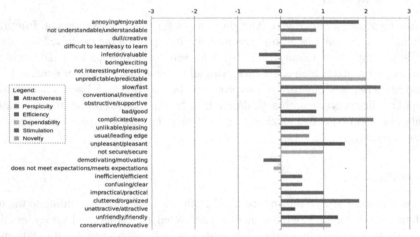

Fig. 7. Average vote per UEQ question (values < −0.8 to be interpreted as negative and values > 0.8 as positive)

and recommendations will be incorporated, in order to encourage exploring individual and group data reports. With more emphasis on the reporting user interface component, the application is expected to trigger more interest and user stimulation. Furthermore, reported analysis is currently limited and focused on descriptive group statistics. Group statistics are deemed interesting to a user, as they enable comparing individual emotions to the group "average" emotions and tendencies. Nevertheless, given the number and constitution of pilot users in this first study, the "group" feature was neither brought forward nor effectively used, rendering group statistics irrelevant. Finally, the motivation to use the application will also depend on its usage context, and more specifically how the awareness information reported is dealt with. This is compliant with the underlying model which views comfort elicitation and optimization as an integral part of the working environment.

6 Conclusion and Future Work

This paper presents a conceptual model for understanding comfort, using an adaptive and global approach. The proposed model includes digital components facilitating comfort elicitation and awareness through automated analysis and reporting. A proof-of-concept application based on the proposed model was developed and tested in a short-term study. The comfort elicitation means implemented in the application were perceived as efficient. Future work includes developing an analyzer with more advanced pattern matching and predictive algorithms. As far as the reporter is concerned, dashboards can be complemented with a more "natural" communication channel. Conversational agents (or chatbots) [23] can interact with users and communicate significant awareness signals and recommendations. For instance, chatbots can inform individual users that a room measured temperature does not lie into their own thermal comfort zone or signal that a significant portion of group members are experiencing some discomfort, in order to trigger communication and adaptive actions. Long-terms experiments will be conducted in order to assess the application's perceived usefulness and hedonic qualities. Longitudinal studies involving the application deployment in real working environments, are also planned in order to assess the impact of individual and group awareness on facilitating negotiations and comfort optimization.

Acknowledgments. This interdisciplinary research work was funded by the SLL (Smart Living Lab) [20]. Anthony Cherbuin, Martin Spoto, Ryan Siow, Yaël Iseli and Joëlle Rudaz have significantly contributed to the application development.

References

1. Haynes, B.P.: The impact of office comfort on productivity. J. Facil. Manag. **6**(1), 37–51 (2008)
2. Rupp, R.F., Vásquez, N.G., Lamberts, R.: A review of human thermal comfort in the built environment. Energy and Build. **105**, 178–205 (2015)
3. Song, Y., Mao, F., Liu, Q.: Human comfort in indoor environment: a review on assessment criteria, data collection and data analysis methods. IEEE Access **7**, 119774–119786 (2019)
4. Smith, A.P., Wadsworth, E.J.K, Chaplin, K., Allen, P.H., Mark, G.: The relationship between work/well-being and improved health and well-being. Report 11.1 IOSH (2011)
5. De Looze, M., Kuijt-Evers, L., Van Dieen, J.: Sitting comfort and discomfort and the relationships with objective measures. Ergonomic **46**(10), 985–997 (2003)
6. Vischer, J.C.: Designing the work environment for worker health and productivity. In: Proceedings of the 3rd International Conference on Design and Health, pp. 85–93 (2003)
7. Nicol, J.F., Humphreys, M.: Understanding the adaptive approach to thermal comfort. ASHRAE Trans. **104**, 991–1004 (1998)
8. Ortiz, M.A., Kurvers, S.R., Bluyssen, P.M.: A review of comfort, health, and energy use: understanding daily energy use and wellbeing for the development of a new approach to study comfort. Energy Build. **152**, 323–335 (2017)
9. De Dear, R., Brager, G.S.: Developing an adaptive model of thermal comfort and preference (1998)
10. Cole, R.J., Robinson, J., Brown, Z., O'shea, M.: Re-contextualizing the notion of comfort. Build. Res. Inf. **36**(4), 323–336 (2008)

11. Nkurikiyeyezu, K., Suzuki, Y., Maret, P., Lopez, G., Itao, K.: Conceptual design of a collective energy-efficient physiologically-controlled system for thermal comfort delivery in an office environment. SICE J. Control Meas. Syst. Integr. **11**(4), 312–320 (2018)
12. Agha-Hossein, M.M., et al.: Providing persuasive feedback through interactive posters to motivate energy-saving behaviours. Intell. Build. Int. **7**(1), 16–35 (2015)
13. El-Bishouty, M.M., Ogata, H., Rahman, S., Yano, Y.: Social knowledge awareness map for computer supported ubiquitous learning environment. Educ. Technol. Soc. **13**(4), 27–37 (2010)
14. Lockton, D., David, H., Neville, S.: Making the user more efficient: design for sustainable behaviour. Int. J. Sustain. Eng. **1**(1), 3–8 (2008)
15. Hancer, M., George, R.T.: Job satisfaction of restaurant employees: an empirical investigation using the Minnesota Satisfaction Questionnaire. J. Hosp. Tour. Res. **27**(1), 85–100 (2003)
16. Cabrita, J., Perista, H.: Measuring job satisfaction in surveys. Comparative analytical report. https://www.eurofound.europa.eu/publications/report/2006/measuring-job-satisfaction-in-surveys-comparative-analytical-report. Accessed 01 Nov 2020
17. Karlsen, R., Andersen, A.: Recommendations with a nudge. Technologies **7**(2), 45 (2019)
18. Williams, G.M., Smith, A.P.: Developing short, practical measures of well-being. In: Anderson, M. (ed.) Contemporary Ergonomics and Human Factors, pp. 203–210. Taylor & Francis (2012)
19. Jazizadeh, F., Becerik-Gerber, B.: Toward adaptive comfort management in office buildings using participatory sensing for end user driven control. In: Proceedings of the Fourth ACM Workshop on Embedded Sensing Systems for Energy-Efficiency in Buildings, pp. 1–8. ACM (2012)
20. Big Building Data. https://www.smartlivinglab.ch/en/infrastructures/bbdata/. Accessed 7 Feb 2021
21. Laugwitz, B., Held, T., Schrepp, M.: Construction and evaluation of a user experience questionnaire. In: Holzinger, A. (ed.) USAB 2008. LNCS, vol. 5298, pp. 63–76. Springer, Heidelberg (2008). https://doi.org/10.1007/978-3-540-89350-9_6
22. Nielsen, J., Landauer, T.K.: A mathematical model of the finding of usability problems. In: Proceedings of the INTERACT 1993 and CHI 1993 Conference on Human Factors in Computing Systems, pp. 206–213 (1993)
23. Zierau, N., Elshan, E., Visini, C., Janson, A.: A review of the empirical literature on conversational agents and future research directions. In: International Conference on Information Systems (ICIS) (2020)

Opportunities of Digitalization and Artificial Intelligence for Occupational Safety and Health in Production Industry

Tim Jeske[✉] [iD], Sebastian Terstegen, and Catharina Stahn

ifaa – Institute of Applied Industrial Engineering and Ergonomics, Uerdinger Straße 56, 40474 Düsseldorf, Germany
{t.jeske,s.terstegen,c.stahn}@ifaa-mail.de

Abstract. Since latest the presentation of the concept of Industry 4.0 digitalization is increasingly implemented in industry and especially in production industry. Along with this development the availability and handling of data in production enterprises have been improved and are still objective of further improvements. Additionally, data are the basis for implementing artificial intelligence and using its potentials for many purposes. One of these can be supporting employees completing their tasks. Both, digitalization, and artificial intelligence lead to changes in work design, work processes and organizational structures. Thus, they also have an impact on occupational safety and health and require identifying and assessing the consequences for the physical and mental health of employees. The risk assessment is an essential part of occupational safety and health. It has to be performed for instance in case that new machines or devices will be procured. Further questions in this context concern possibly arising fears of employees, having little experience with new technologies, or the fit of existing and required skills for new technologies. Structured by informational and energetic types of work as well as the design areas technology, organization, and personnel the opportunities of digitalization and artificial intelligence are described within this contribution. Equally, the impact on occupational safety and health is discussed. Finally, the implementation of digitalization and artificial intelligence is outlined and an outlook on future standardization activities is given.

Keywords: Digitalization · Artificial intelligence · Work design · Occupational safety and health · Production industry

1 Introduction

Since latest the presentation of the concept of Industry 4.0 digitalization is increasingly implemented in industry and especially in production industry. This process is dynamic since digitalization contributes to increasing productivity and profitability by enabling innovative changes and improvements in products, processes, and business models [15]. Along with this development, the handling of data in production enterprises has been improved and is still objective of further improvements. It leads to an availability of data

V. G. Duffy (Ed.): HCII 2021, LNCS 12777, pp. 43–57, 2021.
https://doi.org/10.1007/978-3-030-77817-0_4

via digital networks which allows automated analyses of data and using the results for steering processes based on predetermined rules and cyber-physical systems. Additionally, data are the basis for implementing artificial intelligence (AI) and using its potentials for many purposes. AI helps handling large amounts of data as well as finding structures and relations within these data. Thus, it is a valuable tool for supporting employees completing their tasks – no matter if these tasks are of informational or energetic kind. Both, digitalization, and artificial intelligence lead to changes in work design, work processes and organizational structures. Thus, they also have an impact on occupational safety and health. Besides the opportunities of informational or energetic support for employees, e.g. reducing physical strain by using work assistance systems or reducing mental strain by supplying relevant information on smart devices, it is necessary to identify and assess the consequences for the physical and mental health of employees. To do so, the risk assessment is an essential part of occupational safety and health management. It has to be performed for instance in case that new machines or devices will be procured for implementing digital technologies. Further questions in this context concern possibly arising fears of employees, having little experience with new technologies, or the fit between existing qualifications and competencies and (new) requirements of using new technologies. Therefore, an adequate communication before and while implementing new technologies is crucial for engaging employees and has to be considered as well. Due to that, not only the technical basis of digitalization and AI but also their impact on organizational structures and personnel are subject of standardization activities like they are described in the German Standardization Roadmaps Industry 4.0 [7], Artificial Intelligence [24] and Innovative Working World [6].

2   Background

Crucial for a comprehensive understanding of the afore described development tendencies and the afterwards following discussion of opportunities of digitalization and artificial intelligence for occupational safety and health in production industry is a background in digitalization, artificial intelligence and occupational safety and health which is presented in this chapter.

2.1   Digitalization

Digitalization describes the increasing use of digital technologies in all areas of human life. It started with the concept of digitization and the design of the first computer systems. Since then, digital technologies have been developed with a high dynamism which is often described by the help of Moore's law [8]. Thus, digital technologies and especially the contained computer systems became smaller, more efficient, and more cost effective. This facilitated their increasing use more and more.

Also in production industry, digitalization started slowly with increasing dynamics and is still ongoing. A fully digitalized production industry is often described as smart manufacturing or "Industry 4.0". Both terms describe digitally supported production systems. They consist of cyber-physical systems (CPS) and thus are called cyber-physical production systems (CPPS). A CPS can be any component of a production system as long as it can be integrated into a digital network; for example, a tool machine which can communicate information on its current status and can be controlled digitally. This leads to a horizontal and vertical integration in production enterprises for sharing information and allows setting up decentral steering mechanisms. To do so, the available data are used to implement simple rule-based algorithms which help completing simple tasks as for example, ordering new materials if their stock level falls below a certain predetermined level. Afterwards, further development can be done by an integrated view and analysis of many data and usually requires the implementation of artificial intelligence including deep learning.

On this basis the development of digitalization in production industry can be structured into three steps: (1) information by availability of data, (2) interaction by simple rule-based algorithms, and (3) artificial intelligence including deep learning. These steps are building on each other and are illustrated in Fig. 1.

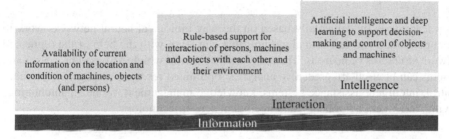

Fig. 1. Stepwise development of digitalization [[10] modified].

Digitalization affects the handling of data. Thus, examples of digitalization can be structured by the steps of the data handling process: collection, transfer, processing, providing and usage of data [25]. In Fig. 2 examples of digitalization in production industry are illustrated along the data handling process.

2.2 Artificial Intelligence

In the course of progressive digitalization in the production industry towards Industry 4.0, intelligent networking of various IT systems as part of vertical integration and the use of networked cyber-physical systems generate extensive data streams that can be combined for a wide variety of evaluations. The resulting data volumes can be systematically analyzed with the aid of appropriate techniques for the purpose of process or product innovation and the development of new business models. The digital availability of information is a central prerequisite, to enable artificial intelligence (AI) methods for being implemented into industrial production processes to realize Industry 4.0 and to enable additional productivity gains here. AI technologies are to be understood as methods and processes that enable technical systems to perceive their environment, work out on what they perceive, and independently solve problems, make decisions, and learn from the consequences of these decisions and actions. The currently very prominently discussed AI term essentially refers to deep learning with artificial neural networks.

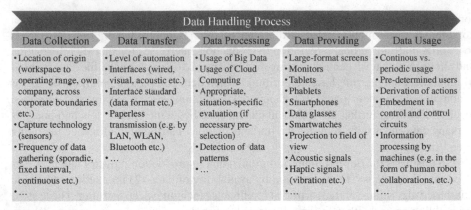

Fig. 2. Examples for digitalization in production industry structured by steps of digitalized data handling [25].

Deep learning is fundamentally based on the way biological neural networks work in the human brain and refers to algorithms that can learn with the help of the replicated network structures of neurons. The main applications in which AI-based processes and systems can be used are predictive analytics, optimized resource management, quality control, intelligent assistance systems, knowledge management, robotics, autonomous driving, intelligent automation, and intelligent sensor technology.

2.3 Occupational Safety and Health

The increasing implementation of digitalization and AI goes along with changes in the design of work, workplaces, and organizational structures. This affects occupational safety and health and can enable physical and mental relief. Additionally, the use of new technologies and a corresponding infrastructure ("Internet of Things", cyber-physical systems) can enhance the quality of the risk assessment: through its integration into existing systems and the receipt of occupational safety and health-relevant data from these systems [17].

The prevention of absences due to illness or occupational accidents, for example, is an essential building block for a healthy working environment. In addition, the humane design of work is an important guiding principle in occupational safety and health. Work must be designed in such a way that, as far as possible, it does not result in any adverse effects on health and performance. Employers have a legal obligation to ensure the safety and health of employees in the workplace. With risk assessment as an essential element of occupational safety and health, hazards are identified, and protective measures are initiated. Even though the responsibility for carrying out the risk assessment lies with the employer, he does not have to carry it out himself, but can commission other actors from the company to do so.

The increased use of digital technologies brings various challenges for employees and companies. It is important for companies to address the question now of what the working world of tomorrow should look like in order to ensure health, work and performance [20]. Aspects relevant to occupational safety and health concern, for example, the changes in strain constellations that the introduction of a new technology may bring. How and when potential users are informed about the technology and its expected benefits is also crucial. In this way, possible reservations on the part of subsequent users can be countered. In view of increasing digitalization, risk assessment loses nothing in terms of topicality and relevance. It can be used to derive and implement preventive protective measures. Ideally, the risk assessment should be carried out before a new technology is acquired, but at the latest before it is introduced.

Digitalization offers a wide range of possibilities for work design and, as a result, new opportunities for occupational safety and health. This applies to both, predominantly mental and predominantly physical activities. To ensure that digitalization and modern occupational safety and health can be implemented successfully, companies are required to take advantage of the wide range of opportunities and find company-specific solutions [14]. In this context, both, managers and employees are challenged to counter the potential hazards of tomorrow's working world. Aspects that contribute to maintaining work and performance in a changing working world are:

- Optimal ergonomic design of the human-machine interface
- Optimal design of work systems/technical systems to support the employees in their work, also with regard to learning supportability
- Enabling lifelong learning and tailor-made further training
- Strengthening personal responsibility
- Live and use occupational safety and health and place greater focus on the preventive aspect to ensure safety and health
- Involve all stakeholders at an early stage before introducing a new technology
- Take into account users' needs and emotional and cognitive states (e.g., in the case of digital assistance systems) [1].

3 Opportunities of Digitalization and Artificial Intelligence for Work Design and Impact on Occupational Safety and Health

The manifold opportunities of digitalization and artificial intelligence (AI) for designing work and their impact on occupational safety and health (OSH) are structured by two basic concepts: The two basic types of work and the three aspects/perspectives of work design [12].

The main structure differentiates the basic types of work (see Fig. 3). This structure has been chosen since both basic types of work can be supported specifically by digitalization and AI and every type of work is composed out of different shares of both basic types of work. Thus, the opportunities of digitalization and AI for any type of work can be composed out of the opportunities of digitalization and AI for both basic types of work. This enables deriving the opportunities of digitalization and AI for the specific circumstances of any application case. Similarly, the impact of digitalization and AI on OSH for any application case can be composed out of the impacts digitalization and AI have on the contained shares of basic types of work.

Both basic types of work are sub structured by three aspects/perspectives of work design. These are technical, organizational, and personal aspects/perspectives of work

Basic types of work	Energetic work			Informational work	
Types of work	Mechanical	Motor	Reactive	Combinative	Creative
What does the completion of the task require from human?	Give off forces	Perform movements	React and act	Combine information	Generate information
	„Mechanical work" in the sense of physics	Precise movement with low force output	Taking in information and reacting to it	Linking information with memory content	Linking of information to "new" information
Which organs or functions are stressed?	Muscles, tendons, skeleton, respiration	Sensory organs, muscles, tendons, circulation	Sensory organs, reactivity, memory and muscles	Thinking and memory skills and muscles	Ability to think, remember and draw conclusions
Example	Carrying	Assembling	Car driving	Constructing	Inventing

Fig. 3. Types of human work and their composition out of basic types of human work [19].

design. The three aspects are influencing each other and thus, have to be considered holistically to design work safe and healthy, and influence the stress-strain situation of employees properly. For safety reasons, possible measures from the different aspects are usually prioritized in the following order: technical measures before organizational measures and organizational measures before personal measures.

3.1 Opportunities for Informational Work

The opportunities of digitalization and AI for supporting informational work or work components result from their opportunities to support each step of the information handlings process: data collection, transfer, processing, providing and usage (see Fig. 2). This leads to numerous approaches to further improve the stress-strain situation of employees by cognitive relief [12].

Technical Design of Informational Work. Technical opportunities for supporting informational work facilitate the access to information as well as their presentation within the process of work [12].

Digital representations of information are advantageous over paper-based documents. They help ensuring the actuality of information when product specifications are changing, or production processes need to be adapted to changing requirements. They also contribute to the accessibility of information when they are immediately available from a single point of truth. Allocating digital information to products requires marking products or workpiece carriers with bar codes, QR codes or RFID tags. They help identifying the product and allow displaying the associated product or process information via projections, displays, tablet computers, smartphones, and smartwatches. Also, data glasses using augmented reality can be suitable for providing information in some cases. Furthermore, the allocated information can be displayed according to defined requirements of certain displays or – in case of work instructions – depending on the progress of a job. Additionally, information on typical mistakes can be displayed according to certain tasks or subtasks for supporting quality management. The location-independent availability of information via digital networks allows supporting mobile activities such as maintenance and repair or field service. Equally, knowledge work can be carried out mobile as long as information and communication technology enables secure and stable data connectivity with sufficient bandwidth.

The adjustment of displayed information to the current work progress of a task as well as the information on typical mistakes can be improved continuously by implementing AI and deep learning.

A proper situational provision of information can relieve employees from searching for information. Additionally, the linking of information with objects, as made possible by augmented reality and projection systems, prevents misunderstandings and mistakes. Both leads to a cognitive relief. Furthermore, the handling of paper-based documents is avoided, which saves time and prevents cuts on sharp paper edges; depending on the respective design of information provision, both hands can remain free for carrying out the actual activity [12].

Organizational Design of Informational Work. Organizational opportunities for supporting informational work facilitate the handling and mastering of large amounts of data as it is required for planning and coordination activities [12].

The allocation of employees to various workplaces requires at least the consideration of attendance and qualification as basic criteria. Informational assistance systems meet these requirements and, in addition allow considering other criteria such as ergonomics. This requires the creation of profiles characterizing each employee and each task, the determination of possible assignments of employees to tasks based on their qualifications, and establishing methods for the automatic ergonomic assessment of all these assignments by the help of well proven assessment tools (e.g. [2–4]). The resulting evaluations of the individual stress-strain situations of each assignment are the basis for identifying and selecting an assignment combination that leads to a minimum strain on the respective group of employees considered [13]. The location-independent access to information enables extensive opportunities for designing knowledge work and any other kind of work which does not require special materials or supplies that are available only within buildings or workplaces of the employer. The opportunities refer to mobile work and home office and require adequate tools which support communication and collaboration processes on distance. These tools increase the requirements on competencies for using them as well as digital literacy in general. They also enable working in the field of remote maintenance and remote control. The flexibility of location-independent work can facilitate access to the labor market for employees who are restricted in their mobility and thus in their choice of work location due to their life situation or for personal reasons.

AI can be applied for improving the outlined methods and tools. The allocation of employees to tasks by consideration of ergonomics allows, for example, also identifying qualification potentials for individual employees that can help improving ergonomics within an entire group of employees.

At the core of industrial production, AI analyzes and interprets sensor data. The sensors measure distributed states in machines and systems in order to carry out actions in process sequences derived from them. Firstly, the industrial data shows where there is potential for optimizing existing production processes, for example, by controlling automatic maintenance of machines or providing indications of malfunctions. Second, the resulting feedback loops reveal new opportunities for services and the further development of smart products. In this way, new knowledge is continuously being generated – together with new ideas, it opens the way to previously untapped markets. With the help of data sharing, the overall plant capacity can be increased and consequently new potential benefits can be tapped.

The consideration of ergonomics for the allocation of employees to workplaces enables an additional contribution to the preservation of health as well as the work and performance capacity of employees [11]. Location-independent work can help reducing stress from commuting to work. On the other hand, one aspect of successful mobile work is the selection and use of ergonomically designed work equipment. Furthermore, it can be assumed that the ergonomic behavior of employees will be more important in this form of work than in stationary work. This also means that instruction in safe and healthy behavior will become even more important [18]. Furthermore, possible impairing consequences such as extended work-related availability or the phenomenon of so-called "interested self-endangerment" can occur. Ideally, therefore, stress factors that could result in adverse consequences should not arise at all. As part of their duty of care, companies must take measures to minimize the adverse effects on safety and health if hazards cannot be ruled out. Employees must support their company in this (§ 15–16 ArbSchG).

Personal Design of Informational Work. Personal opportunities for supporting informational work regard the preparation and presentation of information for specific purposes like securing employees decisions or promoting their creativity and learning [12].

Comprehensive information about a production system, its current status and historical data on order processing can be used to identify possible handling alternatives for production planning or in the event of malfunctions that occur despite predictive maintenance and other preventive measures. In addition, the handling alternatives can be evaluated based on simulation using key figures such as overall equipment efficiency (OEE) or adherence to delivery dates. Historical data on order processing are also helpful for supporting the activities of design engineering: Based on the current design progress potentially reusable parts can be automatically identified and suggested. At the same time, specific faults that occur during the production or assembly of certain components can be visualized and can enable corresponding changes in the current design. In this way, the effort required for the manual search for reusable parts and for unnecessary new designs, as well as the consequences of design faults, can be reduced. Furthermore, the level of detail of work instructions can be adapted to the employees experience. When performing a task for the first time, employees are provided with very detailed instructions. While gaining more experience the amount of information within the work instructions can be reduced to key information and, if necessary, references to special requests from customers. The assistance system for the allocation of employees to tasks described before also allows maintaining required knowledge and a high level of practice by assigning certain tasks to each employee at latest after a predefined period of time.

Methods of AI can help simplifying the implementation and application of the afore described measures and can help improving their effectiveness. E.g., historical data can help AI improving the validity and reliability of simulation results. Equally, tracking user behavior can help to automatically identify approaches for improving software ergonomics.

AI-driven assistance systems also offer enormous potential in the service sector and in classic office work. Customers often expect a comprehensive personal advisory service that is available around the clock and without long waiting times. Chatbots, i.e. AI-based chat programs, can relieve customer service employees here in the future and process routine inquiries independently 24 h a day. Employees will then have more time to deal with more complex inquiries or provide personal support to customers. The same applies to intelligent, i.e. AI-based, image recognition software, which can already create simple analyses based on photos and process the appropriate handling of a service case. Employees then have more resources for processing complicated service cases. In this context, intelligent assistance systems will primarily take over routine activities and rule-based tasks, thus giving employees more room for creative, social and service activities.

The processing of existing information can contribute significantly to cognitive relief, e.g. by simulation-based decision support in complex decision-making situations. Likewise, information can be used to design work in a way that is conducive to learning and to maintain knowledge and practice. In this way maintaining a sufficient level of practice can also help to prevent accidents at work. Against the background of occupational safety and health, it should be noted that, for example, when introducing assistance systems, future users should ideally already be involved in the design process. Likewise, the design of computer and machine systems, visual displays, screen displays and outputs should be adequately ensured for meaningful dialog guidance [1].

3.2 Opportunities for Energetic Work

The opportunities of digitalization and AI for supporting energetic work or work components result from the combination of their opportunities to support each step of the information handlings process (data collection, transfer, processing, providing and usage; see Fig. 2) and the general technological development. This leads to numerous approaches to further improve the stress-strain situation of employees by reducing physically stressful activities or parts of them [12].

Technical Design of Energetic Work. Technical opportunities for supporting energetic work address the transfer of work to technical systems. Often generic technical systems are used for executing simple tasks [12].

For example, simple transport tasks are often suitable to be transferred to driverless transport systems. The easier such systems can be set up and the easier they can take over transport orders (e.g. on demand or by gestures), the more is an increasing spread in the operational practice to be expected. Those facilitations require the collection of data on the surrounding environment of the transport system as well as on the way transport orders are taken over.

Their introduction and use in companies can be simplified and optimized by AI methods. This refers especially to the recognition of surrounding ways, standing and moving obstacles, and humans as well as to the determination of consequences in the movements of the transport system.

In addition, AI-based robots will take on physically heavy work. Ergonomic gains will also enable older employees to work in jobs with high physical stress. There are also opportunities to further reduce accident and health risks in many areas. The AI technology natural language processing can be used to provide speech-based interfaces for picking, for example. Information is transformed into speech via the system and fed to the user via headphones. Commands and confirmations are also made via voice commands. The main advantage of such solutions is the hands-free operation of the system, which is crucial in logistics. AI-based self-controlling machine monitoring can eliminate physically demanding manual maintenance inspections for humans. Sensors monitor various real-time data such as lubrication condition, temperature, vibrations, and forces in machines. The data collected is used to create a virtual image of the current machine and process condition and to control automated maintenance activities such as adding lubricant. If the automated activities do not improve the system status, further sources of error are identified and a maintenance technician is informed via smartphone. In this way, the necessary human maintenance activities are reduced to a minimum.

Thus, the technical opportunities for supporting energetic work can significantly contribute to relieving humans and their musculoskeletal systems from monotonous as well as physically demanding tasks. While the reduction of, for example, monotonous activity is to be welcomed, great importance should be attached to a careful design of work and support systems, otherwise impairing physical consequences such as forced posture and lack of movement may result. In addition, excessive and unindividualized support can lead to monotony, which in turn can have unfavorable consequences for motivation, health, and long-term work ability [1].

Organizational Design of Energetic Work. Organizational opportunities for supporting energetic work are usually considered when technical opportunities are not applicable. They usually address the transfer of work components to technical systems [12]. This requires a targeted distribution of work components between employees and technical systems.

The human-robot collaboration (HRC) is a well-known example for the distribution of work components between employees and technical systems. The consideration of the individual strength of humans (e.g. dexterity and experience) and robots (e.g. high positioning accuracy and high load capacity) and their targeted combination is crucial for a successful implementation of HRC. Since this collaboration usually is implemented without enclosure or fencing of the robots, there is a large amount of data necessary for steering the robots properly and preventing collisions with humans which may lead to injuries. In addition to avoiding collisions also the consequences of collisions can be minimized. This is enabled by the implementation of lightweight robots which lowers the risk of damages or injuries due to their smaller mass. The implementation of lightweight robots is limited by their smaller load capacity (compared to classic industrial robots).

The required data include not only details on the task to be performed, but also on the current positions of the human and the robot as well as predictions on the human's movements for proceeding the task execution. Deep learning can help improving the required coordination and control processes and adapt them to the special characteristics of different tasks as well as on the individual needs and characteristics of different employees [22].

A major obstacle to the introduction of industrial robots is the high cost of training for automation solutions. This effort leads to high setup costs and low flexibility, which so far made such solutions economical only for frequently recurring processes. The combination of various AI technologies, such as multidimensional pattern recognition and action planning algorithms, now allows new processes to be set up by mimicking the movements of humans. Flexible adaptation to process runtime is also increasing by using AI technologies. For example, handoff areas can be defined instead of requiring precise, fixed handoff points when setting up the process. Dynamic detection of the position and orientation of the required components is then performed with the help of image processing and, if necessary, other sensor technology. In addition to flexibility compared to previous automation solutions, this also increases the stability of the processes. Image processing also enables direct HRC without a safety fence. The human-machine interface can also be made more intuitive with the help of natural language processing.

Overall, the organizational support for energetic work by HRC can significantly contribute to relieving humans and their musculoskeletal systems of monotonous and physically demanding work components. Generally, it is recommended to apply a ranking of the applicable measures, e.g. with the 3-step method for determining protective measures. The 1st stage concerns direct safety engineering (eliminate hazards or reduce the risk as far as possible, e.g. increase distances to the hazardous point or modify the design). The 2nd stage is aimed at indirect safety engineering by installing separating or non-separating protective devices against remaining risks (e.g. with hazardous movements, interlocked light curtains or safety doors). In the 3rd stage, indicative safety technology is used by informing and warning users about residual risks (e.g. by means of operating instructions, information signs, optical/acoustic warning devices) [5].

Personal Design of Energetic Work. Personal opportunities for supporting energetic work are usually considered when technical or organizational opportunities are not applicable [12]. They address supporting human activities within the work process by introducing exoskeletons or other assistive devices for handling, absorbing and dissipating forces.

Basically, there are passive and active assistive systems available. Passive systems do usually not require any technical control. For example, springs are currently in use for passive exoskeletons, which help facilitating overhead work where it cannot be avoided. But there are also simpler devices like covers for the tips of the thumbs to facilitate clipping tasks or bandages for wrists to relief strain during lifting and holding tasks. Active systems with own drives require technical control for balancing forces and dissipating them away from employees. In principle, active systems can also provide additional power for increasing human capabilities. For example regarding force, they could enable employees to lift larger loads than it would be possible naturally.

Active systems can be controlled via AI and thus adapt to the user by means of deep learning [22]. This refers especially to individual needs and characteristics of different employees.

The use of AI in companies and the associated increasing possibility of human-machine collaboration have significant implications for future work design. Energetic assistance systems (robots, exoskeletons) can, among other things, keep older and disabled people in the work process longer or integrate them better into it, or enable less qualified employees to perform complex work collaboratively with AI-based machines. In order to take advantage of these opportunities for companies and employees alike, work must be designed to enable efficient collaboration between employees and AI-based machines. For example, workplaces can be adapted in such a way that one-sided physical stresses caused by collaboration is avoided, e.g. with AI-based robots that adapt to the body size and movement patterns of employees.

Exoskeletons and other assistive devices can provide physical relief and help maintaining the employee's ability to work and perform. An enhancement of human capabilities by active exoskeletons does not necessarily lead to relief and must therefore be examined for every use case – also regarding possibly occurring long-term effects.

4 Implementation of Digitalization and Artificial Intelligence

The implementation of digitalization and artificial intelligence in companies is changing the way information and the associated information flows are handled. Thus, existing structures and processes must be reviewed and, if necessary, adapted. Productivity gains result from high availability and targeted use of information based on digitalization and data connectivity throughout the company – in direct and indirect areas alike. This means that information is largely captured, forwarded, and processed automatically. These automated information flows require compliance with fundamental principles of automation and lean management or holistic enterprise systems. Processes, including the information flows associated with them, must therefore be clearly defined and standardized. On this basis, digital information flows can be designed to meet the specific requirements of each application or use case [12].

The implementation of intelligent digitalization with artificial intelligence has special features that arise in particular from the participation and acceptance of employees and have an impact on the work design process [21]. AI technologies in the sense of self-learning algorithms usually require supervised or reinforcement learning for their efficient use. Employees are then usually not only users of the system, but also trainers, partners, or mentors. For achieving the required high level of acceptance of AI technologies, human aspects must be indispensably taken into account in their use.

The goal and purpose of using the AI system should be defined with the employees right from the start. It is helpful to provide information about how an AI system works and to assess the potential and risks of AI for the company, the organization, and the employees. The design of the interface between humans and the AI system should be guided by criteria for a humane and productive implementation of human-machine interaction in the work environment, such as transparency, explainability, or the type of data processed and used by the AI system [21].

An AI system must be suitably integrated into existing or new or changed work processes and organizational structures. This may result in changed task and activity profiles for employees and corresponding qualification measures [9]. AI technologies are characterized by the fact that they are trained on multi-layered (production) data. Since this data changes continuously, an AI system also changes permanently. After the introduction of an AI system, there should therefore be a continuous review and evaluation of the AI deployment to ensure possible adjustments regarding the design of the applications, the organization of work or the further qualification of employees [23].

Part of the transformation – the change towards working with AI technologies, is to define a culture of change, to try out possible uses of AI, to experiment, but also to evaluate, to accept or reject changes. Helpful tools in the introduction of AI systems are pilot projects and experimentation phases, in which experiences can be achieved and possible adaptation needs can be identified regarding the AI systems, qualification requirements or work organization. Successful implementations usually help to identify new opportunities for further digitalization activities and further applications of AI. Therefore, successful implementations often cause self-reinforcing tendencies and increase digitalization dynamism.

If, for example, new technologies or intelligent software is introduced, the risk assessment must be carried out or checked to ensure that it is up to date. The question to be asked here is whether the innovations introduced bring significant changes. On the other hand, these new technologies can be used for an improved risk assessment, for example by using sensors to determine,

- whether work equipment meets the safety requirements.
- whether work equipment is being used that is not suitable or approved.
- which hazardous substances are used and what exposures arise.
- whether the prescribed personal protective equipment (PPE) is being used.

Aspects of data protection must always be taken into account. Furthermore, when considering potential new threats, cross-divisional and cross-interface impacts should be considered in addition to the impact on users, especially with regard to the company's IT department [16].

5 Summary and Outlook

Digitalization is an ongoing process which affects all areas of human life. In production industry digitalization is related to the concepts of smart manufacturing and Industry 4.0. It enables the improvement and new design of products, processes, and business models. Equally, digitalization enables the implementation and use of artificial intelligence and related methods as deep learning. These developments affect human work and the design of workplaces as well as the organizational structures around. In consequence, also for occupational safety and health occur new developments.

The opportunities of digitalization and artificial intelligence as well as their consequences for occupational safety and health are illustrated by the help of examples and analyzed in detail afterwards. The results are structured by informational and energetic types of work as well as the design areas technology, organization, and personnel. Overall, many opportunities for relieving humans from physical strain and mental stress become visible. They complement the extensive opportunities of digitalization and artificial intelligence to increase productivity and profitability.

The implementation requires well proven methods of change management applied for the special opportunities of digitalization and artificial intelligence while considering occupational safety and health. Furthermore, existing implementations help identifying new opportunities for digital technologies and cause self-reinforcing tendencies.

The opportunities of digitalization and artificial intelligence as well as experiences from practical implementations into socio-technical systems result in needs for the adaptation of existing standards and preparing new ones. These needs are described in several standardization roadmaps which now can result in regarding activities of the different standardization organizations on national and international level.

References

1. Apt, W., Schubert, M., Wischmann, S.: Digitale Assistenzsysteme. Perspektiven und Herausforderungen für den Einsatz in Industrie und Dienstleistungen (2018). https://www.iit-berlin.de/de/publikationen/digitale-assistenzsysteme. Accessed 5 Feb 2021
2. BAuA: Leitmerkmalmethode-Heben, Halten, Tragen. Bundesanstalt für Arbeitsschutz und Arbeitsmedizin und Länderausschuss für Arbeitsschutz für Sicherheitstechnik (ed.) (2001)
3. BAuA: Leitmerkmalmethode-Ziehen, Schieben. Bundesanstalt für Arbeitsschutz und Arbeitsmedizin und Länderausschuss für Arbeitsschutz für Sicherheitstechnik (ed.) (2002)
4. BAuA: Leitmerkmalmethode-Manuelle Arbeit. Bundesanstalt für Arbeitsschutz und Arbeitsmedizin und Länderausschuss für Arbeitsschutz für Sicherheitstechnik (ed.) (2012)
5. Deutsche Gesetzliche Unfallversicherung e.V. (DGUV): DGUV Information 209–074. Industrieroboter (2015). http://www.vbg.de/SharedDocs/Medien-Center/DE/Broschuere/Themen/Geraete_Maschinen_Anlagen/DGUV_Information_209_074_Industrieroboter.pdf?__blob=publicationFile&v=2. Accessed 5 Feb 2021
6. DIN, DKE: Deutsche Normungsroadmap Innovative Arbeitswelt. Version 1. DIN/DKE, Berlin/Frankfurt (2021)
7. DIN, DKE: German Standardization Roadmap Industry 4.0. Version 4. DIN/DKE, Berlin/Frankfurt (2020)
8. Eigner, M., Gerhardt, F., Gilz, T., Mogo Nem, F.: Informationstechnologie für Ingenieure. Springer, Heidelberg (2012). https://doi.org/10.1007/978-3-642-24893-1
9. Frost, M., Jeske, T., Terstegen, S.: Die Zukunft der Arbeit mit Künstlicher Intelligenz gestalten. ZWF Zeitschrift für wirtschaftlichen Fabrikbetrieb 114(6), 359–363 (2019)
10. IAO: Innovationsnetzwerk Produktionsarbeit 4.0 des Fraunhofer-Instituts für Arbeitswirtschaft und Organisation IAO (2015)
11. INQA: Initiative Neue Qualität der Arbeit, Thematischer Initiativkreis 30, 40, 50plus – Gesund arbeiten bis ins Alter: Demographischer Wandel und Beschäftigung. Plädoyer für neue Unternehmensstrategien. Memorandum, Dortmund (2005)
12. Jeske, T.: Digitalisierung und Industrie 4.0. Leistung Entgelt (2), 3–46 (2016)
13. Jeske, T., Brandl, C., Meyer, F., Schlick, C.M.: Personaleinsatzplanung unter Berücksichtigung von Personenmerkmalen. In: Gesellschaft für Arbeitswissenschaft e.V. (ed.) Gestaltung der Arbeitswelt der Zukunft – 60. Kongress der Gesellschaft für Arbeitswissenschaft, pp. 327–329. GfA-Press, Dortmund (2014)
14. Jeske, T., Stowasser, S.: Digitalisierung bietet neue Möglichkeiten für den Arbeitsschutz. KANBrief (2), 3 (2017)

15. Jeske, T., Weber, M.-A., Lennings, F., Stowasser, S.: Holistic productivity management using digitalization. In: Nunes, I.L. (ed.) AHFE 2019. AISC, vol. 959, pp. 104–115. Springer, Cham (2020). https://doi.org/10.1007/978-3-030-20040-4_10

16. Koczy, A., Stahn, C., Hartmann, V.: Untersuchung der Veränderung von Kompetenzanforderungen durch Assistenzsysteme im Projekt AWA. In: GfA (ed.) Digitale Arbeit, digitaler Wandel, digitaler Mensch? Bericht zum 66. Kongress der Gesellschaft für Arbeitswissenschaft, contribution A.15.3. GfA-Press, Dortmund (2020)

17. Offensive Mittelstand. Gefährdungsbeurteilung 4.0. (2018). https://www.offensive-mittel stand.de/fileadmin/user_upload/pdf/uh40/2_2_1_gefaehrdungsbeurteilung.pdf. Accessed 2 Sep 2001

18. Sandrock, S., Stahn, C.: Arbeits- und Gesundheitsschutz bei mobiler Arbeit. In: ifaa – Institut für angewandte Arbeitswissenschaft e. V. (ed.) Ganzheitliche Gestaltung mobiler Arbeit, pp. 3–9. Springer, Heidelberg (2020). https://doi.org/10.1007/978-3-662-61977-3_1

19. Schlick, C.M., Bruder, R., Luczak, H.: Arbeitswissenschaft, Springer, Heidelberg (2018). https://doi.org/10.1007/978-3-540-78333-6

20. Stahn, C.: Arbeitswelt 4.0: Chancen und Herausforderungen für Unternehmen und Beschäftigte. Arbeitsschutz in Recht und Praxis. Zeitschrift für Gesundheit und Sicherheit am Arbeitsplatz 1, 24–26 (2020)

21. Stowasser, S., Suchy, O., et al.: Einführung von KI-Systemen in Unternehmen. Gestaltungsansätze für das Change-Management. Whitepaper aus der Plattform Lernende Systeme, München (2020)

22. Terstegen, S., Jeske, T.: Digitalisierung und Künstliche Intelligenz nutzen – Chancen und Anforderungen der Arbeitsgestaltung. ASU Arbeitsmed Sozialmed Umweltmed 56(1), 12–14 (2021)

23. Terstegen, S., Lennings, F., Suchy, O., Schalter, K., Suarsana, D.: Künstliche Intelligenz in der Arbeitswelt der Zukunft – Ansichten u Standpunkte. Leistung Entgelt 3, 3–48 (2020)

24. Wahlster, W., Winterhalter, C.: German standardization roadmap on artificial intelligence. DIN/DKE, Berlin/Frankfurt (2020)

25. Weber, M.A., Jeske, T., Lennings, F.: Ansätze zur Gestaltung von Produktivitätsstrategien in vernetzten Arbeitssystemen. In: Gesellschaft für Arbeitswissenschaft (ed.) Soziotechnische Gestaltung des digitalen Wandels – kreativ, innovativ, sinnhaft. 63. Kongress der Gesellschaft für Arbeitswissenschaft. GfA-Press, Dortmund (2017)

Digital Human Simulation for Fall Risk Evaluation When Sitting on Stepladders

Tsubasa Maruyama$^{(\boxtimes)}$ iD, Haruki Toda iD, Yui Endo iD, Mitsunori Tada iD, Hiroyuki Hagiwara, and Koji Kitamura iD

Artificial Intelligence Research Center, National Institute of Advanced Industrial Science and Technology (AIST), Tokyo, Japan
{tbs-maruyama,haruki-toda,y.endo,m.tada,hiroyuki.hagiwara,
k.kitamura}@aist.go.jp

Abstract. Fall accidents due to the loss of balance on stepladders never go away. Straddling and sitting on the top cap of the stepladders appears to be stable, but working in sitting may lose balance. The purpose of this study is to evaluate the fall risk when sitting on stepladders based on digital human simulation. This study consists of two steps: preliminary experiment and digital human simulation. The preliminary experiment is conducted for estimating the lumbar critical torque. In the experiment, backward tilt motion is measured by optical motion capture system with force plates. Six older people participate in the experiment. After that, the fall risk of stepladder sitting is estimated by the digital human simulation. In the simulation, various reaching postures are generated by the inverse kinematics calculation, and corresponding lumbar torque is further estimated by the inverse dynamics calculation. Our results clarify the reaching postures into falling or stable postures by comparing the measured critical torque with the estimated one.

Keywords: Digital human · Stepladder · Fall risk

1 Introduction

Fall accidents by stepladders have occurred for industrial workers and senior citizens due to the loss of balance [1–3]. As shown in Fig. 1(a), for safety use of stepladders, forward reaching with standing at the steps is recommended. Straddling and sitting on the top cap (Fig. 1(b)) appears to be stable, but working in sitting may lose balance. Such use is restricted, but accidents due to sitting on the stepladders never go away [4]. Thus, quantification and visualization of fall risks are important to reduce the accidents.

Studies have been conducted on the safety of the stepladders. Stability of reaching with standing at the steps were evaluated based on the foot force measurements [5–7] and the inverted-pendulum model [8]. However, it is basically infeasible to apply these approaches to the sitting case due to the difference of the contact parts between the user and the stepladder.

As demonstrated by the previous studies [6, 8], relation of a boundary of base-of-support (BoS) and the body center-of-mass (CoM) has been used for posture stability

© Springer Nature Switzerland AG 2021
V. G. Duffy (Ed.): HCII 2021, LNCS 12777, pp. 58–66, 2021.
https://doi.org/10.1007/978-3-030-77817-0_5

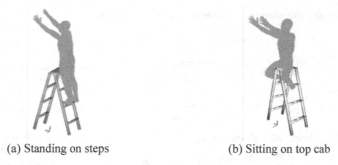

(a) Standing on steps   (b) Sitting on top cab

Fig. 1. Standing and sitting on stepladders using stepladders

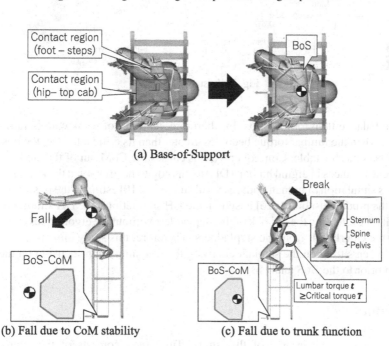

(a) Base-of-Support

(b) Fall due to CoM stability   (c) Fall due to trunk function

Fig. 2. Fall from stepladders

evaluation. The BoS is determined as a convex polygonal region over the contact regions, where the contact regions between the human and the objects such as the floors and chairs are projected onto the horizontal plane. In the case of sitting on the stepladders, as shown in Fig. 2(a), the BoS is determined by the contact regions between the both feet and steps and between the hip and top cap. The body CoM exceeding the BoS leads the falling of the user [6, 8]. The CoM out of BoS is motivated by the active behavior, i.e., the excessive forward reaching (Fig. 2(b)), and the passive behavior, i.e., breaking posture due to the high physical load (Fig. 2(c)). In the case of sitting on the stepladders, the fatal cause of posture breaking is the trunk function. During the sitting, both feet are under the hip joints with hip abduction. In this posture, the trunk function more contributes to

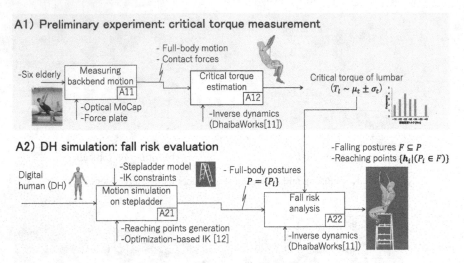

Fig. 3. System overview

maintain balance than lower limbs. Furthermore, inability of trunk causes falling. For example, when the lumbar torque becomes greater than its critical torque, the posture of the user becomes instable. Consequently, this causes the CoM out of the BoS.

Recent advances in digital human (DH) technologies have enabled the kinematics and dynamics simulation of human body. Several studies [9, 10] estimate the posture stability [9] and the product usability [10] based on the DH simulation. The DH simulation has a potential for evaluating the fall risk of the stepladders without the ergonomics experiment making the elderly fall from the stepladders. Therefore, this study aims to evaluate the fall risk when sitting on the stepladders using the DH simulation focusing on the trunk function prior to the BoS analysis.

2   Method

Figure 3 shows an overview of this study. This study consists of two steps: (A1) preliminary experiment and (A2) DH simulation. Details are described below.

(A11) Measuring Backward Tilt Motion

The backward tilt motion was measured by optical motion-capture system with force plates (Fig. 4). Six older people (65 to 75 years) participated in the experiment. They were asked to backward tilt down slowly until they can no longer keep the posture. The full-body motion and the reaction forces on both feet $F_{r,l}$ and chair legs $F_{1\sim4}$ were obtained. The contact force f_p between the hip and chair is estimated as $f_p = F_1 + F_2 + F_3 + F_4$, and its position is estimated by the conditions for the equilibrium of moment. In this

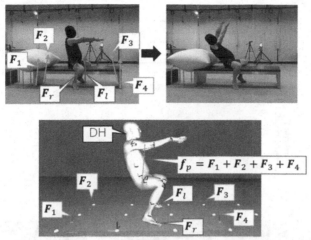

$F_{1,2,3,4}$: contact force b/w floor and chair
$F_{r,l}$: contact force b/w floor and foot

Fig. 4. Preliminary experiments

study, well-measured 17 trials in total were used. The experiment has been approved by the ethical reviewer board in author's institute.

(A12) Critical Torque Estimation

All joint torques were calculated from the measured motions and forces. Inverse dynamics calculation was performed by DhaibaWorks [11], in-house DH platform. In this system, the joint torque t_i is obtained by an optimization method [11] the under the assumption of the conditions for the equilibrium of gravity, inertial, and contact forces:

$$m_G g + f_C^G + f_K^G + f_H^G = 0, \tag{1}$$

and the equilibrium of moment:

$$r_{cog}^G \times m_G g + t_C^G + t_K^G + t_H^G = 0 \tag{2}$$

m_G and g are the mass of the body segment G and the gravity acceleration vector. The forces f_C^G, f_K^G, and f_H^G represent the contact forces for the segment G, the joint reaction forces between the segment G and its parent segment, and the joint reaction forces between the segment G and its child segment. The torques t_C^G, t_K^G, and t_H^G represent the torques for the segment G caused by the forces f_C^G, f_K^G, and f_H^G, respectively. The forces and torques could be written as follows.

$$f_K^G = \sum_{j=0,1,2} x_{K,j}^G e_j, \tag{3}$$

$$t_K^G = \sum_{j=0,1,2} x_{K,j+3}^G e_j, \tag{4}$$

where $x \in X$ represents the optimization variables to describe the forces and torques. e_0, e_1, and e_2 represent the unit vectors $e_0 = i, e_1 = j, e_2 = k$. Finally, all forces and torques

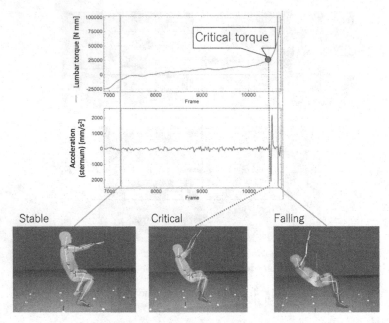

Fig. 5. Critical torque estimation

are estimated under the assumption of minimum sum of squares of contact forces and joint torques, i.e., minimizing the following objective function.

$$F_o = \sum_{x \in X} (w_x x)^2, \tag{5}$$

where w_x is the weight coefficients for x and specified to constant value ($w_x = 1$).

In this study, the forces $\boldsymbol{F}_r$, $\boldsymbol{F}_l$ and $\boldsymbol{f}_p$ were treated as $\boldsymbol{f}_C^G$ for the right foot, left foot, and the pelvis segments.

When the backward tilt posture was broken, a spike acceleration of the sternum was observed (Fig. 5). At this time, the lumbar joint torque t_e in extension (+)-flexion (−) direction was calculated for all participants. Its average μ_t and standard deviation σ_t were treated as the lumbar critical torque $T_l \sim \mu_t \pm \sigma_t$.

(A21) Motion Simulation on Stepladders

In the simulation step, various reaching postures were generated and used for fall risk evaluation. First, as shown in Fig. 6, the target hand points $H = \{\boldsymbol{h}_i\}$ were generated in a radial way from the breast. Then, a set of reaching posture $P = \{P_i\}$ was estimated by the optimization-based inverse kinematics [12] to satisfy the given constraints: both hands contact on $\boldsymbol{h}_i$, both feet contact on the steps, the hip contacts on the top cap, and all joint angles satisfies its range-of-motion. The details of this algorithm are described in [12].

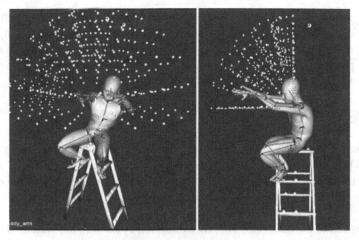

Fig. 6. Target reaching points

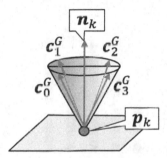

Fig. 7. Friction cone ($N_e = 3$)

(A22) Fall Risk Analysis

The lumbar joint torque t_i of each posture P_i was estimated by the inverse dynamics using the Eqs. (1)–(5). Different from the critical torque estimation process, the contact forces between the user and the stepladders were unknown. Thus, such contact forces were further estimated. In this study, as shown in Fig. 7, the contact force f_C^G is defined by the friction cone

$$f_C^G = \sum_{i=[0,N_e]} x_{C,i}^G c_i^G \tag{6}$$

$$t_C^G = \sum_{j=0,1,2} x_{C,j+3}^G e_j \tag{7}$$

where c_i^G is the unit vector defined on the i th triangular surface of the friction cone. The friction cone is created so that its top vertex and central axis correspond to the contact position and normal vector. Finally, all joint torques, joint reaction forces, and contact forces were estimated by solving the Eq. (5) with the constraints (1)–(4), (6) and (7).

After that, for posture P_i, t_i was compared with the critical torque distribution T_l. In this study, the posture P_i satisfying $t_i \leq \mu_t \pm s\sigma_t$ was categorized into the falling posture $F \subseteq P$ i.e., reaching h_i by hand causes the fall due to inability of lumbar. On the other hand, other posture P_i satisfying $t_i > \mu_t \pm s\sigma_t$ is seemed to be stable posture $S \subseteq P$ i.e., reaching h_i was realized with less lumbar torque. s represents safety factor ($s \geq 1$).

3 Results

Figure 8 shows the result of critical torque estimates by the preliminary experiment (Fig. 3 (A1)). The distribution was calculated from 17 trials performed by six older people (65 to 75 years). As shown in the figure, the distribution of critical torque was $T_l \sim 25.9 \pm 6.7$ Nm. T_l is used as a threshold value to evaluate the fall risk of given posture.

Figure 9 shows the developed fall risk evaluation system. In the system, the posture estimation results were displayed by the digital human model. The lumbar torque and

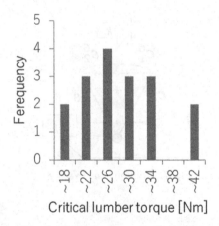

Fig. 8. Critical torque measurements

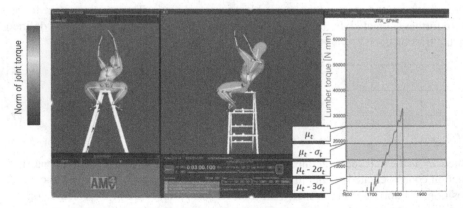

Fig. 9. Fall risk visualization

the distribution T_l is also displayed. In addition, Fig. 10 shows the fall risk estimation results. As shown in Figs. 10(a) and (b), the lumbar torques of these postures were greater than μ_t, so such large backward tilt with torso twist were categorized into falling posture $P_i \in F$ even with $s = 1$. In contrast, the lumbar joint torques of Figs. 10(c)–(f) were less than μ_t, thus its categorization depends on the value of safety factor s. However, the posture in Fig. 10(f) could be considered as stable posture even with $s = 3$. The fall risk tended to increase as the CoM moves backwards. Thus, the fall risk estimation results are seemed to be reasonable.

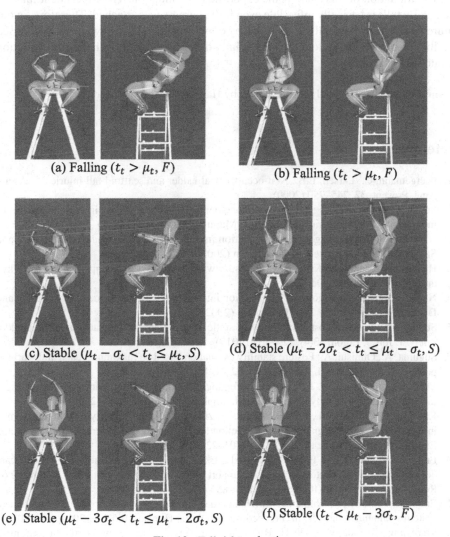

(a) Falling ($t_t > \mu_t$, F)   (b) Falling ($t_t > \mu_t$, F)

(c) Stable ($\mu_t - \sigma_t < t_t \leq \mu_t$, S)   (d) Stable ($\mu_t - 2\sigma_t < t_t \leq \mu_t - \sigma_t$, S)

(e) Stable ($\mu_t - 3\sigma_t < t_t \leq \mu_t - 2\sigma_t$, S)   (f) Stable ($t_t < \mu_t - 3\sigma_t$, $\bar{F}$)

Fig. 10. Fall risk evaluation

4 Conclusion

In this study, the fall risk evaluation system for sitting on stepladders was developed. In this system, the reaching postures were generated by the generated. Then, the lumbar torque was estimated by the inverse dynamics calculation and compared with the critical torque distribution measured by six older people. Our results shows that the estimated reaching posture could be clarified to falling or stable posture based on the user-specified safety factors.

The limitation of this study is the experimental validation. The experiment making the elderly falls is basically infeasible even if the harness was attached. Therefore, in our future work, the system will be validated by comparing the fall risk with the BoS-based stability factors. These factors were essentially different; however, it helps the validation of our system.

Acknowledgment. This study was supported by Hasegawa Kogyo Co., Ltd.

References

1. Faergemann, C., Larsen, L.B.: Non-occupational ladder and scaffold fall injuries. J. Accid. Anal. Prevent. **32**, 745–750 (2000)
2. Suguma, A., Ohnishi, A.: Occupational accidents due to stepladders in Japan: analysis of industry and injured characteristics. Proc. Manuf. **3**, 6632–6638 (2012)
3. Navarro, T., Clift, L.: Ergonomics Evaluation into the Safety of Stepladders: Literature and Standards Review - Phase 1. HSE, London (2002)
4. How to use – safe use of stepladder. https://www.hasegawa-kogyo.co.jp/support/howto/kya tatsu.php. Accessed 27 Oct 2020
5. Navarro, T., Clift, L.: Ergonomics Evaluation into the Safety of Stepladders: User Profile and Dynamic Testing - Phase 2. HSE, London (2002)
6. Suguma, A., Seo, A.: Postural stability of static standing on narrow platform for stepladder safety. J. Jpn. J. Ergon. **53**(4), 125–132 (2017)
7. Suguma, A., Ohnishi, A.: Posture stability evaluation based on maximum reach and working posture on a stepladder. J. Jpn. J. Ergon. **52**(1), 40–48 (2016)
8. Yang, B., Ashton-Miller, J.A.: Factors affecting stepladder stability during a lateral weight transfer: a study in healthy young adults. J. Appl. Ergon. **36**, 601–607 (2005)
9. Kawano, T., Onosato, M., Kazuaki, I.: Visualizing the postural stability of a digital human in working. In: 2003 Digital Human Modeling for Design and Engineering Conference and Exposition. SAE Technical Paper, #2003–01–2222 (2003)
10. Endo, Y., Ayusawa, K., Endo, Y., Yoshida, E.: Simulation-based design for robotic care device: optimizing trajectory of transfer support robot. In: 2017 International Conference on Rehabilitation Robotics (ICORR), pp. 851–856 (2017)
11. Endo, Y., Tada, M., Mochimaru, M.: Dhaiba: development of virtual ergonomic assessment system with human models. In: Proceedings of Digital Human Modeling 2014, #58 (2014)
12. Maruyama, T., Tada, M., Toda, H.: Riding motion capture system using inertial measurement units with contact constraints. Int. J. Autom. Technol. **13**(5), 506–516 (2019)

Study on Evaluation Index of Physical Load of Chemical Prevention Personnel in High Temperature and Humidity Environment

Peng Zhang[1,2], Zhongqi Liu[1,2], Xuemei Chen[1,2], and Qianxiang Zhou[1,2(✉)]

[1] Key Laboratory for Biomechanics and Mechanobiology of the Ministry of Education, School of Biological Science and Medical Engineering, Beihang University, Beijing 100191, China
zqxg@buaa.edu.cn
[2] Beijing Advanced Innovation Centre for Biomedical Engineering, Beihang University, Beijing 102402, China

Abstract. Chemical protection personnel need to wear closed clothing to work in harsh environment. Continuous sweating and outward heat dissipation will lead to high temperature and high humidity inside the chemical protection clothing, which will increase the physical load of chemical protection personnel. In the environment of high temperature and humidity for a long time, the thermoregulation function of chemical prevention personnel is easy to be maladjusted, such as heat stroke, heat spasm, heat failure, etc., which will lead to vague consciousness and even shock. Therefore, accurate monitoring and evaluation of the physical load of chemical protection personnel in high temperature and humidity environment is very important to optimize the operation process and ensure the safety of workers. Firstly, the temperature and humidity of the environment were controlled by simulation experiment, and the core temperature, surface skin temperature, heart rate, blood oxygen, sweating amount and sweat evaporation amount were measured when the chemical protection personnel were wearing chemical protective clothing. The change rules of each index were studied by using statistical analysis method, and the sensitive physical load evaluation index was revealed. Then, the weight coefficient of each index is calculated based on factor analysis method to simplify the independent variable factors of physical load evaluation model. Finally, the regression model of physical load was constructed by combining subjective feelings and physiological indexes. Sixteen healthy men aged 19–25 years participated in the test. The environment temperature and humidity were divided into normal temperature and humidity (23 °C, 45%), low temperature and high humidity (10 °C, 70%) and high temperature and humidity (35 °C and 60%). The core temperature was measured by anus and Cor-temp capsule temperature sensor. The results showed that the core temperature of chemical prevention personnel in normal temperature and humidity environment was relatively stable, while the core temperature in low temperature and high humidity, normal temperature and high humidity environment increased by 0.74 °C, 1.03 °C and 2 °C respectively. There was significant difference in the core temperature of chemical prevention personnel under different temperature and humidity environment ($P < 0.05$), which proved that the core temperature can be used as a sensitive index to evaluate physical load. The surface skin temperature of shoulder, chest, arm, waist,

© Springer Nature Switzerland AG 2021
V. G. Duffy (Ed.): HCII 2021, LNCS 12777, pp. 67–78, 2021.
https://doi.org/10.1007/978-3-030-77817-0_6

neck, hand, thigh and lower leg was measured by temperature inspection instrument. The results showed that the surface skin temperature of chemical protection personnel in high temperature and humidity environment increased significantly (up to 39 °C). There were significant differences in the skin temperature of chemical protection personnel under different temperature and humidity conditions (P < 0.05), indicating that the surface skin temperature can be used as a sensitive index to evaluate physical load. The heart rate data were measured using the ECG band developed by polar team. The results showed that the heart rate of the chemical protection personnel wearing protective clothing was the fastest (up to 180 bpm) in high temperature and humidity environment. There was significant difference in heart rate under different temperature and humidity (P < 0.05), which proved that heart rate can be used as a sensitive index to evaluate physical load. The blood oxygen saturation was measured by finger cuff sensor. The results showed that the oxygen saturation of the chemical protection personnel in the normal temperature and humidity environment was 95%, and the oxygen saturation of the chemical protection personnel wearing protective clothing in the low temperature and high humidity environment, the normal temperature and normal humidity environment and the high temperature and high humidity environment decreased gradually, which were 94%, 93% and 91%, respectively. There was significant difference in blood oxygen saturation among chemical workers under different temperature and humidity (P < 0.05), which proved that blood oxygen saturation could be used as a sensitive index to evaluate physical load. The results showed that the amount of sweat and evaporation increased with the increase of ambient temperature. The average sweating amount was 1.25 kg, accounting for 1.6% of body weight, which reached the limit of human sweating capacity. There were significant differences in the amount of sweat and the amount of sweat evaporation in different temperature and humidity environment (P < 0.05), which proved that the amount of sweat and the amount of sweat evaporation can be used as a sensitive index to evaluate the physical load. The weight coefficient obtained by factor analysis showed that the temperature index was the most important indexes in the evaluation of physical load in high temperature and humidity environment. There are two key factors, core temperature and heart rate, in the stepwise regression equation of physical load established between subjective feelings and sensitive indicators. The fitting degree of the model is as high as 0.917 under the hypothesis test of homogeneity of variance.

Keywords: Chemical protection personnel · Physical load · Evaluation index · High temperature environment · High humidity environment

1 Introduction

Due to the harshness of the working environment such as fire-fighting and nuclear-biochemical treatment, more and more people work in closed clothing. Therefore, we must pay attention to their life safety to avoid casualties and improve the efficiency of the task [1]. Because it is easy to induce overload when working in closed clothes, which leads to the decline of physical efficiency, slow reaction and affects people's working ability and life safety. If the protection is improper, it will lead to the occurrence of life-threatening phenomenon. According to statistics, in the 161 casualty accidents of fire officers and soldiers in China from 1980 to 2008, there were 801 casualties, 225 deaths and 576 injuries. One of the main reasons is their high intensity and overload work. In addition, in the usual training, it is also possible to cause fainting, dyspnea, heart discomfort and other phenomena due to overload training intensity [2]. Similarly, the shipbuilding industry personnel need to wear closed clothing, they will be affected by the high temperature environment and work clothes, which will make the human body produce strong thermal stimulation. In severe cases, it will cause syncope of operators, and even endanger lives [3]. Especially, chemical protection soldiers must wear closed protective clothing and carry a 20 kg compressed air tank when they work, and they will be exposed to toxic gases in the process of performing tasks. They often appear overload state and then affect people's work efficiency and life safety. Therefore, it is of great research value to monitor the vital signs and working ability of the operators of airtight clothing [4–6].

Now we attach great importance to the life safety of staff, and the number of occupations wearing protective clothing is gradually increasing. But at the same time, it also brings many problems, the main problem is the physical load caused by wearing protective clothing for a long time. Wearing protective clothing will increase the wearer's metabolism, and the total increase of metabolism depends on the properties of protective clothing. The number of layers, fitness and weight of clothes will affect the metabolic rate and physiological reaction during activity [7]. The research of Rintamaki et al. found that every 0.5 kg increase of clothing could increase the metabolic rate by 2.7–3.3% [8]. Oksa and Dorman compared 14 different combinations of personal protective clothing and found that the metabolic rate increased by about 2.7% [9, 10]. The correct choice and use of protective clothing in industry can reduce the physiological burden of wearers. Through the experiments of different layers of protective clothing in different environments, it is found that the more layers, the faster the metabolic rate increases and the heavier the physical load.

In the extreme environment, firefighters cannot work without protective clothing. The weight of personal protective equipment will increase the thermal stress, thus increasing the probability of firefighters falling and other injuries. Kiwon Park conducted four simulated fire-fighting experiments on 44 firefighters and found that wearing fire-fighting clothing and protective equipment was more likely to cause high physical load. Through the comparison of the tests before and after the operation, it is found that fatigue will affect the working energy and cause large operation error [11]. Deanna Colburn conducted sensory and motor control tests on firefighters wearing protective equipment. It was found that although wearing masks would affect breathing, it did not have a substantial impact on the stability of the front and rear position or movement of firefighters, but only increased the physical load of firefighters in action [12]. Ming Fu studied the thermal effect of protective clothing for firefighters and proved that the influence of clothing permeability on thermal effect was positively correlated with the core temperature and skin surface temperature of human body [13]. M. Fu, W.G. Weng studied quantitatively the heat flux and thermal protection of the four layers of protective clothing. It was found that the protective clothing with high air permeability could reduce the temperature by sweating, while the protective clothing with low air permeability had the opposite effect [14]. Ann Sofie Lindberg Christer malm studied the physical load of various parts of the body of firefighters with 13 years of experience through a questionnaire. The research shows that exercise is beneficial to the physical and mental load bearing ability of firefighters, so it is very important for firefighters' moderate daily training [15–17]. Anna Marszalek studied the thermal load of mine rescuers under the same physical workload (25% of the maximum oxygen consumption). He used three types of respirators to evaluate the physical load of mine rescuers. The results show that the respirator obviously hinders the heat exchange with the environment and increases the physical load [18].

This paper focuses on the physical load of chemical prevention personnel wearing closed clothing in different temperature and humidity environment. Core temperature, surface skin temperature, heart rate, blood oxygen, sweating volume, sweating volume, subjective perception value and other indicators were measured. Statistical analysis was used to find out the sensitive indexes related to the characteristics of physical load. Finally, combined with the subjective feelings of chemical prevention personnel, the physical load was evaluated to provide technical basis for their safety protection and ability monitoring.

2   Method

2.1   Participants

In this study, 16 healthy male volunteers aged 19–25 were selected. No cold, fever or other symptoms were found in the volunteers during the period of the experiment. All the volunteers did not take part in the similar experiment. They had good sleep quality before the experiment and had no drinking or coffee behavior. During the experiment, the volunteers were familiar with the purpose and process of the experiment and filled in the informed consent form. The basic information of volunteers is shown in Table 1.

2.2   Experimental Environment and Equipment

The experimental scene is a walk-in environmental simulation test chamber which the temperature and humidity can be adjusted according to the requirements of the test. The experimental environment of this experiment is low temperature and high humidity (10 °C, 70%), normal temperature and humidity (23 °C, 45%) and high temperature and high humidity (35 °C, 60%). The rectal temperature is measured by the sensor made by YSI company of USA (model is 4000 A, the range is 0–50 °C, and the resolution is ±0.01 °C). The body temperature was measured by Cor-temp capsule temperature sensor made in USA (The accuracy is 0.01 °C). Heart rate and blood oxygen were tested by polar team management system. Sweating amount and sweat evaporation amount were measured by Kcc150 high precision anthropometric scale (The maximum range is 150 kg and the resolution is 0.0001 kg).

Table 1. Basic information of volunteers

Number	Age (years)	Weight (kg)	Height (cm)
1	23	59	172
2	19	66	173.5
3	20	69	173
4	21	63	180
5	19	68	176
6	18	64	173
7	20	84	177
8	25	76	178
9	24	63	175
10	27	55	170
11	24	57	166
12	27	68	172
13	25	65	170
14	23	82	174
15	24	65	172
16	24	60	171
Mean value	22.68 ± 2.84	66.5 ± 8.18	173.28 ± 3.43

2.3 Experiment Content

In this paper, the control variable method is used to simulate the working environment of chemical protection. By controlling the type of protective clothing, the volunteers were exposed to different temperature and humidity environments (low temperature and high humidity (10 °C, 70%), normal temperature and humidity (23 °C, 45%) and high temperature and high humidity (35 °C, 60%). In different temperature and humidity environment, volunteers wear different protective clothing. Their core temperature, surface skin temperature, heart rate, blood oxygen, sweating, evaporating hair and subjective feeling score were collected.

First, the volunteers wore ordinary clothes and conducted an experiment, which served as a benchmark. Then volunteers wear protective clothing to run on treadmill in different temperature and humidity environment. The basic time is 1H and the speed is 4 km/h. The trial was terminated when the heart rate exceeded 180 bmp or the core temperature increased by 2 °C. In experiment, rectal temperature was measured by inserting 10 cm into the anus of volunteers and core temperature was measured by oral capsule sensor. The 8-channel temperature inspection instrument was used to measure the surface skin temperature at 8 points, including shoulder temperature, chest temperature, arm temperature, waist temperature, neck temperature, hand temperature, thigh temperature and calf temperature. The polar team heart rate meter was used to collect the heart rate of the volunteers during the whole experiment, which the data was recorded once a second. Sweating amount and sweat evaporation amount were measured by weighing method. The amount of sweating was equal to the net weight before the experiment minus the net weight after the experiment. The amount of evaporated hair was equal to the weight of the volunteers before the experiment minus the weight of the volunteers after the experiment. The volunteers and the experimental environment were shown in Fig. 1.

Fig. 1. Human temperature test scene

2.4 Data Analysis

Statistical analysis method was used to analyze the change trend of core temperature, surface skin temperature, heart rate, blood oxygen, sweating volume, sweat evaporation volume and subjective perception value. SPSS software was used to compare and analyze the measurement indexes in low temperature and high humidity, normal temperature and humidity, high temperature and high humidity environment to determine whether there are significant statistical differences. Factor analysis was used to analyze the weight coefficient of sensitivity index of physical load. The weight coefficient of physical load sensitivity index in different temperature and humidity environment was obtained. The physical load intensity was classified by relative heart rate method and the physical load model was established by stepwise regression.

3 Results and Discussion

In this paper, anus temperature sensor and cor temp capsule sensor are selected to measure the core temperature. The core temperature curve of volunteers under different temperature and humidity is shown in Fig. 2. The statistical results show that the core temperature of each state increases with time. Under the conditions of low temperature and high humidity, normal temperature and humidity, and high temperature and high humidity, the corresponding core temperature increases by 0.74 °C, 1.03 °C and 2 °C respectively. The state of high temperature and humidity has reached the tolerance limit of human physiological temperature. The main reason for this phenomenon is that the environmental conditions will affect the heat exchange. Heat exchange is easier when the temperature gradient is larger, that the accumulated heat in the human body will be released in time. The p value of paired t test of core temperature among groups was less than 0.05, so core temperature can be used as a sensitive index of physical load.

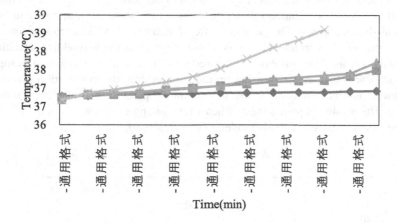

Fig. 2. Core temperature curve under different temperature and humidity. Blue line is normal temperature and humidity without protective clothing. Gray line is normal temperature and humidity with protective clothing. Orange line is low temperature and high humidity with protective clothing. Yellow line is high temperature and humidity with protective clothing. (Color figure online)

The surface skin temperature was measured at 8 points of shoulder, chest, waist, neck, hand, arm, thigh and leg. The average skin temperature curve of volunteers under different temperature and humidity conditions is shown in Fig. 3. The surface skin temperature showed an upward trend with the increase of time, which was mainly caused by the environmental gradient and the sweat evaporation of wearing protective clothing. The p value of paired t test of surface skin temperature among groups was less than 0.05, so surface skin temperature can be used as a sensitive index of physical load.

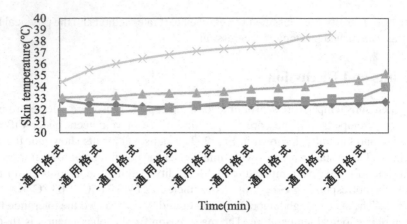

Fig. 3. Skin temperature curve under different temperature and humidity. Blue line is normal temperature and humidity without protective clothing. Gray line is normal temperature and humidity with protective clothing. Orange line is low temperature and high humidity with protective clothing. Yellow line is high temperature and humidity with protective clothing. (Color figure online)

In this paper, the polar heart rate meter is used to measure the heart rate of volunteers. The heart rate curve of volunteers under different temperature and humidity conditions is drawn as shown in Fig. 4. The metabolic rate of human body will increase accordingly with the increase of environmental temperature to maintain the normal life activities of human body. The heart rate must be accelerated with the increase of oxygen consumption and blood flow speed. When wearing protective clothing, the evaporation process of human sweat is hindered, and the rise of human temperature will also accelerate the heart rate. The p value of paired t test of heart rate among groups was less than 0.05, so heart rate can be used as a sensitive index of physical load.

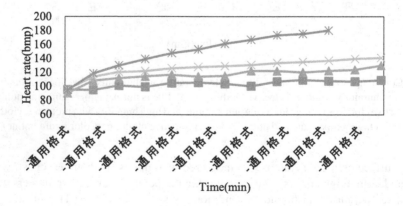

Fig. 4. Heart rate curve under different temperature and humidity. Blue line is normal temperature and humidity without protective clothing. Gray line is normal temperature and humidity with protective clothing. Orange line is low temperature and high humidity with protective clothing. Yellow line is high temperature and humidity with protective clothing. (Color figure online)

Blood oxygen saturation is an important physiological index to judge whether the body is anoxic or not. When the body is in mild hypoxia, the volunteers will have poor breathing. When the body is in severe hypoxia, the volunteers will have shock. In this paper, a finger cuff sensor is used to measure blood oxygen saturation. The change curve of blood oxygen saturation of volunteers under different temperature and humidity is shown in Fig. 5. The results showed that in the environment of low temperature and high humidity, normal temperature and humidity, and high temperature and humidity, the lack of oxygen supply of volunteers was gradually aggravating. The p value of paired t test of blood oxygen saturation among groups was less than 0.05, so blood oxygen saturation can be used as a sensitive index of physical load.

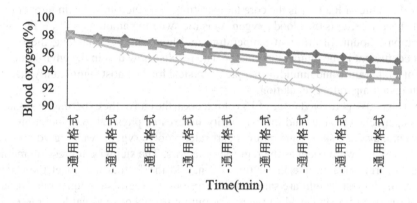

Fig. 5. Blood oxygen saturation curve under different temperature and humidity. Blue line is normal temperature and humidity without protective clothing. Gray line is normal temperature and humidity with protective clothing. Orange line is low temperature and high humidity with protective clothing. Yellow line is high temperature and humidity with protective clothing. (Color figure online)

In the environment of low temperature and high humidity, normal temperature and humidity, and high temperature and high humidity, sweating amount and sweat evaporation amount are increasing. This is mainly because when the skin surface temperature reaches the critical temperature of sweat activity, it begins to reduce the temperature through sweat. Therefore, the higher the temperature, the greater the amount of sweating, and then the amount of sweating will increase. In the high temperature and humidity environment, the amount of sweating has reached 1.25 kg. According to the calculation, the tolerance limit sweating of human body in high temperature and humidity environment accounts for 1.6% of body weight, which has exceeded 1.5%. At this time, the body's heat resistance also began to decline, accompanied by heart rate and body temperature rise. The p value of paired t test of sweating amount and sweat evaporation amount among groups were less than 0.05, so sweating amount and sweat evaporation amount can be used as a sensitive index of physical load.

The formula of factor analysis is as follows:

$$F = 0.61F_1 + 0.20F_2 + 0.19F_3 \tag{1}$$

$$F_1 = 0.657x_1 + 0.766x_2 + 0.209x_3 - 0.475x_4 + 0.487x_5 - 0.023x_6 \tag{2}$$

$$F_2 = 0.644x_1 + 0.550x_2 + 0.942x_3 - 0.837x_4 + 0.126x_5 + 0.134x_6 \tag{3}$$

$$F_3 = 0.152x_1 + 0.170x_2 + 0.143x_3 - 0.140x_4 + 0.788x_5 + 0.954x_6 \tag{4}$$

F represents a comprehensive physiological index. The smaller the value of F, the smaller the value of load. x_1 is the core temperature, x_2 is the surface skin temperature, x_3 is the heart rate, x_4 is the blood oxygen, x_5 is the sweating amount and x_6 is the sweat evaporation amount. In different temperature and humidity environment, the biggest weight coefficient is the temperature factor. The results show that in the environment of different temperature and humidity, people's physical load is most significantly affected by their own temperature regulation.

The subjective perceived value of 16 volunteers at the end of the experiment was taken as the dependent variable, and the sensitivity indexes of physical load including core temperature, average skin temperature, heart rate, blood oxygen, sweating volume and sweating volume were taken as the regression factors. The stepwise regression method is used to carry out multiple linear regression, and the factors that meet the criteria and have the largest weight are selected to carry out the regression equation. Through the analysis of SPSS statistical software, the output results of physical load regression model are shown in Table 2. It can be seen from Table 2 that there are two variables in the regression model, which are core temperature and heart rate. The R^2 adjusted by regression model is 0.917, which indicates that the regression equation is well fitted.

Table 2. Results of physical load regression model

Model	Items in the model	Coefficient	t value	P value
Regression	Constant	−271.731	−7.056	0.000
	Core temperature	6.937	6.232	0.000
	Heart rate	0.176	5.403	0.000

4   Conclusion

In this paper, the physiological indexes of 16 young male volunteers were measured under different temperature and humidity environment. Through statistical analysis, core temperature, surface skin temperature, heart rate, blood oxygen, sweating amount and sweat evaporation amount can be used as sensitive indicators of physical load. The weight coefficient obtained by factor analysis showed that the temperature index was the most important indexes in the evaluation of physical load in high temperature and humidity environment. There are two key factors, core temperature and heart rate, in the stepwise regression equation of physical load established between subjective feelings and sensitive indicators. The results obtained in this paper can be used to evaluate physical load. It can provide theoretical support for the health monitoring of chemical protection personnel.

References

1. Lanzotti, A., Vanacore, A., Tarallo, A., et al.: Interactive tools for safety 4.0: virtual ergonomics and serious games in real working contexts. Ergonomics **63**(3), 324–333 (2020)
2. Lin, W., Wang, Z.: Study on common risk factors in fire fighting and rescue process of fire fighting forces. Fire Tech. Prod. Inf. (12), 22–25 (2012)
3. Li, X.: Analysis of occupational hazard risks and protective measures in shipbuilding industry. In: National Conference on Labor Health and Occupational Diseases, vol. 9, no. 03, pp. 87–93 (2013)
4. Nicholas, R., Pascal, I., Ollie, J., et al.: Steady-state sweating during exercise is determined by the evaporative requirement for heat balance independently of absolute core and skin temperatures. J. Physiol. **589**(13), 2607–2619 (2020)
5. Otani, H., Kaya, M., Goto, H., Tamaki, A.: Rising vs. falling phases of core temperature on endurance exercise capacity in the heat. Eur. J. Appl. Physiol. **120**(2), 481–491 (2020). https://doi.org/10.1007/s00421-019-04292-6
6. Horn, G.P., Blevins, S., Fernhall, B., et al.: Core temperature and heart rate response to repeated bouts of firefighting activities. Ergonomics **56**(9), 1465–1473 (2013)
7. Pokorny, J., Fiser, J., Fojtlin, M., et al.: Verification of Fiala-based human thermophysiological model and its application to protective clothing under high metabolic rates. Build. Environ. **126**(12), 641–651 (2017)
8. Holmér, I.: Protective clothing in hot environments. Ind. Health **44**(3), 404–413 (2006)
9. Oksa, J., Kaikkonen, H., Sorvisto, P., et al.: Changes in maximal cardiorespiratory capacity and submaximal strain while exercising in cold. J. Therm. Biol. **29**(7–8), 815–818 (2004)
10. Dorman, L.E., Havenith, G.: The effects of protective clothing on energy consumption during different activities. Eur. J. Appl. Physiol. **105**(3), 463–470 (2009). https://doi.org/10.1007/s00421-008-0924-2
11. Park, K., Rosengren, K.S., Horn, G.P., et al.: Assessing gait changes in firefighters due to fatigue and protective clothing. Saf. Sci. **49**(5), 719–726 (2011)
12. White, S.C., Hostler, D.: The effect of firefighter protective garments, self-contained breathing apparatus, and exertion in the heat on postural sway. Ergonomics **60**(8), 1137–1145 (2016)
13. Fu, M., Weng, W., Han, X.: Effects of moisture transfer and condensation in protective clothing based on thermal manikin experiment in fire environment. Procedia Eng. **62**(8), 760–768 (2013)
14. Fu, M., Weng, W.G., Yuan, H.Y.: Quantitative assessment of the relationship between radiant heat exposure and protective performance of multilayer thermal protective clothing during dry and wet conditions. J. Hazard. Mater. **276**(5), 383–392 (2014)
15. Lindberg, A.S., Malm, C., Oksa, J., et al.: Self-rated physical loads of work tasks among firefighters. Int. J. Occup. Saf. Ergon. **20**(2), 309–321 (2014)
16. Beach, T.A.C., Frost, D.M., Mcgill, S.M., et al.: Physical fitness improvements and occupational low-back loading-an exercise intervention study with firefighters. Ergonomics **57**(5), 744–763 (2014)

17. D'Artibale, E., Laursen, P.B., Cronin, J.B.: Profiling the physical load on riders of top-level motorcycle circuit racing. J. Sports Sci. **36**(39), 1–7 (2017)
18. Marszałek, A., Bartkowiak, G., Dąbrowska, A., et al.: Mine rescuers' heat load during the expenditure of physical effort in a hot environment, using ventilated underwear and selected breathing apparatus. Int. J. Occup. Saf. Ergon. **24**, 1–13 (2018)

Human Body and Motion Modeling

The Wearable Resistance Exercise Booster's Design for the Elderly

Xiangtian Bai[1], Jun Ma[2], and Duan Dai[1]($\boxtimes$)

[1] School of Architecture and Art, Central South University, Changsha, Hunan, China
[2] Xiang Ya Nursing School, Central South University, Changsha, Hunan, China

Abstract. Nowadays, the phenomenon of aging is becoming more and more serious. The elderly people suffer from various illness, like degenerative osteoarthropathy and sarcopenia, which seriously hinder the ability of elders' daily activities and affect their quality of life, and even induce other more serious diseases. The medical and health care design that focuses on such problems is extremely important and urgent. Some evidence indicated that resistance exercise was an appropriate treatment method for early-staged degenerative osteoarthropathy and sarcopenia. Based on the basic principle of resistance exercise and the digital human modeling (DHM) technical expertise, a set of wearable exercise boosters was designed, and with it the elders can perform appropriate resistance activities without any external assist, and maintain the mobility of lower limbs. The wearable exercise booster combines concepts of anthropometry, biometrics, motion capture and prediction. Firstly, the signals of flexion and extension of limbs can be transmitted to the servo motor by the pressure sensor placed in the device pad. Then, the servo motor drives the external kneepad by rotating in a specified direction and gives proper resistance to the stretching motion, and finally, the wearers can do resistance exercise by themselves gradually with the booster's help. For patients who need different levels of exercise, artificial intelligence technology can be applied beforehand to make changes of strength, speed and frequency in different treatment courses, to fully meet the requirements of users for home-based rehabilitation physiotherapy. This research is a good application of the DHM in medical and nursing fields, and has certain innovative and practical significance.

Keywords: Resistance exercise booster · Activities of daily living · DHM · Ergonomics · Aging

1 Introduction

The aging of the Chinese population is becoming more and more serious, and the elderly generally suffer from various lower limb diseases such as degenerative osteoarthropathy and sarcopenia. The statistical data of the WHO indicated that there are 355 million patients with degenerative osteoarthropathy worldwide, and in particular, almost everyone suffers from different degrees of joint disease or is unable to sit or move as a result of degenerative joint disease in people aged over 60 [1]. Sarcopenia is also a common disease in the elderly. Studies found that the quality and quantity of skeletal muscle

© Springer Nature Switzerland AG 2021
V. G. Duffy (Ed.): HCII 2021, LNCS 12777, pp. 81–91, 2021.
https://doi.org/10.1007/978-3-030-77817-0_7

decreased about 8% per year from 40 years old, and doubles over the age of 70. These afflictions seriously hinder the ability of elders' daily activities and affect their quality of life. As of 2020, bone Joint disease will become the fourth most disabling disease in the world [2], bringing a heavy economic burden to society and the country. Sarcopenia is also a common disease in the elderly. Such diseases will reduce the ability of daily living of the elderly to varying degrees and affect their quality of life in their later years [3].

However, the pathogenesis of these diseases is not yet clear, and there is no exact cure method. In 2018, the Chinese Orthopaedic Association *"Osteoarthritis Diagnosis and Treatment Guidelines"* proposed that the stepped treatments of knee osteoarthritis include basic treatment, drug treatment, restorative treatment and reconstruction treatment [4], and the exercise-based treatments are accepted by most patients for the advantages in efficacy, side effects and price [5]. Hence, the medical and health care design that can assist exercise treatments might be a major gap that we need to pay attention to due to long-lived possibilities of these diseases.

Some evidence indicated that resistance exercise was an appropriate treatment method for early-staged degenerative osteoarthropathy and sarcopenia since it can effectively improve flexibility and stiffness, reduce pain and stiffness of joints, enhance stability of the whole joint and readjust the stress distribution on the joint surface [6]. Besides, resistance exercise can improve the strength and quality of skeletal muscle independently. With short-term resistance exercise, the elderly who lack of exercise can maintain basic function of lower limb, or the protein synthesis rate and neuromuscular adaptability of whom can even reach a similar level with young people [7].

Therefore, in this project, we conducted interview investigations, analyzed the information of behaviors and psychological conditions of patients, analyzed the design points of the rehabilitation equipment, combined concepts of rehabilitation and physiotherapy of lower extremity diseases and the principle of resistance exercise and digital human modeling (DHM), and eventually designed a wearable resistance exercise booster that is expect to explore the research path about the function setting, human machine interactive optimization, product modality, etc. of resistance exercise booster aids for elderly patients with bone and joint diseases, effectively improve the joint flexibility, the joint stiffness, and the strength and quality of skeletal muscles, and meet the needs of the elderly for home rehabilitation physiotherapy.

2   Research Methods

2.1   Investigation Objects and Time

In Changsha, Hunan Province, with community recommendation and informed consent procedure, we did a simple interview with 63 senior citizens with degenerative osteoarthropathy or sarcopenia, and according to the type and degree of diseases in the inclusion and exclusion criteria, 22 senior citizens were enrolled. The project coordinator collected their demographic information and conducted in-depth interviews about their exercise rehabilitation needs.

Taking the important influence of temperature differences, clothing thickness and other factors on the medical experience into account, 11 senior citizens in the sample pool were interviewed in December 2019 (Winter), and the other 11 senior citizens were interviewed in September 2020 (Summer). And the time of in-depth interview were controlled within 30 min.

2.2 Investigation Information

The contents of the in-depth interview were roughly divided into two parts. Part 1: demographic information, including the senior citizen's age, address, disease symptoms, medical treatment methods/places, treatment frequency, calf and thigh circumference, etc. Part 2: exercise rehabilitation information. a) The transport method between hospital and home. b) The specific behavior or process of "registration – inquiry – treatment" in the hospital. c) The effect of rehabilitation and physiotherapy for a period of time. d) The cost incurred during the treatment, the proportion of national reimbursement and payment, the impact on the family economy, etc. Take Mrs. Liu from Yuelu District, Changsha City, Hunan Province as an example, extract and draw the key information (see Fig. 1).

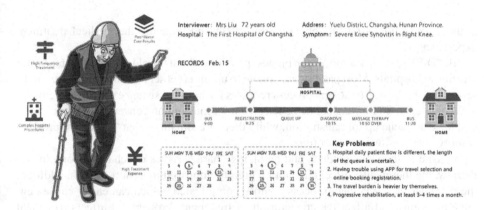

Fig. 1. Recovery journey map based on the key information.

Now we perform a pie chart of these main information such as treatment methods/places, treatment frequency in Part 1 (see Fig. 2). It is found that 73% of elderly patients with joint degenerative osteoarthropathy or sarcopenia will choose "all in hospital" or "hospital + home" physiotherapy model. It's worth noting that there are also a certain proportion of patients with mild or normalized follow-up visits. In terms of their diagnosis and treatment efficiency, going to the hospital involves too much energy obviously.

At the same time, it mainly focuses on the summary analysis of the rehabilitation experience information in Part 2.

A. "Difficult traffic" is the primary problem for elderly patients in seeking medical treatment. Although the government and bus companies have the travel benefit policy such as "senior citizen bus card". And the commuting between the bus station and home

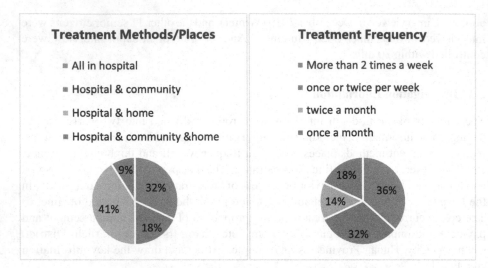

Fig. 2. Treatment methods/places, treatment frequency.

is the crux of hindering the rehabilitation effect and reducing the medical treatment experience.

B. "Difficult registration" is the biggest problem which the elderly patients face after arriving at hospitals. Most patients are unable to use internet services by themselves and a series of complicated treatment process requires the active assistance of family members and volunteers. So they cannot be benefit from various online convenient functions and still have to queue up for registration, while there are situations that "no-sign source" or "empty queue" situation most time.

C. Due to the slow, gradual, and recurring characteristics of rehabilitation physiotherapy, the therapeutic effect may not be greatly improved in a short time. In addition, the diagnosis and treatment process is more complicated, which can easily cause negative emotions and affect the cooperation of treatment. Probably, it affects treatment adversely.

D. Finally, the economic situation. Although the cost of each hospital treatment is not high, the particularity of long-term treatment of such diseases will still exert certain economic pressure on elderly patients, and also have many adverse effects on treatment.

2.3 Design Points

First of all, the conclusion of A, B, and C is that though hospital visits are the necessary guarantee for the rehabilitation of degenerative osteoarthropathy and sarcopenia, but elderly patients should also make better choices due to their needs like home rehabilitation training with advanced equipment, to avoid unnecessary exhaustion physically and mentally. And original model even has a negative effect on rehabilitation. The research should focus on the optimizing design based on the existing re-habilitation equipment in community and family.

Secondly, in order to meet the elderly patients' needs for using equipment frequently, the equipment should to be easily to operate and can handle independently by elders. To be more specific, artificial intelligence and machine learning related technologies should be introduced [8]. In addition, it is also necessary to consider the scientific such as treatment frequency, and consider the effective integration of medical rehabilitation planning to use flexibly. And in terms of specific structure, a mechanical structure that can accurately control the speed and angle must be set to ensure the physical therapy accuracy under the control of artificial intelligence technology.

3 Research Foundation

3.1 Theoretical Foundation

Activity of Daily Living (ADL). In rehabilitation medicine, ADL means the daily life activity, reflects the most basic ability of people in the family, medical institution and the community [9]. Therefore, ADL is the most basic and important content in rehabilitation medicine. ADL has gradually formed since childhood, and has developing gradually until the perfection with the practice. It is simple and feasible for healthy people, but for the patient, the injured, the disabled, it may become quite difficult and complicated. If they have no ability to complete daily life activity behavior, this phenomenon could lead to the loss of self-esteem and confidence, and then can aggravate the capacity loss of life [10].

The Activity of daily living scale developed by Lawton and Brody in the United States is an important indicator to evaluate health, living quality and independent mobility of the elderly. It can more intuitively reflect the self-care of the elderly and reflect the physiology health condition [11]. Degenerative osteoarthropathy is one of the common diseases of ADL damage. The elderly with ADL damage might have more medical service needs. The more severe the damage, the bigger the medical services demands. From another perspective, the elderly with whole ADL function and less damage should be encouraged to choose the "hospital + home" comprehensive rehabilitation physiotherapy model to avoid unnecessary medical resources consumption and improve the rehabilitation physiotherapy effectiveness as a whole.

Resistance Exercise. Resistance exercise, also known as strength training or resistance training, refers to the exercise method in which the body fully relies on its own muscle strength to fight against a certain external resistance to achieve muscle growth and strength increase [12]. Studies have shown that scientific resistance exercise can improve the patients physical function, and also help control the disease effectively. Meanwhile, it has certain clinical guiding significance [13]. For this research, the specific effect is that it can relieve degenerative osteoarthropathy patients' condition, reduces joint pain, improves joint function, and improves muscle strength.

Digital Human Modeling (DHM). DHM is the virtual representation of body in the computer simulation environment. The content includes external geometry, physical hierarchy, kinematic characteristics, dynamics and biomechanical information, and emotional perception, etc. [14].

In the process of design, research and development, it was often necessary to use physical models to test the comfort and safety of products. With the development of computer graphics, three-dimensional scanning and other technologies, digital models and virtual environment will become the mainstream. DHM usually has the physiological attributes of specific populations. It makes the product's defect identification becomes more and more simple, reduces or even eliminates the needs of physical models or real human trials, and which can quickly reduce design costs and shorten design cycles.

3.2 Technical Support

Servo Motor. Servo control means the effectively and accurately control such as the displacement, velocity, acceleration, angular velocity and angular acceleration of the controlled object movement. The driving core is the servo motor (see Fig. 3), it has been gradually applied to the lower limb rehabilitation exoskeleton equipment designing. The advantage of the servo motor lies on its excellent controllability in the operation process of starting, stopping, steering, etc. The speed can be adjusted efficiently with the change of the control signal, and the speed range is wider. It can achieve start and stop quickly because of the large starting torque and its small inertia [15]. Usually, it working condition is stable and its failure rate is almost nonexistent.

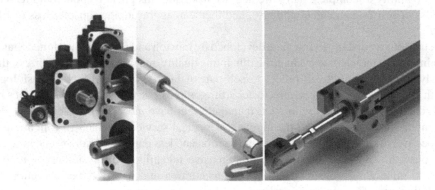

Fig. 3. The various servo motor.

Pressure Sensor. The pressure sensor is commonly used in industrial design. The detection system based on the pressure sensor is simple and easy to operate, and has a high cost performance [16]. From the external structure, the thin film pressure sensor [17] is relatively easy to install and use due to its small size and high flexibility. Fully meet the pressure collection requirements of this type of equipment (see Fig. 4). Combined with the thin film pressure sensor to monitor the pressure change between the device and the leg when the patient squats up, and then map these signals to the joint angle. At the same time, the data is transmitted to the control system for data processing and reference. Finally, the exoskeleton artificial intelligence control system blocks out the corresponding assistance rehabilitation exercise strategies.

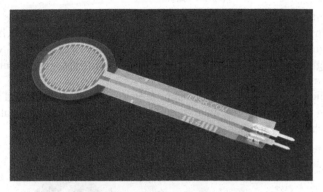

Fig. 4. The thin film pressure sensor.

4 Project Research

4.1 Brainstorming

Based on the interview data, the key design points, as well as the medical theoretical basis and feasible technical support that have been combed through multi-dimensional comparison, the design is made by using sketch and rhino modeling (see Fig. 5).

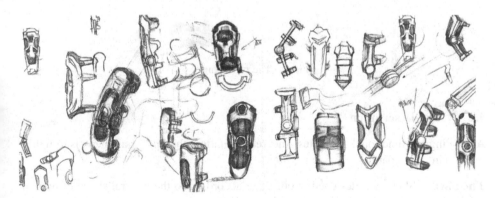

Fig. 5. The sketching.

Considering the booster' project medical attributes, it is necessary to focus on design research principles such as comfort, convenient operation, and design semantics. The final design effect is shown (see Fig. 5).

(1) Comfort

The booster is in contact with the knee directly. The comfort of wearing and ergonomic should be taken into consideration, so that the elderly can wear without stiffness and move flexibly throughout the whole process.

(2) Convenient operation

Considering the difficulty of operation accepted by the elderly, the booster must pay attention to the convenient operation in multiple processes of wearing and supporting. It can be started with one key and be controlled intelligently.

(3) Design semantic

For specific users and specific application environment, medical and health facilities' form must be soft and natural, color can be referred to medical white-blue, medical white-gray o other schemes for combination (Fig. 6).

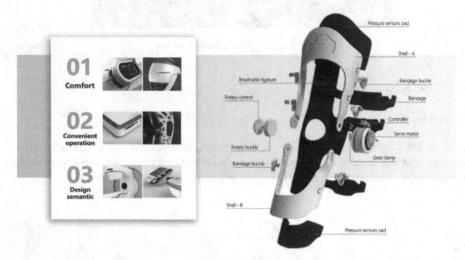

Fig. 6. The rendering.

4.2 Design Description

According to functional attributes, the rehabilitation therapy equipment is roughly divided into five parts:

The Shells. Shell-A is designed to optimize according to the general shape of human thighs. The four bandage buckles on the left and right sides are integrally formed, and the bandage is used to fix the device on the thigh. Similarly, Shell-B is designed to optimize according to the general shape of human calf. Two bandage buckles on the side to fix equipment by bandage passing through.

The Pressure Sensor Pad. There is a pressure sensor inside this part for keen monitoring the body signal of squatting up and sitting down. And the outer surface is treated with the soft materials to improve the comfort of body.

The Servo Motor. The booster transmits the squatting signal to the servo motor through the thin film pressure sensor inside the equipment pad. The servo motor militates and drives the external kneecap by giving rotation in the specified direction, and then assists the leg, thus making it easier for the wearer to squat (see Fig. 7).

The Rotary Control. After the servo motor completes the rotation in the specified direction, the rotary control fix the device' opening and closing angle for a short time, waiting for the wearer's next limb movement signal (Fig. 7).

The Breathable Ligature. It fits the form of people's bones to the maximum extent and provide assistance power when sitting up.

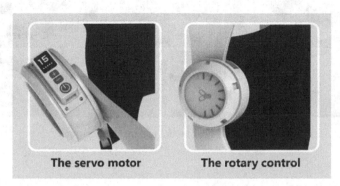

Fig. 7. The servo motor and the rotary control.

In order to meet the rehabilitation needs of most elderly patients as much as possible, the average value of the calf and thigh circumferences in the preliminary investigation was calculated. The size and the rotation range of the resistance exercise booster were set, and this booster was optimized according to DHM. The final figure Model size as shown (see Fig. 8).

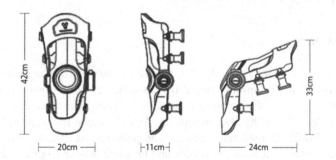

Fig. 8. The model dimension.

Prototype is the first step to verify the feasibility of product. It is the most direct and effective way to find out the defects, deficiencies, and shortcomings of the designed product, so as to make targeted improvements to the defects [18]. Using the high-precision 3D printer in laboratory to output each component models. And performing painting, assembly and other work (see Fig. 9). At the same time, five of the 22 elderly patients were selected for the experience testing. After wearing test, the experience was great, and no inappropriate was found. It also further explained the operability of the "Basic Data Analysis-Digital Human Modeling Optimization" practice path for human-machine medical product design.

Fig. 9. The physical model making and testing.

4.3 Function Extension

Taking the possibility of different symptoms in different patients into account, "Artificial Intelligence" is embedded in the controller module. The patient can set the booster's power, speed, frequency and other attributes on the mobile terminal in advance. When the user doing rehabilitation physiotherapy exercise, the booster adjusts the most suitable mode in a short time. These behaviors can improve user experience and treatment effects further. At the same time, the device controller is also in the process of continuous intelligent optimization, and its fine-tuning process will be recorded. All working can optimize the physical therapy mode further.

5 Conclusion

This research is based on the principle of resistance exercise and digital human modeling (DHM) to optimize the design of a wearable resistance exercise booster that targeted, the rehabilitation treatment of elderly patients with lower extremity diseases such as degenerative osteoarthropathy and sarcopenia. And aims to solve effectively the existing problems of difficult medical treatment and poor results. The research combines feasible technologies such as Servo Motor and Pressure Sensor to give the wearer the appropriate boosting attributes in the rehabilitation process. Then, elderly patients can perform resistance rehabilitation physical therapy activities independently. At the same time, Artificial Intelligence (AI) technology is also used to adjust the booster's power, speed and frequency according to the different patients' needs. This research is a good application of the DHM in medical and nursing fields, and has certain innovative and practical significance. Then, this project can combine with other bone and joint diseases to refine the assist mode and conduct comparative studies to further verify the feasibility of this method path.

References

1. Hu, C.C.: Usability design of home adjuvant medical products for elderly knee joint. Tianjin Polytechnic University, Tianjin (2015)
2. Bijlsman, J.W., Berenbaum, F., Lafeber, F.P.: Osteoarthritis: an update with relevance for clinical practice. J. Lancet **377**(9783), 2115–2126 (2011)
3. Cawthon, P.M.: Recent progress in sarcopenia research: a focus on operationalizing a definition of sarcopenia. J. Curr. Osteoporos. Rep. **16**(6), 730–737 (2018). https://doi.org/10.1007/s11914-018-0484-2
4. Osteoporosis Group of Chinese Orthopaedic Association: The guidelines for the osteoarthritis diagnosis and treatment. J. Chin. J. Orthop. **54**(03), 458–462 (2019)
5. Wang, J.M., Wang, A.P.: Research progress on exercise therapy nursing program for patients with knee osteoarthritis. J. Chin. J. Nurs. **54**(03), 458–462 (2019)
6. Xie, X., Chen, H.: The application of exercise therapy in patients with rheumatoid arthritis. J. Chin. J. Nurs. **50**(09), 1100–1103 (2015)
7. Dong, H.: The influence of the resistance training on the muscle mass and exercise capacity of the elderly people with sarcopenia. Inner Mongolia Normal University, Hohhot (2020)
8. Gao, Q.Q., Lv, J.Y.: Intelligent healthcare: opportunities and challenges for public health in the age of artificial intelligence. J. E-Gov. (11), 11–19 (2017)
9. Qi, H.J.: Study on non-communicable diseases and its influence on activities of daily living of the elderly rural China. Hebei United University, Tangshan (2014)
10. Lv, Y., Li, S., Ni, Z.Z.: The status of chronic conditions among the elderly and the influencing factors related to ADL of old people. J. Acta Universitatis Medicinalis Anhui (01), 29–32 (2001)
11. Hu, D., Chen, H., Jiang, Y.T., et al.: Service needs analysis of the institutional elderly based on daily living ability assessment. J. Health Econ. Res. **36**(10), 55–57 (2019)
12. Feigenbaum, M.S., Pollock, M.L.: Prescription of resistance training for health and disease. J. Med. Sci. Sports Exerc. **31**(1), 38–45 (1999)
13. Leng, Y.F., Hu, J.Q., Zhan, L.L., et al.: Application effect of resistance exercises in patients with rheumatoid arthritis: a systematic review. J. Chin. Nurs. Res. **34**(17), 3041–3048 (2020)
14. Ren, J.D., Fan, Z.J., Huang, J.L.: An overview on digital human model technique and its application to ergonomic design of vehicles. J. Autom. Eng. (07), 647–651 (2006)
15. Dong, Y.M.: Study and realization of the training control system of a rehabilitation exoskeleton orthosis for lower limbs. Zhejiang University, Hangzhou (2008)
16. Bao, H.Q.: Design and optimization of the pressure sensor. Southeast University, Nanjing (2016)
17. Pang, W.Q., Yi, J.Y., Jia, S., et al.: Preparation and characteristics of flexible pressure film sensor. J. Electron. Compon. Mater. **39**(12), 53–57+76 (2020)
18. Wu, D.J.: The importance of sample model in industrial design process. J. Zhejiang Bus. Technol. Inst. **8**(01), 49–50 (2009)

3D Model of Ergonomic Socket Mechanism for Prostheses of Transtibial Amputees

Isabel Carvalho[✉], Victor Nassar[✉], Gabriel Prim[✉], Jonathan Nishida[✉], Eliete Ourives[✉], Tainá Bueno[✉], and Milton Vieira[✉]

Universidade Federal de Santa Catarina, Florianópolis, Brazil
milton.vieira@ufsc.br

Abstract. This work presents a model for the development of a socket mechanism for transtibial prosthesis. A survey was carried out with Brazilian amputee users, based on interviews to understand the context of use and to be able to identify problems of balance, ergonomic and friction problems in the prostheses' socket. With this, a list of requirements was defined, and a semantic map was created, which guided the development of a 3D model of a prosthetic socket, aiming to minimize the mechanical friction, allowing the regulation of the pressure exerted on the stump and the adjustment of fit according to the need of user.

Keywords: Assistive technology · Transtibial prosthesis · Design · Brazilian culture

1 Introduction

The complexity of the health sector opens up spaces for multidisciplinary incorporation, where in design is able to offer solutions and different applications. In this way, certain design concepts are associated with the development of prostheses, such as methodologies for solving problems of the most varied origins with a common focal point: working with people and for those same people [7].

Thus, design can act as an innovation process centered on Brazilian prosthesis users, as it uses approaches that, once focused on the human being, are capable of making tangible the processes of observation and collaboration in visualizing ideas and prototyping [8]. Thus, this study makes a connection between the design process and the inclusion of prosthesis users in its creation, considering the cultural references they have in relation to comfort, flexibility, ease of use, among other relevant aspects for an ergonomic prosthesis.

In the context of amputation, it is highlighted that the lower limb amputee may have difficulties in maintaining static balance, which can lead to falls, and consequently fractures. The use of prostheses has the function of physically and psychologically stabilizing the individual in the face of a critical moment in their life, seeking to restore to the amputee the integrity of the anatomical and functional elements [1, 3].

V. G. Duffy (Ed.): HCII 2021, LNCS 12777, pp. 92–99, 2021.
https://doi.org/10.1007/978-3-030-77817-0_8

It is salutary that, for an individual who uses a prosthesis to regain independence, a process of rehabilitation and readaptation must take place, aimed at promoting a balanced gait and carrying out daily activities with quality, reinserting them into society. However, the gait pattern after an amputation depends on the lost structure and the potential for control, as well as the type of prosthesis used [2, 6].

Within the rehabilitation team, Pullin [5] highlights a specific role for the designer, integrating a systemic and interdisciplinary view to the daily problems faced by people who had lower limbs amputated, to create solutions to improve the usability of the prostheses.

Given the above, it should be noted that this research was limited to exploring the experience of users with transtibial prostheses, with the aim of developing a new prosthetic socket mechanism. From interviews with amputee users, it was possible to analyze the problems faced in the use of prostheses. Issues such as balance, ease in donning the prosthesis, the texture against the residual limb, user mobility, comfort and movement were considered. The developed model aims to minimize the mechanical friction, by means of regular and uniform distribution of the force fields exerted on the prosthesis during the gait.

2 Materials and Methods

As the objective is to develop a mechanism for the socket, there will be no prototype of the feet, suspension and tubular structure components. Thus, it was defined that the element to be prototyped is the one responsible for the interface between the stump and the prosthesis, designated as the socket. The prosthesis socket creation process can be divided into three stages: 1) Immersion, 2) Analysis and synthesis and 3) Prototyping. The immersion phase aims to bring the team closer to the context of the problem, which, furthermore, can either be a preliminary or in-depth immersion. In the analysis and synthesis phase, the insights obtained during the immersion phase are organized in order to obtain patterns and to create challenges that help in understanding the problem. In the prototyping stage, concepts are generated, and solutions are created that are in accordance with the project context [8].

2.1 Immersion

This stage is aimed at investigating socket problems in the prostheses of transtibial amputees. Initially, movement tests were performed to analyze balance with users, such as: walking, sitting, searching for objects on the floor, climbing up and down steps. Afterwards, individual interviews were carried out, seeking to understand the context of the use of transtibial prostheses and to list the problems pointed out, determining the limiting factors for the problem not yet being solved, also contemplating the economic viability of current solutions. The survey recruited nine prosthetic Brazilian volunteers with transtibial amputation. The individuals met the following inclusion criteria: Age between 18 and 65 years; Unilateral transtibial amputation; Used prosthesis for more than 1.5 years; Does not have musculoskeletal changes that make it impossible to remain standing.

2.2 Analysis and Synthesis

At this stage, a semantic panel was built, with the joint participation of users and the general listing of the problems presented in the use of prostheses. The semantic panel provides a visual mode capable of stimulating and inspiring the process of project development, "which must be considered because they are more logical and empathetic to the design context than the traditional approach centered on verbal code" [4]. For each requirement, users should list previously separated images in the database. In the case that one considered that no image would reflect the word, new searches on the internet would be made.

2.3 Prototyping

From the analysis of the prosthesis problems raised by the users and the respective construction of the semantic panel, the requirements that guided the creation of the new socket model for transtibial prosthesis were defined. With that, the basis was created for the creation of the 3D model of the new transtibial prosthesis socket. The model adopted the points raised in the user's analysis stage as form and functionalities. With the creation of the prototype of the socket model for transtibial prostheses, there was an assessment of how the product can act in order to meet the problems diagnosed in the analysis stage with the users. Thus, this stage also included a discussion on how assistive technologies act in the rehabilitation process and to promote the quality of life of amputees.

3 Results

3.1 Balance Observations

In the collective observations of prosthesis users, difficulties were observed during movements to reach an object in front of them. This difficulty is believed to be related to the inability to apply force with the prosthetic tip of the foot when projecting the balance center forward. There were also difficulties to pick up objects on the floor and to rotate 360°. These difficulties are believed to be related to the inability to apply force with the prosthetic toe and the decrease in the degree of freedom of rotation of the amputated limb. Difficulties were noted in supporting the entire body weight in the prosthesis, which may be related to the materials, the socket system and the suspension system of the prosthesis.

3.2 Balance Observations

In the interviews, complaints about injuries to the stump were observed, also, difficulties in making certain movements that require straining inside the socket of the prosthesis. Regarding comfort levels of the material of the prosthesis, volunteers showed dissatisfaction with the comfort, due to the stiffness of the socket which caused pain. Problems with cleaning and smell have also been reported. Thus, relevant points reported by users were:

- Volunteer 1: Does not report complaints of pain or injury to the stump. Uses a silicone coating around the stump.
- Volunteer 2: Has diabetes. Complains of pain and injury to the stump. Was uncomfortable when performing balance tests.
- Volunteer 3: Does not complain of pain or injury to the stump. They underwent physiotherapy after amputation. Young individual, physically active.
- Volunteer 4: Does not complain of injuries to the stump. Individual reports arthrosis in the hip and poor calcification in the right shoulder. Uses prosthesis with components in titanium, carbon and silicone. Prosthesis equipped with suction system.
- Volunteer 5: Complains of frequent injuries to the stump, discomfort with socket material and cleaning. Balance tests point to difficulties in reaching objects in front of them and making rotating movements of the body.
- Volunteer 6: Complains of frequent injuries to the stump, discomfort with socket material and cleaning. Uses crutches for assistance. They present significant bone loss. Movement restricted by the use of a fixative, being unable to maintain orthostatism. Showed low performance in the control of balance.
- Volunteer 7: Complains of pain where the prosthesis and stump are in contact, inconvenient for cleaning. Volunteer complains that they have had the same prosthesis for three years.
- Volunteer 8: Has hypertension. Complains of stump injuries. Prosthetic foot is in poor condition, requiring component replacement. Stump shape makes fitting difficult.
- Volunteer 9: Has hypertension. Complains of pain, but not of injuries to the stump. Uses an internal femoral prosthesis and screw implant in the right foot.

3.3 List of Requirements for the Model Definition of an Ergonomic Socket Mechanism

From the analysis of users of transtibial prostheses in the previous steps, the semantic panel (Figs. 1, 2 and 3) was created with the requirements raised for the development of the model for this project, in which there were greater complaints and difficulties in the performance of the patient's movements. Thus, the following requirements were defined: Texture, Shape and Use. For each requirement, volunteers were invited to define related keywords and subsequently gather images that could express the concepts. In this way, the requirements for formatting the semantic panel were divided: Texture Requirements (Light, Soft, Comfortable, Clean), Shape Requirements (Organic, Aerodynamic, Versatile, Minimalist and Technological) and Requirements for use (Easy, Agile and Flexible). With that, semantic panels were created and used as a basis for the generation of the socket model.

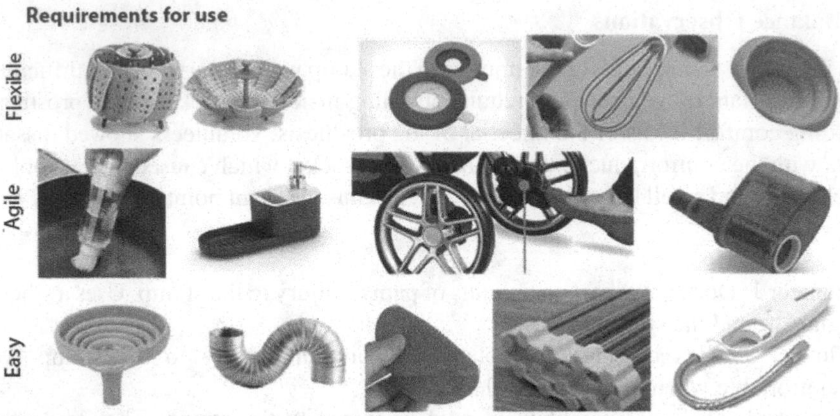

Requirements for use

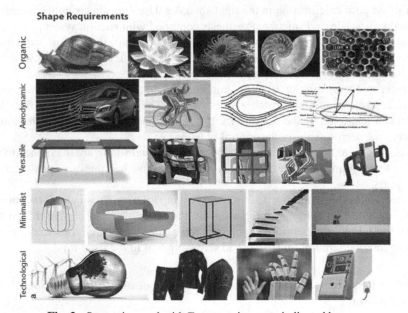

Fig. 1. Semantic panel with the Usage requirements indicated by users

Shape Requirements

Fig. 2. Semantic panel with Form requirements indicated by users

3.4 3D Development of the Prosthetic Socket Model

In order to develop a better fitting socket mechanism, this research sought to establish the concept of a prosthesis in order to provide comfort, fixation, size adjustment and compatibility between prostheses of different specifications. In addition to better prosthesis fixation, better balance, ease in donning the prosthesis, better feel and texture of the prosthesis against the residual limb, good mobility with low energy consumption for its use accompanied by the appropriate weight of the prosthesis were taken into consideration. The prosthesis socket system aims to minimize mechanical friction without

Texture Requirements

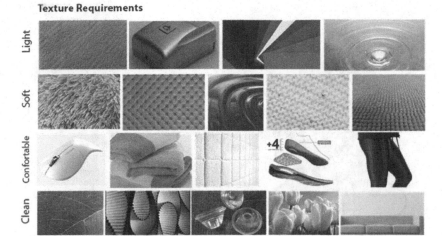

Fig. 3. Semantic panel with Texture requirements specified by users

causing injuries or wounds. In this configuration, the developed solution considers the regular and uniform distribution of the force fields exerted on the prosthesis during the amputee's gait, opening the socket according to the user's need (Fig. 4).

The socket mechanism constitutes the link between the stump and the prosthesis. It allows the regulation of the pressure exerted on the stump, making the adjustment according to the user's need. When rotating the base (a) clockwise, the support (b) decompresses, allowing the "opening" of the flaps (c). By rotating the base (a) counterclockwise, the flaps (c) perform a "closing" movement. In this way, the fitting of the socket onto the stump can be adjusted according to the desired pressure, size or comfort (Fig. 5).

Fig. 4. Simulation of the opening of the prosthetic socket

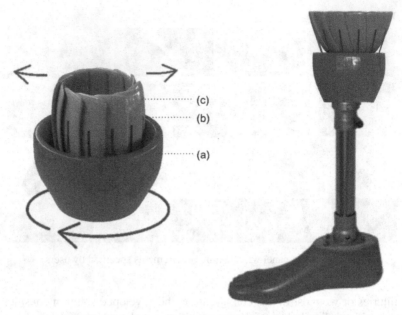

Fig. 5. Socket operation and positioning in the prosthesis

4   Conclusion

The prostheses seek to restore the integrity of the anatomical and functional elements to the amputee. The lower limb amputee may have difficulties in maintaining static balance, which can lead to falls or fractures. Thus, there is relevance in the development of new models of prostheses once the results achieved are able to improve the quality of life of prosthesis users. More than its functional rehabilitation, the prosthesis can mean one's reinsertion into society and one's independence.

In view of the products and technologies related to the use of prostheses, there are several factors to be considered regarding the usability of prostheses for transtibial amputees. Issues that touch on its usefulness and mobility, such as fit, balance, comfort and mobility in different environments. It is necessary to consider factors related to the health of the residual limb, such as blisters and injuries. The prostheses also involve factors such as appearance, acceptance by the partner and family and active social life.

The socket system of the prostheses distributed by the Brazilian Unified Health System (SUS) does not have a vacuum fixation system, which has a high cost. Without the vacuum system, the appearance of wounds and blisters is common due to the friction generated at the interface between the residual limb and the prosthesis. It is also important to remember that there is a human factor in the process. The orthopedic doctor and the prosthetic technician are responsible for prescribing the most appropriate materials and technologies for each case.

The model presented for a socket mechanism in transtibial prosthesis aims to meet requests generated from the complaints from the users themselves. By bringing the patient into the discussion of how the product could be developed, a better understanding of the needs and what kind of solutions can be obtained as well as be tested, immersing themselves in the cultural reality of the patients. Thus, the contexts related to use, texture and shape for the fit between stump and prosthesis were highlighted, seen as these were the major complaints by the user group. Afterwards, certain requirements such as flexibility, comfort, lightness, softness and versatility, helped in determining what kind of aspects the product would have. In this sense, the use of the semantic panel construction stage was relevant for the materialization of the users' thoughts and desires, as well as the systematization of references and the guidance of the design team for the creation of the 3D project. It is also worth mentioning the use of users' references according to the Brazilian cultural context in which the research is inserted.

It is noteworthy that the product of this research is a concept that has yet to have its performance validated through balance assessment methods. Thus, for the future of this research, the technical specification of the proposed solution is expected in order to understand the materials to be used and the product components, as well as the technical design, establishing the product dimensions and modules, the development of the prototype function of the ergonomic prosthesis socket system and the respective tests in order to obtain evidence of the results with prosthesis users.

References

1. Baraúna, M.A., et al.: Avaliação do equilíbrio estático em indivíduos amputados de membros inferiores através da biofotogrametria computadorizada. Bras. J. Phys. Ther. **10**(1), 83–90 (2006). https://doi.org/10.1590/S1413-35552006000100011
2. Boccolini, F.: Reabilitação: amputados, amputações e próteses. Robe Livraria e Editora, São Paulo (2001)
3. Carvalho, J.A.: Amputações de Membros Inferiores: em Busca de Plena Reabilitação, 2a edn. Manole, São Paulo (2003)
4. McDonagh, D., Denton, H.: Exploring the degree to which individual students share a common perception of specific mood boards: observations relating to teaching, learning and team-based design. Des. Stud. **26**(1), 35–53 (2005). https://doi.org/10.1016/j.destud.2004.05.008
5. Pullin, G.: Design Meets Disability. The MIT Press, Cambridge (2009)
6. Ramos, A.R., Alles, I.C.D.: Aspectos clínicos. Fisioterapia: aspectos clínicos e práticos da reabilitação. In: Borges, D., Moura, E.W., Lima, E., Silva, P.A.C. (eds.) Artes Médicas, São Paulo, pp. 234–262 (2005)
7. Skrabe, C.: Chegou a hora e a vez do design. In: Anuário Hospital Best. Eximia Comunicação, São Paulo (2010)
8. Vianna, M., et al.: Design Thinking: Inovação em Negócios. MJV, Rio de Janeiro (2012)

Evaluating the Risk of Muscle Injury in Football-Kicking Training with OpenSim

Jing Chang[1], Wenrui Wang[2], Damien Chablat[3(⊠)], and Fouad Bennis[4]

[1] Tsinghua University, Beijing 100084, China
les_astres@tsinghua.edu.cn
[2] École Centrale de Nantes, 44300 Nantes, France
[3] Laboratoire des Sciences du Numérique de Nantes, UMR CNRS 6004, 44300 Nantes, France
damien.chablat@cnrs.fr
[4] École Centrale de Nantes, LS2N, UMR CNRS 6004, 44300 Nantes, France
fouad.bennis@ec-nantes.fr

Abstract. Football, as the most popular sport in the world, has a very wide spread worldwide. With the wide spread of football, more and more people participate in football activities. Football is a very strenuous sport and athletes are easily injured. This article examines the problem of kicking through two experiments, one is the normal kicking process, and the other is the process of imitating the kicking. The two sets of experiments use the same motions, but their applied external forces are different. In the normal kicking, the football will receive a force on the foot during the kicking process. Conversely, in the imitation kicking, the foot is not in contact with the football and no extra force is apply on the foot. Analyze the impact of football on the body by comparing the above two experiments. OpenSim software is used to calculate the forces of each muscle by simulating the process of kicking a ball to analyze the muscle fatigue. It is judged that those muscles are vulnerable to injury during the kick. Athletes should focus on strengthening the exercise of these muscles, increase the strength of related muscles, and focus on protecting related muscles during exercise to reduce injuries.

Keywords: Football · Football injury · Football kicking · OpenSim · Muscle fatigue · Fatigue model

1 Introduction

As one of the most popular and physically demanding games around the world, football is reported to bring about 12 to 35 injury incidences per 1000 h outdoor games [1]. Most of the injury is caused by impact trauma [1], followed by overuse injury, which takes 34% of all [2]. Researches on retired football players have shown that they are faced with twice the incidence of coxarthrosis compared with normal people [3, 4]. In fact, the lifelong occurrence of musculoskeletal problems in former football athletes is reported to be even higher than that of former long-distance runners or shooters [5].

© Springer Nature Switzerland AG 2021
V. G. Duffy (Ed.): HCII 2021, LNCS 12777, pp. 100–109, 2021.
https://doi.org/10.1007/978-3-030-77817-0_9

Kicking football is a basic training specific for football players. A normal football, weighing about 0.44 kg could reach up to 200 km/h in a shot, which may bring heavy load to athletes. Body parts that form the kicking-related kinetic chain such as the back, hip, and knee are reported to be the most fragile parts in terms of musculoskeletal injuries [2]. To prevent related impact and overuse injuries, it is necessary to have an evaluation on the muscle loads as well as a prediction on the fatigue process in football-kicking training.

OpenSim is one of the main biomechanical human modeling platforms [6]. Various kinematical and dynamical calculations are available to simulate human motion as well as to estimate body loads. Furthermore, algorithms such as Static optimization (SO), Compute muscle control (CMC) were developed to estimate the activities of individual muscles [6]. In previous researches, the OpenSim platform has been used to study muscle contributions to sports such as running [7], to determine the risky muscle groups in physical works such as overhead drilling [8], and to study the ways of human-machine interaction from the aspects of body load distribution, such as to compare the unilateral and bilateral crutch gaits [9]. OpenSim will be effective to study the muscle contribution in football-kicking.

Muscle fatigue is an important contributing factor to overuse muscle injuries as well as musculoskeletal disorders. To date, very few studies have investigated the muscle fatigue induced by football-kicking. The muscle fatigue process has been described by the decline of muscle maximal voluntary contraction force (MVC) [10]. As illustrated by the Dynamic muscle fatigue model, the rate of force decline is dependent on the current muscle loads as well as the subject-specific trait. By the time, the muscle MVC declines to a level close to its current load, the risk of overuse injury increases.

In this study, we seek to understand how different muscle groups contribute to football-kicking training as well as to predict the fatigue process in this training. Null hypotheses include:

1) Muscle groups near the acting point of external force (i.e., the calf and knee) contribute more than that of the farther (i.e., the hip and trunk muscles);
2) Muscles of left and right sides differ in contribution. The dominant side that applies football-kicking contributes more than the other.
3) The lower leg and knee muscles contribute especially to accelerating the football.

Results of this study will expand our knowledge about the kinetics of football-kicking and help prevent both impact and overuse injuries in football.

2   Methods

This is a biomechanical simulation study. A football-kicking motion is simulated and muscle activations with and without the action force of football are calculated with OpenSim. Muscle fatigue process is indicated by muscle MVC declines in constant repetitive football-kicking training.

2.1   OpenSim Model

In this study, a generic OpenSim model, gait2354 is used for simulation. It is one of the most widely-used models with satisfactory effectiveness (for details see https://simtk-con fluence.stanford.edu/display/OpenSim/Gait+2392+and+2354+Models).   Muscles   are categorized by four groups. The trunk group includes three pairs of muscle (the internal and external obliques, and the erector spine); the hip group includes 18 pairs of muscle that connects the pelvis and leg; the knee group include seven pairs of muscle that cross the knee joint; the calf group includes 4 pairs of muscles.

2.2   Data and Simulation

For kicking football, athlete lifts the dominant foot and swings forward to reach the ball, during which ground reaction force acts on the supporting foot and football-accelerating force on the dominant foot. In this study, we compare the case with or without the accelerating force. Motion and force data come from OpenSim document (https://simtk.org/frs/index.php?group_id=679, copyright open from Stanford University), which represents a subject kicking football with the right foot. The kicking motion lasts for 1.5 s (Fig. 1).

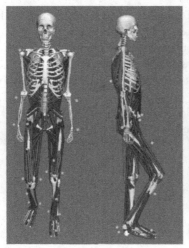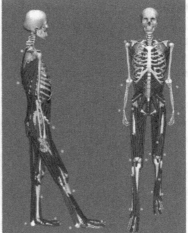

Fig. 1. The simulated football-kicking motion at t = 0.45 s (left) and t = 0.9 s (right).

Muscle contribution is indicated by computed muscle activation. Inverse kinematics and inverse dynamics are computed to estimate joint positions and joint moments; then Residual reduce algorithm and CMC are applied to estimate the muscle activations.

2.3 Muscle Fatigue Analysis

The Dynamic muscle fatigue model is presented as Eq. 1. In this study, we approximate the maximal muscle ability $(F_{max}(t))$ as the MVC. With the computed muscle activation from OpenSim simulation, the profile of maximal muscle force is predictable. As illustrated in Introduction, the muscle would be at risk for overuse injury by the time its maximal force declines near the required muscle load. In this study, we analyze the muscle fatigue process in repetitive football-kicking motions to check athlete's maximal endurance time. The subject-specific muscle fatigability is set to 1 min^{-1}, indicating average fatigue resistance [8].

$$\frac{dF(t)}{dt} = -k\frac{F_{load}(t)}{F_{max}(t)}F(t) \tag{1}$$

With

- $F_{cem}(t)$ N   Current existing maximal muscle ability
- $F_{load}(t)$ N   Muscle load
- $F_{max}(t)$ N   Maximal muscle ability
- k min^{-1} Subject-specific fatigability
- $F(t)$ 1   Muscle activation

3 Results

3.1 Muscle Contribution in Football-Kicking

The estimated muscle activations are summarized in Table 1. In general, muscle group that contribute the most are the knee and the hip, instead of the calf; the first hypothesis is not supported. Muscles on the right side (dominant side in this simulation) are more activated, which supports the second hypothesis. However, significant difference only presents in the knee and calf. Finally, contrary to the third hypothesis, acting force from football only makes significant difference in the trunk muscle group. Both the left and right trunk are much more activated in simulation with football (2.18% vs. 24%), suggesting that football acceleration force mainly depends on the trunk muscles.

Table 1. The calculated muscle activations in football-kicking training. Muscles are compared between left and right side.

Muscle group	Number of muscles	Muscle activation (%)			
		R-with football	R-without football	L-with football	L-without football
Hip	18	35.64	36.77	33.23	32.11
Knee	7	40.54	41.53	28.65	27.20
Calf	4	18.22	17.49	6.85	5.48
Trunk	3	2.18	24.21	2.18	23.97

3.2 Fatigue Process of Football-Kicking Training

The Muscle Force Profiles. Muscles that activated the most in each muscle group are chosen to study the fatigue process. They are the *iliacus* on the hip, the *biceps femoris-long head (bifemih)* on the knee, the *tibialis anterior (tib_ant)* of the calf, and the *internal oblique (intobl)* of the trunk. Mean activation of these muscles are shown in Table 2, and their force profiles are presented in Fig. 2.

Table 2. The typical muscle activation of each muscle group in football-kicking training.

Muscle group	Name of muscle	Muscle activation (%)			
		R-with football	R-without football	L-with football	L-without football
Hip	*Iliacus*	67.1	74.9	65.0	65.5
Knee	*Bifemih*	35.8	33.1	25.9	26.9
Calf	*Tib_ant*	31.8	32.3	15.0	8.9
Trunk	*Intobl*	2.1	29.8	2.1	29.1

The Fatigue Process and Maximal Endurance Time

The fatigue process in 200 repetitive football-kicking motions of the four typical muscles are shown in Fig. 3, 4, 5 and 6. Red line indicates the muscle force ability while green lines indicates the muscle force requirement at each moment. The intersection of the two indicates the time when current existing muscle force ability declines to the requirement of the motion, so-called the maximal endurance time (MET). After that, the muscle would enter into a risky situation for overuse injuries. It can be found from the figures that the right *iliacus* in kicking-with-football motion has the shortest MET (12.39 s, about 8 cycles), followed by the right *introbl* in kicking-with-football motion (22.85 s, about 15 cycles).

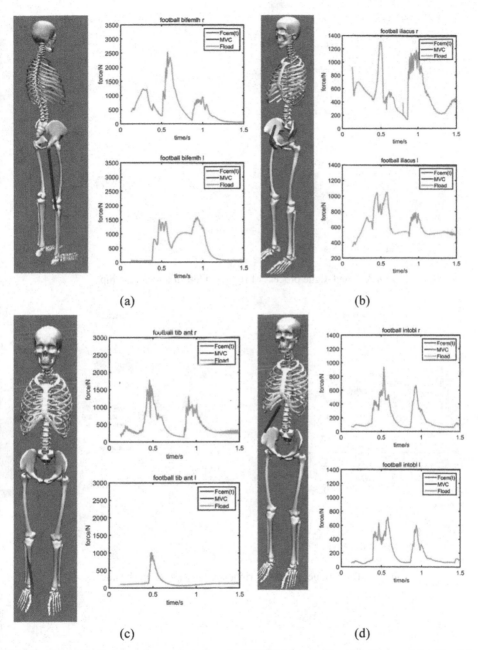

Fig. 2. The estimated muscle exertions in a football-kicking motion. (a) *iliacus* of the hip; (b) *biceps femoris-long head (bifemlh)* of the knee; (c) *tibialis anterior (tib_ant)* of the calf; (d) *internal oblique (interobl)* of the trunk.

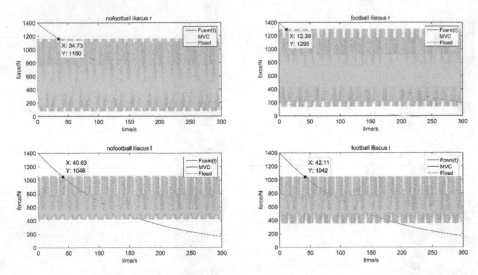

Fig. 3. The fatigue process of right and left *iliacus* on the hip.

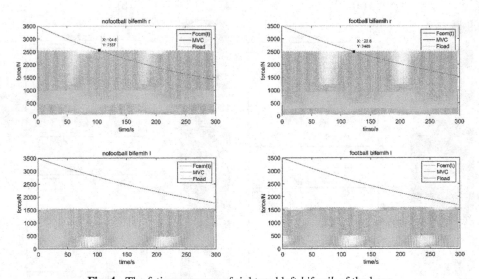

Fig. 4. The fatigue process of right and left *bifemih* of the knee.

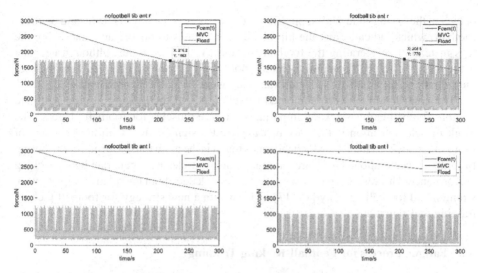

Fig. 5. The fatigue process of right and left *tib_ant* on the calf.

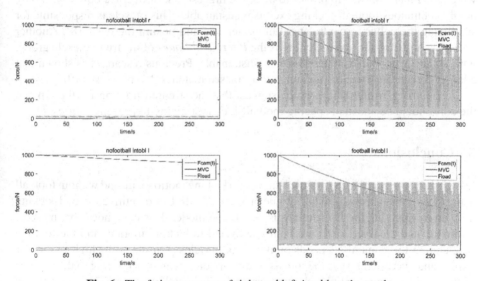

Fig. 6. The fatigue process of right and left *intobl* on the trunk.

4 Discussion

4.1 Contribution of Different Groups of Muscle in the Football-Kicking Motion

The first surprising result about muscle loads in kicking motion is that the hip muscle group is highly activated (more than 30% on average). This result may explain the high incidence of hip and groin injury in football players [12–14]. In fact, the hip and groin injury is reported to be the most common non-time-loss injury in football players [13]. Results of this study also show that the loads of hip muscles present little difference between the swing side and supporting side, or between motions with and without football, which indicates that the hip mainly contributes to posing and stabilizing the legs instead of accelerating the football. Besides, the calf muscles, although near the acting point of football reaction force, are not highly activated. The result emphasizes the importance of a holistic view in examining workloads in ergonomics [11].

The comparison between simulated muscle loads of the kicking motion with and without football emphasizes the importance of core muscles for football players. The trunk muscle activation is the only that aggravates significantly with the presence of football (about 2% vs. 24%), which indicates that it is the main muscle group contributing to football acceleration. Therefore, stronger trunk muscles may generate better kicking performance. This result expands our previous knowledge about the relationship between strength and football velocity [16, 17], from whom a new strategy for football kicking training may come out.

4.2 Fatigue Process for Football-Kicking Training

The fatigue process analysis of the typical muscles has outlined the fragile muscles, in which the *iliacus* of the hip proves to be at the highest risk of overuse injury with only height continuous football-kicking exercises sustainable. This muscle is responsible for stabilizing the pelvis in contralateral hip extension and posing the legs [18]. Another muscle at high risk for overuse injury is the *internal obliques* of the trunk muscle group, with about 15 football-kicking exercises sustainable. Previous research has shown that a larger core muscle reduces the number of missed matches due to injury [19].

In summary, results of this study suggest that the strength training for the hip and the core should be ahead of specific football-kicking training to prevent injuries.

5   Conclusions

In this study, we examine the muscle behavior in kicking motion with and without football using OpenSim, then evaluate the fatigue process and MET of repetitive football-kicking training by applying the Dynamic Muscle Fatigue model. It is concluded that muscles of the hip and the knee joints are highly activated in kicking motion, and the football acceleration force mainly depends on the trunk muscles. Muscle at the highest risk for fatigue and overuse injury is the *iliacus* of the hip joint, which, according to the settings of this study, sustains only height continuous football-kicking cycles. The results may offer a reference for the coaches, athletes, and physiotherapists about the football-kicking training and related injuries.

References

1. Junge, A., Dvorak, J.: Soccer injuries. Sports Med. **34**(13), 929–938 (2004)
2. Nielsen, A.B., Yde, J.: Epidemiology and traumatology of injuries in soccer. Am. J. Sports Med. **17**(6), 803–807 (1989)
3. Klünder, K.B., Rud, B., Hansen, J.: Osteoarthritis of the hip and knee joint in retired football players. Acta Orthop. Scand. **51**(1–6), 925–927 (1980)

4. Lindberg, H., Roos, H., Gärdsell, P.: Prevalence of coxarthrosis in former soccer players: 286 players compared with matched controls. Acta Orthop. Scand. **64**(2), 165–167 (1993)
5. Räty, H.P., Kujala, U.M., Videman, T., et al.: Lifetime musculoskeletal symptoms and injuries among former elite male athletes. Int. J. Sports Med. **18**(08), 625–632 (1997)
6. Delp, S.L., Anderson, F.C., Arnold, A.S., et al.: OpenSim: open-source software to create and analyze dynamic simulations of movement. IEEE Trans. Biomed. Eng. **54**(11), 1940–1950 (2007)
7. Hamner, S.R., Seth, A., Delp, S.L.: Muscle contributions to propulsion and support during running. J. Biomech. **43**(14), 2709–2716 (2010)
8. Chang, J., Chablat, D., Bennis, F., Ma, L.: A full-chain OpenSim model and its application on posture analysis of an overhead drilling task. In: Duffy, V.G. (ed.) HCII 2019. LNCS, vol. 11581, pp. 33–44. Springer, Cham (2019). https://doi.org/10.1007/978-3-030-22216-1_3
9. Chang, J., Wang, W., Chablat, D., Bennis, F.: Evaluating the effect of crutch-using on trunk muscle loads. In: Stephanidis, C., Duffy, V.G., Streitz, N., Konomi, S., Krömker, H. (eds.) HCI International 2020 – Late Breaking Papers: Digital Human Modeling and Ergonomics, Mobility and Intelligent Environments: 22nd HCI International Conference, HCII 2020, Copenhagen, Denmark, July 19–24, 2020, Proceedings, pp. 455–466. Springer International Publishing, Cham (2020). https://doi.org/10.1007/978-3-030-59987-4_32
10. Ma, L., Chablat, D., Bennis, F., et al.: A new simple dynamic muscle fatigue model and its validation. Int. J. Ind. Ergon. **39**(1), 211–220 (2009)
11. Chang, J.: The risk assessment of work-related musculoskeletal disorders based on OpenSim. PhD Thesis École centrale de Nantes (2018)
12. Werner, J., Hägglund, M., Waldén, M., et al.: UEFA injury study: a prospective study of hip and groin injuries in professional football over seven consecutive seasons. Br. J. Sports Med. **43**(13), 1036–1040 (2009)
13. Langhout, R., et al.: Hip and groin injury is the most common non-time-loss injury in female amateur football. Knee Surg. Sports Traumatol. Arthrosc. **27**(10), 3133–3141 (2018). https://doi.org/10.1007/s00167-018-4996-1
14. Feeley, B.T., Powell, J.W., Muller, M.S., et al.: Hip injuries and labral tears in the national football league. Am. J. Sports Med. **36**(11), 2187–2195 (2008)
15. Nesser, T.W., Huxel, K.C., Tincher, J.L., et al.: The relationship between core stability and performance in division I football players. J. Strength Condition. Res. **22**(6), 1750–1754 (2008)
16. McGuigan, M.R., Wright, G.A., Fleck, S.J.: Strength training for athletes: does it really help sports performance? Int. J. Sports Physiol. Perform. **7**(1), 2–5 (2012)
17. Young, W.B., Rath, D.A.: Enhancing foot velocity in football kicking: the role of strength training. J. Strength Condition. Res. **25**(2), 561–566 (2011)
18. Andersson, E., Oddsson, L., Grundström, H., et al.: The role of the psoas and iliacus muscles for stability and movement of the lumbar spine, pelvis and hip. Scand. J. Med. Sci. Sports **5**(1), 10–16 (1995)
19. Hrysomallis, C.: Injury incidence, risk factors and prevention in Australian rules football. Sports Med. **43**(5), 339–354 (2013)

New Approaches to Movement Evaluation Using Accurate Truck Ingress Data

Martin Dorynek[1]([⊠]) [iD], Hongtao Zhang[1], Norman Hofmann[2], and Klaus Bengler[1] [iD]

[1] Chair of Ergonomics, Technical University of Munich, Boltzmannstraße 15, 85747 Garching, Germany
martin.dorynek@tum.de
[2] Institute for Mechatronics e.V., Reichenhainer Straße 88, 09126 Chemnitz, Germany
norman.hofmann@ifm-chemnitz.de

Abstract. The importance of ergonomic studies will increase in the future, particularly with regard to occupant comfort, safety and health, especially in view of an aging society that is working longer. Therefore, there is a need to integrate these studies into the digital product development process of vehicle manufacturers. For this purpose, a technology for the motion prediction and evaluation of occupants on/in the vehicle model with digital human models is required in order to obtain ergonomic statements about the design in an early development phase. However, this technology is not yet available with the human models currently in use, since on the one hand the prediction of movements still requires a very high manual effort and on the other hand the ergonomic evaluation of movements cannot be calculated validly. Within the project, a connection between subjective measured variables and objective kinematic and dynamic data is to be established.

Keywords: Ingres/egress · Digital-Human-Model (DHM) · Movement analysis/evaluation · Biomechanics

1 Introduction

Of the many research areas in the field of human anthropometry and digital human modeling, ingress and egress are particularly customer-relevant product features. A vehicle's geometric restrictions can cause a high level of strain on the human movement system. With regard to demographic change, comfortable vehicle ingress and egress is becoming an increasingly important purchase criterion in our aging society. At present, however, there are only limited possibilities of analytically assessing the ease of vehicle entry and exit, as evaluation procedures are predominantly subjective. This is why it has been such a heated topic of debate in the ergonomic research community for so many decades.

The risk of injury to truck drivers is not limited to the driving phase but often occurs while the vehicle is stationary. Truck driver injuries sustained in a stationary vehicle occur, for example, when boarding, as shown in a study by Lin and Cohen (1997). According to this study, 27% of truck driver accidents are due to slips and falls. Heglund and Cavagna (1987) also show that truck driver injuries often occur on entering or exiting

© Springer Nature Switzerland AG 2021
V. G. Duffy (Ed.): HCII 2021, LNCS 12777, pp. 110–121, 2021.
https://doi.org/10.1007/978-3-030-77817-0_10

the cab. Truck driver falls are usually caused by tripping, misstepping, or losing balance (Lin and Cohen 1997). Typically, injuries are sustained to the back as well as to knee, wrist, ankle and shoulder joints. Given the severe consequences of truck driver injury, an important goal is to adapt truck design by devising preventive measures (Michel 2014). In order to better understand the inherent difficulties encountered during boarding, Hebe and Bengler (2018) investigated a wide variety of truck boarding strategies. They found that there are no clear core strategies.

Since passengers interact dynamically with a vehicle, motion and movement studies are needed to ensure their ergonomic protection. There are currently several physical models available for conducting tests involving subjects. However, such tests are overly complicated, time-consuming and cost-intensive. Studies are also costly in terms of both time and pressure to obtain rapid vehicle developments. In addition to the time required, trials based on questionnaires additionally suffer from ambiguity of words used in the survey, which impacts the evaluation. A test person's individual experience inevitably plays a role, as does the fact that the limbic system in the evaluation is not consciously accessible to humans (Bubb 2015; Chateauroux et al. 2012).

2 Materials and Methods

2.1 Experimental Procedure

For the aforementioned reasons, equipment is required for predicting movement and evaluating the vehicle model, together with digital human models, to obtain ergonomic design information at an early phase of development. The *'Dynamic Evaluation of Vehicle Passenger'* (DELFIN) scheme was set up by the Federal Ministry of Education and Research to create software technology to facilitate the ergonomic assessment of predicted motions for the purpose of optimizing ergonomic design workflows. The general usability of technologies in vehicle development focuses on trucks, but it will also be available for other applications in the future.

Realistic motion data are needed to form the data basis for a model-based approach such as this. A measurement mock-up was designed for the project to study subjects' ingress motions. The measurement mock-up consists of three components: a system for varying the structural parameters, a motion capture system to record human movements, and a force measurement system to determine the interaction forces between the human and the mock-up.

Mock-Up
The mock-up framework of is made of aluminum profiles (Bosch) to enable structural variation. The height, width and angle of the steps can be varied as can the door opening. For example, step height can be adjusted within the range 280–400 mm, which covers the step distances found in typical truck models. The required variation ranges were determined by extensive research. The front link design is the one primarily used in Europe, so this design will be examined in more detail. All access openings used by European manufacturers are positioned in front of the front axle. This means that the front wheel protrudes into the door cutout and the steps are arranged on the left-hand side. Handrails on the A and B pillars support the ladder-like entry. The entry height is

scaled with either three or four steps. (Latka 2020) The possible variations are shown in Fig. 1.

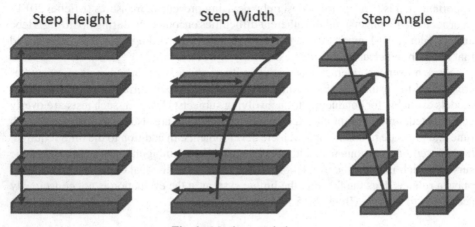

Fig. 1. Mock-up variations

The mock-up itself is fixed to the ground.

Motion Capture System

A motion capture system made by ART is used to record motions. It is a real-time system that uses rigid bodies (targets) with reflective markers. A target comprises several markers and indicates its position and orientation in 3D space (6DOF – six degrees of freedom). Nineteen targets are applied to the human body to record the motion trajectories of the segments. Further targets are also applied to parts of the mock-up to record these motions. These are the door, seat and steering wheel, as well as the mock-up itself. The wiring can be seen in Fig. 2.

A combination of fifteen ATrack-5 cameras were used for motion recording. These were attached to a profile setup which was independent of the mock-up. Motions were captured at a recording frequency of 150 Hz.

Force-Measurement-System

Force sensors were installed in the mockup to measure the interaction forces. They comprised six mobile force plates (Kistler Type 9286BA) and four 3D force sensors (Kistler Type 9327C). The six force plates were attached to the aluminum profiles using specially manufactured adapters and reflected the tread surface of the steps. The four 3D force sensors were attached to the handrails and the aluminum profiles with special adapters. The 3D force sensors were connected to a DAQ box via a charge amplifier (Kistler LabAmp). As the force plates they have a built-in charge amplifier, they were connected directly to the DAQ box. A Kistler Sdk unit was used to control the functionality of the DAQ box and to start and stop the measurement procedure (Fig. 3).

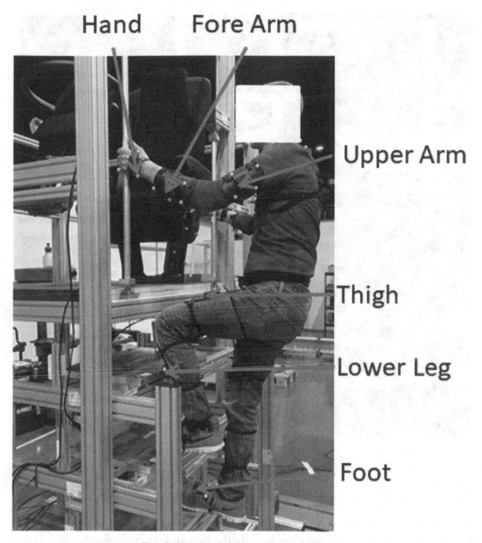

Fig. 2. Subject with targets on mock-up

To create an overall measurement system, all subsystems had to be integrated into a temporally and spatially unified model. For this reason, all force measurement sensors were calibrated in the global coordinate system to ensure their spatial positioning. A motion capture system with a measurement tool was used for this purpose. Synchronization of the data streams was established via a hardware interface (TTL signal) using the master-slave principle. Here, the force measurement system is the master and the motion capture system is the slave.

Fig. 3. Mock-up with force sensors

2.2 Transfer of the Movement to the Dynamicus Digital Human Model

The 'Dynamicus' human model is used for modeling the human body. The 'alaska' general-purpose simulation software regards the human body as a multi-body system (MBS). The Dynamicus model consists of non-deformable bodies representing the various segments of the human body. The rigid bodies are kinematically coupled by idealized joints [DHM and Posturography].

The Dynamicus model is designed to represent an individual subject as best as possible. To do this, the subject's anthropometric data must be precisely determined; this refers to the lengths, widths, and circumferences etc. of the segments. Based on these dimensions, it is then possible to parameterize the Dynamicus as a multi-body system. They include both kinematic dimensions (coordinates of the joints, segment lengths) and mass distribution properties (coordinates of the center of mass and moments of inertia of each body of the mode).

The recorded movements are transferred to the multi-body model using the method of motion reconstruction. This applies to both human motion and the motion of the mock-up components. Motion reconstruction by inverse kinematics uses an optimization procedure to create the best possible match between the model and the measured motion capture data. Motion reconstruction enables the following to be determined:

- Joint angles and positions of the segments or joints in space;
- Velocities of the segments and the joint angle velocities;
- Position and velocity of the center of mass of the entire model or of the individual segments.

The inverse dynamics method is applied to the overall model based on the data from the motion reconstruction and the joint forces and joint torques calculated. In relation to the human model, joint torques are also referred to as muscle torques. They represent the sum of all torques resulting from the reduction of muscle forces to the joint center (Winter 2009). They are also referred to as net joint torques (Zaciorskij 2002). The inverse dynamics method enables the joint torques and joint forces to be determined.

Together, the results of the motion reconstruction and inverse dynamics are referred to as the biomechanical parameters. An overview of the data flow and calculation methods is given in Fig. 4.

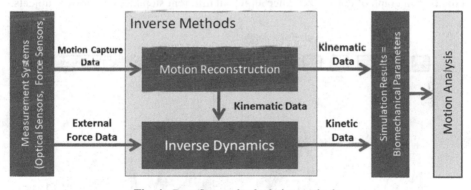

Fig. 4. Data flow and calculation methods

2.3 Data Processing

The movement required to gain ingress into a truck is a very complex one, as it involves all four human interactors – both hands and both feet. As these interactors are used at different times and for different lengths of time, the partial movements vary both intra-individually and inter-individually. To perform a movement analysis based on biomechanical parameters, comparable data or comparable data sections have to be generated. For this purpose, the overall process was divided into eleven sub-processes (Fig. 5), classified according to the kinematic data and the forces measured on the force plates. The following figure presents an example of the keyframes and associated sub-processes.

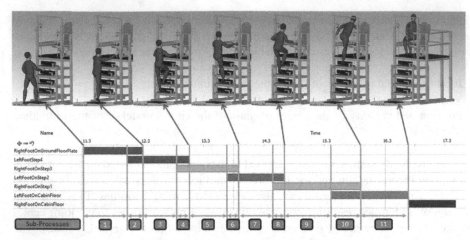

Fig. 5. Keyframes and sub-processes

After classifying the sub-processes, the calculated biomechanical parameters are normalized and are then available for further evaluation. Figure 6 presents an example in the form a graph of normalized knee angles at different step heights for two subjects.

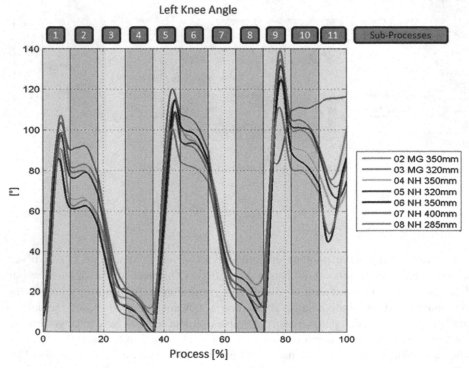

Fig. 6. An example illustration of the normalized knee angle of two subjects at varying step heights

2.4 Data Recording

Data recording is not only a very time-consuming process, it is also physically and mentally demanding for the subject. The subject is required to enter the measurement mock-up at least 120 times over a period of approximately seven hours and complete twelve different measurement mock-ups. Each variation is repeated ten times. There are several breaks, during which the measurement mock-up is modified and the test person fills in a digital questionnaire. To exclude any effects of movement learning, the order of the variations is randomized.

3 Data Clustering and Analyzation

After the data pre-processing step is complete, all ingress movement data are reconstructed for further time-series clustering methods. These generally consist of several key steps, including similarity calculations and the implementation of clustering algorithms (Aghabozorgi et al. 2015).

It is apparent from the literature review that multiple methods of time-series similarity calculation are available. These can be categorized into either shape-based measurements or distance-based measurements. The distance-based method focuses more on mathematical calculation and delivers the difference in the mathematical model of the movement, while the shape-based method focuses more on the movement's details and features in particular areas over time. The aim of this study is to compare different movements in detail and thus to deliver the key movement behavior for use in design and development. This means that in our case, shape-based similarity measurement is the more appropriate method.

Various research studies focus on time-series clustering, and there are multiple clustering algorithms and frameworks that can be applied to the system. Clustering algorithms are classified by mathematical model; they include hierarchical clustering, partitioning clustering, model-based clustering, and density-based clustering, as presented in the work by (Ergüner Özkoç 2021). The partitioning clustering method has been widely used in similar time-series clustering analyses and is therefore the method selected for this study.

A clustering evaluation is required to analyze and compare all the methods. In addition, multiple configurations have to be set for clustering. A best practice involves combining all optimum methods in each clustering step. Of all the evaluation methods, some require external data, such as the true label of time-series data or the data's predicted label. However, such data is not available in this study, so only the internal clustering evaluation tools can be applied to evaluate the system (Rousseeuw 1987).

The solution proposed in this study evaluates a movement on the basis of the similarity index. Here, each new movement is compared with each reference movement. If the movement is good, i.e., common in terms of the movement data already observed in the system, it should be similar to one of the reference movements. If not, it is regarded as a bad, i.e., unusual, movement as it can collide with the mechanism. All in all, the evaluation succeeds in comparing the new movement with each of the reference movements and analyzes whether or not it is similar to any of them (Cassisi et al. 2012).

Figure 7 shows all the motions recorded for one body joint. These were segmented into three main movements by clustering, as shown in Fig. 8.

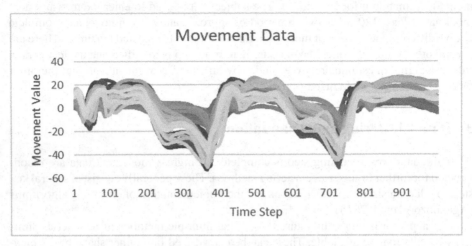

Fig. 7. Collection of various ingress movements for one configuration and one body part

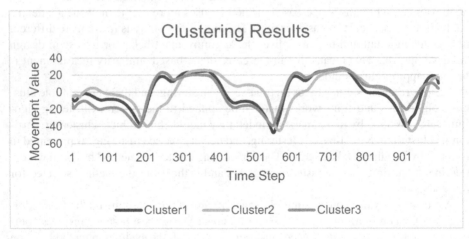

Fig. 8. After clustering, three clusters remain

4   Results

A mock-up for recording entry movements was constructed during the course of the study, in which both the height and width of the steps could be varied. Their depth relative to each other could also be adjusted. An adjustable door was also created to enable even more realistic entry, allowing entry movements to be manipulated in different ways and the comfort ranges of the test subjects to be exploited to the full. The extensive measurement setup enabled both joint angles and joint torques to be recorded for further movement evaluation.

The movement data was correctly labeled and classified using advanced data analysis methods such as clustering and correlation analysis. To achieve the goal, many procedures were tested and compared. From the aspect of human factor engineering, each index's reference movement was individually analyzed according to the nature of each index. In addition, surveys of the tests were conducted to ascertain subjects' opinions as to the convenience of a convenient. The aim is that each index should display different limit configurations.

This study encompasses three major systems: database, clustering and evaluation systems. In each system step, the configuration is optimized by different methods to set the best configuration for the respective parameters.

The key platform for the database system is Access, which is used to collect the input data for each individual index. Basic pre-processing tools are applied beforehand to ensure that the data from the simulation (biomechanical parameters) are in the correct format. Datasets are split and stored in different locations in the database and retrieved for different purposes during system setup. In the next step, the system exports the data for the clustering operation.

The clustering system uses the R environment, which analyzes and applies the data for each individual index. The computation script is implemented and composed in RStudio. Many different clustering approaches have been trialed for use in the method comparison, based on the serval clustering evaluation index. The most outstanding result for each index is delivered by the clustering strategy based on the "dtwclust" external open-source package and raw scripting (Sardá-Espinos 2021). The best result of the applied methods and configuration can vary in each time series data scenario. With the aid of the evaluation index, the system is able to optimize the precise configuration for an optimal method to be calculated. This optimized strategy sets different parameters in a set of orders to find the best configuration. An additional system clusters the data as a pre-processing method for outlier detection. In all, the data from each body part index are clustered into three reference movements for further analysis.

The evaluation system also uses the R environment, which directly applies the clustering results to calculate the reference data for the evaluation process. The evaluation can currently be conducted by comparing the clusters with the new movement data using a similarity index. The evaluation limitation parameter can be set by applying the concept based on the convex hull theory. Thus, each index's new movement data can be evaluated in an R environment, and the result can be illustrated in the RStudio plotting interface. In addition, all the relevant results can be obtained from the workspace and saved for subsequent use. The system can be optimized using subjective methods, including feedback from testers regarding the movement involved. Other methods of evaluation may deliver similar or better results, which can be applied to the system in future work.

5   Discussion

As many parameters are involved in the design of a truck and these parameters have complex interrelationships, predicting motion and discomfort during entry and exit is a major challenge for manufacturers. With COE trucks in particular, the cab is located far above the ground, so ascending the steps may produce a feeling of discomfort. There are several studies that present quantitative methods of determining discomfort relating to body movement or posture. These methods use kinetic or kinematic data to determine the level of discomfort.

The data and correlations obtained from the study data are subsequently used to create a mathematical model, which should be as simple as possible. It can draw on kinematic data (joint angles) and dynamic data (joint moments) as a basis for evaluation. This research is interdisciplinary and combines big data analysis with human factor engineering. The study is still at an early stage, as no related advanced work exists. The only studies available are either in the field of ergonomic engineering, focusing on the subjective, step-by-step analysis of movement behavior, or else in the field of data science, focusing on clustering in other scenarios. The application of clustering methods, in this case time-series clustering, in analyzing movement data is a brand-new field of research.

This field offers an immense research potential. The clustering system based on time-series data can provide strong reference data showing the kinds of movement that are the most common of all, resulting in a better and more human-friendly design concept. This research is not limited to ingress motion but can also be applied to the analysis of other movements. It can benefit from a big data clustering analysis resulting in a design that better matches for common movement behavior and providing a more ergonomic design solution.

In future work, there are still numerous research challenges that need to be overcome. These are mainly related to the use of machine learning in data science and ergonomic research, where the major research potential is located.

6 Conclusion

An objective evaluation of movement data related to vehicle entry is the research project's focus. The general aim of this study is to build and implement a cognitive computation system to evaluate ingress movement data. It can be divided into two subsystems: the time-series data clustering system and the time-series data evaluation system. Various methodologies can be applied to carry out the cluster and evaluation operations. The methods that deliver the best outcomes are determined as key methods and implemented on the study's core platform. The next step is to expand the data base and complete the evaluation.

Acknowledgments. This work is funded by the German Research Foundation (BMBF) within the scope of the research project "Dynamische Evaluierung von Fahrzeuginsassen", grant MA 01IS18084C/D. The project period is from May 2019 to April 2022. We would like to thank our colleagues Heike Hermsdorf (IfM), Volker Enderlein (IfM), Danny Möbius (IfM), Dr. Hans-Joachim Wirsching (Human Solutions), Dr. Armin Weiss (A.R.T.) and project partners Roland Stechow (Daimler Trucks), Dr. Raphael Bichler (BMW) and Melf Mast (Airbus) for the good discussions and support.

References

Aghabozorgi, S., Seyed Shirkhorshidi, A., Ying Wah, T.: Time-series clustering – a decade review. Inf. Syst. **53**, 16–38 (2015). https://doi.org/10.1016/j.is.2015.04.007

Bubb, H.: Automobilergonomie. ATZ/MTZ-Fachbuch. Springer Vieweg (2015). http://search.ebscohost.com/login.aspx?direct=true&scope=site&db=nlebk&AN=959251

Cassisi, C., Montalto, P., Aliotta, M., Cannata, A., Pulvirenti, A.: Similarity measures and dimensionality reduction techniques for time series data mining. In: Karahoca, A. (ed.) Selecting Representative Data Sets. INTECH Open Access Publisher (2012). https://doi.org/10.5772/49941

Chateauroux, E., Wang, X., Roybin, C.: Analysis of truck cabin egress motion. Int. J. Human Factors Modell. Simul. **3**(2), 169 (2012). https://doi.org/10.1504/IJHFMS.2012.051095

Ergüner Özkoç, E.: Clustering of time-series data. In: Birant, D. (ed.) Data Mining: Methods, Applications and Systems. IntechOpen (2021). https://doi.org/10.5772/intechopen.84490

Hebe, J., Bengler, K.: How do people move to get into and out of a European cabin-over-engine truck? In: Bagnara, S., Tartaglia, R., Albolino, S., Alexander, T., Fujita, Y. (eds.) IEA 2018. AISC, vol. 823, pp. 142–151. Springer, Cham (2019). https://doi.org/10.1007/978-3-319-96074-6_15

Heglund, N.C., Cavagna, G.A.: Mechanical work, oxygen consumption, and efficiency in isolated frog and rat muscle. Am. J. Physiol.-Cell Physiol. **253**(1), C22–C29 (1987). https://doi.org/10.1152/ajpcell.1987.253.1.C22

Latka, J.: Nutzerzentrierte entwicklung von ein-und ausstiegskonzepten im nutzfahrzeugbereich unter der betrachtung von bewegungsstrategien (2020). https://d-nb.info/1215837704/34

Lin, L.-J., Cohen, H.H.: Accidents in the trucking industry. Int. J. Ind. Ergon. **20**(4), 287–300 (1997). https://doi.org/10.1016/S0169-8141(96)00060-1

Michel, B.: Ergonomische Analyse der Fahrerumgebung im Fernverkehrs-Lkw (2014). https://mediatum.ub.tum.de/1256350

Rousseeuw, P.J.: Silhouettes: a graphical aid to the interpretation and validation of cluster analysis. J. Comput. Appl. Math. **20**, 53–65 (1987). https://doi.org/10.1016/0377-0427(87)90125-7

Sardá-Espinosa, A.: Comparing Time-Series Clustering Algorithms in R Using the dtwclust Package (2021). http://cran.uni-muenster.de/web/packages/dtwclust/vignettes/dtwclust.pdf

Winter, D.A.: Biomechanics and Motor Control of Human Movement, 4th edn., Wiley (2009). http://onlinelibrary.wiley.com/book/10.1002/9780470549148, https://doi.org/10.1002/9780470549148

Zaciorskij, V.M.: Kinetics of human motion. Human Kinetics (2002)

A Two-Step Optimization-Based Synthesis of Squat Movements

Bach Quoc Hoa[1](✉), Vincent Padois[2], Faiz Benamar[1], and Eric Desailly[3]

[1] Institute for Intelligent Systems and Robotics (ISIR), Sorbonne University,
Place Jussieu, 75005 Paris, France
`hoa@isir.upmc.fr`, `faiz.ben_amar@sorbonne-universite.fr`
[2] Auctus, Inria/IMS (Univ. Bordeaux/Bordeaux INP/CNRS UMR52181),
33405 Talence, France
`vincent.padois@inria.fr`
[3] Fondation Ellen Poidatz, 77310 St. Fargeau-Ponthierry, France
`eric.desailly@fondationpoidatz.com`

Abstract. In this paper, we explore the use of numerical optimization techniques to synthesize realistic human-like squat motions. For this purpose, a two-step optimization-based synthesis scheme, inspired by whole-body controllers from robotics, is proposed. In step I, a reduced set of physically-relevant criteria is optimized to produce the state and torque patterns with a joint-actuated model. Afterwards, muscle activities are computed in step II with a muscle-actuated model. To validate the approach, the synthesized kinetic and muscle activities of two squat strategies obtained through the scheme are analyzed and compared to captured movement and electromyographic data. The outcome shows that it is feasible to synthesize human-like squats without motion capture data while exhibiting several main features of the motor function strategies. However, disparities related to the simple modeling of the actuators are observed.

Keywords: Human modeling · Realistic human-like movement synthesis · Optimization

1 Introduction

Squat is one of the most popular and important exercises in physical rehabilitation to develop strength and power of the lower limbs [3, 10]. In consequence, squat simulation has been studied extensively in the literature. In [1], a real-time estimation of lower limb and torso kinematics was developed with a single inertial measurement unit (IMU) placed on the lower back. The planar IMU orientation and vertical displacement were estimated and then used to compute the joint angles of the lower limbs by means of Jacobian pseudoinverse matrix and null-space decoupling. In [2], joint torques during squat motions were estimated by using a simplified inverse dynamic model and motion capture data. In these studies, the models were joint-actuated models, in which the muscles actuating

© Springer Nature Switzerland AG 2021
V. G. Duffy (Ed.): HCII 2021, LNCS 12777, pp. 122–138, 2021.
https://doi.org/10.1007/978-3-030-77817-0_11

a joint were lumped and represented by an equivalent joint torque. Thanks to their simplicity and computational efficiency, skeletal models are commonly used in human movement simulation [22]. On the other hand, there are some particularities of the human motor system strongly influencing the way we move that cannot be accounted for using such models but can, to some extent, be reflected through muscle-actuated models such as the unilateral nature (a muscle can only pull) and the actuation redundancy [20]. For this reason, muscle-actuated models are largely developed and applied in the synthesis of human movements to determine the causality between biomechanical principles and movements as well as to predict the effects of changes in the musculoskeletal system. For example, the synthesis of squat-to-stand motion by optimal control in [6] produced results showing considerable activity of extensor muscles, which is a major feature of squat movement. In [23], a muscle-actuated model of the lower limb was developed to predict the coordination of the muscles during a rising squat. Optimal control was formulated to compute muscle activations with a minimum fatigue criterion based on endurance time and muscle stress.

In our work, we propose to synthesize human-like squat movements by a two-step optimization-based scheme which takes advantage of both the low complexity of joint-actuated models and the characters of muscle-actuated models. Step I of the scheme synthesizes the desired squat motions and the joint torque patterns on a joint-actuated model via a reactive optimization-based dynamic task controller. This approach draws inspiration from robotics [18] and has shown interesting results for human-aware automated synthesis and optimization of collaborative robots [15]. In this step, one of our objectives is to find the minimum number of tasks allowing to produce different strategies of human-like squat. Step II is a post-processing procedure using the state and torque trajectories obtained in step I to compute muscle activity patterns with a muscle-actuated model. No motion capture data is required thanks to the optimization-based reactive controller. Motor functional strategies are identified through the value of the weighting coefficients. To demonstrate our approach, we synthesize two different strategies of human-like squat and evaluate the results with the motion capture and electromyographic (EMG) data.

2 Human Models

The models, constructed with OpenSim [5], a physiologically-based simulator, are two planar 4-DOFs models sharing the same skeletal structure. They consist of the torso, two arms, the pelvis, the right leg and the right foot which is fixed to the ground (Fig. 1). All the joints are revolute joints. The rigid-body dynamics can be expressed in the Lagrangian form

$$M(q)\dot{\nu} + c(q, \nu) + g(q) = \tau \tag{1}$$

with $q \in \mathbb{R}^n$, n the number of joints, the vector of joint angles, ν the generalized velocities, M the inertia matrix, c the centrifugal and Coriolis effects vector, g the gravity force vector and τ the joint torques generated by actuators.

The expression of the joint torques τ depends on the model, particularly the topology of the actuator system in consideration. Given the control input vector $u \in \mathbb{R}^{n_a}$, n_a the number of actuators, the joint torques produced on the joint-actuated model by the torque generators can be formulated as

$$\tau = S u \tag{2}$$

with S the selection matrix. As the torque generators apply torques proportional to the control signals, the selection matrix S is a diagonal matrix whose elements are

$$S_{i,i} = \tau_{max,i} \tag{3}$$

with $\tau_{max,i}$ the maximum available torque of the ith torque generator. It is worth noting that the range of the control inputs is $[-1, 1]$, meaning the torque actuators can generate both extension and flexion torques.

On the other hand, for the muscle-actuated model, the active movements are generated by path actuators, which are basically tensionable ropes representing muscles. The produced forces, proportional to the muscle activation a, create torques around the joint axes.

$$\tau = S a \tag{4}$$

The selection matrix takes into account the moment arms of the muscles and its elements are expressed as

$$S_{i,j} = F_{max,j} \, d_{i,j}(q) \tag{5}$$

with $F_{max,j}$ the maximum force of the jth actuator and $d_{i,j}(q)$ the moment arm with respect to (w.r.t) the ith joint. Due to the spatial attachment configuration of muscles, their moment arm is configuration dependent and calculated internally by OpenSim according to [21]. Since the muscle can only pull, the range of the control inputs is $[0, 1]$. Nine muscles are implemented, among which six are uni-articular and three are bi-articular. Specifically, the hip joint is flexed by the iliopsoas (ILIO) and the rectus femoris (RF) and extended by the gluteus maximus (GLU) and the hamstring (HAM). The knee joint is extended by the vasti (VAS) and the RF, whereas its flexion is produced by the gastrocnemius (GAS), the bicep femoris short head (BIFEMSH) and the HAM. At the ankle, dorsiflexion is produced by the tibialis anterior (TA) and plantar-flexion by the soleus (SOL) and the GAS respectively. The last two path actuators at the lumbar joint (blue) allow extension and flexion of the torso with respect to w.r.t the pelvis.

3   Synthesis Scheme

The two-step synthesis scheme (Fig. 2) starts by synthesizing the desired squat motion on the joint-actuated model. The formulation of the reactive optimization-based dynamic task controller is based on the works on the whole-body control in [4,14,18], Specifically, we consider a human-like movement as

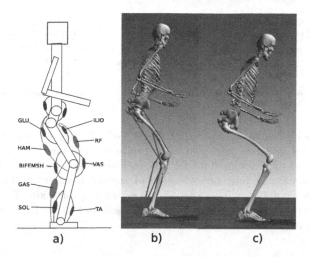

Fig. 1. The muscle layout a) of the planar 4-DOFs models b) and the joint-actuated model c). The muscle-actuated model has 9 muscles (path actuators): 6 uni-articular (red) and 3 bi-articular (green). The blue path actuators in the layout actuating the lumbar joint are not studied. The right foot is fixed to the ground. The joint-actuated model shares the same skeletal structure with the muscle-actuated model. Please note that the torque actuators are not represented visually. (Color figure online)

the outcome of performing multiple tasks of different priority simultaneously in an optimized manner while respecting certain constraints. These tasks can represent physically-relevant high-level objectives such as lifting the head, maintaining balance, reducing joint torques and minimizing angular momentum (AM) variation. In terms of inputs, step I requires task objectives such as head target heights and zero variation of angular momentum as well as the duration of a squat phase (the ascent phase or the descent phase as we consider them having the same duration). At the end of step I, the trajectories of joint torques and state (generalized angles and velocities) are obtained and inputed into step II, where the post-processing procedure is carried out on the muscle-actuated model. The muscle activations are then estimated by solving a double-objective optimization problem. Below are the details of the steps.

3.1   Motion Synthesis

At each time step, the controller solves a multi-objective optimization formulated based on the current state of the model. The control problem is formulated as

$$
\begin{aligned}
\operatorname*{argmin}_{\chi} \quad & \sum_{i=1}^{n_{task}} w_i f_i(\chi) + w_0 f_0(\chi) \\
\text{s.t} \quad & G\chi \le h \\
& A\chi = b
\end{aligned}
\tag{6}
$$

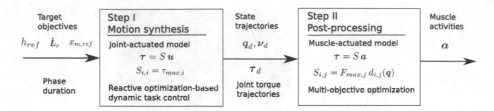

Fig. 2. The two-step squat movement synthesis method. Step I relies on the reactive optimization-based dynamic task control to produce the desired movement and the joint torques on the joint-actuated model. The task objectives are reaching head target heights h_{ref}, maintaining reference variation of angular momentum $\dot{L}_r$, maintaining center of mass set-point $x_{m,ref}$ as well as respecting the duration of a squat phase. Step II is a sequence of optimizations computing the muscle activity patterns a on the muscle-actuated model.

f_i is the cost function of the i_{th} task expressed in terms of χ, the optimization variables. The smaller its value is, the better the task is performed. A global cost function is then constructed as the weighted sum of all individual cost functions. G and h represent to the equality constraint while A and b define the inequality constraints. The chosen optimization variable vector is

$$\chi = \begin{bmatrix} \dot{\nu} \\ u \end{bmatrix}$$

Solving an optimization problem yields a control set of torque actuators and the resulting generalized accelerations. At the end of the step I, we obtain the control history of the torque actuators, hence the torque profiles and the resulting state trajectory of the synthesized movement.

Head Vertical Displacement. We consider that a squat cycle consists of two phases starting by the descent phase and finishing with the ascent phase, as shown in Fig. 3. The purpose of the task is approaching the controlled point located at the top of the head towards the two target heights. For the ascent phase, the target height 2 is achieved when the body stands up straight. For the descent phase, the target height 1 is considered as the body lowers to the minimum height. This position task is converted to an acceleration task by means of task servoing [14]. The task performance indicator is formulated as

$$f_1(\chi) = \| \ddot{h} - \ddot{h}_{des} \|_2^2 \tag{7}$$

with $\ddot{h}$ the acceleration of the controlled point. The desired acceleration is expressed in Cartesian space through a PD controller

$$\ddot{h}_{des} = \ddot{h}_{ref} + K_p(h_{ref} - h) + K_v(\dot{h}_{ref} - \dot{h}) \tag{8}$$

with K_p and K_v the position and the velocity gains, h_{ref}, $\dot{h}_{ref}$ and $\ddot{h}_{ref}$ the target height, vertical velocity and vertical acceleration respectively. In case of

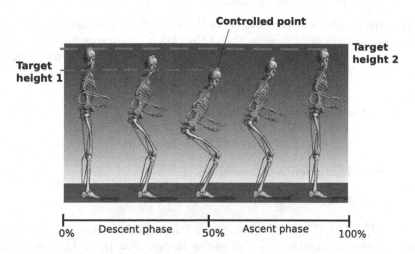

Fig. 3. The squat cycle starts with the descent phase and finishes with the ascent phase. Each phase has a target height for the controlled point of the head.

squat movements, we set $\dot{h}_{ref} = 0$, $\ddot{h}_{ref} = 0$ and h_{ref} to either target head 1 or target head 2. To drive these errors to zero in a critically damped fashion, the velocity gains can be chosen such as $K_v = 2\sqrt{K_p}$. The vertical acceleration of the controlled point is computed as $\ddot{h} = (J_{sp}\dot{\boldsymbol{\nu}} + \dot{J}_{sp}\boldsymbol{\nu})\begin{bmatrix}0 & 1 & 0\end{bmatrix}^T$ with $\dot{J}_{sp}(\boldsymbol{q})$ the Jacobian w.r.t the controlled point.

Maintaining Balance. To ensure the equilibrium of the system, we aim to maintain the projection of the center of mass (CoM) close to a set-point $x_{m,ref}$ inside the convex hull of the foot-support area. As the model is planar, only the coordinate x_m represented along the sagittal axis of the body of the CoM ground projection is considered. The task performance indicator is formulated as an acceleration task:

$$f_2(\boldsymbol{\chi}) = \| \ddot{x}_m - \ddot{x}_{m,des} \|_2^2 \tag{9}$$

where the CoM acceleration can be computed as

$$\ddot{x}_m = \frac{\boldsymbol{S}_m}{M} \sum_i m_i (J_{m,i}\dot{\boldsymbol{\nu}} + \dot{J}_{m,i}\boldsymbol{\nu}) \tag{10}$$

with $J_{m,i}$ the Jacobian w.r.t the CoM of the body i^{th} and m_i its mass, $M = \sum_i m_i$ the total mass of the system and $\boldsymbol{S}_m = [1\ 0\ 0]$ the row vector to select the component x of the whole body CoM position vector. The desired CoM acceleration is expressed in Cartesian space through a PD controller

$$\ddot{x}_{m,des} = \ddot{x}_{m,ref} + K_p^m(x_{m,ref} - x_m) + K_v^m(\dot{x}_{m,ref} - \dot{x}_m) \tag{11}$$

The reference acceleration $\ddot{x}_{m,ref}$ and velocity $\dot{x}_{m,ref}$ are set as null.

Minimizing Angular Momentum Variation. The formulation of the task is based on the work in [4]. The objective of the task is to improve balance stability. The variation of angular momentum (AM) about the CoM of the whole body $\dot{L}$ is controlled linearly

$$f_3(\chi) = \| \dot{L}_d - \dot{L} \|_2^2 \tag{12}$$

The desired AM variation is computed as

$$\dot{L}_d = k_p(\dot{L}_r - \dot{L}) \tag{13}$$

The current AM variation is expressed as

$$\dot{L} = PJ\dot{\nu} + (\dot{P}J + P\dot{J})\nu \tag{14}$$

with $J = [J_1^T \cdots J_{n_b}^T]^T$ the concatenation of Jacobian matrices mapping generalized velocities to angular velocities of the bodies, $P = [I_1 \cdots I_{n_b}]$ the concatenation of inertia matrices about the CoM of the bodies and n_b is the number of bodies in the model. We set the reference AM variation $\dot{L}_d = 0$.

Regularization Task. To narrow down the solution space, we add to the cost function a regularization term. It's a weighted sum of squared optimization variables

$$f_0(\chi) = \sum_{i=1}^{n_{opt}} \alpha_i \chi_i^2 \tag{15}$$

with n_{opt} the number of optimization variables. More details are in Sect. 4.1.

Posture Task. The objective of the task is to stop the movement in a damping manner at the end of each phase. As soon as the vertical distance between the controlled point on the head and the current target height is less than a predefined margin, the task is activated and maintained until the end of the current phase. When the task is "switched on", all the other tasks of step I are "switched off", meaning all their weights are set to zero. The task performance indicator is formulated as

$$f_b(\chi) = \| \dot{\nu} - \dot{\nu}_{p,des} \|_2^2 \tag{16}$$

where the desired acceleration is expressed through a proportional controller

$$\dot{\nu}_{b,des} = K_p^p(\nu_{ref} - \nu) \tag{17}$$

with $\nu_{ref} = \mathbf{0}$.

Constraints. Constraints imposed on the control scheme are related to the dynamic equation and the mechanical limits of the model. This section presents these constraints formulated in terms of χ.

Equation of Motion. The evolution of χ is enforced by the dynamic equation (1). It can be rewritten in terms of χ as

$$A^d \chi = b^d \tag{18}$$

with $A^d = \begin{bmatrix} M(q) & -S \end{bmatrix}$ and $b^d = g(q) + c(q, \nu)$.

Joint Limits. The angular joint limits can be expressed as an inequality on q

$$q_{min} \leq q \leq q_{max} \tag{19}$$

To formulate this constraint, q needs to be calculated by second-order approximation

$$q(t + h) = q(t) + h\nu(t) + \frac{h^2}{2}\dot{\nu}(t) \tag{20}$$

where h is the control period. Replacing (20) in (19) yields

$$\dot{\nu}_{min} \leq \dot{\nu} \leq \dot{\nu}_{max} \tag{21}$$

with

$$\dot{\nu}_{min} = \frac{2}{h^2}(q_{min} - q - h\nu)$$

$$\dot{\nu}_{max} = \frac{2}{h^2}(q_{max} - q - h\nu).$$

Control Input Limits. Similar to the joint limits, the control input constraint can be written as

$$u_{min} \leq u \leq u_{max} \tag{22}$$

Control Input Variation Limits. As the model torque generator model does not represent the dynamics of muscle contraction, the actuators can adopt any value of control input and can provoke sudden change of acceleration and potentially instability. Therefore, we impose a constraint limiting the variation of control input expressed as

$$\dot{u}_{min} \leq \dot{u} \leq \dot{u}_{max} \tag{23}$$

3.2   Post-processing

The joint torques obtained in step I are reproduced on the muscle-actuated model by finding the optimal control inputs a^* of the path actuators. For this purpose, the optimization problem is formulated as

$$a^* = \underset{a}{\operatorname{argmin}} \quad w_\tau f_\tau(q_d, \nu_d, \tau_d, a) + w_0 f_0(a)$$

$$\text{s.t} \qquad a_{min} \leq a \leq a_{max} \tag{24}$$

$$\dot{a}_{min} \leq \dot{a} \leq \dot{a}_{max}$$

with a the muscle activations, τ_d the desired torques and (q_d, ν_d) the desired state obtained in step I. The two tasks implicated are tracking joint torques and minimizing total control inputs.

Tracking Joint Torque. Since the path actuator model does not take into account the dynamics of muscle contraction, the torques produced by the path actuators are only configuration dependent. The task can be expressed as

$$f_\tau(\boldsymbol{q}_d, \boldsymbol{\nu}_d, \boldsymbol{\tau}_d, \boldsymbol{a}) = \| S(\boldsymbol{q}_d)\boldsymbol{a} - \boldsymbol{\tau}_d \|_2^2 \qquad (25)$$

Minimizing Total Muscle Activations. The task is defined as minimizing the weighted sum of squared muscle activations

$$f_0(\boldsymbol{a}) = \| \boldsymbol{a} \|_2^2 \qquad (26)$$

4 Simulation and Validation

Based on the formulation in the previous section, the squat movement is simulated by solving the optimization problems. In this section, we cover the details of the simulation and the validation method by experiments with two different strategies of squat.

4.1 Simulation

The dynamic simulation is carried out using OpenSim. Due to the linear nature of the actuators, we can express all optimization problems as a Linear Quadratic Program (LQP) optimization problems. The implementation and the resolution of the LQP are performed with qpOASES [9], an open-source solver based on online active set strategy. Two strategies of squat are simulated. Strategy I imposes the back to be as straight as possible throughout the movement. Strategy II requires the hip to move as far back as possible while descending to reduce the knee joint torque and as a consequence, the head is lowered deeper. The duration of a simulation is around 12 min, in which only 1 min is devoted to step I.

Weight Tuning Method. In multi-objective optimization, task weights dictate how the QP computes an optimum and thus influence strongly the results. In step I, to create the two movement strategies, we choose to only consider the influence of the main tasks on the outcome (Table 1). To this aim, the weights α_i of the terms in the regularization task are kept unchanged when simulating both squat strategies. For step II, the torque tracking task is associated by a weight value of 1 while the task of minimizing total control activities weighted 0.01.

The distinction between the simulations of the squat strategies is mainly related to the weight associated to the angular momentum task. Indeed, choosing a greater weight for this task keeps the back erected during the squat cycle and leads to strategy I, while allowing more angular momentum variation leads to strategy II. We also increase the weight of the generalized lumbar acceleration for the ascent phase of strategy II as wider range of motion is observed by using the same value as in the descent phase. On the other hand, the purpose of adopting different values for the head vertical displacement task is only to fine-tune the kinetic results more closely to the captured joint angle profiles. This fine-tuning adjustment is not mandatory as the synthesis scheme does not required any predefined trajectory.

Table 1. Weighting coefficients for tasks and optimization variables for step I

Squat strategy	Strategy I		Strategy II	
Phase	Descent	Ascent	Descent	Ascent
Task				
Head vertical displacement	0.013	0.006	0.015	0.008
Angular momentum variation	0.040	0.040	0.010	0.010
Balance	0.400	0.400	0.400	0.400
Control				
All actuators	0.010	0.010	0.010	0.010
Generalized acceleration				
Ankle	0.003	0.003	0.003	0.003
Knee	0.003	0.003	0.003	0.003
Hip	0.003	0.003	0.003	0.003
Lumbar	0.014	0.014	0.014	0.020

4.2 Validation

The data was collected from a healthy male subject. His height is 163 cm and his body mass is 55 kg. His participation was voluntary, and a written informed consent, as approved by the Sorbonne University, was obtained prior to the experiments. The subject was instructed to perform three repetitions of squat cycles of the two different movement strategies (Fig. 4). The experimental data was normalized by dividing the cycle duration, which is the sum of the descent phase and the ascent phase durations. The acquisition is performed with a Vicon system. Captured motion of the markers is then used to scale the dimensions, mass and inertial properties of the body segments of the OpenSim models. EMG data are acquired in 7 muscles (HAM, GLU, RF, VAS, GAS, SOL, TA) through 14 Delsys sensors 2000 Hz.

Joint Movements and Torques. Overall, it can be seen that several features of the captured squats are predicted in the synthesized squats (Fig. 5). First, the transfer from the descent to the ascent phase occurs simultaneously at all joints at around half of the squat cycle. This is marked by the shift from flexion to extension after the joint angles have reached their peak values, which takes place

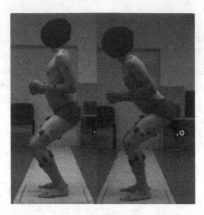

Fig. 4. Squat strategy I (left) with straight back and strategy II (right) with hip pushed behind to reduce knee joint torque.

at the same time as the torque actuators reached their maximal torques (Fig. 6). Secondly, in strategy I, the ankle and knee joints have a wider range of motion whereas the hip and lumbar joints are more engaged in strategy II. The trend is also reflected in the synthesized torques where a substantially higher torque is produced at the knee joint than other joints in strategy I, whereas in strategy II, these torques have considerably closer values one to another. This can be explained partly that the straight back in strategy I increases the gravity effect on the knee. In reality, passive knee torque [16] also contributes to the dynamic equation, but our modeling does not take this phenomenon, among others, into account.

On the other hand, some disparities between the simulation and the captured data are present, notably the evolution of joint speeds. In the captured data, the joint speeds reach their peak values towards the beginning of descent phase and the end of ascent phase while the synthesized peak joint speeds appear toward 50% of the cycle. Additionally, several artifacts are observed towards the end of the phases. They are related to the trigger of the posture task and the simple linear model of the actuators.

Muscle Activities and Forces. We investigate the qualitative characteristics of muscle activities and forces between EMG data and the simulation (Fig. 8). Due to the simple model of path actuators, the synthesized forces are proportional to the activations (Fig. 7). Both in synthesized activities and measured EMG, VAS shows the highest activity among all muscles while no considerable activity is obtained for HAM, GAS and SOL.

Although in the literature GAS and HAM have been observed, through the recorded EMG signals, to be less active than VAS and RF [12,13,19], they co-contract with the vastus muscles and RF to improve knee stability [7,8]. Additionally, thanks to the collagenous structures holding the muscle fibers together and resisting stretch even when the muscle is relaxed [17], muscles can still pro-

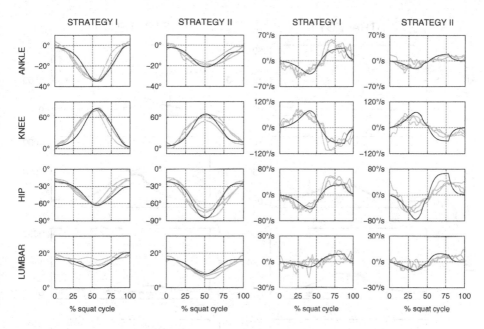

Fig. 5. The synthesized squat cycle (black) has the joint angles (first and second columns) and the joint speeds (third and forth columns) staying in the area of movement captured data (gray).

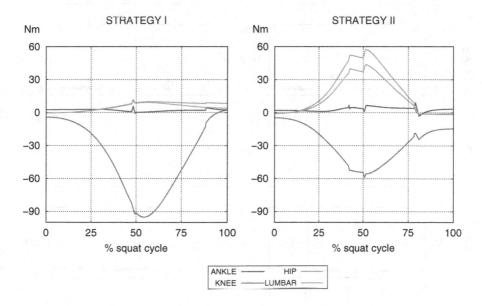

Fig. 6. Distinct synthesized torque profiles between the two strategies.

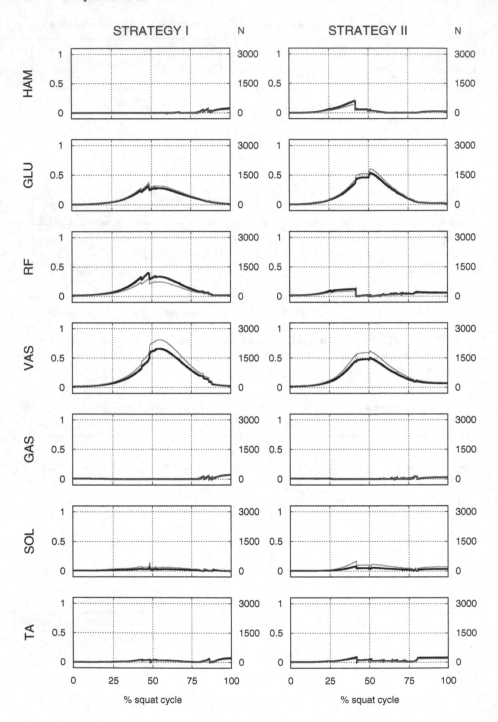

Fig. 7. Synthesized muscle activations (black) and forces (green) during a squat cycle. (Color figure online)

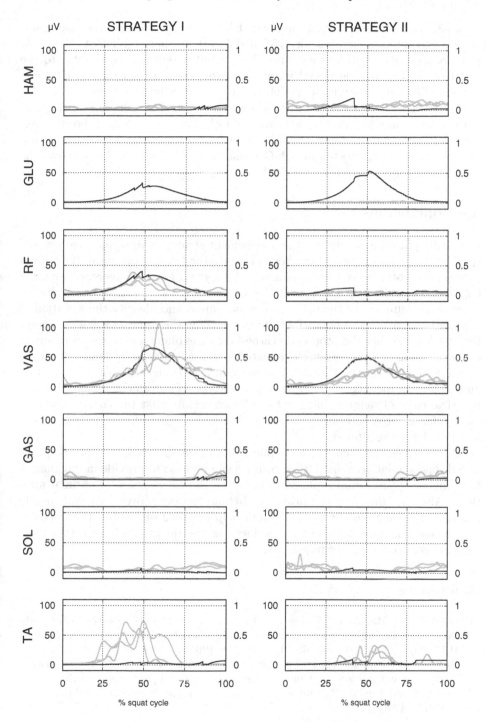

Fig. 8. Synthesized muscle activations (black) and EMG signals (gray) in during a squat cycle.

duce passive forces while exhibiting little EMG activity. On the other hand, our synthesized forces generated for GAS and HAM are not significant enough to produce co-contraction between knee flexors and extensors. This is due to the simplicity of our muscle model which does not integrate elastic and damping elements like Hill-type muscle models [11] to modelize passive forces.

Comparing the data between the two strategies reveals some interesting disparities between EMG and the synthesis. Firstly, the simulations of both strategies yield substantial values of GLU, for which only minor EMG signals are observed. Secondly, substantial EMG signals are observed for TA whereas the synthesized control inputs are negligible.

5   Conclusions

Physically plausible solutions of two movement strategies of squat were synthesized by the proposed two-step scheme. Despite the low complexity of the human models, the obtained results demonstrated a certain level of coherence with the captured data. Furthermore, with the low number of tasks, we were able to observe the influence of the tasks on the movement and identify the variation of angular momentum as a potential factor influencing the squat movement. Therefore, we believe that the proposed synthesis scheme offers a potential framework of synthesizing motions of muscle-actuated systems. However, the manual tuning is the weak point of the method, especially in case other types of movement or altered human models are considered as each type of movement requires its own practical rules of weight tuning. Also, it's not certain that the tuned weighting factors for healthy movement of a model would predict the movement of the same model being altered.

Perspectives are open for the application of this approach. As the computational time is relatively small, the synthesis can be used to provide initial guesses for a global optimization problem to facilitate the convergence of optimal solutions. Also, insights into the principles behind human movements and muscle functions gained from the method could help improve motor function analysis and decision making for surgeons performing treatments such as orthopaedic surgery on a given type of impairment.

References

1. Bonnet, V., Mazza, C., Fraisse, P., Cappozzo, A.: Real-time estimate of body kinematics during a planar squat task using a single inertial measurement unit. IEEE Trans. Biomed. Eng. **60**(7), 1920–1926 (2013)
2. Bordron, O., Huneau, C., Le Carpentier, É., Aoustin, Y.: Joint torque estimation during a squat motion. In: Congrès Français de Mécanique (Brest) (2019)
3. Comfort, P., Kasim, P.: Optimizing squat technique. Strength Conditioning J. **29**(6), 10 (2007)

4. De Lasa, M., Mordatch, I., Hertzmann, A.: Feature-based locomotion controllers. ACM Trans. Graph. (TOG) **29**(4), 1–10 (2010)
5. Delp, S.L., et al.: OpenSim: open-source software to create and analyze dynamic simulations of movement. IEEE Trans. Biomed. Eng. **54**(11), 1940–1950 (2007)
6. Dembia, C.L., Bianco, N.A., Falisse, A., Hicks, J.L., Delp, S.L.: OpenSim Moco: Musculoskeletal optimal control. BioRxiv 839381 (2019)
7. Draganich, L., Jaeger, R., Kralj, A.: Coactivation of the hamstrings and quadriceps during extension of the knee. J. Bone Joint Surg. Am. Vol. **71**(7), 1075–1081 (1989)
8. Escamilla, R.F.: Knee biomechanics of the dynamic squat exercise. Med. Sci. Sports Exerc. **33**(1), 127–141 (2001)
9. Ferreau, H., Kirches, C., Potschka, A., Bock, H., Diehl, M.: qpOASES: a parametric active-set algorithm for quadratic programming. Math. Program. Comput. **6**(4), 327–363 (2014)
10. Fry, A.C., Smith, J.C., Schilling, B.K.: Effect of knee position on hip and knee torques during the barbell squat. J. Strength Conditioning Res. **17**(4), 629–633 (2003)
11. Haeufle, D., Günther, M., Bayer, A., Schmitt, S.: Hill-type muscle model with serial damping and eccentric force-velocity relation. J. Biomech. **47**(6), 1531–1536 (2014)
12. Isear Jr., J.A., Erickson, J.C., Worrell, T.W.: EMG analysis of lower extremity muscle recruitment patterns during an unloaded squat. Med. Sci. Sports Exerc. **29**(4), 532–539 (1997)
13. Kongsgaard, M., et al.: Decline eccentric squats increases patellar tendon loading compared to standard eccentric squats. Clin. Biomech. **21**(7), 748–754 (2006)
14. Lober, R.: Task compatibility and feasibility maximization for whole-body control. Theses, UPMC, November 2017. https://hal.archives-ouvertes.fr/tel-01685182
15. Maurice, P., Padois, V., Measson, Y., Bidaud, P.: Human-oriented design of collaborative robots. Int. J. Ind. Ergon. **57**, 88–102 (2017)
16. Riener, R., Edrich, T.: Identification of passive elastic joint moments in the lower extremities. J. Biomech. **32**(5), 539–544 (1999)
17. Amankwah, K., Triolo, R.J., Kirsch, R.: Effects of spinal cord injury on lower-limb passive joint moments revealed through a nonlinear viscoelastic model. Biomedical Engineering Department, Case Western Reserve University, Cleveland, OH (2004)
18. Salini, J., Padois, V., Bidaud, P.: Synthesis of complex humanoid whole-body behavior: a focus on sequencing and tasks transitions. In: 2011 IEEE International Conference on Robotics and Automation, pp. 1283–1290. IEEE (2011)
19. Schwanbeck, S., Chilibeck, P.D., Binsted, G.: A comparison of free weight squat to smith machine squat using electromyography. J. Strength Conditioning Res. **23**(9), 2588–2591 (2009)
20. Seth, A., Sherman, M., Reinbolt, J.A., Delp, S.L.: OpenSim: a musculoskeletal modeling and simulation framework for in silico investigations and exchange. Procedia IUTAM **2**, 212–232 (2011)
21. Sherman, M.A., Seth, A., Delp, S.L.: What is a moment arm? Calculating muscle effectiveness in biomechanical models using generalized coordinates. In: ASME 2013 International Design Engineering Technical Conferences and Computers and Information in Engineering Conference. American Society of Mechanical Engineers Digital Collection (2013)

22. Xiang, Y., Arora, J.S., Abdel-Malek, K.: Physics-based modeling and simulation of human walking: a review of optimization-based and other approaches. Struct. Multi. Optim. **42**(1), 1–23 (2010)

23. Yang, Y., Wang, R., Zhang, M., Jin, D., Wu, F.: Redundant muscular force analysis of human lower limbs during rising from a squat. In: Duffy, V.G. (ed.) ICDHM 2007. LNCS, vol. 4561, pp. 259–267. Springer, Heidelberg (2007). https://doi.org/10.1007/978-3-540-73321-8_31

Ergonomics-Based Clothing Structure Design for Elderly People

Jingxiao Liao[✉] and Xiaoping Hu[✉]

School of Design, South China University of Technology, Guangzhou,
People's Republic of China

Abstract. This research takes Guangdong and Jiangxi in southern China as examples for actual investigation. The actual measurement of the body shape data of the elderly over 65 years of age, the area where the changes in the body shape of the elderly are inferred, and the integration of the data of the elderly body in the form of graphs and tables; through the recording of the color and shape of the clothing worn by the measured subjects on that day, the psychological needs of their clothing colors are analyzed, and their clothing shape graphs are integrated to determine the clothing shape preferred by the elderly. By combining the characteristics of the elderly's body form, we drew up the dress style and structure diagram to fit the elderly, and provided data reference and shape suggestion for making the dress style more suitable for the elderly in South China.

Keywords: Ergonomics · The elderly · Clothing Structure · Somatic Data

1 Introduction

Advances in medical technology have contributed to the continuous extension of the average life span of human beings and the increasing number of the elderly over 65 years old, making "aging of population" one of the inevitable trends of the present era. The 7th Nationwide Census in China will begin on November 1, 2020, and it has been ten years since the 6th Nationwide Census. The 6th Nationwide Census in 2010 showed that the total population of China was 1.37 billion people as of that time [1]. All along, China's continuous adjustments to its population structure policies have deeply affected the age ratio of the Chinese population, so the continuous increase of the elderly population is an inevitable trend in history. Guangdong Province is one of the more developed provinces in southern China, attracting a large number of young people from other regions and constantly changing the proportion of the population of Guangdong Province. The census data in 2010 showed that the number of elderly people aged 65 and above in Guangdong Province reached 7,086,000, accounting for 6.79% of the permanent population in Guangdong Province [2]. Jiangxi Province and Guangdong Province are contiguous, according to the population data released by the Jiangxi Provincial Bureau of Statistics in 2016, as of the end of 2015, Jiangxi Province's population of 65 years old and above accounted for 9.44% of the total population, increased by 0.32% compared to 2014, and the province's aging degree continued to deepen [3].

© Springer Nature Switzerland AG 2021
V. G. Duffy (Ed.): HCII 2021, LNCS 12777, pp. 139–151, 2021.
https://doi.org/10.1007/978-3-030-77817-0_12

The transformation of human clothing from loose garment culture to fitting garment culture is the result of the continuous improvement of human clothing structure. The emergence of ergonomics makes the focus of clothing improvement constantly shift from decorative purpose to functional purpose. Unlike young people, the clothes of the elderly pay more attention to the laws of ergonomics while pursuing beauty and comfort. For the elderly with declining body functions, the demand for clothing is more focused on shifting from aesthetics to comfort. Clothing ergonomics is a discipline comprehensively analyzing human body structure, psychological preferences and other issues with the methods of anthropometry, psychology and physiology. The application of ergonomic principles to clothing is conducive to designing more scientific clothes, and is of great theoretical significance to the structural improvement of clothing.

Somatic data is the basis for the combination of clothing design and ergonomics. China conducted a nationwide survey of body dimensions of adults in the 1980s, and later released "GB10000-88 Body Dimensions of Chinese Adults" became China's basic body dimension data [4]. With the continuous expansion of the elderly market, the existing standard clothing sizes cannot meet the consumer market of the elderly and the lack of physical data for the elderly also shows the necessity of somatic data measurement. While the value of the elderly population continues to rise, the consumer demand of the elderly population increases, and more and more attention is paid to functional products serving the elderly. This research combines ergonomics and clothing design, and uses surveying as the starting point to explore the relationship between the physical characteristics of the elderly and the clothing structure, and provide references for designing clothing products that better meet the needs and needs of the elderly.

2   Research Methods

2.1   Human Body Measurement

Determine the Measurement Subjects. In Jiangxi and Guangdong provinces in southern China, 60 elderly people who are capable of taking care of themselves and over the age of 65 were randomly selected as the measurement subjects. The measurement period was from December 2020 to January 2021.

Measurement Methods and Instruments. The manual measurement method was used to collect data from the measurement subjects. When the measurement was taken, the measurement subjects wore a single piece of close-fitting clothing, kept their bodies standing straight, with their feet close together and their eyes looking forward, and their arms hanging naturally with their palms facing the inside of their bodies. The measuring tools included: soft tape measure, steel tape measure, height and weight measuring instrument, data recorder, etc.

Measurement Items. We measured 10 items, including height, weight, neck circumference, shoulder width, abdominal circumference, hip circumference, arm length, arm lift angle, arm spread angle, and bending ability. In the measurement items, its starting point is to determine the shape of the elderly and whether they have trouble putting on and taking off clothing, which can make the design of the top clothing shape of the elderly as the target of measurement.

2.2 Clothing Record

Since the measurement time was winter in China, the subjects of the human data measurement wore coats in their daily life. The jacket worn by the subjects on that day was the measurement target, and they measured and recorded the shape of the jacket. During the measurement, the subjects' jackets were spread flat on a flat area with the lapels aligned and the sleeve cages stretched to their natural state, where the collars were folded to the wearing state, and the data were recorded with a soft tape measure.

3 Data Collection

3.1 Anthropometric Measurements

Sixty elderly women aged 65 years or older with self-care ability were randomly selected in South China, and the measurement sites were elderly activity centers where the elderly gathered. The age distribution of the measurement subjects is shown in Fig. 1, and the majority of the sample were women aged between 70 and 74 years old.

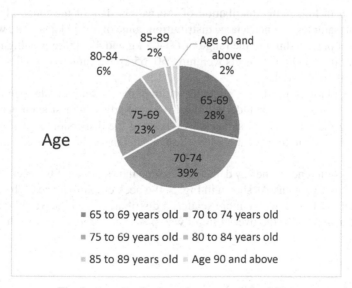

Fig. 1. Age distribution of measurement subjects

The height distribution of the measured samples is shown in Fig. 2, and 48% of the elderly women were between 150 and 154 cm in height. The lowest height of the measurement sample was 135 cm and the highest was 164 cm. Different from young people, the physical characteristics of the elderly will change with age, such as cartilage elasticity decline, muscle atrophy, deterioration of exercise ability, etc. [5].

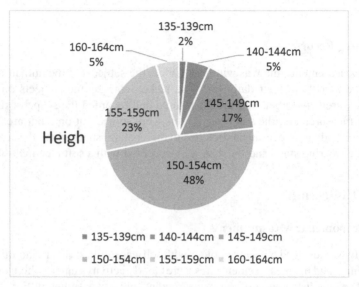

Fig. 2. The height data of the measurement subjects

As shown in Fig. 3, the distribution of the weight data of the randomly selected measurement samples spanned a large distribution range of 30–74 kg, among which, the number of people weighing in the range of 60–65 kg and 40–45 kg was higher. It was observed that the height of subjects weighing 60–65 kg was higher overall than that of subjects weighing 40–45 kg.

As shown in Fig. 4, the data of shoulder width of the random sample spanned a wide range, with the narrowest shoulder width of 37 cm and the widest shoulder width of 46 cm among the 60 measured subjects. Analysis of the dispersion of shoulder width showed that the overall trend of shoulder width and height of the measured samples was positive.

Neck circumference is the key data to determine the structure of the neck circumference of the upper garment. As shown in Fig. 5, the neck circumference of the measured subjects spanned 12 cm, with a more scattered distribution, and the 31–33 cm interval accounted for more, and the overall trend was positively proportional to the shoulder width.

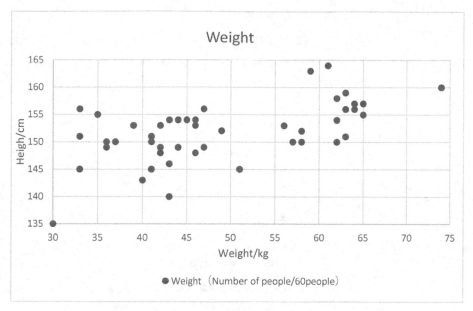

Fig. 3. Distribution of body weight of female elderly

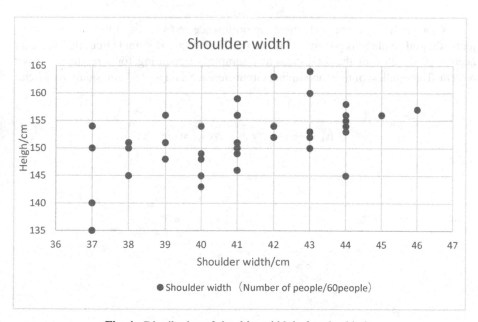

Fig. 4. Distribution of shoulder width in female elderly.

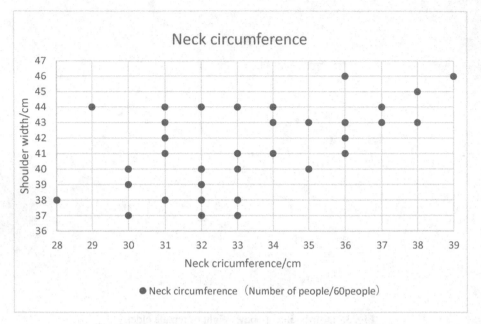

Fig. 5. Distribution of neck circumference of female elderly

As shown in Fig. 6, the abdominal circumference and weight of the measured subjects, showed an obvious positive relationship. 75–80 cm abdominal circumference data accounted for 28% of the total measured samples, accounting for a relatively heavy weight. The smallest of their abdominal circumference data was 63 cm, spanning 41 cm.

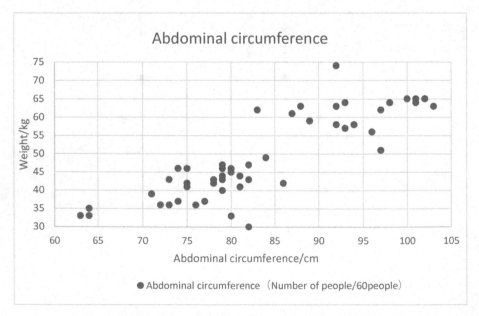

Fig. 6. Distribution of abdominal circumference in female elderly

As shown in Fig. 7, the hip circumference of the measurement subjects was distributed between 78–108 cm, with a relatively even distribution and a small difference in the percentage of each interval. Overall, hip circumference showed a positive relationship with body weight.

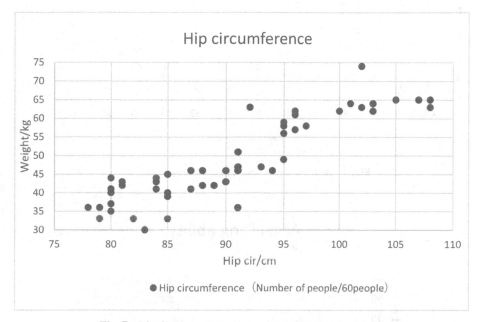

Fig. 7. Distribution of hip circumference in female elderly

As shown in Fig. 8, the arm lengths of the measurement samples were mainly in the range of 47–55 cm, and the arm lengths were centered at 50 cm and extended up and down with a span of 14 cm.

As shown in Fig. 9, the angle at which the measured subjects were able to open their arms when they were horizontal to their bodies and the angle at which they raised their arms high and up was recorded. Ninety-eight percent of the randomly selected female elderly were able to open and lift their arms without difficulty.

The bending ability of the subjects was recorded, and the standard was whether the arms could reach the ground when the subjects bent over. As shown in Fig. 10, the majority of female elderly with self-care ability could reach the ground when they bent over.

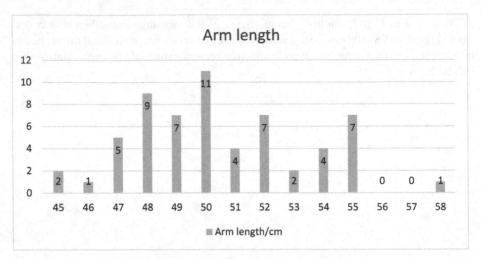

Fig. 8. Distribution of arm length of female elderly

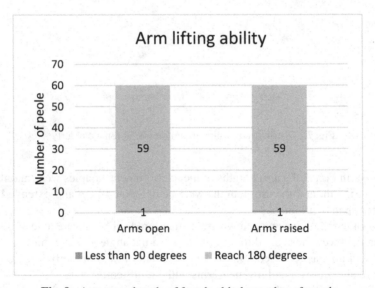

Fig. 9. Arm spread angle of female elderly number of people

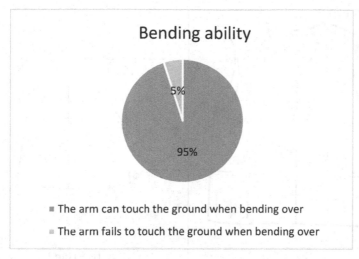

Fig. 10. Bending ability of elderly women

3.2   Dress Form Records

According to the survey, there are fewer sizes available for the elderly [6]. By measuring the coats worn by the subjects on that day and drawing the coat structure diagram, it is not difficult to find that the repetition rate is high. The elderly clothing market has been in a downturn, the main reason is that clothing cannot meet the needs of the elderly [7]. Among the tops measured in this survey, the four top structure diagrams with the highest repetition rate were selected. Figure 11 shows the overlapping images of the four top structure diagrams, and Fig. 12a, b, c, d shows the form structure diagrams of the four tops.

Fig. 11. Overlapping diagrams of four types of tops

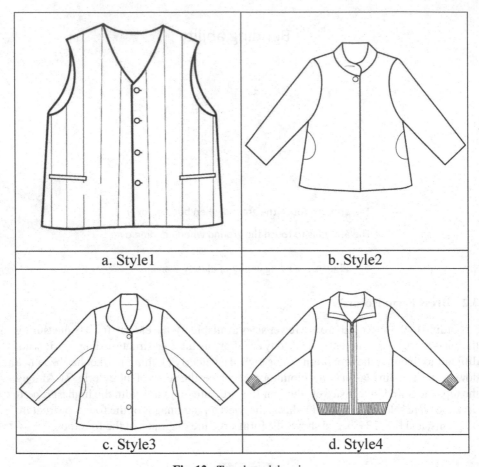

Fig. 12. Top-shaped drawing

4 Analysis and Discussion

4.1 Body Shape

The data of hip circumference, abdominal circumference and shoulder width of the sample were measured, and their distribution spanned a wide range, with hip circumference ranging from 78–108 cm; abdominal circumference ranging from 63–103 cm; the data of shoulder width ranging from 37–46 cm, and the length of the arms mainly distributed between 47–55 cm. It is not difficult to observe that the shoulder width of women over 65 years old is similar to that of ordinary adult women, while the abdominal circumference is large, showing a pattern of small upper and wide lower. The weight and shoulder width of elderly women are proportional to their height; neck circumference is related to shoulder width; abdominal circumference and hip circumference are proportional to their weight; arm lifting and spreading ability is better, and they can complete the normal dressing and undressing process.

In order to adapt to the physical characteristics of the elderly, in the design of tops, the amount of the abdomen of the dress should first be appropriately increased to accommodate the abdominal circumference of elderly women, unlike adult women, the abdominal circumference of the elderly is generally larger. In the design of the top structure, the waist province can be reduced or eliminated. Secondly, the size should be increased appropriately to enrich the clothing choices of elderly women with different shapes. Furthermore, the neck circumference data of female elderly is more scattered and proportional to the shoulder width, and the collar circumference of the apparel in the market should take into account the factor that the neck circumference data of the elderly spans a wide range.

4.2 Analysis of Upper Garment Shape

Since the measurement period was from December to January, it was winter in southern China and the temperature of the region was around 10–16°. Older people wear more clothes in daily life. According to the actual observed clothing worn by the measurement subjects, it was found that their coats were mainly tweed coats and knitted woolen sweaters. They wore fewer light and warm down coats as well as cotton coats for the elderly. Woolen fabric is the fabric that grows with the elderly as opposed to light and thin down clothing. The weight distribution of older adults spans a wide range. According to the size of the tops worn by the measured sample subjects, they, however, did not have a significant span change, in which the top structure as a whole showed a loose and fat characteristic, and the thin elderly people chose mostly jackets of more generous size for their own body.

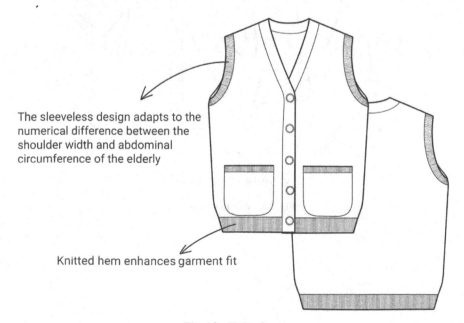

The sleeveless design adapts to the numerical difference between the shoulder width and abdominal circumference of the elderly

Knitted hem enhances garment fit

Fig. 13. Knitted vest

4.3 Top Style Design

Scheme 1. As shown in Fig. 13, the knitted undershirt style can better solve the problem of the ratio of shoulder width to waist circumference of the elderly, effectively increase the activity of the abdomen of the elderly, and the tightened cuffs and hem, effectively prevent wind more warm.

Scheme 2. According to the measurement results, the elderly have a large arm span, so the movable detachable cuff structure can flexibly change the sleeve length and increase the fit of the garment. As shown in Fig. 14, the double zipper design of the placket increases the movement of the abdomen and helps to reduce the accumulation of wrinkles produced by the garment when the elderly are in a sitting position.

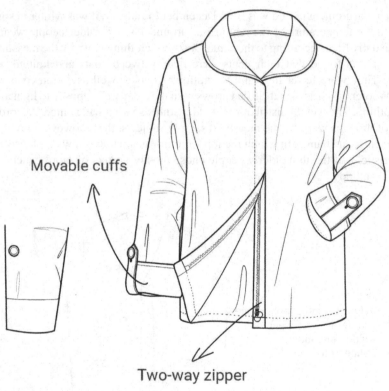

Movable cuffs

Two-way zipper

Fig. 14. Woolen jacket

5 Summary

In this study, manual measurement method was uses. In this study, the actual body data of 60 elderly women over 65 years old in South China were measured using the manual measurement method, and it was concluded that the form data of elderly women spanned a wide range, as well as the distribution of each data such as height, shoulder width, neck circumference, abdominal circumference and hip circumference was scattered within each interval. The observation method and manual measurement method were used to measure the daily wear of the elderly, and the four top styles with the highest repetition rate were mapped. It is proposed that (1) older women in South China are used to wearing familiar fabrics that grow up with them, such as wool and tweed; (2) the design of older people's clothing should pay more attention to the span of their sizes. Finally, a brief discussion on the body shape and psychological needs of dresses of older women in South China was made, and two top structure design suggestions were put forward in the hope of providing data reference for the senior citizens' apparel market.

References

1. The data of the sixth nationwide population census from the National Bureau of Statistics of the People's Republic of China (2011)
2. Guangzhou Statistics Bureau 2015 1% Population Sampling Survey. Statistics Bureau of Guangdong Province (Table 1–9) (2015)
3. Jiangxi Province Statistics Bureau 2015 1% Population Sampling Survey. Statistics Bureau of Jiangxi Province (2015)
4. Yongmei, L., Xiaoxue, Z., Yunxin, G.: Survey and analysis on domestic and overseas human body database for garments' use. J. Textile Res. **06**, 141–147 (2015)
5. Human Dimensions of Chinese Adults (GB/T10000-1988) (1998)
6. Zeng, X.: Chinese aged people health comprehensive analysis. J. Popul. Econ. **5**, 89–95 (2010)
7. Hu, X., Feng, X., Men, D., Chen, R.C.C.: Demands and needs of elderly chinese people for garment. In: Stephanidis, C., Antona, M. (eds.) UAHCI 2013. LNCS, vol. 8010, pp. 88–95. Springer, Heidelberg (2013). https://doi.org/10.1007/978-3-642-39191-0_10
8. He, J.: Study on consumer demands and consumer market of Chinese aged people. J. Popul. Econ. **4**, 104–111 (2004)

Comparisons of Hybrid Mechanisms Based on Their Singularities for Bone Reduction Surgery: 3-PRP-3-RPS and 3-RPS-3-PRP

Annisa Pratiwi[1], Sinh Nguyen Phu[2], Terence Essomba[2], and Latifah Nurahmi[1]([envelope]) [ORCID]

[1] Department of Mechanical Engineering, Institut Teknologi Sepuluh Nopember, Surabaya, Indonesia
latifah.nurahmi@me.its.ac.id
[2] Department of Mechanical Engineering, National Central University, Taoyuan City, Taiwan

Abstract. This paper presents comparisons of two hybrid mechanisms for bone reduction surgery based on the singularity analysis. These hybrid mechanisms are named Hybrid mechanisms I and II which are composed of two different parallel mechanisms, namely a planar mechanism and a 2T1R spatial mechanism. Both parallel mechanisms are mounted in series. Initially, transformation matrices of both parallel mechanisms are obtained. The products of both transformation matrices define the operation modes of Hybrid mechanisms I and II. Time derivative of transformation matrices are performed to derive Jacobian matrices. Jacobian matrices play the key role to derive singularity conditions. Eventually, singularity loci of Hybrid mechanisms I and II can be illustrated and compared.

Keywords: Hybrid mechanisms · Parallel mechanisms · Operation modes · Singularity

1 Introduction

The thigh bone (femur) is the longest bone in human body. The broken femur is called femoral fracture and severe femoral fractures require a surgical treatment, namely bone reduction surgery. This surgery aims to realign and to put the bone pieces in close proximity to one another so the healing can occur. During the surgical procedure, an incision is made in the skin to visualize the broken bone to the surgeons. Due to the unique nature of femur anatomy, the surgeons should apply significant amount of forces to relocate the bone pieces. This open procedure exposes great risks to the patients, for example bleeding, infections, inflammation and scar tissue.

Recent advanced procedure, namely minimally invasive surgery, has been developed over the past decades. A set of nails are inserted into the bone segments

V. G. Duffy (Ed.): HCII 2021, LNCS 12777, pp. 152–162, 2021.
https://doi.org/10.1007/978-3-030-77817-0_13

by making a small incision no larger than the nail cross section. Based on the real time images, the surgeons may adjust the position of bone segments. A complete bone reduction surgery is performed by moving the bone segments in three linear motions and three rotational directions. Therefore, a robot having a six Degree-of-Freedom (DOF) motion is the most suitable system for this procedure.

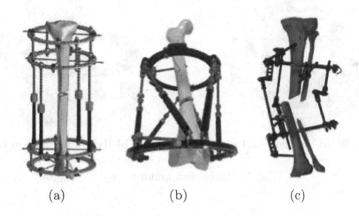

(a)   (b)   (c)

Fig. 1. (a) Ilizarov apparatus, (b) Ortho-Suv frame, (c) Taylor Spatial frame

The first robot performing bone reduction surgery was proposed by Dr. Gavril Abramovich Ilizarov in 1992 [1,2] and it was named Ilizarov fixator. The robot is mounted on one bone segment by surrounding the patient's limb as shown in Fig. 1(a). For complex fractures, this robot cannot achieve one-time surgery and re-assemblage is needed. To overcome this issue, Taylor Spatial Frame was fabricated based on Hexapod architecture as shown in Fig. 1(b). This robot was introduced by Charles and Harold Taylor in 1999 [3,4]. A software-based robot was developed by Ortho-SUV Ltd in 2006 [5] as shown in Fig. 1(c). The robot consists of a fixed ring and a mobile ring connected by six telescopic struts, which has better accuracy, higher rigidity and shorter correction time. The above mentioned robots are fully-parallel structures which have limited workspace due to collisions and small joint range of motions about vertical axis.

Motivated by these issues, this paper aims to study two hybrid mechanisms for bone reduction surgery which have been proposed by Esseomba *et al.* [6–8]. These hybrid mechanisms consist of two parallel mechanisms mounted in series. Both hybrid mechanisms have 6-DOF and its rotation about vertical axis is unlimited. The operation modes and singularities of both hybrid mechanisms will be analysed based on the algebraic geometry approach.

2   Robot Architectures and Applications

Figures 2(a)–2(b) show the architectures of hybrid mechanisms I and II, respectively. These mechanisms are composed of two distinct parallel mechanisms,

(a) Hybrid mechanism I   (b) Hybrid mechanism II

Fig. 2. Mechanism architectures

namely 3-RPS[1] and 3-PRP, attached in series. The compositions of hybrid mechanisms I and II are as follows:

– Hybrid mechanism I: 3-PRP-3-RPS
– Hybrid mechanism II: 3-RPS-3-PRP

Figure 3(a) depicts the 3-PRP parallel mechanism that has been introduced by Daniali *et al.* [9]. It is a planar mechanism that is composed of double platforms of equilateral triangles. The bottom and upper platforms are respectively defined by $A_1A_2A_3$ and $B_1B_2B_3$. The circumradius of both platforms are defined by a and b, respectively. The edges of both platforms are equipped with prismatic joints. The prismatic joints of the bottom and upper platforms are denoted by M_i and N_i, where $(i = 1, 2, 3)$. Both prismatic joints are connected by revolute joint and three prismatic joints of the bottom platform are actuated. The displacements of prismatic joint M_i are defined by r_1, r_2, r_3 respectively from points A_1, A_2, A_3. The displacements of prismatic joint N_i are defined by l_1, l_2, l_3 respectively from points B_1, B_2, B_3.

The coordinate frame (U, V, W) is located in the middle of bottom platform. The position coordinates of prismatic joints M_i and N_i are as follows:

$$\mathbf{m_1} = \begin{bmatrix} 1 \\ a - \dfrac{\sqrt{3}r_1}{2} \\ \dfrac{r_1}{2} \\ 0 \end{bmatrix} \quad \mathbf{m_2} = \begin{bmatrix} 1 \\ -\dfrac{a}{2} \\ \dfrac{\sqrt{3}a}{2} - r_2 \\ 0 \end{bmatrix} \quad \mathbf{m_3} = \begin{bmatrix} 1 \\ -\dfrac{a}{2} + \dfrac{\sqrt{3}r_3}{2} \\ -\dfrac{\sqrt{3}a}{2} + \dfrac{r_3}{2} \\ 0 \end{bmatrix} \quad (1)$$

---

[1] S, P and R denote spherical, prismatic and revolute joints.

$$\mathbf{n}_1 = \begin{bmatrix} 1 \\ b - \dfrac{\sqrt{3}l_1}{2} \\ \dfrac{l_1}{2} \\ 0 \end{bmatrix} \quad \mathbf{n}_2 = \begin{bmatrix} 1 \\ -\dfrac{b}{2} \\ \dfrac{\sqrt{3}b}{2} - l_2 \\ 0 \end{bmatrix} \quad \mathbf{n}_3 = \begin{bmatrix} 1 \\ -\dfrac{b}{2} + \dfrac{\sqrt{3}l_3}{2} \\ -\dfrac{\sqrt{3}b}{2} + \dfrac{l_3}{2} \\ 0 \end{bmatrix} \quad (2)$$

The 3-RPS parallel mechanism is a spatial mechanism that has been proposed by Hunt [10]. It consists of two platforms of equilateral triangles. The bottom platform is confined by revolute joints of points B_i with circumradius b. The upper platform is confined by spherical joints of points C_i with circumradius c. Both platforms are linked by three RPS legs. Revolute and spherical joints are attached to the bottom and upper platforms, respectively. Prismatic joint of each leg is actuated and its displacement is denoted by r_4, r_5, r_6. Different structure of 3-RPS parallel mechanism having two operation modes, was developed in [11–13] for ankle rehabilitation device.

The coordinate frame (PQR) is located in the middle of bottom platform. The position coordinates of point B_i and C_i are as follows:

$$\mathbf{b}_1 = \begin{bmatrix} 1 \\ b \\ 0 \\ 0 \end{bmatrix} \quad \mathbf{b}_2 = \begin{bmatrix} 1 \\ -\dfrac{b}{2} \\ \dfrac{\sqrt{3}b}{2} \\ 0 \end{bmatrix} \quad \mathbf{b}_3 = \begin{bmatrix} 1 \\ -\dfrac{b}{2} \\ -\dfrac{\sqrt{3}b}{2} \\ 0 \end{bmatrix} \quad (3)$$

$$\mathbf{c}_1 = \begin{bmatrix} 1 \\ c \\ 0 \\ 0 \end{bmatrix} \quad \mathbf{c}_2 = \begin{bmatrix} 1 \\ -\dfrac{c}{2} \\ \dfrac{\sqrt{3}c}{2} \\ 0 \end{bmatrix} \quad \mathbf{c}_3 = \begin{bmatrix} 1 \\ -\dfrac{c}{2} \\ -\dfrac{\sqrt{3}c}{2} \\ 0 \end{bmatrix} \quad (4)$$

3 Operation Modes

In this section, the operation modes of 3-PRP mechanism, 3-RPS mechanism, Hybrid mechanism I, and Hybrid mechanism II will be analysed. Initially, transformation matrices of 3-PRP mechanism and 3-RPS mechanism should be determined separately based on Quaternion parameters. Then, transformation matrices of Hybrid mechanism I and II are obtained from the product of transformation matrices 3-PRP mechanism and 3-RPS mechanism. These transformation matrices are key point to physically interpret operation mode.

3.1 3-PRP Mechanism

As stated in Sect. 2, the translational displacements of upper platform are described by (U, V, W). The rotational parameters used in the analysis of 3-PRP

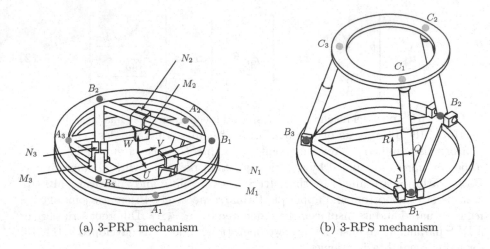

(a) 3-PRP mechanism   (b) 3-RPS mechanism

Fig. 3. Coordinate systems

mechanism is defined by (p_0, p_1, p_2, p_3). Kinematic analysis of the 3-PRP parallel mechanism was provided in [14], while the dynamic modelling was presented in [15]. According to [14], 3-PRP mechanism performs 3-DOF planar motion, which can be described by the following transformation matrix:

$$
\mathbf{T}_{\text{3-PRP}} =
\begin{bmatrix}
1 & 0 & 0 & 0 \\
U & p_0^2 - p_3^2 & -2p_0p_3 & 0 \\
V & 2p_0p_3 & p_0^2 - p_3^2 & 0 \\
0 & 0 & 0 & 1
\end{bmatrix}
\tag{5}
$$

This transformation matrix shows that the 3-PRP mechanism performing two translational motions along U and V directions; and one rotation about vertical axis. The rotational motion is defined by p_0, p_3 that should satisfy $p_0^2 + p_3^2 - 1 = 0$.

3.2   3-RPS Mechanism

The linear displacements of 3-RPS mechanism are defined by P, Q, R. The rotational parameters used to define this mechanism is (q_0, q_1, q_2, q_3). According to the study in [16–18], the 3-RPS mechanism has two operation modes. In this paper, only one operation mode will be investigated and it is described by the transformation matrix as follows:

$$
\mathbf{T}_{\text{3-RPS}} =
\begin{bmatrix}
1 & 0 & 0 & 0 \\
b(q_1^2 - q_2^2) & (q_0^2 + q_1^2 - q_2^2) & 2q_1q_2 & 2q_0q_2 \\
-2q_1q_2b & 2q_1q_2 & q_0^2 - q_1^2 + q_2^2 & -2q_0q_1 \\
R & 2q_0q_2 & 2q_0q_1 & q_0^2 - q_1^2 - q_2^2
\end{bmatrix}
\tag{6}
$$

This transformation matrix tells that the 3-RPS mechanism is able to move along vertical direction defined by R. This mechanism is also able to perform 2-DOF rotations defined by q_0, q_1, q_2 that should fulfil $q_0^2 + q_1^2 + q_2^2 - 1 = 0$.

3.3   Hybrid Mechanisms I and II

Hybrid mechanisms I and II perform 6-DOF, however their motion types (operation modes) are different. Transformation matrix of Hybrid mechanism I is determined by the product of transformation matrices of 3-PRP and 3-RPS mechanisms, as follows:

$$\mathbf{T_I} = \mathbf{T}_{3\text{-PRP}}\ \mathbf{T}_{3\text{-RPS}}$$

$$= \begin{bmatrix} 1 & 0 & 0 & 0 \\ U + (p_0^2 - p_3^2)(q_1^2 - q_2^2)c + 4p_0p_3q_1q_2c & \sigma_1 & \sigma_2 & \sigma_3 \\ V + 2p_0p_3c(q_1^2 - q_2^2) - (2(p_0^2 - p_3^2))q_1q_2c & \sigma_4 & \sigma_5 & \sigma_6 \\ R & & \sigma_7 & \sigma_8 & \sigma_9 \end{bmatrix} \quad (7)$$

where

$$\sigma_1 = (p_0^2 - p_3^2)(q_0^2 + q_1^2 - q_2^2) - 4p_0p_3q_1q_2$$
$$\sigma_2 = (2(p_0^2 - p_3^2))q_1q_2 - 2p_0p_3(q_0^2 - q_1^2 + q_2^2)$$
$$\sigma_3 = (2(p_0^2 - p_3^2))q_0q_2 + 4p_0p_3q_0q_1$$
$$\sigma_4 = 2p_0p_3(q_0^2 + q_1^2 - q_2^2) + (2(p_0^2 - p_3^2))q_1q_2$$
$$\sigma_5 = 4p_0p_3q_1q_2 + (p_0^2 - p_3^2)(q_0^2 - q_1^2 + q_2^2)$$
$$\sigma_6 = 4p_0p_3q_0q_2 - (2(p_0^2 - p_3^2))q_0q_1$$
$$\sigma_7 = -2q_0q_2 \quad \sigma_8 = 2q_0q_1 \quad \sigma_9 = q_0^2 - q_1^2 - q_2^2$$

The transformation matrix $\mathbf{T_I}$ describes the motion of Hybrid mechanism I. This mechanism is able to perform a pure translation along vertical direction defined by R. The horizontal translations are parasitic motions which is a combination between translations of 3-PRP mechanism and rotations of 3-PRP and 3-RPS mechanisms $(p_0, p_3, q_0, q_1, q_2)$.

The product of transformation matrices of 3-RPS and 3-PRP mechanisms yields transformation matrix of Hybrid mechanism II, as follows:

$$\mathbf{T_{II}} = \mathbf{T}_{3\text{-RPS}}\ \mathbf{T}_{3\text{-PRP}}$$

$$= \begin{bmatrix} 1 & 0 & 0 & 0 \\ (q_0^2 + q_1^2 - q_2^2)U + 2q_1q_2V + c(q_1^2 - q_2^2) & \lambda_1 & \lambda_2 & \lambda_3 \\ 2q_1q_2U + (q_0^2 - q_1^2 + q_2^2)V - 2q_1q_2c & \lambda_4 & \lambda_5 & \lambda_6 \\ R - 2Uq_0q_2 + 2Vq_0q_1 & & \lambda_7 & \lambda_8 & \lambda_9 \end{bmatrix} \quad (8)$$

where

$$\lambda_1 = (q_0^2 + q_1^2 - q_2^2)(p_0^2 - p_3^2) + 4q_1q_2p_0p_3$$
$$\lambda_2 = -(2(q_0^2 + q_1^2 - q_2^2))p_0p_3 + 2q_1q_2(p_0^2 - p_3^2) \quad \lambda_3 = 2q_0q_2$$
$$\lambda_4 = 2q_1q_2(p_0^2 - p_3^2) + (2(q_0^2 - q_1^2 + q_2^2))p_0p_3$$
$$\lambda_5 = -4q_1q_2p_0p_3 + (q_0^2 - q_1^2 + q_2^2)(p_0^2 - p_3^2) \quad \lambda_6 = -2q_0q_1$$
$$\lambda_7 = -2q_0q_2(p_0^2 - p_3^2) + 4q_0q_1p_0p_3$$
$$\lambda_8 = 4q_0q_2p_0p_3 + 2q_0q_1(p_0^2 - p_3^2) \quad \lambda_9 = q_0^2 - q_1^2 - q_2^2$$

The transformation matrix $\mathbf{T_{II}}$ illustrates the motion types performed by Hybrid mechanism II. It turns out that all translational motions are parasitic motions. The horizontal translations are a combination between translations of

3-PRP mechanism and rotations of 3-RPS mechanisms (q_0, q_1, q_2). The vertical translation is also a parasitic motion which is a combination between the vertical motion and rotations of 3-RPS mechanism (R, q_0, q_1, q_2), translational motions of 3-PRP mechanism (U, V).

4   Singularity

Let the rotational parameters (p_0, p_3) and (q_0, q_1, q_2) be defined by Euler angles, such that:

$$
\begin{aligned}
p_0 &= \cos(\alpha) \\
p_3 &= \sin(\alpha) \\
q_0 &= \cos(\frac{\theta}{2}) \\
q_1 &= \sin(\frac{\theta}{2}) \sin(\phi) \\
q_2 &= \sin(\frac{\theta}{2}) \cos(\phi)
\end{aligned}
\tag{9}
$$

The rotational motions of Hybrid mechanisms I and II are described by the angles ϕ, θ, α and the translational motions are characterized by U, V, R. Since 6-DOF motions are now parametrized by six parameters, the velocity operator can be performed as follows:

$$\Omega = \dot{\mathbf{T}}\mathbf{T}^{-1} \tag{10}$$

where

$$
\Omega =
\begin{bmatrix}
0 & 0 & 0 & 0 \\
v_{ox} & 0 & -\omega_z & \omega_y \\
v_{oy} & \omega_z & 0 & -\omega_x \\
v_{oz} & -\omega_y & \omega_x & 0
\end{bmatrix}
\tag{11}
$$

Let $\mathbf{t}$ and $\dot{\mathbf{x}}$ be the moving platform twist and output velocity. They are expressed as follows:

$$\mathbf{t} = \begin{bmatrix} \omega_x & \omega_y & \omega_z & v_{ox} & v_{oy} & v_{oz} \end{bmatrix} \tag{12a}$$

$$\dot{\mathbf{x}} = \begin{bmatrix} \dot{\theta} & \dot{\phi} & \dot{\alpha} & \dot{x} & \dot{y} & \dot{z} \end{bmatrix} \tag{12b}$$

The relationship between moving platform twist $\mathbf{t}$ and output variables $\dot{\mathbf{x}}$ is through Jacobian, as:

$$\mathbf{t} = \mathbf{J}\dot{\mathbf{x}} \tag{13}$$

Jacobian of the 3-PRP mechanism, 3-RPS mechanism, Hybrid mechanism I, and Hybrid mechanism II is obtained by applying Eq. (10) into the corresponding transformation matrices. The hybrid mechanisms I and II will be subjected to singularity if and only if one of the following five conditions is fulfilled, namely:

1. 3-PRP mechanism is in singularity and 3-RPS mechanism is not in singularity, i.e. $\det(\mathbf{J}_{3\text{-PRP}}) = 0$ and $\det(\mathbf{J}_{3\text{-RPS}}) \neq 0$

2. 3-PRP mechanism is not in singularity and 3-RPS mechanism is in singularity, i.e. $\det(\mathbf{J}_{3\text{-PRP}}) \neq 0$ and $\det(\mathbf{J}_{3\text{-RPS}}) = 0$

3. 3-PRP mechanism and 3-RPS mechanism are simultaneously in singularities, i.e. $\det(\mathbf{J}_{3\text{-PRP}}) = \det(\mathbf{J}_{3\text{-RPS}}) = 0$

4. 3-PRP mechanism and 3-RPS mechanism are not in singularities but Hybrid mechanism I is in combined singularity, i.e. $\det(\mathbf{J}_{3\text{-PRP}}) \neq 0$, $\det(\mathbf{J}_{3\text{-RPS}}) \neq 0$, $\det(\mathbf{J}_{\mathrm{I}}) = 0$.

5. 3-PRP mechanism and 3-RPS mechanism are not in singularities but Hybrid mechanism II is in combined singularity, i.e. $\det(\mathbf{J}_{3\text{-PRP}}) \neq 0$, $\det(\mathbf{J}_{3\text{-RPS}}) \neq 0$, $\det(\mathbf{J}_{\mathrm{II}}) = 0$.

Therefore, the vanishing conditions of determinant of Jacobian should be computed as:

$$\det(\mathbf{J}_{3\text{-PRP}}) = \cos^2(\alpha) + \sin^2(\alpha) - 1 = 0 \tag{14a}$$

$$\det(\mathbf{J}_{3\text{-RPS}}) = 2R(32\cos^6(\phi) - 48\cos^4(\phi) + 18\cos^2(\phi) - 3)c^2 BA \cos^5(\tfrac{\theta}{2})$$

$$+2ABCD\sin(\phi)c^2(ABc + b)\sin(\tfrac{\theta}{2})\cos^4(\tfrac{\theta}{2}) - R(128\cos(\phi)^6 - 192\cos^4(\phi)$$

$$+72\cos(\phi)^2 - 13)c^2 BA \cos(\tfrac{\theta}{2})^3 - 2ABCD\sin(\phi)c(2ABc^2 + 3R^2 + 2b^2)\sin(\tfrac{\theta}{2})$$

$$\cos^2(\tfrac{\theta}{2}) - R(-64AB\cos^6(\phi)c^2 + 96AB\cos^4(\phi)c^2 - 36AB\cos^2(\phi)c^2 + 2AB$$

$$Ebc - 4b^2 BA + 6c^2 BA - ER^2)\cos(\tfrac{\theta}{2}) - 2\sin(\phi)R^2(b - c)\sin(\tfrac{\theta}{2})ABCD = 0 \tag{14b}$$

$$\det(\mathbf{J}_{\mathrm{I}}) = \mathbb{I} \tag{14c}$$

$$\det(\mathbf{J}_{\mathrm{II}}) = 4\cos(\tfrac{\theta}{2})^4\cos(\phi)^4 + 4\cos(\tfrac{\theta}{2})^4\cos(\phi)^2\sin(\phi)^2 - 4\cos(\tfrac{\theta}{2})^4\cos(\phi)^2$$

$$- 8\cos(\tfrac{\theta}{2})^2\cos(\phi)^4 - 8\cos(\tfrac{\theta}{2})^2\cos(\phi)^2\sin(\phi)^2 + 8\cos(\tfrac{\theta}{2})^2\cos(\phi)^2 + 4\cos(\phi)^4$$

$$+4\cos(\phi)^2\sin(\phi)^2 - 2\cos(\tfrac{\theta}{2})^2 - 4\cos(\phi)^2 + 1 = 0 \tag{14d}$$

where:

$$A = \cos(\tfrac{\theta}{2}) - 1 \qquad B = \cos(\tfrac{\theta}{2}) + 1$$
$$C = 2\cos(\phi) - 1 \qquad D = 2\cos(\phi) + 1$$
$$E = 2\cos^2(\tfrac{\theta}{2}) - 1$$

Equation (14a) shows that the 3-PRP mechanism is in singularity at home position, namely when $\alpha = 0$. Equation (14b) defines singularity equation of the 3-RPS mechanism which is affected by the design parameter (b, c) and moving platform altitude R. Equation (14c) describes imaginary solutions of combined singularity of Hybrid mechanism I which means that combined singularity of Hybrid mechanism I will never be encountered. Equation (14d) depicts combined singularity of Hybrid mechanism II which is not influenced by either the design parameters or moving platform altitude.

Singularity loci of the 3-RPS mechanism (Eq. (14a)) and the Hybrid mechanism II (Eq. (14d)) are illustrated in Figs. 4, 5 and 6 by the red and blue curves, respectively. Singularity loci of the 3-RPS mechanism is affected by the increment of moving platform altitude R. With the altitude is getting higher, the workspace inside singularity loci is getting smaller.

Hybrid mechanism II will encounter combined singularity when the moving platform tilts $\theta = 1.57$ rad. In this configuration, any rotational motions generated by the 3-PRP mechanism fails to rotate the moving platform about vertical axis.

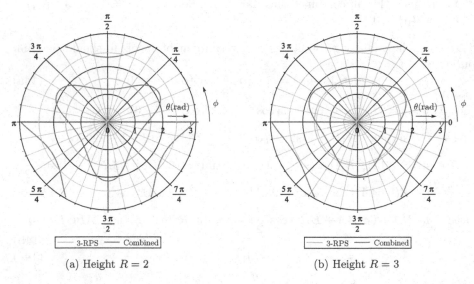

(a) Height $R = 2$ (b) Height $R = 3$

Fig. 4. Singularity loci of Hybrid mechanism II at $a = \dfrac{1}{2}, b = 1, c = 1$

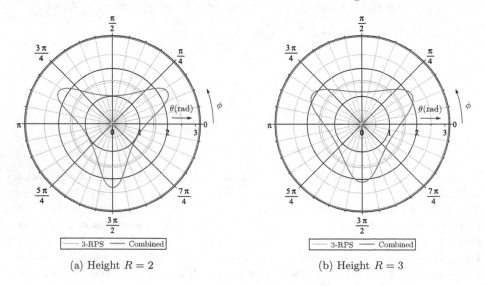

(a) Height $R = 2$ (b) Height $R = 3$

Fig. 5. Singularity loci of Hybrid mechanism II at $a = 1, b = 1, c = 1$

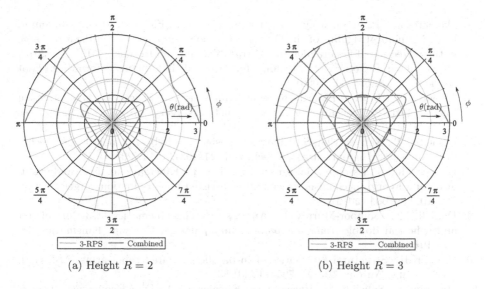

(a) Height $R = 2$ (b) Height $R = 3$

Fig. 6. Singularity loci of Hybrid mechanism II at $a = 2, b = 1, c = 1$

5 Conclusions

This paper investigated two hybrid mechanisms for bone reduction surgery based o their singularities. These hybrid mechanisms are composed of two distinct parallel mechanisms mounted in series, namely 3-RPS and 3-PRP parallel mechanisms. Hybrid mechanism I consists of 3-PRP-3-RPS and Hybrid mechanism II consists of 3-RPS-3-PRP. Transformation matrices of 3-PRP and 3-RPS parallel mechanisms were initially derived. The transformation matrices of Hybrid mechanisms I and II were obtained from the product of transformation matrices of 3-PRP and 3-RPS parallel mechanisms. Time derivatives of transformation matrices were computed to find Jacobian. Determinant of Jacobian was enumerated and five singularity conditions were identified. It revealed that Hybrid mechanism I does not encounter combined singularity, while Hybrid mechanism II encounters combined singularity when the moving platform tilts up to 90 deg. Loci of combined singularity was also depicted.

References

1. Ilizarov, G.A., Leydaev, V.I.: The replacement of long tubular bone defects by lengthening distraction osteotomy of one of the fragments. Clin. Orthopaedics Related Res. **280**, 7–10 (1992)
2. Seide, K., Wolter, D., Kortmann. H. R.: Fracture reduction and deformity correction with the hexapod Ilizarov fixator. Clin. Orthopaedics Related Res. **363**, 186–195 (1999)
3. Solomin, L.N., Paley, D., Shchepkina, E.A., Vilensky, V.A., Skomoroshko, P.V.: A comparative study of the correction of femoral deformity between the Ilizarov apparatus and Ortho-SUV Frame. Int Orthopaedics **38**, 865–872 (2013)

4. Skomoroshko, P.V., Vilensky, V.A., Hammouda, A.I., Fletcher, M.D.A., Solomin, L.N.: Mechanical rigidity of the OrthoSUV frame compared to the Ilizarov frame in the correction of femoral deformit. Strat. Trauma imb Reconstr **10**, 5–11 (2015)

5. Taylor, J.C.: Perioperative planning for two-and-three-plane deformities. Foot Ankle Clin. **13**, 69–121 (2008)

6. Essomba, T., Nguyen Phu, S., Kinematic analysis and design of a six-degrees of freedom 3-RRPS mechanism for bone reduction surgery. ASME J. Med. Devices **15**(1), 011101 (2021)

7. Essomba, T., Nguyen Phu, S.: Kinematic design of a hybrid planar-tripod mechanism for bone reduction surgery. Mech. Ind. **21**(403), 1–14 (2020)

8. Nguyen Phu, S., Essomba, T., Idram, I., Lai, J.-Y.: Kinematic analysis and evaluation of a hybrid mechanism for computer assisted bone reduction surgery. Mech. Sci. **10**, 589–604 (2019)

9. Daniali, M., Zsombor-Murray, P., Angeles, J.: The kinematics of 3-DoF planar and spherical double-triangular parallel manipulators. Comput. Kinematics **28**, 153–164 (1993)

10. Hunt, K.H.: Structural kinematics of in-parallel-actuated robot-arms. ASME. J. Mech. Trans. Autom. **105**(4), 705–712 (1983)

11. Nurahmi, L., Solichin, M., Harnany, D., Kurniawan, A.: Dimension synthesis of 3-RPS parallel manipulator with intersecting R-axes for ankle rehabilitation device. In: 18th International Conference on Advanced Robotics (ICAR), pp. 269–274 (2017)

12. Nurahmi, L., Solichin, M.: Motion type of 3-RPS parallel manipulator for ankle rehabilitation device. In: International Conference on Advanced Mechatronics, Intelligent Manufacture, and Industrial Automation (ICAMIMIA), pp. 74–79 (2017)

13. Nurahmi, L., Caro, S., Solichin, M.: A novel ankle rehabilitation device based on a reconfigurable 3-RPS parallel manipulator. Mech. Mach. Theory **134**, 135–150 (2019)

14. Chablat, D., Staicu, S.: Kinematics of A 3-PRP planar parallel robot. UPB Sci. Bull. Ser. D Mech. Eng. **71**(1), 3–16 (2009)

15. Staicu, S.: Dynamics of the 3-PRP planar parallel robot. Rom. J. Tech. Sci. Appl. Mech. **54**(2), 125–142 (2009)

16. Schadlbauer, J., Walter, D., Husty, M.: The 3-RPS parallel manipulator from an algebraic viewpoint. Mech. Mach. Theory **75**, 161–176 (2014)

17. Schadlbauer, J., Nurahmi, L., Husty, M., Wenger, P., Caro, S.: Operation modes in lower-mobility parallel manipulators. Interdisc. Appl. Kinematics **26**, 1–9 (2013)

18. Nayak, A., Nurahmi, L., Wenger, P., Caro, S.: Comparison of 3-RPS and 3-SPR parallel manipulators based on their maximum inscribed singularity-free circle. In: Wenger, P., Flores, P. (eds.) New Trends in Mechanism and Machine Science. MMS, vol. 43, pp. 121–130. Springer, Cham (2017). https://doi.org/10.1007/978-3-319-44156-6_13

The Measurement and Analysis of Chinese Adults' Range of Motion Joint

Qianxiang Zhou[1,2], Yu Jin[1,2], and Zhongqi Liu[1,2](✉)

[1] Key Laboratory for Biomechanics and Mechanobiology of the Ministry of Education, School of Biological Science and Medical Engineering, Beihang University, Beijing 100191, China

[2] Beijing Advanced Innovation Centre for Biomedical Engineering, Beihang University, Beijing 102402, China

Abstract. There have been many studies on range of motion (ROM) of joint at home and abroad, but they were generally measured on a certain age group, a certain group of people, and a certain area. So far, no large-scale measurement research on Chinese adults has been carried out systematically. Based on the regional characteristics of China, this study selected three places of Hangzhou, Xi'an, and Dalian as sampling points, and 818 Chinese adults' data of ROM were collected whose age ranged from 18 to 67 years old. And their careers involved university teachers, staff, undergraduate students, graduate students, farmers, workshop workers, etc. Forty parameters of ROM were measured including shoulder, elbow, wrist, fingers, neck, spine, hip, knee, ankle, etc. After analyzing the effects of age, gender, BMI index, region and labor intensity to the ROM, it was found that the most females' ROM were larger than males'. In generally, female's neck, wrist, hip, shoulder, ulna and finger joints were more flexible than male's. There was no obvious difference in flexibility between men and women about spine thoracolumbar, elbow, knee and ankle joints. The effect of age on ROM was more obvious. The overall trend was that the ROM decreased with age, and the smallest reduction was hip adduction, by 2.1%, and the largest reduction was wrist radial flexion, by 25.2%. The smallest degree reduction also was hip adduction (0.6°), and the largest was wrist flexion (13.2°). Among the 40 parameters measured, 33 parameters decreased with the increase of BMI index. The largest decrease was elbow extension (29.1%), and the smallest decrease was shoulder abduction (2.7%). The ROM of each joint varied greatly in different regions, ranging from 2° to 19.4°. The smallest was shoulder abduction (2°), and the largest was shoulder internal rotation (19.4°). By analyzing the data of subjects with different labor intensity, it could be found that as the labor intensity increase, the ROM become smaller.

Keywords: Range of motion (ROM) · Adult · Gender · Age · BMI · Region · Labor intensity

1 Introduction

The angle of joint motion is also called the range of motion (ROM) of joint, which refers to the maximum angle when the joint rotate from the neutral position or zero position to

© Springer Nature Switzerland AG 2021
V. G. Duffy (Ed.): HCII 2021, LNCS 12777, pp. 163–177, 2021.
https://doi.org/10.1007/978-3-030-77817-0_14

the limit position. The measurement of ROM was originally taken by Camus and Amar in the early 20th century [1], which began with the assessment of disability caused by post-war injuries, and was later widely used in the fields of industry, agriculture, aerospace, medicine, and sports science, for example, industrial mechanical equipment design, public facilities and product design, design and evaluation of workspace, design and evaluation of clothing and personal protective equipment. The ROM is mainly related to age, gender, race, body type and training.

Boone et al. (1979) measured the ROM of 109 normal male subjects ranging in age from 18 months to 54 years old. The results showed that children twelve years old or younger had more backward extension of the shoulder, ankle flexion, and foot eversion than did the other subjects. In comparing the youngest group (five years old or less) with the rest of the subjects, the youngest group had greater pronation and supination of the forearm; flexion, radial deviation of wrist, and inward and outward rotation of the hip. Children who were six to twelve years old had slightly more horizontal extension of the shoulder, elbow extension, and wrist extension [2]. In order to determine the effect of age on ROM, Nancy et al. (1993) collected 23 parameters of white males (25 to 54 years old). Their results indicated a decrease in joint ROM with age, with decreased from 4% to 30% [3]. This implied that the aging population with reduced ROM might be at a higher risk of injury for manual material handling and cumulative trauma disorders.

Agustin et al. (1997, 1998) analyzed data from elderly people (65–79 years old) in the San Antonio area to determine the influencing factors of ROM [4]. The results of hips and knees found that more than 90% of the elderly's bending angles of hip and knee were greater than 90°; the higher the BMI index, the smaller the bending angles of hip and knee; women's bending angles of hip and knee were smaller than men's; Mexicans' bending angles of hip and knee are were smaller than other races; if the knee was painful, the knee bending angle was smaller; men's bending angles of shoulder and elbow were smaller than women's; Mexicans' bending angles of shoulder were smaller than other races. Generally speaking, the ROM of most elderly people could be competent for basic activities of daily living, but obesity and arthritis were two potential threats that affect the ROM. Veronique et al. (1998) measured the neck joints' ROM of people aged 14 to 70 years [5]. The results showed that the ROM in the sagittal plane was 122°, and the neck bending angle was slightly larger than the extension angle. The neck joints' ROM was not relate to gender, but related to age, and decreased significantly with age.

Yoon Hoon-Yoog et al. (2000) of Dong-A University in Busan, South Korea measured the ROM for Korean adults of the age between 18 and 60 [6]. The results showed that there was no obvious difference between the sexes. Female subjects had larger ROM than male subjects in hip movement (hip adduction and abduction), knee movement (knee rotation medial and lateral), neck movement (right flexion, dorsal flexion, right rotation), wrist movement (wrist extension and adduction), elbow flexion and shoulder extension; male subjects had larger range of movements than female subjects in wrist abduction, wrist flexion, forearm supination, shoulder rotation (lateral), shoulder adduction, knee flexion (standing), ankle flexion, hip flexion, and hip rotation medial (sitting). In general, the ROM tends to decreased with age, especially the reduction of shoulder activities (adduction, abduction, rotation), neck activities (forward flexion, extension, right flexion, right rotation) was very obvious, hip flexion and knee flexion also decreased with age, however, some range of joint movements such as wrist flexion and extension increased with ages for both male and female subjects.

Kang Yuhua et al. (2001) took middle-aged and elderly people (50 to 89 years old, 100 men and women each) as the research objects, and measured the ROM of shoulders, elbows, forearms, wrists, marrow, knees, ankles, etc. [7]. The results found that the normal value of ROM in the 4 groups of 50–59, 60–69, 70–79, and 80–89 years old decreased with the increase of age, especially after the age of 60, the ROM decreased rapidly. It might be related to the decrease in the amount of activity and the degenerative changes of the joints after aging. Hu Haitao (2006) and others used digital camera photography to measure the ROM of 105 elderly people in Beijing [8]. The results showed that there was no significant difference in most ROM between 65–74 years old and over 75 years old, and there was no significant difference between genders.

In order to establish a database of ROM of Taiwanese workers and study the influence of age and gender on ROM, Chung Meng-Jung et al. (2007) measured Taiwan 1134 ROM of workers (16–64 years old) [9]. The statistical results showed that age and gender had a significant impact on the most ROM. With the increase of age, the data of ROM showed a downward trend, but it was related to the joints, the neck and wrists were the most obvious, and the maximum decline rate was 26%. The joint mobility of women was significantly greater than that of women, and the joint mobility of the elbow, wrist and forearm was significantly greater than that of men. This difference in the shoulders might be related to osteoporosis which was more common in women. When the disease occurred, the position of the scapula changed, which led to the decrease of the women's ROM.

In order to study the effect of left and right joints on ROM, Allander et al. (1974) measured the ROM of 309 Icelandic women aged 33–60 years old and 411 (208 women and 203 men) Swedes aged 45–70 years old [10]. The results showed that among Ice landers, there was no significant difference in the ROM of the left and right joints; among Swedes, the ROM of the wrist and metacarpophalangeal joints of some age groups was significantly smaller than that of the left, and the joints of the left hip were significantly smaller than the right. Gunal et al. (1996) measured the active and passive arcs of motion of the shoulder, elbow, forearm, and wrist in 1000 healthy male subjects who were right-hand dominant and who ranged of age from eighteen to twenty-two years [11]. The ranges of motion on the right side were significantly smaller than those on the left. They concluded that the contralateral, normal side might not always be a reliable control in the evaluation of restriction of motion of a joint. Christopher et al. (2002) measured the data of 280 subjects (4 to 70 years old) [12]. Among these subjects, 254 were right-handed and the rest were left-handed. Among these subjects, 258 were white, 13 were African American, and 9 were Asian. It was found that whether the arm was in abduction or adduction during the measurement, the angle of external rotation of the dominant hand was significantly greater than that of the non-dominant hand; the internal rotation and extension of the non-dominant hand were significantly greater than that of the dominant hand. There was no obvious difference between the forward and abduction angles of the dominant hand and the non-dominant hand. If the above differences were true, it was inappropriate to use the contralateral joint range of motion data to evaluate the pre-injury joint range of motion, because it might lead to excessive distraction of the joint and cause the joint to be injured. However, some researchers obtained different results from the above. Roaas et al. (1982) measured the ROM data on the left and right sides in healthy male subjects, 30–40 years old, in a randomized sample from the population in the city of Gothenburg, Sweden. There were no statistically significant differences between the motions of the right and left side [13].

In order to explore the mechanism of airflow injury and provide data on the ROM, Wu Guirong and Zhang Yunran of the China Institute of Aerospace Medicine measured the range of motion data of 190 active pilots aged 20 to 50 [14]. The relationship between ROM and body type, age and height was studied. They obtained the ROM for pilots of different body types and obtained the regression equations with age. The body types of 190 pilots were classified according to three standards: standard body type, lean body type and fat body type. The ROM changed regularly with the increase of body size, and the ROM gradually decreased from thin to fat. The statistical results were significantly different. This might be the less exercise of the obese people, leading to the more fat body. Because of the thick limbs of obese people, the movement of the joints was affected during flexion. In addition, obese people might have poor mobility. People who exercised often generally had stronger muscle strength, thicker ligaments, and stronger mobility. Relevant studies had also confirmed that people with lean body types had a larger range of motion. According to the order of movement range from small to large, the crowd was divided into fat, muscle, medium and thin. The study divided the pilots into three age groups, 20 to 23 years old, 30 to 34 years old, and 40 to 50 years old. The results showed that as age increased, the range of joint motion showed a decreasing trend. There were significant differences in data between age groups which might be related to the natural laws of human growth, development, and aging. In order to explore the relationship between height and ROM, the study selected two groups of pilots above 1.75 m and below 1.67 m in the standard body type group for comparative analysis. The results showed that there was no significant difference between the two groups, which mean that the effect of height on the ROM was not obvious.

From the above study, it could be seen that age and gender were the two most prominent factors that affect ROM. In addition, ROM was also affected by factors such as race, region, occupation, and obesity. Although there had been a large number of measurement and study on the ROM at home and abroad, due to the influence of various factors of the ROM, the research of the Chinese adults' ROM has not been carried out. Therefore, it is necessary to carry out measurement research on Chinese adults' range of motion joint.

2   Method

2.1   Parameters to be Measured

The joints of the human body include shoulder joints, elbow joints, wrist joints, neck joints, spine thoracolumbar joints, hip joints, knee joints and ankle joints. According to the degrees of freedom and movement directions of above joints, the study measured 40 parameters which are shown in Table 1. The definition of each parameter refered to [15–17].

Table 1. ROM parameters in the experiment

Parameters	Abbr	Parameters	Abbr
Shoulder abduction	Shoulder AB	Hip abduction	Hip AB
Shoulder adduction	Shoulder AD	Hip extension	Hip EX
Shoulder internal rotation	Shoulder IR	Hip inward rotation	Hip IR
Shoulder external rotation	Shoulder ER	Hip outward rotation	Hip OR
Shoulder flexion	Shoulder F	Hip forward bend (knee flexion)	Hip FB(KF)
Shoulder backward extension	Shoulder BE	Hip forward bend(knee straight)	Hip FB(KS)
Shoulder flexion horizontal	Shoulder FR	Knee extension	Knee EX
Shoulder extension horizontal	Shoulder EH	Knee flexion	Knee F
Elbow extension	Elbow EX	Ankle dorsiflexion	Ankle D
Elbow flexion	Elbow F	Ankle Plantar flexion	Ankle PF
Forearm pronation	Forearm PR	Neck right flexion	Neck RF
Forearm supination	Forearm SU	Neck left flexion	Neck LF
Wrist dorsiflexion	Wrist DOR	Neck flexion	Neck F
Wrist flexion	Wrist F	Neck extension	Neck EX
Wrist radial deviation	Wrist RD	Neck right rotation	Neck RR
Wrist ulna deviation	Wrist UD	Neck left rotation	Neck LR
Thumb ulnar abduction	Thumb UB	Spine flexion	Spine F
Thumb abduction	Thumb AB	Spine extension	Spine EX
Finger flexion	Finger F	Spine left flexion	Spine LF
Hip adduction	Hip AD	Spine right flexion	Spine RF

2.2   Equipment Used for Measurement

The measuring equipment for the ROM mainly included a photographic measuring system and an electronic joint angle ruler, and their respective measured parameters were shown in Table 2.

The photogrammetry system (Fig. 1) included software system and hardware system. The hardware system mainly included a digital camera, tripod, notebook computer and data cable. The software system mainly included remote control camera photographing software, photo analysis and processing software. When measuring the joint angle, the camera was fixed on a tripod, and the remote control camera photographing software was used to control the camera to capture various subjects' joint activities. And photos were automatically transferred to the hard disk for storage through the data cable between the camera and the laptop. The photo analysis and processing software loaded the photos, and manually click 3 points on the joints that need to be measured (Fig. 2): a point on the movable arm, a point on the joint between the fixed arm and the movable arm, and a point on the reference surface. Three points were connected into two lines. The angle, which

Table 2. Equipment and corresponding measuring parameters

Number	Equipment	Corresponding measuring parameters
1	Electronic joint angle ruler	Neck LR
2		Elbow EX
3		Thumb UB
4		Thumb AB
5		Finger F
6		Knee EX
7		Elbow EX
8	Photographic measuring system	Other 33 parameters

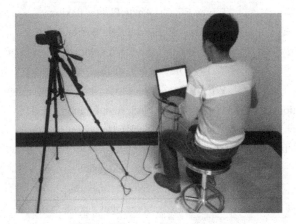

Fig. 1. Photogrammetric system

was the ROM, between the two lines at the joint connection could be easily calculated by mathematical methods.

The electronic articulation angle ruler was also composed of a fixed arm and a movable arm liked the traditional articulation angle ruler. The difference between them was that the former had an additional digital display on the movable arm, which could automatically display the movement angle of the joint (Fig. 3).

2.3 Measured Sample Size Distribution

Three places of Hangzhou, Xi'an, and Dalian were selected as sampling points, and 818 Chinese adults' data of ROM were collected whose age ranged from 18 to 67 years old. The specific sample size distribution was shown in Table 3 and Table 4.

Fig. 2. Measurement and calculation of joint angles

Fig. 3. Electronic joint angle ruler

Table 3. The male sample size sampled and counted by age group in 3 regions

Age	Hangzhou	Xi'an	Dalian	Total
18–25	56	43	15	114
26–35	45	47	31	123
36–59	85	35	38	158
60–67	15	0	0	15
Total	201	125	84	410

Table 4. The female sample size sampled and counted by age group in 3 regions

Age	Hangzhou	Xi'an	Dalian	Total
18–25	81	19	13	113
26–35	35	48	36	119
36–59	95	36	42	173
60–67	3	0	0	3
Total	214	103	91	408

2.4 Requirements of the Measurement Process

During the measurement, the subject should wear as little clothing as possible, be bare-foot and without a crown. The planes contacted by body parts include standing surface (ground), sitting surface (chair sitting surface and backrest), backrest surface (chair back, wall or other surfaces that could be relied on), and lying plane (bed or other platform on which you can lie down). These planes should be flat, horizontal and non-deformable.

3 Results

3.1 The Effect of Gender on the ROM

Gender is an important factor that affects the ROM. The independent t test method was used to calculate the effect of gender on the ROM. The results were shown in Table 5. It could be seen that 23 of the 40 measurement parameters have reached different degrees of significant differences, involving various joints of the human body except the knee joint and the elbow joint. On the whole, the most of females' ROM was greater than males'. The greatest difference was spine flexion, which was 8.2° larger for female than male, and the lest was the ulnar curvature of the wrist, which was 1.2° larger for female than male. Generally speaking, females' neck, wrist, hip, shoulder, ulna and finger joints were more flexible than males'. There was no obvious difference in flexibility between male and female in the spine thoracolumbar, elbow, knee and ankle joints. The results of domestic and foreign studies on the effect of gender on ROM were quite different, but the more consistent result was that most of female's ROM were better than males' [7, 10].

3.2 The Effect of Age on the ROM

Age is also an important factor affecting the ROM. This study set up 4 age groups of 18 to 25 years, 26 to 35 years, 36 to 59 years, and 60 to 67 years, and used a one-way analysis of variance to calculate the effect of age on the ROM. The results of one-way analysis of variance showed that in addition to the left-handed and right-handed neck, the other 38 measurement parameters reached the significant level ($P < 0.05$). Table 6 showed the average of 38 ROM of different ages with significant differences.

Table 5. Parameters of joint motion with significant differences between men and women

Parameters	Sex	Average (°)	Difference	Parameters	Sex	Average (°)	Difference
Neck LR	M	75.1	***	Forearm SU	M	114	***
	F	79.6			F	121.7	
Neck RR	M	75.8	***	Thumb UB	M	80.7	*
	F	79.3			F	82.1	
Neck LF	M	41.2	***	Thumb UB	M	84.2	***
	F	46.8			F	87.8	
Neck LF	M	41.8	***	Spine F	M	57	***
	F	46.6			F	65.2	
Neck EX	M	65.7	***	Hip FB(KF)	M	110.9	*
	F	72.4			F	112.6	
Shoulder EH	M	115.9	***	Hip FB(KF)	M	78.6	***
	F	122.1			F	85.6	
Shoulder BE	M	51	***	Hip EX	M	32.2	***
	F	54.4			F	35	
Shoulder AB	M	175.3	***	Hip OR	M	32.8	***
	F	177			F	38.5	
Elbow EX	M	4	***	Hip AD	M	26.1	***
	F	5.6			F	31.5	
Wrist F	M	63.2	***	Ankle D	M	38	***
	F	66			F	35.7	
Wrist F	M	57.8	*	Ankle PF	M	46.4	***
	F	59.7					
Wrist U	M	32.8	*		F	53.8	
	F	34.1					

There are 4 changes in the ROM with age. Firstly, the ROM decreased with age. There was no significant change in the ROM for people aged 18 to 35. Compared with other age groups, the ROM was greatest at 18 to 35 years old, and then gradually decreased. Among the 40 parameters, the parameters that met the above conditions were the most. There were 25 items in total. These involve all the joints of the body, such as all 4 parameters of the spine joints, all 7 parameters of the hip, all 3 parameters of the finger joints, and radius all 2 parameters of the joint, as well as the parameters of other joints of the body. Secondly, the ROM decreased with age. There were 8 parameters in this case, involving 5 joints of the shoulder, elbow, wrist, neck and ankle. Thirdly, ROM first increased and then decreased. The ROM increased first in the age group of 26 to 35 years old, and then decreased. The ROM in the 18 to 25 years old age group was only

Table 6. Mean values of ROI with significant differences in different age (°)

Parameters	Age range				Parameters	Age range			
	18–25	26–35	36–59	60–67		18–25	26–35	36–59	60–67
Shoulder FR	50.3	49.4	42.8	39.5	Neck F	54.7	58.5	51.6	46.6
Shoulder EH	123.8	118.7	116.1	114.7	Neck EX	75.4	71.5	63.5	57.4
Shoulder F	185.3	182.2	173.9	162.6	Neck LF	47.1	45.8	41.1	34.4
Shoulder BE	52.6	54.9	51.3	51.4	Neck RF	46.8	46.2	41.4	35.7
Shoulder AB	179.2	177.8	173.3	165.5	Spine F	65.3	63.9	56.9	47.4
Shoulder AD	44.2	46.9	39.7	33.7	Spine EX	34.2	32.8	28.4	22
Shoulder ER	28.5	28.6	22.7	19.7	Spine LF	47.2	47.9	40.1	31.6
Shoulder IR	93.6	100.5	91.1	84.3	Spine RF	47	48	40.6	33.1
Elbow F	149.4	148.6	145.2	148.5	Hip AD	28.9	29.9	28.3	23
Elbow EX	6.3	4.3	4.2	3.9	Hip AB	54	54.7	52.5	47.6
Wrist DOR	65.3	60.8	53.6	42.5	Hip FB(KF)	114.4	112.7	109.7	101.2
Wrist F	71.9	67.2	58.7	46.2	Hip FB(KS)	83.5	82.8	81	74.2
Wrist RD	22.2	21.4	16.6	13.5	Hip EX	38.1	36.5	29.1	20.3
Wrist UD	35.8	34.7	31.1	28.1	Hip IR	36.1	37.3	34.1	32.5
Forearm PR	80.2	80.8	77.4	74.2	Hip OR	37.1	36.6	34.2	29.5
Forearm SU	124.7	120.4	112.3	99.2	Knee F	125.3	125.5	119.4	114.1
Thumb AB	88.1	87.4	83.8	79.1	Knee EX	5.7	4.7	6.1	6.5
Thumb UB	83.2	82.5	79.4	79.1	Ankle D	37.1	38	36.1	34.6
Finger F	105.2	104.4	99.9	95.7	Ankle PF	52.8	50.5	48.5	38.7

lower than that in the 26 to 35 years old age group and larger than other age groups. In this case, there were only 3 parameters for the shoulder and 1 parameter for the neck. Last, there was no obvious change. In this case, there was only one parameter of knee extension. Combining the four situations, age had a more obvious influence on ROM. The overall trend was that the ROM decreased with age, which was consistent with the existing literature [4, 6–8, 10, 15]. The smallest degree of reduction was hip adduction (0.6°), and the largest was wrist flexion (13.2°).

3.3 The Effect of BMI on the ROM

BMI (Body Mass Index) is the body mass index. It is a number obtained by dividing the weight in kilograms by the height in meters squared. And it is currently a commonly used international standard to measure the degree of body weight and health. In this study, one-way analysis of variance was used to calculate the effect of BMI index (<18.5,

[18.5, 24), [24, 28), ≥28) on the ROM. The results of one-way analysis of variance showed that in addition to the 6 parameters of left-handed neck, right-handed neck, thumb ulnar abduction, hip abduction, radial ulnar pronation, and ankle dorsiflexion, the other 34 measurement parameters reached significance level (P < 0.05). Table 7 showed the average value of 34 ROM of different BMIs with significant differences.

Table 7. Mean values of ROM with significant differences in different BMIs (°)

Parameters	BMI				Parameters	BMI			
	<18.5	[18.5, 24)	[24, 28)	≥28		<18.5	[18.5, 24)	[24, 28)	≥28
Shoulder FR	49.4	48.1	44.6	42.4	Neck F	57	55.6	52.8	49.7
Shoulder EH	124.4	120.4	116.4	112.8	Neck EX	77.6	70.6	65.5	62.1
Shoulder F	181.6	180.5	177.5	174.8	Neck LF	46.8	45.4	41.3	40.3
Shoulder BE	55.6	53.6	51.5	48	Neck RF	47.2	45.3	42.1	40.2
Shoulder AB	178.3	176.8	175	173.4	Spine F	66.8	62.8	58.1	54.2
Shoulder AD	47.4	44.3	40.8	36.6	Spine EX	33.5	31.9	29.5	29.5
Shoulder ER	27.2	27.2	23.9	23.4	Spine LF	46.6	45.3	42.5	40.1
Shoulder IR	100.2	95.5	92.6	87.7	Spine RF	46.8	45.3	43.1	40.5
Elbow F	149.3	148.4	146.1	143.5	Hip AD	32.9	29.4	27.2	25.7
Elbow EX	5.5	5.3	3.9	3.9	Hip FB(KF)	117.9	113.7	108.4	103.5
Wrist DOR	60.9	60	56	56.7	Hip FB(KS)	83.8	83.4	80.1	78.1
Wrist F	69.6	66.4	61.3	57.9	Hip EX	38.5	34.9	30.6	29.9
Wrist RD	21.5	20.2	18	17.8	Hip IR	37.1	35.9	35.2	33.2
Wrist UD	34.6	34	32.1	32.4	Hip OR	40.7	36.2	33.7	32.4
Forearm SU	123.9	121	113.1	106.1	Knee F	130.2	124.7	119.2	113.7
Thumb AB	89.2	86.3	85.1	84	Knee EX	4.5	5.4	6	6.6
Finger F	106.3	103.8	100.9	96.8	Ankle PF	52.9	51.1	47.9	47.5

It could be seen from Table 7 that, except for knee extension, the other 33 parameters generally decreased with the increase of BMI index, which was consistent with the results of related studies [15]. Literature [15] thought that due to thick limbs, joint movement was affected during flexion. In addition, people who were obese might have poor mobility. People who exercised much more had stronger muscle strength, thickened ligaments, and greater mobility. Among the 33 parameters, the greatest reduction was the radial ulnar supination (17.8°), and the lest decrease was elbow extension (1.6°).

3.4 The Effect of Region on the ROM

China has a great territory, and the ROM of people in different regions may vary. The sampling population at the three sampling sites represented three regions of the south-west, northwest and northeast of China. The independent one-way analysis of variance method was used to calculate the influence of region on the ROM. The results showed that 29 measurement parameters reached the significance level (P < 0.05). Table 8 showed the average value of 29 joint activity parameters in different regions with significant differences. It could be seen that ROM varied greatly between regions, ranging from 2° to 19.4°. The smallest difference was shoulder abduction (2°), and the greatest difference was shoulder internal rotation (19.4°).

Table 8. Mean values of ROM with significant differences in different regions (°)

Parameters	Hangzhou	Xi'an	Dalian	Parameters	Hangzhou	Xi'an	Dalian
Shoulder FR	45.7	46.3	49.9	Neck LR	79	74.7	76.8
Shoulder EH	123	113.5	116.6	Neck RR	78.9	75.2	77.2
Shoulder BE	49.3	52.9	60.5	Spine F	58.5	61.7	66.5
Shoulder AB	175.2	177.2	176.9	Spine LF	40.1	47.7	49.3
Shoulder AD	37.2	44	55.7	Spine RF	40.7	47.5	49.3
Shoulder ER	24.4	26.7	28.9	Hip AD	26.2	27.8	36.6
Shoulder IR	87.9	96.3	107.3	Hip AB	50.9	52.4	61.1
Elbow EX	6.2	3.6	3.2	Hip FB(KF)	109.5	115.3	112.3
Wrist DOR	59.8	56.4	59.4	Hip FB(KS)	81	81.8	85.1
Wrist F	62.9	64.9	68.3	Hip EX	31.1	36.1	36.3
Wrist RD	17.6	21.5	21.4	Hip IR	34.5	36.8	36.5
Wrist UD	32.2	34.2	35.5	Hip OR	33.9	35.9	39.3
Thumb AB	84.6	85.3	90	Knee F	121.1	125	123.6
Thumb UB	80.7	81.5	82.9	Knee EX	7.4	3.7	3.6
Neck F	50.1	58.8	59.2				

3.5 The Effect of Labor Intensity on the ROM

The sampled population had a wide range of occupational sources (Table 9). Different occupations have different labor intensity(LI). Different LI may affect the strength of muscles, bones, and ligaments, which in turn may cause differences in ROM. With reference to related literature [18], this study divided all sampled populations into three levels of LI, mild, moderate, and heavy, as shown in Table 9.

A one-way analysis of variance method was used to calculate the effect of LI on the ROM. The results showed that 36 measurement parameters reached the significance level (P < 0.05). Table 10 was the average of 36 joint activity parameters with significant differences. It could be seen that the difference in ROM of each joint parameter caused by LI ranged from 1.2° to 13°. The biggest difference was ulnar and radial supination (13°), and the least difference is knee extension (1.2°).

Table 9. The labor intensity of the sampling population

LI	sampling population
mild	University student, Teacher, Technicist, Designer, administrator, Researcher, White collars, Salesman, Librarian
moderate	Security staff, Equipment maintenance personnel, Workshop worker, College dorm administrators, University support staff, Driver, Cleaner,
heavy	Farmer, Food related personnel, The operator and stevedore in the factory, building worker

Table 10. Mean values of ROM with significant differences in different LI (°)

Parameters	mild	moderate	heavy	Parameters	mild	moderate	heavy
Shoulder FR	49.7	47.3	42.7	Neck RF	47.3	43.5	41.6
Shoulder EH	125.3	115.2	117	Neck LF	79.5	75.7	77.2
Shoulder F	184.4	179	173.9	Neck RF	79.5	75.9	77.5
Shoulder AB	178.9	175.6	173.8	Spine F	65.7	61.3	55.5
Shoulder AD	43.8	43.9	40.6	Spine EX	33.9	30.9	28.4
Shoulder ER	29	25.3	23.5	Spine LF	46.3	44.4	41.5
Elbow F	149.2	147.5	145.3	Spine RF	46.3	44.7	42
Elbow EX	6.3	4.1	4.1	Hip AD	29.9	28.3	28.3
Wrist DOR	64.8	57.4	53.8	Hip AB	54	54.4	51.7
Wrist F	70.8	63	59.6	Hip FB(KF)	114.4	111	109.7
Wrist RD	21.9	18.7	18	Hip FB(KS)	84.1	81.7	80.4
Wrist UD	35.4	33.4	31.1	Hip EX	37.7	32.4	30.7
Forearm SU	124.9	116.4	111.9	Hip IR	36.6	35.6	34.4
Thumb AB	88.9	85.4	83.4	Hip OR	37.6	34.8	34.5
Thumb UB	83.1	81.1	79.8	Knee F	125.4	122.2	120.5
Finger F	104.8	103.1	99.5	Knee EX	6.2	5	5.6
Neck EX	75.1	67.4	64.3	Ankle D	37.7	36.3	36.7
Neck LF	47.2	43.2	41.4	Ankle PF	52.9	48.9	48.6

3.6 The Impact of Multi-factor Interaction on the ROM

From the results of the above single-factor analysis of variance, it could be seen that the five variables of gender, age, BMI index, region and LI had a significant impact on ROM. Among them, age had the largest impact, followed by and BMI index, followed by region and gender. Was there any interaction between the five factors? Through the multi-factor analysis of variance, it was found that firstly, there was no interaction between the region and the other 4 variables; secondly, there was no interaction between the other 4 variables; finally, there was an interaction between three factors. The details were shown in Table 11.

Table 11. Parameters that interact with multiple factors

Parameters	Three factors interaction		Two factors interaction			
	Age*LI*BMI	Gender*career*BMI	LI*BMI	Gender*BMI	Age*BMI	Age*LI
Spine F	*		**			
Spine LF			*			
Spine RF			*			
Hip EX				*		
Elbow F			*			
Wrist DOR	*		*			
Thumb UB		*	*			
Thumb AB					*	
Finger F						**

It could be seen from Table 11 that there were only two groups with three-factor interaction. The interaction of age, labor intensity, and BMI only affected spine flexion and wrist dorsiflexion; the interaction of gender, occupation and BMI only affected the ulnar abduction of the thumb. There were four groups of variables with interaction of two factors: LI and BMI, gender and BMI, age and BMI, and age and LI. Age and LI affected only one parameter of index finger flexion; age and BMI only affected one parameter of volar abduction of thumb; gender and BMI only affected one parameter of hip extension; labor intensity and BMI affected a relatively large number of parameters, including spine flexion, left spine flexion, right spine flexion, elbow flexion, wrist dorsiflexion and thumb ulnar abduction.

Generally speaking, age, gender, BMI index, region and labor intensity these five factors basically affected the ROM individually. The ROM affected by the combined effect of multiple factors was very small.

4   Conclusion

Through sampling at 3 measurement points in East China, Northwest and Northeast, the study collected data on 40 joint motion parameters of 818 people. After statistical analysis of the measurement data, it can be seen that gender, age, BMI index, region and labor intensity will have a significant impact on most of ROM. The specific conclusions are as follows:

(1) The most females' ROM were larger than males'. In generally, female's neck, wrist, hip, shoulder, ulna and finger joints were more flexible than male's.

(2) The overall trend of age's effect on ROM is that the ROM decreases with age.

(3) As the BMI index increases, ROM decreases.

(4) The ROM varies greatly with different LI, decreases with the increase of LI.

References

1. Allander, E., Bjornsson, O.J.: Normal range of joint movements in shoulder, hip, wrist and thumb with special reference to side: a comparison between. Two populations. Int. J. Epidemiol. **3**(3), 253–261 (1974)
2. Boone, D.C., Azen, S.P.: Normal range of motion of joints in male subjects. J. Bone Joint Surg. **61**(5), 756–759 (1979)
3. Nancy, B.S., Jeffrey, E.F., William, M.G.: Normative data on joint ranges of motion of 25- to 54-year-old males. Int. J. Ind. Ergon. **12**, 265–272 (1993)
4. Esealante, A., Llehtensteln, M.J., Hazuda, H.P.: Determinants of shoulder and elbow flection range: results from the San Antonio longitudinal study of ageing. Am. Coll. Rheumatol. **12**(4), 277–286 (1999)
5. Veronlque, F., Benolt, R.: Normal global motion of the cervical spine: an electrogoniometric study. Clin. Biomech. **14**, 462–470 (1999)
6. Hoon, Y.Y., Sang, D.L., Dong, C.L.: A study on range of joint movement for Korean adults. In: The Proceedings of the IEA 2000/HFES 2000 Congress, vol. 44, pp. 328–332 (2000)
7. Kang, Y.H., Zhang, W.G., Qu, L.: Range of motion of healthy elders. Chin. J. Phys. Med. Rehabil. **23**, 221–223 (2001)
8. Hu, H.T., Li, Z.Z., Yan, J.B., et al.: Measurements of voluntary joint range of motion of the Chinese elderly living in Beijing area by a photographic method. Int. J. Ind. Ergon. **36**, 861–867 (2006)
9. Meng, J.C., Mao, J.J.: The effect of age and gender on joint range of motion of worker population in Taiwan. Int. J. Ind. Ergon. **39**, 596–600 (2009)
10. Allander, E., Bjornsson, O.J.: Normal range of joint movements in shoulder, hip, wrist and thumb with special reference to side: a comparison between two populations. Int. J. Epidemiol. **3**(3), 253–261 (1974)
11. Gunal, I., Kose, N., Erdogan, O., Gokturk, E., Seber, S.: Normal range of motion of the joints of the upper extremity in male subjects, with special reference to side. J. Bone Joint Surg. Am. **78**, 1401–1404 (1996)
12. Christopher, J.B., Van, S.M.D., Richard, A., et al.: The effects of age, sex, and shoulder dominance on range of motion of the shoulder. J. Shoulder Elbow Surg. **10**(3), 242–246 (2002)
13. Roaas, A., Andersson, G.B.: Normal range of motion of the hip, knee and ankle joints in male subjects, 30–40 years of age. Acta Orthop. Scand. **53**, 205–208 (1982)
14. Wu, G.R., Zhang, Y.R.: Measurement of the range of motion of human joints. Space Med. Med. Eng. **2**(2), 123–131 (2002)
15. GJB/Z 131-2002, Ergonomic design manual for equipment and Facilities (2002)
16. Shao, X.Q.: Anthropometric manual, Shanghai Dictionary Publishing House, vol. 6 (1985)
17. Yu, D.S.: Handbook of rehabilitation Medical Evaluation. Huaxia Press, Beijing (1993)
18. GB/T 6565–2015, Class classification and code (2015)

Language, Communication
and Behavior Modeling

Modeling Rapport for Conversations About Health with Autonomous Avatars from Video Corpus of Clinician-Client Therapy Sessions

Reza Amini[1](✉), Maya Boustani[2](✉), and Christine Lisetti[1](✉)

[1] Knight Foundation School of Computing and Information Sciences, Florida International University, Miami, FL 33199, USA
{ramin001,lisetti}@cs.fiu.edu
[2] School of Behavioral Health, Department of Psychology, Loma Linda University, Loma Linda, CA 92350, USA
mboustani@llu.edu

Abstract. In human face-to-face conversations, non-verbal behaviors (NVB), such as gaze, facial expressions, gestures, and body postures, can improve communication effectiveness, by creating a smooth interaction between the interlocutors - called *rapport*. During human interactions with embodied conversational agents (ECAs) (a.k.a. virtual humans), a key issue for the success of the interaction is the ability of an ECA to establish and maintain some level of rapport with its human counterpart. This need is particularly important for ECAs who interact in contexts involving socio-emotional content, such as education and entertainment, or in the role of health assistants delivering healthcare interventions, as in the context of this study. Because clinical psychologists are trained in establishing and maintaining rapport, we designed an ECA that learns offline from such an expert, which NVBs to display, when to display them, when not to display them, in real time. We describe our data-driven machine learning approach to modeling rapport from a corpus of annotated videos of counseling sessions, that were conducted by a licensed practicing clinical psychologist with role-playing patients. Results of a randomly controlled experiment show that, in its role of delivering a brief screening health intervention, our ECA improved user's attitude, intention to (re-)use the ECA system, perceived enjoyment, perceived sociability, perceived usefulness, social presence, and trust.

Keywords: Modeling rapport · Intelligent virtual agent · Behavior health intervention

1 Introduction

In human face-to-face conversations, non-verbal behaviors (NVB, e.g. gaze, facial expressions, gestures, and postures), can improve communication effectiveness

V. G. Duffy (Ed.): HCII 2021, LNCS 12777, pp. 181–200, 2021.
https://doi.org/10.1007/978-3-030-77817-0_15

by creating a smooth interaction between the interlocutors. That feeling of flow, or of connection, is known as *rapport*. Grahe [6] has shown that rapport is mostly correlated with nonverbal behaviors. Given their emerging role as a prevalent new metaphor in human-computer interaction, it is important to enable embodied conversational agents (ECAs, a.k.a. virtual humans) to establish rapport with their users with appropriate NVB animations, so as to improve users' acceptance of, and engagement with ECAs, in a variety of domains involving socio-emotional content (e.g. healthcare, medicine, education).

According to Tickle-Degnen and Rosenthal's seminal work [25], the three essential components of rapport are *mutual attentiveness* (e.g., mutual gaze, mutual interest, and focus during interaction), *positivity* (e.g., head nods, positive facial expressions, eye contact) and *coordination* (e.g., postural mirroring, synchronized movements, balance, and harmony).

Listeners frequently nod, and use para-verbals, such as "uh-huh" and "mm-hmm", when someone is speaking. Such behaviors, *back-channel continuers*, are considered by a speaker as signals that the communication is working and that she/he should continue speaking. *Nods, postural mirroring*, and *mirroring of head gestures* (e.g., gaze shifts) are a few examples of back-channel continuers [3].

Whereas Tickle-Degnen and Rosenthal [25] posited that *positive emotions* are a part of the fundamental non-verbal behavior structure of rapport, they further point out, that while eye contact is usually indicative of positive feelings, in competitive conditions, it may indicate aggressiveness [25]. Similarly, smiling may be a positive expression of warmth or a negative expression of anxiety [4]. Hence the use of non-verbal acts must be viewed as *context-dependent*, although we will argue that learning NVBs from clinical psychologists (who are expert at rapport), might provide a gold standard for modeling rapport in a variety of contexts.

We present our approach for generating models of NVB toward establishing rapport (diagrammed in Fig. 1), using machine learning (ML) techniques from annotated video of conversations which we recorded, transcribed and annotated. These conversations are counseling sessions between a licensed therapist and a role-playing patient. In an attempt to account for the richness of human rapport, our approach models synchronized multimodal NVBs (head gestures, head movements, eye gaze, smiles, hand gestures, emotional facial expressions, eyebrow movement, and lean), with verbal features generated from the session transcripts. We describe an experiment that we conducted to evaluate our ECA NVBs against a neutral ECA, in the role of delivering a brief screening health intervention. We looked at user's attitude, intention to use, perceived enjoyment, perceived sociability, perceived usefulness, social presence, trust, and social influence.

Because of the major facilitating role of rapport in human-human communication and social interactions, and given the recent progress on embodied conversational agents (ECAs) – also referred to as virtual humans – as a emerging modality for human-computer user interfaces, it has become important to enable these virtual agents to establish rapport with their users so as to improve user acceptance and engagement with the agents.

Most of the current approaches taken to date use rule-based techniques to provide the agent with some rapport ability, where rules are manually created by

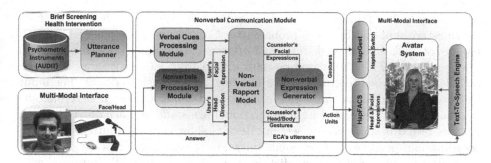

Fig. 1. Virtual health assistant architecture overview.

the virtual agent designers, based on what they can extract from social communication literature research. Whereas some of these rule-based systems have been successful in creating a sense of rapport, the process of generating non-verbal behaviors with these approaches is not automated.

We describe a data-driven approach to modeling rapport from annotated video corpora of counseling sessions between a clinical psychologist and a patient. We discuss how we evaluated our rapport model with objective measures, and how we integrated it in a healthcare behavior change intervention to evaluate its impact on users' subjective experience.

2   Related Research on Modeling Rapport

Unlike rule-based approaches to modeling rapport (in which "literature-based" hand-crafted rules for controling the ECA's NVBs animations are generated by the ECA developer from interpreting social communication literature [2,9,19] machine-learning (ML) approaches to modeling rapport use a multi-modal corpus of recorded human behaviors (nonverbals and surface texts) that is annotated (manually or automatically), and used to learn behavioral patterns for the automatic generation of an ECA's NVBs.

Lee et al. [18] used the Hidden Markov Model (HMM) ML technique for which a sequence of observations is available [24], to create a *head nod model* from annotated video corpora of face-to-face human interactions. The sequential nature of the input - a sequence of NVB and verbal feature combinations (vectors) representing each word of the dialog surface text - lends itself to using HMMs, as our approach also uses. Lee et al. [20] expanded their head nod model [18] by using *affective information* during the learning process to predict the *speaker's head nods*. The affective information consisted of the detected emotion label of each word in the surface text, and emotion label of the whole sentence. Their results show that using that affective information, especially in *sentence level* vs. word level, improves the prediction metrics compared to the same model without affective information.

Huang et al. [13] built on [7] to develop Rapport 2.0, in which simple behavior rules are replaced by three probabilistic Conditional Random Field (CRF) models of *backchannel* prediction, *end-of-turn* (turn-taking opportunity), and *affective feedback* (smile), based on data driven from video corpora. The CRF models predict when to give feedback and how to give such feedback. The input features used are *silence, head nod, eye gaze* and *smile*, and the non-verbal output features (i.e., generated ECA animations) are *smile* and *head nod*. Rapport 2.0 was tested in an interview setting. Results show that the mutual attention, coordination, positive emotion communication (or affective response), rapport, naturalness, and backchannel prediction of the Rapport Agent [7] improved with Rapport Agent 2.0. In [14], a model non-verbal facial expressions (e.g., smile, laugh, eyes open/closed) for face-to-face communication with an ECA automatically learns to update the agent's facial expressions based on the user's expressions using an unsupervised deep neural network trained on interaction videos.

Our non-verbal rapport model is most similar to the Rapport Agent 2.0 [13]. We could not directly compare it with ours, however, given that we use different systems and 3D graphics, and that there are differences between the approaches, which we discuss next.

3   Overview of Our Approach to Modeling Rapport by Learning from Videos of an Expert in Action

We present a machine learning approach with Hidden Markov Models (HMM) which uses both verbal and NVB as features of the interaction to predict the best NVBs for animating an ECA with the goal of simulating aspects of human rapport, in the context of a healthcare intervention.

Similarly to Rapport Agent 2.0 [13], our rapport model focuses on Tickle-Degnen and Rosenthal's three main components of rapport [25]. However, we model (1) mutual *attentiveness* and *coordination* using the hand gestures, body lean, head gestures, and eye gaze models; and (2) we model *positivity* using the head nod, smile, emotional facial expressions, and eyebrow movement models.

Our approach to modeling rapport for an ECA further advances current research in computational models of rapport: (1) we **learn our NVB models from a professional expert in establishing rapport** (Sect. 3.1); (2) we model **both NVB and verbal features** of the interaction to predict the best NVB for animating an ECA for a health intervention Sect. 4.2; (2) we model the NVBs for an ECA's in **both a Speaker role and in a Listerer role** (Sect. 3.2); (3) we evaluate each NVB model with **objective metrics** (Sect. 5.1), but also evaluate **subjective end-user's perception** of the NVB models after they have been integrated in our health intervention (Sect. 5.2); (4) we learn a **significantly larger number of multimodal social cues** than current approaches (Sect. 2).

3.1   Learning from an Annotated Video Corpus of a Pro

Because establishing and maintaining rapport with patients is essential to the success of counseling sessions [22], we learn our NVB models for rapport-enabled (or rapport-aspiring) ECAs from video-recordings of motivational interviewing (MI) counseling sessions. These were conducted by a licensed clinical psychologist with role-playing clients. Previous rapport modeling approaches (Sect. 2) do not learn from data gathered from clinical psychologists "in action". In [13], the corpus consists of actors role-play story telling monologues to a non-speaking, but nonverbally attentive agent; in [5] the corpus dialogues are about choosing tiles while redesigning bathrooms; in [18] the corpus used consists of recordings of business meetings in a conference room, where employees discuss development of a new TV remote control.

Clinical psychologists are, however, experts at establishing and maintaining rapport, and can therefore provide a golden standard of verbal and non-verbal behaviors to learn from. We integrated the NVB models learned from our expert in a brief MI health screening intervention that our ECA delivered to participants. Section 5.2 briefly describes the health intervention, and the evaluation of our ECA's NVBs in action.

3.2   ECA that Can Speak, but Also Listen, to the User with Appropriate Social Cues

During conversations, humans do not display the same social cues when they speak or when they listen (unless they have poor social skills), as rapport involves mutual attentiveness and coordination [25]. Our ECA learns which NVBs are relevant to display when in both the **Speaker Role** (Fig. 2), and in the **Listener Role** (Fig. 3). It alternates between roles when it asks users screening questions in the health intervention, and when it listens to the user's answers.

Our video corpora therefore includes videos of the counseling MI sessions with a frontal view of the clinical psychologist/counselor, and the corresponding

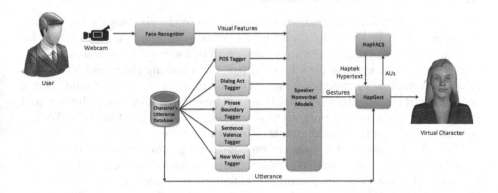

Fig. 2. Runtime process for the ECA in the **Speaker role.**

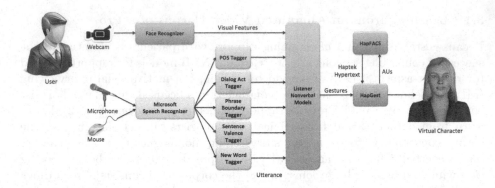

Fig. 3. Runtime process for the ECA in the **Listener role**.

video of the frontal view of a role-playing individual with at-risk behaviors. We synchronized the pair of video streams in our annotation process (Sect. 4.2), and constructed NVB models for each relevant features in both roles (Sect. 4.7).

4   Machine Learning of Multimodal Social Cues from Videos of Counseling Sessions

4.1   Data Collection

The input to our ML algorithm is data derived from the annotated video corpora and the conversation transcript of the Motivational Interviewing (MI) counseling session conducted by a licensed clinical psychologist expert in MI [22] and a role-playing adult client.

For this work, we annotated 40 min of the video, including 20 min from the counselor, and its corresponding 20 min of the client. For *each* of the non-verbal behaviors, the dataset includes 5,281 samples.

4.2   Data Annotation and Schema

We automatically performed the data annotation of the counselor's and client's NVBs portrayed in the videos, and of the verbal conversation transcripts, for most of the features using software tools described below. For a small number of nonverbal features we identified in the videos when making the inventory of each unique non-verbals in the videos, no reliable automatic tool was found. Hence we annotated these features manually using *Anvil* [16] annotation software, and a specialized XML annotation schema we designed for these features. We also used *Anvil* to align individual annotation features.

To validate automatic annotations, a human annotator randomly re-annotated 25% of the automatic annotations. We calculated Cronbach α as a measure of the correlation between the automatic and manual annotations. For all features, the Cronbach α value was greater than 0.7, which indicates the reliability of the automatic annotations.

Annotation and Runtime Modes. Because we used the same automatic recognizers in both the offline annotation mode (OA), and in runtime recognition mode (RR) during the human interaction with the ECA at runtime (see Figs. 2 and 3, and Sect. 4.7), we specify the inputs and outputs (I/O) of each automatic recognizers in both OA and RR modes. The I/O, OA and RR modes for the Nonverbals Processing module are described in Sect. 4.2. For each of the verbal utterance taggers in the Verbal Processing Module (Fig. 1, Sect. 4.2) discussed in this article:

– I/O in **offline annotation (OA) mode**: the *input* are text files with the complete transcript of the video-recorded counseling sessions, for the counselor's and client's utterances respectively; the *output* are annotated text files for the counselor's and client's utterances, respectively;
– I/O in **runtime recognition (RR) mode**: the *input* is a single utterance, which can either be the ECA's next utterance when the ECA is in its Speaker Role (see Fig. 2), or the answer from the user (transcribed into text) when the ECA is in its Listener Role (see Fig. 3); the *output* are the annotated text files for the counselor's and user's utterances (respectively), which are then passed to the relevant Speaker or Listener NVB Models modules, respectively.

Nonverbals Processing Module. We implemented the Nonverbals Processing Module utilizing the C++ *SightCorp InsightSDK* commercial Face Analysis Toolkit. The nonverbal features that we process are:

1. **Head gestures** of the counselor: *neutral*, head *nod* (AUM59), head *shake* (AUM60), head *nod-shake*, and lateral head *sweep*.
2. **Head movements** of the client and counselor: head *yaw* (left or AU51, right or AU52), head *pitch* (up or AU53, down or AU54), head *roll* (roll-left or AU55, roll-right or AU56), and all 12 combinations of the head AUs (see above).
3. **Hand gestures** of the counselor: *neutral, formless flick, point, contrast, iconic* (represents some object or action), *opened,* and *closed* gestures.
4. **Eye gaze** of the client and counselor: *forward, left* (AU61), *right* (AU62), *up* (AU63), and *down* (AU64).
5. **Smile** of the client and counselor: *neutral, subtle* smile (AU12), and *open-mouth large* smile (AU12 + AU25 + AU26).
6. **Emotional facial expressions** of the client and counselor: *neutral, happy* (AU6 + AU12), *sad* (AU1 + AU4 + AU15), *angry/puzzled* (AU4 + AU5 + AU7 + AU23), *afraid* (AU1 + AU2 + AU4 + AU5 + AU20 + AU26), *surprised* (AU1 + AU2 + AU5 + AU26), and *disgusted* (AU9 + AU15 + AU16).
7. **Eyebrow movements** of the client and counselor: *neutral, up* (AU1 + AU2), and *down* (AU4 + AU42).
8. **Lean** of the counselor: *neutral*, lean *forward*, lean *left*, lean *right*, and lean *back*.

In *OA mode*, the Nonverbals Processing Module takes as *input* the counselor's video file and the client's video file recorded during the therapy sessions, and produces two *output* text files with the visual feature annotations for the counselor's NVB features and for client's NVB features, respectively.

In *RR mode*, the Nonverbals Processing Module takes the video stream of the user's face captured by camera (640 × 480 pixels, user-screen at 60 cm distance) while the user interacts with the ECA in realtime, and produces a stream of feature recognition results, that are passed, through message passing, to the NVB Models module in our main ECA application, in order to control the ECA's animations (facial expressions, gestures) in realtime.

Verbal Part of Speech (POS) Tagger. For POS tagging, we used the *Stanford Natural Language Processing (NLP) POS tagger API* [26], which assigns POS tags to each word in a text, according to the following (abbreviations in parentheses are used in the Value column in Tables 3 and 4, according to [26] terminology): **preposition** (IN), **Adjective** (JJ), **Noun singular or mass** (NN), **Noun plural** (NNS), **personal pronoun** (PRP), **possessive pronoun** (PRP$), **adverb** (RB), **interjection** (UH), **verb based form** (VB), and **verb non-3rd person singular present** (VBP).

The text files that the POS Tagger generates contain PO-annotated utterances for each word in the utterance(s) it is passed (Sect. 4.2 and Figs. 2 and 3).

Verbal Dialog Act Tagger. We implemented a Dialog Act Tagger using a collection of phrases and words that are most frequently used in different dialog acts. We first tokenize the input sentence with *Stanford NLP parser*, and if a word/phrase from the possible dialog acts is found, the sentence is tagged with that dialog act. The complete list with more examples is provided below (abbreviations in parentheses are used in the 1st column for Value in Tables 3 and 4):

1. **Affirmation** (Aff.): true, OK, yes, yeah, right, I am, he/she is, you/we are, all right, I/we have, he/she has, I/we do, and he/she does.
2. **Assumption** (Assu.): I guess, I suppose, I think, maybe, perhaps, could, probably, and assume.
3. **Contrast** (Con.): but, however, although, though, whereas, and while.
4. **Inclusivity** (Inc.): every, all, whole, several, plenty, and full.
5. **Intensification** (Inten.): really, very, quite, completely, wonderful, lot, great, absolutely, gorgeous, huge, fantastic, amazing, important, and much.
6. **Interjection** (Inter.): all right, of course, well, right, yes, yeah, no, and nope.
7. **Negation** (Neg.): nothing, cannot, can't, not, no, none, and nope.
8. **Response request** (RR): you know.
9. **Word search** (WS): um, uh, well, mm, hmm, like, kind of, and I mean.
10. **Question** (Ques.): WH questions with one of the following words in the beginning of the sentence: do, does, have, has, is, are.
11. **Obligation** (Obl.): have to, has to, need to, ought to, and should.

12. **Greeting** (Greet.): hi, hello, how are you, good morning, good afternoon, good evening, how do you do, what's up, how is it going, and how are you doing.

The input/output of the Dialog Act Tagger in OA and RR mode is discussed in Sect. 4.2, and the textfiles it generates contain Dialog-act-annotated utterances of the utterance(s) it is passed as input.

To evaluate the Dialog Act Tagger, we asked 3 participants to tag the sentences used by the ECA. Each sentence was tagged by all three subjects and the union of the subjects' tags was used as the set of tags for each sentence. Then, we tagged the same sentences using the *Dialog Act Tagger*, and calculated its performance metrics. Results show an accuracy of 0.9581, precision of 0.7119, recall of 0.9225, and F1-measure of 0.8036.

Verbal Phrase Boundary Tagger. We implemented a Phrase Boundary Tagger using the *Stanford NLP* API. Based on previous studies [18,20] found that, among other phrase boundaries in a sentence, some are the most useful during NVB generation. Therefore, we used these for the *phrase boundary* feature: **noun phrase start/end** (NPS/NPE), **verb phrase start/end** (VPS, VPE), and **sentence start/end** (SS, SE). If a word is not tagged with any of the above values, it is tagged with the **"None"** tag.

The textfiles that the Phrase Boundary Tagger generates contain Phrase-boundary-annotated words, for each word in the utterance(s) it is passed as input, depending upon the current OA/RR mode (Sect. 4.2) and the ECA's Speaker/Listener role (Figs. 2 and 3).

Verbal New Word Tagger. We implemented a New Word Tagger using dictionaries of words. The new-word tagger includes two sets of words, one for the client and one for the counselor. When a sentence is passed to the New Word Tagger, it checks the corresponding list for every single word in the sentence, and tags them as **new** if they have not been used before by that person, otherwise words are tagged as **old**. Every time a word is checked against a dictionary, it is added to the dictionary for next look ups, if it is a new word.

The input/output of the New Word Tagger in OA and RR mode is discussed in Sect. 4.2, and the textfiles it generates contain New-word-annotated words with their tags (new, old), for each word in the utterance(s) it is passed as input.

4.3   Multimodal Data Pre-processing

To prepare the data to be used by our ML algorithm (Sects. 4.5 and 4.6), we normalized all the annotation results, and converted all annotation values to integer values. We then put together every three consecutive words (and their corresponding feature vectors) to form our dataset for ML: a set of trigrams. An example of feature annotations for "How often do you have a drink containing alcohol?" - one of the sentences uttered by the ECA during its interaction with the user (Sect. 5.2) - is shown in Table 1 (see abbreviations in Sect. 4.2; and Psy stands for the clinical psychologist and Clt stands for the Client on the videos; Forw. stands for forward lean/gaze/head; Neut. stands for Neutral).

For each trigram, a target gesture is determined by the majority vote method: if 2 or 3 out of 3 words co-occur with the target gesture, the trigram is classified as an instance of the target gesture. For example, if we have three consecutive feature vectors of $\{\vec{a}, \vec{b}, \vec{c}\}$ with the output labels of $\{notNod, nod, nod\}$, this trigram generates a data sample with input of $\{\vec{a}, \vec{b}, \vec{c}\}$ and output label of $\{nod\}$. An example derived from Table 1 is shown in Table 2 for the Head Nod model and the sentence "How often do you have a drink containing alcohol?".

4.4   Multimodal Data Alignment

We aligned each word in the sessions transcript with the vector of visual and textual features that co-occur with that word. The annotated data set for ML is a set of vectors, each of which co-occurs with one word in the transcript. For the manually annotated features, the alignment process is done by the *Anvil* annotation software (Sect. 4.2). For the visual features that are annotated auto-

Table 1. Annotations for utterance "How often do you have a drink containing alcohol?"

Sentence	POS Tags	Dialog Act	Phrase Bound.	Clt's Head	Psy's Hand	Psy's Gaze	Psy's Smile	Clt's Smile	Clt's Brow	Psy' Brow	Psy's Head
How	Wh-RB	Ques.	SS	Forw.	Up	Down	Neut.	Neut.	Down	Up	Shake
often	RB	Ques.	None	Forw.	Up	Down	None	Neut.	Neut.	Up	Shake
do	VB	Ques.	VPS	Forw.	Neut.	Forw.	Neut.	Neut.	Neut.	Neut.	Left
you	PRP	Ques.	None	Forw.	Neut.	Forw.	Neut.	Neut.	Neut.	Neut.	Left
have	VB	Ques.	VPE	Forw.	Neut.	Forw.	Neut.	Neut.	Neut.	Neut.	Forw.
a	Det	Ques.	NPS	Forw.	Neut.	Forw.	Neut.	Neut.	Neut.	Neut.	Forw.
drink	NN	Ques.	InNP	Forw.	Neut.	Forw.	Neut.	Neut.	Up	Neut.	Nod
containing	VBGerd	Ques.	INP	Forw.	Neut.	Forw.	Subtle	Neut.	Up	Up	Nod
alcohol?	NN	Ques.	SE	Forw.	Neut.	Forw.	Large	Subtle	Up	Up	Nod

Table 2. Trigrams for head nod model for "How often do you have a drink containing alcohol?"

Trigram	Indiv. output	Classified output
(How, often, do)	notNod, notNod, notNod	**notNod**
(often, do, you)	notNod, notNod, notNod	**notNod**
(do, you, have)	notNod, notNod, notNod	**notNod**
(you, have, a)	notNod, notNod, notNod	**notNod**
(have, a, drink)	notNod, notNod, nod	**notNod**
(a, drink, containing)	notNod, nod, nod	**nod**
(drink, containing, alcohol)	nod, nod, nod	**nod**

matically, we matched and aligned the frame numbers reported by *Anvil* and the automatic annotator, to align the frames and consequently the words to their corresponding annotations.

4.5   Multimodal Feature Selection

For best results with ML given a limited number of data samples, the number of features must be kept low to eliminate uncorrelated features, i.e. features that do not affect the target gestures. We hence took a two-phase feature selection approach. In the *first* phase, for each target gesture, we reduced the number of features by counting the frequency of the gesture co-occurrence with each feature value, and by selecting a subset of them that have the maximum frequency, as recommended by [18, 20]. The resulted list of features is the F_{mf} vector. Since some feature values may never appear in the data, or may appear very few times, we can then remove those feature values from that feature.

Since the data is extracted from recorded videos of human-human interactions, it is possible that, in some video intervals, a specific gesture, say G, is expressed very rarely (or not expressed at all). Hence, those data intervals are not good for training and cross validation of the G model. To prevent this problem, in the *second* phase of the feature selection or the model selection, we used the selected list of features in the first phase F_{mf} as input, and used a 10-fold cross validation phase over multiple splits of data to select the best features from them. For this purpose, we performed step-wise backward elimination approach.

Tables 3 and 4 show the final list of features selected for each of the modeled gestures for speaker and listener roles after cross validation (model selection) phase.

4.6   Model Induction

We used a "one-versus-all" approach for modeling each of the gesture classes, i.e., instead of multi-class classification, we performed a binary classification for each individual gesture class. A binary classification for gesture G classifies the input data into either class G or Not-G. This approach enables us to generate an individual model for each non-verbal behavior.

To determine whether a trigram should be classified as a target gesture G, we trained a Hidden Markov Model (HMM) [24] for G classification. HMM is a statistical model that is used for learning patterns where a sequence of observations is given. In our application, the input is a sequence of feature vectors representing consecutive words. So, the sequential property of this problem led us to use HMMs to predict gestures.

The *input* to the modeling process is a vector of visual and textual features representing each spoken word (by client or counselor) during the session. The *output* of each gesture model is: a category (which represents presence/absence of the target gesture), and the likelihood of the classification (i.e., classification correctness probability).

Table 3. Final set of multimodal features selected for **Speaker** models.

Group	Feature	Value	Head Nod	Hd. NodShak	Head Shake	Subtle Smile	Gaze Left	Gaze Right	Happy	Surprised	Angry	Disgust	Eyebrow Up	Eyebrow Down	Hand Flick	Hand Point	Hand Contrast	Hand Iconic	Hand Closed	Hand Opened	Lean Forward	Lean Left
Counselor	New-Word	Old	-	-	✓	-	-	-	-	-	✓	✓	-	-	✓	-	-	✓	✓	✓	✓	-
		New	-	-	✓	-	-	-	-	-	✓	✓	-	-	✓	-	-	✓	✓	✓	✓	-
	POS	IN	-	-	-	-	-	-	-	✓	-	-	-	✓	✓	-	✓	✓	-	-	-	-
		JJ	-	-	-	-	-	-	-	-	-	-	-	-	-	-	-	✓	-	-	-	-
		NN	-	✓	-	-	-	-	-	-	-	-	-	-	-	-	-	✓	-	-	-	-
		NNS	-	-	-	-	-	-	-	-	-	-	-	-	-	-	-	✓	-	-	-	-
		PRP	-	-	-	-	-	-	-	✓	-	-	✓	✓	✓	-	-	✓	-	-	-	-
		PRP$	-	-	-	-	-	-	-	-	-	-	-	-	-	✓	-	-	-	-	-	-
		RB	-	-	-	-	-	-	-	-	-	-	-	-	✓	-	-	✓	-	-	-	-
		UH	✓	-	-	-	✓	✓	-	✓	-	-	-	-	-	-	-	-	-	-	-	-
		VB	-	-	-	-	-	-	-	-	-	-	-	-	✓	-	-	✓	-	-	-	-
		VBP	-	-	-	-	-	-	-	-	-	-	-	-	✓	-	-	✓	-	-	-	-
	Dialog Act	Aff.	✓	✓	-	✓	-	-	✓	✓	-	-	✓	-	✓	-	-	✓	✓	✓	✓	✓
		Assu.	-	-	-	-	✓	✓	-	-	-	-	-	-	✓	-	-	✓	-	-	-	-
		Con.	-	-	-	-	✓	✓	-	✓	-	✓	-	-	✓	-	-	✓	-	-	-	✓
		Inc.	-	✓	-	✓	✓	✓	✓	✓	-	-	✓	✓	✓	-	-	✓	✓	✓	✓	✓
		Inten.	-	-	-	-	✓	✓	-	-	-	-	✓	✓	✓	-	-	✓	-	-	-	-
		Inter.	✓	✓	✓	-	✓	✓	✓	✓	✓	✓	-	✓	✓	-	✓	✓	✓	✓	✓	✓
		Neg.	✓	✓	✓	-	✓	✓	-	✓	✓	✓	-	✓	✓	-	✓	✓	-	✓	✓	✓
		RR	-	-	-	-	✓	✓	-	-	-	-	-	✓	✓	-	✓	-	-	-	-	-
		WS	-	✓	-	-	✓	✓	-	✓	✓	✓	-	✓	✓	-	✓	✓	-	✓	✓	✓
		Ques.	-	-	-	-	-	-	-	-	-	-	✓	-	-	-	-	-	-	-	-	-
	Phrase Bound.	SS	✓	-	-	✓	✓	✓	-	✓	-	-	✓	✓	-	✓	-	✓	-	✓	-	-
		NPS	-	-	-	✓	-	-	-	✓	-	-	✓	✓	-	✓	-	✓	-	✓	-	-
		NPE	-	-	-	✓	✓	✓	-	-	-	-	-	-	-	-	-	-	-	-	-	-
		VPS	-	-	-	✓	-	-	-	✓	-	-	✓	✓	-	✓	✓	-	✓	-	-	-
	Head Gest.	Neu.	-	-	-	✓	-	-	✓	-	✓	-	✓	-	✓	✓	✓	✓	✓	✓	-	✓
		Nod	-	-	-	✓	-	-	✓	-	✓	-	✓	-	-	-	-	-	-	-	-	-
		Shake	-	-	-	-	-	-	-	-	✓	-	-	-	-	-	✓	-	-	-	-	-
	Hand Gest.	Neu.	✓	-	-	✓	✓	✓	✓	✓	-	✓	✓	-	-	-	-	-	-	-	-	✓
		Cont.	-	-	✓	-	-	-	-	✓	-	-	-	-	-	-	-	-	-	-	-	-
		FF	-	-	-	-	✓	✓	-	✓	-	✓	✓	-	-	-	-	-	-	-	-	✓
		Icon	-	-	-	-	-	-	-	✓	-	✓	✓	-	-	-	-	-	-	-	-	-
		Close	-	-	-	✓	-	-	✓	-	-	-	-	-	-	-	-	-	-	-	-	-
	Eye Gaze	Fwd	✓	-	✓	✓	-	-	✓	-	-	-	-	-	-	✓	✓	-	-	-	✓	✓
		Left	✓	-	✓	✓	-	-	✓	-	-	-	-	-	-	-	-	-	-	-	✓	✓
		Right	✓	-	✓	✓	-	-	✓	-	-	-	-	-	-	-	-	-	-	-	-	-
	Smile	Neu.	-	✓	-	-	-	-	✓	-	✓	✓	-	✓	-	-	-	✓	-	✓	-	-
		Sub.	-	-	-	-	-	-	✓	-	-	-	-	-	-	-	-	-	-	✓	-	-
		Big	-	-	-	-	-	-	✓	-	-	-	-	-	-	-	-	-	-	-	-	-
	Facial Emotion	Neu.	-	✓	-	-	-	-	-	-	-	-	✓	✓	✓	-	✓	-	✓	-	✓	-
		Hap.	-	-	-	✓	-	-	-	-	-	-	-	-	-	-	✓	-	✓	-	-	-
		Sur.	-	✓	✓	-	-	-	-	-	-	✓	-	-	-	-	✓	-	-	-	✓	-
		Ang.	-	-	-	-	-	-	-	-	-	✓	-	-	-	-	-	-	-	-	-	-
	Eyebrow Mov.	Neu.	-	-	-	-	-	-	-	-	✓	-	✓	-	-	✓	-	-	✓	-	-	-
		Down	-	-	-	-	-	-	-	-	✓	✓	-	-	✓	-	-	-	-	-	-	-
	Lean	Neu.	-	✓	-	✓	✓	✓	-	✓	✓	✓	-	-	-	✓	✓	✓	-	✓	-	-
		Fwd	-	✓	-	✓	✓	✓	-	✓	✓	✓	-	-	-	✓	✓	✓	✓	✓	-	-
		Left	-	-	-	-	-	-	-	-	✓	-	-	-	-	-	-	-	-	-	-	-
Client	Head Mov.	Fwd.	-	-	-	-	-	-	-	-	-	-	-	✓	-	-	-	✓	-	-	-	✓
	Eye Gaze	Fwd	✓	✓	-	-	✓	✓	✓	-	✓	-	-	✓	✓	✓	✓	✓	-	✓	✓	✓
		Left	✓	✓	-	-	✓	-	-	-	-	-	-	-	-	-	-	✓	-	-	-	-
		Right	✓	-	-	-	-	✓	-	-	-	-	-	-	-	-	-	-	-	-	-	-
	Eyebrow Mov.	Neu.	-	-	-	-	-	-	-	-	✓	✓	✓	✓	-	-	-	-	-	-	-	-
		Down	-	-	-	-	-	-	-	-	✓	-	-	-	-	-	-	-	-	-	-	-

Table 4. Final set of multimodal features selected for **Listener** models.

Group	Feature	Value	Head Nod	Subtle Smile	Gaze Left	Gaze Right	Happy	Surprised	Angry	Disgust	Eyebrow Down	Hand Closed	Lean Forward
Client	New-Word	Old	✓	✓	-	-	-	-	✓	-	-	-	-
		New	✓	-	-	-	-	-	-	-	-	-	-
	POS	PRP	✓	-	-	-	✓	-	-	-	-	-	-
		RB	✓	-	-	-	-	-	-	-	-	-	-
		UH	-	-	-	-	✓	-	-	-	-	-	-
	Dialog Act	Aff.	✓	✓	✓	✓	✓	✓	-	✓	✓	✓	✓
		Assu.	-	-	-	-	-	-	-	✓	-	-	-
		Inc.	✓	✓	✓	✓	✓	✓	✓	✓	✓	✓	✓
		Inten.	✓	-	✓	✓	-	✓	-	-	-	✓	-
		Inter.	✓	-	✓	✓	✓	✓	✓	✓	✓	✓	✓
		Neg.	✓	-	✓	✓	✓	✓	✓	✓	✓	✓	✓
		WS	✓	-	✓	✓	✓	✓	✓	✓	✓	✓	✓
		Con.	-	-	✓	✓	✓	✓	✓	-	✓	-	-
	Phrase Bound.	SS	✓	-	-	-	-	-	-	-	✓	-	-
		NPS	✓	-	✓	-	-	✓	-	-	✓	-	-
		NPE	-	-	-	-	-	-	-	-	✓	-	-
		VPS	✓	-	-	-	-	✓	-	-	✓	-	-
	Head Mov.	Fwd.	✓	-	✓	✓	✓	✓	✓	-	-	-	-
		Roll-L	✓	-	-	-	-	-	-	-	-	-	-
	Eye Gaze	Fwd	✓	✓	✓	✓	✓	-	✓	✓	-	-	-
		Left	✓	✓	✓	✓	✓	-	✓	✓	-	-	-
		Right	-	-	✓	✓	✓	-	-	-	-	-	-
	Smile	Neu.	-	-	✓	✓	✓	✓	✓	✓	-	✓	-
	Facial Emotion	Neu.	-	✓	✓	✓	✓	✓	✓	✓	✓	-	✓
	Eyebrow Mov.	Neu.	-	-	-	-	✓	✓	✓	-	-	-	-
		Down	-	-	-	-	-	-	-	✓	-	-	-
Counselor	Head Mov.	Fwd.	-	-	✓	✓	✓	✓	✓	✓	✓	✓	✓
	Hand Gest.	Neu.	-	✓	-	-	✓	-	✓	✓	✓	-	✓
		Close	-	-	-	-	✓	-	✓	✓	✓	-	✓
	Head Gest.	Neu.	-	✓	✓	✓	✓	✓	✓	✓	✓	✓	✓
		Nod	-	✓	✓	✓	✓	✓	✓	✓	✓	✓	✓
	Eye Gaze	Fwd	✓	✓	-	-	-	-	✓	✓	-	-	✓
		Left	✓	✓	-	-	-	-	✓	✓	-	-	✓
	Smile	Neu.	-	-	-	-	✓	✓	✓	✓	-	✓	-
		Sub.	-	-	-	-	✓	-	-	-	-	-	-
	Facial Emotion	Neu.	-	-	-	-	-	-	-	-	✓	✓	✓
		Hap.	-	-	-	-	-	-	-	-	-	-	✓
		Ang.	-	-	-	-	-	-	-	-	✓	✓	✓
	Eyebrow Mov.	Neu.	✓	✓	✓	✓	✓	✓	✓	✓	-	✓	-
		Down	-	-	-	-	✓	-	✓	✓	-	✓	-
	Lean	Neu.	✓	✓	✓	✓	✓	✓	-	✓	-	✓	-
		Fwd	✓	✓	-	-	✓	-	-	✓	-	✓	-

As mentioned earlier, one of the novelties of our approach is that, **for each target gesture of the ECA, we trained two models, one as a speaker and one as a listener**, because the non-verbal behaviors of a speaker and those of a listener are different (see Figs. 2 and 3). We used 60% of the total dataset for the training purpose.

When using HMM, we do not observe the actual sequence of states (i.e., the gesture). Rather, we can only observe some feature values that happened at each state (i.e., visual and textual features). In brief, an HMM is a Markov model, for which there is a series of observations $x = \{x_1, x_2, ..., x_T\}$ drawn from an input alphabet $V = \{v_1, v_2, ..., v_{|V|}\}$, i.e., $x_t \in V, t = 1..T$. Also, there is a series of states $y = \{y_1, y_2, ..., y_T\}$ drawn from a state alphabet $S = \{s_1, s_2, ..., s_{|S|}\}$, i.e., $y_t \in S, t = 1..T$, but the values of the states are unobserved. The transition between states i and j is represented by the corresponding value in the state transition matrix A_{ij}, where $A \in \mathbb{R}^{(|S|+1) \times (|S|+1)}$. The value A_{ij} is the probability of transitioning from state i to state j at any time t.

The probability of an observation is modeled as a function of the hidden state. We make the *observation independence assumption* (i.e., current observation is statistically independent of the previous observations) and define:

$$P(x_t = v_k | x_1, ..., x_T, y_1, ..., y_T) = P(x_t = v_k | y_t = s_j) = B_{jk} \qquad (1)$$

where matrix B encodes the probability of observing v_k given that the state at the corresponding time was s_j.

First we solved HMM *learning problem* to calculate the model parameters A and B. Then, for each sentence, we solved the *decoding problem*, in order to find the most probable sequence of states (i.e., gestures) for the input sequence of observations (i.e., visual and textual features). We used the Accord.NET framework for implementing the HMMs.

4.7   Runtime Operation

As shown in Figs. 1, 2 and 3, at runtime: (1) the Verbal Cues Processing Module recognize the part of speech, dialog acts, phrase boundaries, and word newness of the dialog content of the user and ECA; and (2) the Nonverbals Processing Module uses the camera as its input, and returns its classifications (i.e., emotional facial expressions, eyebrow movements, head movements, smile, and gaze) to the rapport model, using message passing.

Since we model the ECA's non-verbal behavior in either speaker and listener roles, we provided the ability for the user to speak his/her answers to answer the ECA. We used the Microsoft Speech Recognizer to recognize the clients' verbal answers, and increased its accuracy by limiting the vocabulary and asking the user to read their answers out-loud, from multiple possible answers displayed next to the ECA on the monitor.

For each sentence uttered by the speaker (ECA or user), or listened to by the ECA, all the above features are recognized and returned to the non-verbal behavior models (i.e., composite non-verbal rapport model). This set of feature values are used as the observations of the non-verbal behavior HMMs. The

HMMs return the sequence of non-verbal behaviors to be expressed when this sentence is being uttered or listened to by the ECA. In order to generate the facial expressions, we use the hypertexts provided by the free open source Hap-FACS software [23].

In the **Speaker role** (Fig. 2), utterances come from the database and are passed to the Verbal Cues Processing Module. The latest visual features of the user are also perceived using the camera and the visual feature recognizer. All these feature values are passed to the speaker inducted models and their outputs are passed to HapFACS and our gesture generator (HapGest, see Fig. 1).

In the **Listener role** (see Fig. 3), responses are perceived from the user using microphone (or mouse, if the speech recognizer cannot recognize the user's voice). Then, similarly to the speaker role, these inputs are passed to the feature recognizers. Feature recognizers send their outputs to the listener inducted models, which decide about the best gestures and sent their decision to HapGest gesture generator. Since the non-verbal behaviors are modeled based on the video corpus of the interactions of rapport-building counselors with clients, we used the combination of the learned non-verbal models to model the ECA's NVB communication as speaker and listener.

5   Evaluation

5.1   Objective Evaluation of the Non-verbal Models

To evaluate our approach, we measured the performance of each individual learned model using 20% of our annotated dataset (test dataset), which was kept unseen during the feature selection and learning phases. We applied the test data to the learned models and calculated the **accuracy** (ratio of gestures correctly expressed), **precision** (ratio between the number of gestures expressed correctly and the total number of expressed gestures), **recall** (ratio between the number of gestures expressed correctly and the number of gestures in the actual data), and **F1-measure** (weighted harmonic mean of precision and recall) of the learned model. Table 5 shows the evaluation results of the objective measures for the NVB speaker and listener models, respectively.

As stated in Sect. 2, few research studies use ML to model a human's NVB, and none model as many NVB features as we do. **Our performance on the features that can be compared is high.** For example, Lee et al. [18] modeled head nods of a human speaker with accuracy of 0.8528, precision of 0.8249, recall of 0.8957, and F1-measure of 0.8588. Lee et al. [20] expanded their head nod model later with affective information with accuracy of 0.8957, precision of 0.8909, recall of 0.9018, and F1-measure of 0.8963. Our speaker head nod model metrics are comparable to the model presented by Lee et al. [18,20]. In an other study [17], which uses both hand crafted rules and ML to generate the gestures (facial expression, gaze, and head movement), the maximum models' cumulative evaluation metrics reported were 0.338 precision and 0.321 recall, which are much lower than in our study.

Table 5. Objective Evaluation Results of **Speaker** and **Listener** Nonverbal Behavior Models

(a) Results of the **Speaker** NVB Models.

Model	Acc.	Prec.	Rec.	F1
Head Nod	0.703	0.750	0.871	0.803
Head Shake	0.982	0.997	0.984	0.991
H. Nod-Shake	0.890	0.992	0.895	0.939
Subtle Smile	0.768	0.991	0.765	0.851
Gaze Left	0.611	0.603	0.374	0.437
Gaze Right	0.773	0.860	0.882	0.860
Happy	0.876	0.981	0.881	0.925
Surprised	0.759	0.914	0.811	0.855
Angry	0.836	0.975	0.849	0.904
Disgust	0.885	0.959	0.915	0.934
E. Brow Up	0.893	0.995	0.897	0.942
E. Brow Down	0.750	0.787	0.921	0.847
Hand Flick	0.743	0.905	0.771	0.830
Hand Point	0.904	0.993	0.909	0.948
Hand Contrast	0.827	0.966	0.842	0.895
Hand Iconic	0.771	0.951	0.794	0.864
Hand Closed	0.814	0.934	0.830	0.879
Hand Opened	0.806	0.975	0.822	0.888
Lean Forw.	0.619	0.733	0.739	0.692
Lean Left	0.902	1.000	0.902	0.948
Average	0.8056	0.9131	0.8327	0.8616

(b) Results of the **Listener** NVB Models.

Model	Acc.	Prec.	Rec.	F1
Head Nod	0.759	0.885	0.747	0.808
Subtle Smile	0.846	0.973	0.862	0.912
Gaze Left	0.559	0.533	0.454	0.473
Gaze Right	0.746	0.854	0.848	0.845
Happy	0.827	0.985	0.826	0.891
Surprised	0.813	0.912	0.880	0.894
Angry	0.738	0.976	0.743	0.841
Disgust	0.763	0.967	0.776	0.852
Brow Down	0.719	0.795	0.844	0.816
Hand Closed	0.845	0.928	0.879	0.902
Lean Forw.	0.672	0.767	0.717	0.713
Average	0.7515	0.8694	0.7825	0.8131

5.2   Subjective Evaluation of the Character

Context of Interaction: A Brief MI Screening Healthcare Intervention. To evaluate the user's perceived rapport and perceived naturalness of the ECA, we integrated the NVB models in a health intervention delivering the same content as the first part of the evidence-based Drinker's CheckUp (DCU) intervention [11]. The ECA's role is to screen individuals for at-risk drinking behaviors using MI principles [22] by asking them a series of question using two DCU psychometrics instruments (AUDIT and DrInc). The system architecture and interface are depicted in Fig. 1.

Experiment Design. We designed an experiment to compare the user's acceptance and perceived ECA features of: (1) the rapport-building ECA described earlier, and (2) a neutral ECA (same ECA, with a neutral expression and no NVBs gestures). We hypothesized that the rapport-building ECA will be better accepted by users and that its ECA features will be better perceived than the neutral ECA. Our **null-hypothesis is "Characters with different levels of rapport abilities (rapport-enabled vs. neutral) have the same effects on the users according to our measures"**.

Measures. We used selected portions of validated questionnaires (available upon request), to debrief participants after their interaction experience with the ECA: Heerink's [10] questionnaire for user acceptance; Bartneck's [1] Godspeed questionnaire for ECA features, and some Rapport scale presented in [8,12,15].

Experiment Procedure. A total of 56 college students were recruited through fliers. Subjects included 39 males with an average age of 25.5 years old and 17 females with an average age of 26.5 years old. Subjects included 21% White, 11% Black, 45% Hispanic, 14% Asian, 5% Caucasian, and 4% Indian ethnicities. Subjects were randomly assigned to either the neutral or the rapport-enabled ECA (27 subjects to neutral ECA and 29 subjects to rapport-enabled ECA). Because we were not interested in evaluating the impact of the interaction with the ECA on drinking health outcomes, we told participants they did not have to answer truthfully. We asked the subjects to answer each question verbally by reading their choice from possible answers displayed on the screen next to the ECA. A web camera was used to recognize visual features and to record the interaction. After the interaction, subjects were directed to a website, where an after-experiment questionnaire asked them to assess their experience with the ECA.

Subjective Evaluation Results and Discussion. The set of questions were asked from each user. Subjects answered each question in a 5-level Likert scale (-2 to $+2$). So, for each question, a 2×5 table is created to compare the two experiment conditions (rapport-enabled vs. neutral ECA). The table rows are the experiment conditions, and the columns are the Likert scales ($-2, -1, 0, +1$, and $+2$). Users' responses were analyzed using the Mantel-Haenszel-Chi-Square statistical method (degree of freedom $df = 1$) [21].

Therefore, under the assumption of the null-hypothesis, a Chi-Square p value of less than 0.05 ($df = 1$) rejects the null-hypothesis. Chi-Square analyses (6) show that the ECA's rapport-building made a significant difference vs. the neutral, except for *perceived ease of use*, and *perceived precision of expressions*.

We also compared the mean values of the same statements in the two experimental conditions to calculate their possible improvement/deterioration upon each other. As indicated in Table 6, the *rapport-enabled* ECA was perceived positively in all measured aspects. Although the *neutral* ECA was also perceived positively in many of the measured aspects, it was perceived negatively in terms of intention to use, perceived sociability, social presence, rapport, recall of expressions, *anthropomorphism*, animacy, and expressiveness.

Table 6. Subjective evaluation mean value comparison and Chi-Square test results.

Evaluated aspect	ECA	Mean	Std. dev.	χ^2	p	Improvement	Null hypothesis
Attitude	Neutral	0.22	1.12	27.92	0.0000	**26.53%**	*Rejected*
	Rapport	1.28	0.71				
Intention to use	Neutral	−0.15	1.24	16.53	0.0000	**34.54%**	*Rejected*
	Rapport	1.23	0.88				
Perceived enjoyment	Neutral	0.00	1.19	30.82	0.0000	**30.42%**	*Rejected*
	Rapport	1.22	0.78				
Perceived ease of use	Neutral	1.26	0.58	3.78	0.0518	**7.69%**	*Not rejected*
	Rapport	1.57	0.56				
Perceived sociability	Neutral	−0.29	1.12	71.66	0.0000	**32.18%**	*Rejected*
	Rapport	1.00	0.75				
Perceived usefulness	Neutral	0.22	1.10	10.33	0.001	**22.78%**	*Rejected*
	Rapport	1.13	0.80				
Social presence	Neutral	−0.38	1.12	45.71	0.0000	**30.12%**	*Rejected*
	Rapport	0.82	0.86				
Trust	Neutral	0.31	1.01	17.22	0.0000	**18.80%**	*Rejected*
	Rapport	1.07	0.75				
Rapport	Neutral	−0.38	1.08	58.38	0.0000	**28.03%**	*Rejected*
	Rapport	0.74	0.82				
Precision of expressions	Neutral	0.78	1.23	0.005	0.9432	**0.56%**	*Not rejected*
	Rapport	0.8	1.11				
Recall of expressions	Neutral	−1.11	0.83	20.53	0.0000	**42.78%**	*Rejected*
	Rapport	0.60	1.33				
Anthropomorphism	Neutral	−0.69	1.09	95.99	0.0000	**35.06%**	*Rejected*
	Rapport	0.71	0.87				
Likability	Neutral	0.53	0.96	62.95	0.0000	**22.17%**	*Rejected*
	Rapport	1.42	0.69				
Animacy	Neutral	−0.11	1.21	40.42	0.0000	**28.29%**	*Rejected*
	Rapport	1.02	0.81				
Perceived intelligence	Neutral	0.15	1.19	22.90	0.0000	**25.88%**	*Rejected*
	Rapport	1.18	0.85				
Expressiveness	Neutral	−0.70	1.33	23.42	0.0000	**45.09%**	*Rejected*
	Rapport	1.10	0.75				

6   Conclusion

We modeled human NVBs from video and conversation text corpora, using HMM, for both speaker and listener roles of an ECA, including: head gesture subtle smile, hand gestures (i.e., formless flick, pointing, contrast, iconic, closed, and opened), emotional facial expressions eyebrow movement, and lean. We evaluated each individual non-verbal behavior using objective tests, and evaluated their combination as a rapport model using subjective tests during randomly controlled experiment. Evaluation results show high accuracy of the individual models and improvements of a rapport-enabled character over a neutral one, for rapport, attitude, intention to use, perceived enjoyment, perceived ease of use, perceived sociability, perceived usefulness, social presence, trust, likability, and perceived intelligence.

Acknowledgment. This work was partially funded by research grant number CISE IIS-1423260 from the National Science Foundation to Florida International University.

References

1. Bartneck, C., Kulic, D., Croft, E.: Measuring the anthropomorphism, animacy, likeability, perceived intelligence and perceived safety of robots. In: Proceedings of the Metrics for Human-Robot Interaction Workshop in Affiliation with the 3rd ACM/IEEE International Conference on Human-Robot Interaction (HRI 2008), Technical report 471, vol. 471, pp. 37–44. University of Hertfordshire, Amsterdam (2008)
2. Cassell, J., Vilhjálmsson, H., Bickmore, T.W.: BEAT: the behavior expression animation toolkit. In: Proceedings of the 28th Annual Conference on Computer Graphics and Interactive Techniques (SIGGRAPH 2001), pp. 477–486. ACM (2001). https://doi.org/10.1145/383259.383315
3. Chartrand, T.L., Bargh, J.A.: The chameleon effect: the perception-behavior link and social interaction. J. Pers. Soc. Psychol. **76**(6), 893–910 (1999)
4. Ekman, P., Freisen, W.V., Ancoli, S.: Facial signs of emotional experience (1980). https://doi.org/10.1037/h0077722
5. Foster, M.E., Oberlander, J.: Corpus-based generation of head and eyebrow motion for an embodied conversational agent. Lang. Resour. Eval. **41**(3–4), 305–323 (2008). https://doi.org/10.1007/s10579-007-9055-3
6. Grahe, J.: The importance of nonverbal cues in judging rapport. J. Nonverbal Behav. **23**(4), 253–269 (1999)
7. Gratch, J., et al.: Virtual rapport. In: Gratch, J., Young, M., Aylett, R., Ballin, D., Olivier, P. (eds.) IVA 2006. LNCS (LNAI), vol. 4133, pp. 14–27. Springer, Heidelberg (2006). https://doi.org/10.1007/11821830_2
8. Gratch, J., Wang, N., Gerten, J., Fast, E., Duffy, R.: Creating rapport with virtual agents. In: Pelachaud, C., Martin, J.-C., André, E., Chollet, G., Karpouzis, K., Pelé, D. (eds.) IVA 2007. LNCS (LNAI), vol. 4722, pp. 125–138. Springer, Heidelberg (2007). https://doi.org/10.1007/978-3-540-74997-4_12
9. Gratch, J., et al.: Can virtual humans be more engaging than real ones? In: Jacko, J.A. (ed.) HCI 2007. LNCS, vol. 4552, pp. 286–297. Springer, Heidelberg (2007). https://doi.org/10.1007/978-3-540-73110-8_30
10. Heerink, M., Krose, B., Evers, V., Wielinga, B.: Measuring acceptance of an assistive social robot: a suggested toolkit. In: The 18th IEEE International Symposium on Robot and Human Interactive Communication, RO-MAN 2009, pp. 528–533. IEEE (2009)
11. Hester, R.K., Squires, D.D., Delaney, H.D.: The Drinker's Check-up: 12-month outcomes of a controlled clinical trial of a stand-alone software program for problem drinkers. J. Subst. Abuse Treat. **28**(2), 159–169 (2005)
12. Huang, L., Morency, L.-P., Gratch, J.: Learning backchannel prediction model from parasocial consensus sampling: a subjective evaluation. In: Allbeck, J., Badler, N., Bickmore, T., Pelachaud, C., Safonova, A. (eds.) IVA 2010. LNCS (LNAI), vol. 6356, pp. 159–172. Springer, Heidelberg (2010). https://doi.org/10.1007/978-3-642-15892-6_17
13. Huang, L., Morency, L.-P., Gratch, J.: Virtual rapport 2.0. In: Vilhjálmsson, H.H., Kopp, S., Marsella, S., Thórisson, K.R. (eds.) IVA 2011. LNCS (LNAI), vol. 6895, pp. 68–79. Springer, Heidelberg (2011). https://doi.org/10.1007/978-3-642-23974-8_8

14. Joo, H., Simon, T., Cikara, M., Sheikh, Y.: Towards social artificial intelligence: nonverbal social signal prediction in a triadic interaction. In: Proceedings of the IEEE Computer Society Conference on Computer Vision and Pattern Recognition, June 2019, pp. 10865–10875 (2019). https://doi.org/10.1109/CVPR.2019.01113

15. Kang, S.h., Watt, J.H., Gratch, J.: Associations between interactants' personality traits and their feelings of rapport in interactions with virtual humans. Paper Presented at the Annual Meeting of the International Communication Association, Marriott, Chicago, IL, pp. 1–25 (2009)

16. Kipp, M.: Anvil - a generic annotation tool for multimodal dialogue. In: Proceedings of the 7th European Conference on Speech Communication and Technology (Eurospeech), pp. 1367–1370 (2001)

17. Kipp, M.: Creativity meets automation: combining nonverbal action authoring with rules and machine learning. In: Gratch, J., Young, M., Aylett, R., Ballin, D., Olivier, P. (eds.) IVA 2006. LNCS (LNAI), vol. 4133, pp. 230–242. Springer, Heidelberg (2006). https://doi.org/10.1007/11821830_19

18. Lee, J., Marsella, S.C.: Learning a model of speaker head nods using gesture corpora. In: Decker, Sichman, Sierra, Castelfranchi (eds.) 8th International Conference on Autonomous Agents and Multiagent Systems (AAMAS 2009). No. Aamas, International Foundation for Autonomous Agents and Multiagent Systems (www.ifaamas.org), Budapest, Hungary (2009)

19. Lee, J., Marsella, S.: Nonverbal behavior generator for embodied conversational agents. In: Gratch, J., Young, M., Aylett, R., Ballin, D., Olivier, P. (eds.) IVA 2006. LNCS (LNAI), vol. 4133, pp. 243–255. Springer, Heidelberg (2006). https://doi.org/10.1007/11821830_20

20. Lee, J., Prendinger, H., Neviarouskaya, A., Marsella, S.: Learning models of speaker head nods with affective information. In: 3rd International Conference on Affective Computing and Intelligent Interaction (ACII 2009), pp. 1–6. IEEE (2009)

21. Maura E. Stokes, Davis, C.S., Koch, G.G.: Categorical Data Analysis Using the SAS System, 2nd edn. SAS Institute and Wiley (2003)

22. Miller, W.R., Rollnick, S.: Motivational Interviewing: Preparing People for Change, vol. 2, 2nd edn. Guilford Press, New York (2002). https://doi.org/10.1026/1616-3443.34.1.66

23. R. Amini, C.L., Ruiz, G.: HapFACS 3.0: FACS-based facial expression generator for 3D speaking virtual characters. IEEE Trans. Affect. Comput. PP(99), 1–13 (2015)

24. Rabiner, L.R.: A tutorial on hidden Markov models and selected applications in speech recognition. Proc. IEEE 77(2), 257–286 (1989)

25. Tickle-Degnen, L., Rosenthal, R.: The nature of rapport and its nonverbal correlates. Psychol. Inq. 1(4), 285–293 (1990)

26. Toutanova, K., Klein, D., Manning, C.D., Singer, Y.: Feature-rich part-of-speech tagging with a cyclic dependency network. In: Proceedings of HLT-NAACL, pp. 252–259 (2003)

Finding a Structure: Evaluating Different Modelling Languages Regarding Their Suitability of Designing Agent-Based Models

Poornima Belavadi$^{(\boxtimes)}$, Laura Burbach , Martina Ziefle ,
and André Calero Valdez

Human-Computer Interaction Center, RWTH Aachen University,
Campus Boulevard 57, 52076 Aachen, Germany
{belavadi,burbach,ziefle,calero-valdez}@comm.rwth-aachen.de

Abstract. Several approaches to standardize the creation of agent-based models exist, but there is no perfect way to do it yet. In this study we analyze, whether two modelling languages (i*Star, UML) can help in designing agent-based models. We identified requirements for building agent-based models and analyzed to what extent the requirements can be met by applying modeling languages. We reflect whether the application of modeling languages can profitably facilitate the creation of agent-based models. We found that modeling languages can meet some requirements for creating agent-based models. Finally, modeling languages offer an added value to the creation of agent-based models, but their application also requires more time than creating a model without their application. However, when creating agent-based models, a considerable amount of time should be spent to decide what the model would depict. Our approach can be helpful in the future for creation of agent-based models.

Keywords: Agent-based modelling · Modelling languages ·
Programming languages · Simulation · NetLogo · UML · i* · i*Star

1 Introduction

Agent-based models have been built for many decades [32], but have only recently been applied in the social and social-ecological sciences [37]. For most of the time, the process of development has been highly individual and has not followed standardized criteria. To facilitate **reuse and replication**, it would be desirable to use **standardized approaches in agent-based modeling** that allow describing models as concisely and completely as math can be described in the universal language of mathematics [17].

As it is not always clear to the developers of agent-based models at what level of detail the models should be described and where, how, and what kind of information should be given, **many descriptions are difficult to read**.

V. G. Duffy (Ed.): HCII 2021, LNCS 12777, pp. 201–219, 2021.
https://doi.org/10.1007/978-3-030-77817-0_16

Similarly, it is often difficult to replicate a published model, which is complicated by the fact that agent-based model descriptions are often incomplete [17].

For this reason, Grimm et al. [16,18] designed the ODD protocol. They believed that many **features of agent-based models are common** and thus enable a common language. The acronym stands for Overview, Design concepts, and Details and the protocol is intended to serve as a standard form for describing agent-based models.

In this article, we reflect on the suitability of different approaches to build agent-based models. To date, agent-based models are most commonly created using NetLogo, which is a simulation environment. In addition, other models have been created in general-purpose programming languages (such as Java, Python or Julia). The **ODD protocol provides a standardized process** towards creating agent-based models using guideline questions. We examine whether it makes sense to **additionally use one of the two class languages UML and i*Star** (actually written i* and pronounced i-Star) when creating agent-based models.

2   Related Work

We first show some fundamental underlying aspects of agent-based modeling: Emergence, complexity vs. simplicity, and realism. Next, we introduce the method agent-based modelling. Then, we show how models are created (simulation environment, programming language, ODD-protocol). Last, we introduce the modelling languages UML and i*Star.

2.1   Aspects of Agent-Based Modelling

Agent-based models simulate individuals or agents whose behavior is guided by simple rules. The behavior and properties of the agents are described at the micro-scale, revealing complex behavior at the macro-scale [31].

Emergence. The whole is more than the sum of its parts. This statement points to a strength of agent-based models. We normally look at individual sub-components of a system and infer the behavior of the whole system from them, the overall behavior does not simply result from just observing the components. Moreover, it is often difficult to look at the overall behavior. Instead, it is easier to look at individual behavior. **Emergence refers to systems that are not merely the sum of the individual components**, but where the individual components complement and influence each other, resulting in hard-to-predict systems.

With agent-based models we can create individual agents and shape their behavior to follow individual rules at micro level. Agents reside in an environment and interact with both the environment and other agents, creating hard-to-predict social patterns. We can thus see emergence or emergent behavior [5].

Complexity, Simplicity, and Realism. Complex systems consist of different onto-logical levels, which can also be considered as interacting subsystems and take place on a micro and macro level [8]. To understand why a system is complex, it is important to look at how the system is (structurally) built [36]. Systems can be both complex and complicated, but they are not always both. Both terms refer to a system that is made up of components, but they refer to different aspects of the system. If there are many subcomponents that affect each other and it is therefore difficult to predict the system behavior, the system is complex. **Complexity depends on the structure of interactions and the underlying dynamics** of a system [6,36,38]. A system is merely complicated if it is difficult for us humans to understand, such as a mathematical equation [6,38].

Using simulations we can analyze complex systems well. Modelling the individual parts of a system makes the overall behavior visible [12].

2.2   General Idea of Agent-Based Models

In agent-based models, agents can be in various forms (such as individuals, trees, atoms) and an environment in which the agents move [4]. Agent-based models also have a topology, which indicates how the agents are connected to each other.

Agent-based models represent a way of thinking rather than a technology [4]. Agent-based models cannot represent reality and they are never fully realistic. As is common for models, they depict reality in a simplified way. They allow to observe emergent behaviors in complex systems by mapping simple rules. Thus, it is possible to **observe and understand the behavior of complex systems without knowing the entire complex system**. Agent-based models are used to analyze systems and patterns from the bottom up. In this process, the agents exhibit heterogeneous behavior, which means that different agents exhibit individually different behavior. Furthermore, agent-based models contain stochasticity, meaning they can vary randomly [20].

In agent-based models, the agents are created programmatically as a template. They move in the environment and make decisions in the simulation depending on how they perceive that environment. Their perception influences their behavioral intent. Often, **agents are connected to other agents through a network**. The network then usually ensures that the agents influence each other.

The modeler can decide whether **agents behave deterministically or randomly**. Random behavior can be used, when not all aspects of the model need to be specified to answer the research question. This reduces complexity and the model can still represent behavior approximating real world concepts [39].

2.3   The ODD Protocol

Many have criticized that it is difficult to relate and build upon existing data, methods, and models. This has led scientists to develop several approaches in parallel to address the *replication crisis* [13,27,28] One of these approaches is the *ODD protocol*, which was developed in 2006 [16] and extended in 2010 [18] and 2020 [17] and has already been used by a lot of modelers (e.g. [29]).

The *ODD protocol* (*Overview, Design concepts, Details*) is intended to **provide guidelines for writing and reading agent-based models** and thus facilitate the standardized creation of models (see Fig. 1). The three categories *overview, design concepts*, and *details* are further divided into seven elements. First, an *overview* of the model is provided. *Design* shows how the important design concepts to the creation of agent-based models have been implemented. *Details* look at all the other details of the model [17].

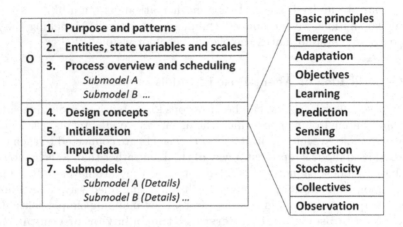

Fig. 1. ODD protocol: structure of model description; used from Grimm et al. [17]

Eleven different *design concepts* can be described. If *design concepts* do not apply, they can be omitted. Modelers should consider all 11 *design concepts* and particularly should decide **which key processes** in their model **are governed by empirical parameters and rules, and which processes are characterized by agents making adaptive decisions.** Typically, only a few processes can be adaptive, so it is important to consider and justify for which processes adaptive adaptation makes the most sense [17].

Through the *ODD protocol*, requirements are placed on modelers: They should describe their models in detail. They should specify the individual parts of their models and, in particular, provide the *design concepts*, which are unique to agent-based models. Through these requirements, modelers must also **reflect, explore, investigate, and justify the parts of the model design** [30].

Even though many modelers from different disciplines have used the *ODD protocol*, **still many papers about agent-based models are published without the use of it** [17]. As the description using the *ODD protocol* often becomes longer than describing the model without the protocol, it discourages some modelers from using it. In addition, there are specification languages that are more concise than *ODDs* (e.g., Z notation; [40]). However, it is difficult to read these specification languages if one is not familiar with them.

Reading the computer code of the model is a good way of understanding the workings of the model and replicating it. In contrast, *ODD* is more narrative, which makes many modelers feel it is less accurate and complete. In their view, *ODD* provides less opportunity to reproduce the model [2]. On the other hand, computer code can also be difficult to understand. Grimm et al. [17] recommend that to understand models accurately, modelers might consider an *ODD* in combination with the model code if they find the written description of the *ODDs* ambiguous [17].

2.4 Modelling Languages

Agent-based modelling has become a popular method for studying complex phenomena. However the available methods to design agent based models are not suitable for non-agent experts [19]. **Modelling languages are used to help in the design and construction of specific components or parts of a system** by following a systematic set of rules and frameworks. They can be either textual or graphical. In this section, we describe process modelling and goal modelling languages and their suitability for the research questions (see Sect. 1) we answer in this paper.

Process Modelling Languages. Process modelling languages are used to depict an actual process in an abstract manner by selecting the process elements that are considered important for the model's purpose. A Process model provides guidance for building a system by breaking down the process description into sufficient details [9]. Humphrey and Kellner [21] define a process as "a set of partially ordered steps intended to reach a goal." A *process element* is any component of a process and a *process step* is an individual or atomic action in a process. A process model is made up of individual model elements: *agent, role, artefact.* An *agent* performs the process element. An ordered set of process elements grouped together and assigned to an agent form a *role.* The outcome or the product created or modified by performing the process is an *artefact.* **Process modelling focuses on the interacting behaviour of agents** [9]. Issues handled by process models range from understanding a process to performing the process.

Some of the important characteristics of process modelling languages include modelling support, which takes care of all the process elements and communication between different agents and parallel activities. They also provide support to start a new task asynchronously, keep track of the unfinished tasks and provide visual notations for better understanding of the process by humans [43]. A process model provides **several perspectives to the underlying process**: In the *functional* perspective, the model focuses on *what* process elements are being executed and what are the relevant data and other entities required. *Behavioural,* focuses on *when* the process elements are executed and *how* they are done. *Organisational,* focuses on *where* and by *whom* in the organization are the processes being performed. *Informational* is related to the entities that are produced as a result of one or more process actions. A process modelling language focuses on one or more of these perspectives [9]. **Unified Modelling Language (UML) is a popular process modelling language** that we consider in this paper to be suitable for designing ABMs.

Goal Modelling Languages. Goal modelling languages help in understanding the requirements of a system. Goal modelling assists in **identifying the system's goals** by asking questions like *what the system needs to do?*, *why a particular functionality is needed?* and *how it can be implemented?* [26]. Goal modelling has gained popularity because of its efficiency in Requirements Engineering (RE). Goal modelling not only helps in elaborating the requirements of the system but also in validating the completeness and correctness of the requirements [22].

There are a lot of goal modelling languages in the literature, however there is no standard construct for them as each language offers their own syntax, semantics and process. This is reported to be the main reason for these languages not being widely accepted [25]. This has motivated the research on goal modelling languages for understanding the effectiveness and efficiency to solve modelling problems. In a typical simulation, software agents are independent entities that interact with one another, cooperate and coordinate to achieve goals. Goal oriented languages are also well suited for agent based simulations. **Many goal modelling language constructs focus on agent-based simulation concepts** and a lot of research has gone into understanding the effectiveness of these languages for modelling agent-based systems [26]. Therefore, we further look into i*Star goal modelling language in this paper, for its suitability in designing ABMs.

3   Requirements Identification

In this study, we first considered different ways to design agent-based models. Second, we identified requirements that are necessary to design agent-based models. Third, we looked at questions each type of modelling language answers.

3.1   Different Ways to Design Agent-Based Models

There are **several ways to design an agent-based model:** One option is to build on existing theory—to evaluate, whether the assumptions from the theory also apply to the context under consideration or—to reflect, whether the theory needs to be updated. Besides, an agent-based model can be based on theoretical assumptions and empirical results as well. Subsequent to a profound literature review, for example an online survey can be conducted and the agent based model can be based on the survey results. This enables to measure theoretical or new assumptions using a specific sample. This ensures, that the agent-based model built on these results can be—at least for the considered sample—more realistic. Models built using either of these approaches can be additionally verified against real data (e.g.: data collected from social media).

3.2 Requirements of Agent-Based Models

In this section **we identify the necessary requirements when designing agent-based models**. Among other things, we have oriented ourselves on the steps and components of the *ODD protocol* [1], as well as adding our own considerations. A list of all collected requirements can be seen in Table 1.

To create an agent-based model, we first need a *suitable idea*, what we want to simulate—a research question—to be analyzed using agent-based modeling. We must reflect, why agent-based modeling is a well-suited method to our question and which *added value* a simulation offers compared to other empirical methods.

For other modellers to understand our model, they must understand the *model's purpose*. For this, **a general purpose of the model should be determined before determining a more specific purpose**. General purposes can be *prediction, explanation,* or *description* of the model. To keep the purpose of the model specific, it should state what components the model includes or what is not included: The goal is that **all entities and mechanisms contained in the model are necessary to achieve its purpose**. To avoid imprecise purposes, they should be deliberately phrased as a question (e.g., *do mechanisms A, B, and C explain observed phenomena X, Y, and Z*) [7].

One added value of agent-based models can be that it is possible to observe and analyze an *emergent aspect* (see Sect. 2.1). Therefore, when designing a model, it might be useful to **think about what potential unexpected outcomes might appear** in the simulation runs. Likewise, we can think of **potential *dynamics* or *dynamic processes*** in the simulation.

Different Ways to Design Agent-Based Models. As mentioned in Sect. 3.1, there are different *ways to design agent-based models* and we need to decide, on which we want to base our agent-based model. First, we need to identify *theoretical assumptions* addressing our research question/interest. Then, we can decide, whether an *empirical analysis* (e.g.: online survey) is needed to get a more realistic simulation (see Sect. 3.1). For empirical analysis, we consider **which processes in the simulation should be based on empirical results**. Besides, we check the possibility of *verifying the simulation against real data* and if so, which real data to use and which parts of the simulation can be verified using the data.

Adaptive Key Processes. As described in Sect. 2.3, we must also **decide which key processes** in our model **should be adaptive** versus based on empirical parameters and rules. For that, we need to reflect and reason, why we have chosen this process(es) to be adaptive.

Contexts Well-Suited for Agent-Based Models. We can also think of *contexts well-suited to agent-based models* or questions that lend themselves to be examined with an agent-based model. Agent-based models are particularly useful, if the focus is on the question of **how a system can adapt to changing conditions (robustness)**. Besides, they are useful, when we consider complex problems. Another suited use case for agent-based models are simulations that involve emergence (see Sect. 2.1). Also a form of interaction, social influence, learning, or dynamics can be considered well in agent-based models.

Entities, State Variables, and Scales. The third element of the *ODD protocol* describes three interconnected parts of an agent-based model. The first part considers *entities*, independent objects or actors behaving as a unit. Entities can be *spatial entities* (e.g., grid cells or GIS polygons), *individual agents* and *collectives* (groups of agents with the same behaviors and attributes) [1]. So, when designing an agent-based model, it is also important to consider **what types of entities the model contains** (see Table 1), **which entities** occur in the model and **why they occur**, as well as **how many types of entities** occur. Each type of entity should be described separately. In Table 1, we listed what should be considered when describing *agents*. The *environment entity* describes how other entities perceive the environment and specifies the time of the simulation [1].

The second part of the third *ODD element* describes the *state variables* or *attributes* for each type of entity. **The state variables indicate *what state an entity is currently in*.** The state variables distinguish an entity from other entities of the same type. The *state variables* can also indicate how an entity changes over (the simulated) time. The characteristics of the *state variables* like *what the variables represent* and *what unit they have* should be explained while defining the *state variables*. Furthermore, **variables can change over time and be dynamic or static**. The type of variable (*integer, floating point number, text string, coordinate set, Boolean (true/false) value, a probability*) and the range they encompass should also be considered.

In addition, the *spatial* and *temporal scale* of the model should be described (3rd part of the *ODD element*). So, for our agent-based model, we should consider how we want to realize space and time as well as scale and shape in the simulation. This includes **specifying what a *spatial unit* in the model represents in reality as well as what a *time step* means in reality** [1].

Processes of the Agent-Based Model. The third *ODD element* summarizes **what happens in the model and in what order**. So, when creating our agent-based model, we should consider the time step and the sequence in which *individual processes* (see Table 1) occur. To monitor this, we should create a sequence of *actions*, for each action, we should decide *how and which entity(ies)* are needed, and *which state variables change* as a result, as well as the *order* in which the entities exhibit their behavior [1].

Design Aspects. The fourth *ODD element* looks at *design concepts*. Some of these are also relevant for our approach to design agent-based models. The concept *fundamental principles* includes reference to already established theories, idea, hypotheses, and prior modeling approaches. For the development of our agent-based model, we check **whether the model considers an idea that has already been addressed in theory** and decide whether we want to use a theory for agent behavior.

As shown earlier, *emergence* is a fundamental feature of agent-based models. We should also consider which mechanisms predictably lead to which outcomes as well as **which outcomes are not predictable (*emergent*) for our model.**

The concept *adaptation* specifies the adaptive behavior of agents. For our model, we should also describe each stimuli and its triggered responses in **agents**, i.e., **when they change their behavior and to what extent adaptively.** We can decide whether agents choose a behavior that directly serves their goal (*direct goal seeking*) and therefore choose a measure to (probabilistically) weigh which behavior is most likely to achieve the goal.

According to the concept *learning*, agents gain experience and change how they adaptively adjust their behavior over time based on their experience. Here, learning does not mean that state variables cause agents to adapt their behavior, but that **agents change the methods of how they make decisions** (e.g., algorithms). For our model, we should define whether there is a form of learning and how it should be implemented if so.

According to the concept *prediction*, we can **specify whether and how agents predict future conditions and decision consequences.** To do this, we need to consider what internal models of future conditions and decision consequences our agents should have to make predictions for decision making. There are *explicit* and *implicit predictions*.

The concept of *sensing* considers **what agents know and what information they possess.** Knowledge determines how agents behave. For our model, we should specify what information (limited/only local) agents possess. We have to decide how an agent perceives the state variables of which entities. Similarly, we need to define which entities (e.g., spatial unit they reside on) they collect values from. Agents can solicit values not only locally, but also across networks and globally.

Agents can *interact* (*concept*) with each other globally, but also locally. The agents can interact *directly* or in a *mediated* manner. If an agent *directly interacts* with other agents it is a *direct interaction*. In contrast, in *mediated interaction*, agents influence each other only indirectly, for example, when they produce a common resource. *Interaction* also includes communication, which is the exchange of information in simulations. For our model, we need to specify which agents interact with each other and how [1].

The concept *stochastic* describes which processes are determined by pseudo-random numbers and how. ***Stochastic processes* are useful when we want to achieve variation in the model,** but do not want to specify which mechanisms cause the variability and how. *Stochastics* is often used for randomly creating state variables at the beginning of agent-based models. In addition, random numbers are used to shape the behavior of agents so that they exhibit different behaviors with the same frequency as observed in real people. For our model, we should also decide, whether pseudorandom numbers should be implemented and for which.

Collectives represent an intermediate level in the organization of agent-based models. They are **aggregations of agents that influence agents and are**

influenced by agents (e.g., social groups, schools of fish). *Collectives* can either be implemented as an *emergent* property of agents (e.g., flock of birds) and not explicitly represented in the model, or *explicitly* defined as an entity type (with shared state variables and behaviors) (e.g., dog packs, political parties).

Observation considers **how information from the agent-based model is collected and analyzed**. Thus, for our model, we should also consider how we collect the information from the agent-based model, or rather, which outcomes we observe (since not all outcomes can be observed) to analyze them later.

Initialization. At one point we should consider **what we need to set up the model** (see *ODD concept 5 Initiation*). We should consider which processes or sub-models we will implement only at the beginning of the simulation. To do this, we should assign numbers to entities, consider what locations the agents are in at the beginning, how the agents are networked together, and what collectives exist at the beginning. In addition, we should consider whether we want to simulate only a specific case or study system or whether it should be more generic and applicable to different sites. Further, we can **decide if our model is always initialized the same way or if we want to generate different scenarios with different initialization** (like different number of agents). So, we should consider whether we are interested in the results regarding different initial states or the results due to the change of aspects during the model. We also need to consider what data we want to use to build our model (for example, to initialize the agent populations). We should justify why we want to use which initialization methods. For example, we should explain which state variables vary between entities and in what way. We can also consider whether it makes sense to run different simulation experiments to visualize the effects of different initialization assumptions [1].

Model Dynamics. In addition to initializing the model, we also need to consider the dynamics of the model. **The model can be dynamic in that the input data can include time series of variable values or outcomes that affect the simulation**. Frequent use is made of environmental variables that change within simulation runs. Input data are often values observed in reality and therefore have statically realistic properties. External models may also be used to generate the input. Similarly, input data can be specified by external events affecting the model during the simulation (for example, times when new agents are created) [1].

Concretization of Idea. Before we can start to actually implement the agent-based model, it is important to have a *concrete idea* of **what the agent-based model should show** respectively which question it should answer. Thus, we must reflect, why the agent-based model should be build.

Basic Elements. When we think about what aspects we need to create agent-based models, we can also think of the basic elements (see Sect. 2.2) of every agent-based model: *agents, environment, network/topology* (see Table 1).

Table 1. Requirements to design agent-based models

Requirements
1. Idea/suitable research question/purpose of model
2. Added value
3. Identify emergent aspect/Identify a kind of dynamic
4. Decide for a way to design agent-based models
5. Choose processes and adaptive key processes
6. Think of contexts well-suited for agent-based models
7. Define entities, state variables, and scales
8. Design concepts of model
9. Define initial state of agent-based model
10. Define model dynamics
11. Concretization of idea
Agents:
12. Heterogeneity/Homogeneity? Different subgroups? Appearance
13. Deterministic vs. random behavior
14. Which behavior should agents show?
15. Define (sets or subsets of) attributes (for defined state)
16. Define interactions between agents
Environment:
17. Which information is given to the agents?
18. How does it influence the actions of agents?
Topology:
19. What should it represent? Physical/geographical/social... network
20. Static vs. dynamic
21. Define number of topologies (1 or more)

Agents. To design the *agents*, we must decide, **whether and *how many different groups of agents* we have or whether each agent is different**. We can consider how the *agents should look like*: Like humans, like animals or anything else? Should all agents look the same? Further, we can decide, whether we want the agents to **behave *deterministically or randomly*** (see Sect. 2.2) and **what the agents can do** in the simulation. We can reflect, whether we want to have a realistic aging process with agents that are born and die. Additionally, we have a lot of options, what the agents can do in the simulation, such as learn, interact physically, exchange opinions, adapt, infect each other, change and they can have emotions, beliefs, desires, goals, intentions and plans.

When we want to design agents, we need to consider, that **some characteristics (4) of agents are essential, whereas others are optional.** Wooldridge and Jennings [41] collected characteristics common to most agents and other studies explained the characteristics further [11,15,24,42]: Agents always have a boundary (*self-contained*). They behave independently and gain information by interactions with other agents and the environment (*autonomous*) [24]. Based on the information, they make independent decisions. They can interact with other agents in at least a certain range of situations. This interaction does not necessarily affect their autonomy. Thus, agents are also active rather than purely passive [7]. In addition, agents have a *defined state* consisting of sets or subsets of attributes. All agent states combined with the state of the environment form the system state. Further, agents interact with other agents (*social*) [24].

Besides, agents can show optional characteristics. In the simulation, agents may modify their behavior according to rules (*adaptive*). Further, they probably adjust their behavior to reach a goal (*goal-directed*). Additionally, agents can be diverse in their attributes and their behavior (*heterogeneous*)[1] [24]. Normally autonomous individuals evolve. If there are groups of agents, they have usually formed from the bottom up by similar autonomous individuals joining together [7].

That agents (can) exert influence independently in a model makes them *active*. Agents can be active in different ways: They can be *proactive/goal-oriented* and seek to achieve goals through their behavior. Agents can also be *reactive/perceptive* and are aware of or have a sense of their environment in the simulation. They may have prior knowledge, such as a mental map of their environment, which increases their awareness of other entities, obstacles, or desired targets in the environment. Agents can also be active by being *interactive/communicative*. They can communicate with other agents within their neighborhood or environment in the simulation and, for example, request certain attributes. They may ignore input that contradicts a desired threshold. In addition, agents are *mobile*. They can move around the environment of the model. Finally, agents can also be able to learn or adapt their behavior adaptively and then have a kind of memory [7].

Environment. **Agents are located in the environment and operate within the space defined by the environment** [7]. The environment also **provides the topology and supports the interaction of agents with each other and the environment**. Thus, to create the environment, we must know how the agents are connected to each other. Additionally, we can decide, *which information the environment provides to the agents* and *how the environment influences the actions of the agents* [24].

Topology. The topology indicates, **how agents are connected to each other**[2]. We can decide, whether the topology should represent a ***physical/geographical network or e.g., a social network*** and whether it is ***static or dynamic***. Further, we should consider, whether our model includes only *one or different*

---

[1] Examples of an agent-based simulation with homogeneous are the well-known *forest fire* and *schelling* [33] model.
[2] Examples for topology include a 2-dimensional grid, network topology or geographic information system topology.

topologies. For example, agents can have different neighborhoods (e.g. geographical, social, ...). Usually only local information is available to the agents. This is typically information from an agent's neighbors [24].

3.3 Suitability of Modelling Languages for Designing Agent-Based Models

We know that modelling languages have been used to design agent-based or other simulations. We understand the specifics of each type of modelling languages from Sect. 2.4. In this section, we discuss the suitability of specific modelling languages (i*Star, UML) and why they can be used to design agent-based models.

i*Star Modelling Language. With agent-oriented modelling becoming popular, several modelling languages have been proposed for the construction of agent-oriented models. **i*Star**, being a goal modelling language **allows modellers to define goals, actors and roles** in the model as well as **dependencies between them in a clear way**. It proposes use of two models: *Strategic Dependency (SD)* which represents the actors as *nodes* and their dependencies as *relationships*. The connected actors will have a common objective, which is represented as *intentional elements*. The intentional elements can be *resources, goal, or softgoals.* The second model is the *Strategic Rationale (SR)* model, which links the relationships defined in SD model into the boundary of the actor and refines the SD model with reasoning. Elements in the SR model are linked in two ways: *Means-end links,* where *mean* are one or more intentional elements that contribute to an end—which can be goal, task, resource or softgoal. *Task decomposition,* which relates to the decomposition of a task into different intentional elements [3]. To get an intuitive overview of the environment and the actors being modelled, the graphical notations provided by the language can be used [34]. The literature points out that i*Star language does not have a language definition and that this was intentional as it gives the language flexibility. But, this flexibility also has given rise to ambiguity while using the language notations [3].

Unified Modelling Language (UML). As the name suggests, the Unified Modelling Language was defined as a *group* or *union* of modelling languages, where several modelling languages are combined each being able to model a specific aspect of a system. Unified Modelling Language is the most popular language for modelling object oriented systems and has been standardized with the main purpose of having an agreement on the commonly accepted notation and abstract syntax for all the diagram types [10,23]. UML was not intended to be a new language but a language that includes all best approaches of available modelling languages when it was introduced. UML follows the traditionally distinguished aspects of the system and provides sub-languages to model *structural* and *behavioural* parts of the system. It provides *class* and *object* diagrams which are derived from the *Entity-Relationship Diagrams* to model structural system aspects. Objects are described by attributes and operations which might change the object's state. The structural relationships are defined by associations and constraints. UML provides several types of diagrams for modelling behavioural aspects of the system. *Use-case diagrams* help in getting the overall functionality (use cases) of a system by defining the actors and their use cases. *Activity diagrams* help to depict the control-flow of the system, *Sequence diagrams* depict the behaviour of a system in a specific scenario, *State-machine diagrams* describe the behaviour of an object over time [10].

Comparison of Languages. As we described, every language comes with its own unique properties and addresses a very specific problem in the modelling world. There are several ways in which the modelling languages are compared in the literature [14,23,26,35]. We found the **semiotic approach to suit our requirements for comparing the modelling languages** the best [23,26].

Semiotic Framework. **Semiotics focuses on the functions that are used to communicate either verbally, non-verbally, or visually**. The semiotic method fits well to our approach as we intend to use the modelling language mainly for communicating the nuances of ABM. We refer the semiotic framework used by Matulevič ius and Heymans [26] to check if the requirements we developed fits a standard framework. Although the semiotic framework has been used to compare the quality of modelling languages, in this paper **we use the framework to check the suitability of modelling languages to design agent-based models**. We then compare the requirements of the agent-based models against the requirements fulfilled by each model, to understand which modelling language approach suits best for designing agent-based models.

The semiotic quality *(SEQUAL) framework* represents a constructivistic world-view, where model creation is seen as a part of communication between the team or users knowledge about the domain, which changes as the modelling takes place. **The framework divides the language quality into five areas:** *Domain appropriateness* that relates the language to the domain, which means that there are no domain statements that cannot be expressed using the language. *Participant knowledge appropriateness* that adheres to the knowledge the participant has about the language which need not be static. *Knowledge externalizability appropriateness* which takes care of how relevant knowledge of the participant can be expressed in the language. *Comprehensibility appropriateness* relates to the understanding of all the statements in the language by the language user. *Technical actor interpretation appropriateness* relates to the formal language requirement by the technical actor (tools).

4   Evaluation of Modelling Languages

As the languages we compare are very different from each other, we use the principles defined by *SEQUAL framework* as a structure for a common ground for mapping our requirements and evaluating other modelling languages.

Sequel Framework	Criteria	ABM Requirements	i* language	UML
Domain Appropriateness	What are the views covered by language? (structural, functional, behavioural, rule-based, actor, role)	Identify the emergent aspect	SD and SR diagrams	NA
		Identify a kind of dynamic	SD and SR diagrams	NA
		Deterministic vs random behaviour?	Not well defined	Activity diagrams,
		Which behaviour must agent show?	Not well defined	Use-case, State-machine diagrams
Domain Appropriateness	Requirement definition to model the ABM	Concretization of the Idea	SD diagrams	Class diagrams
		Decide for a way to design ABM	SD diagrams	Use-case / Class diagrams
		Additional empirical Analysis?	Intentional elements	NA
		Additional verification against real data?	SD Diagrams	NA
		Theoretical assumptions?	SD Diagrams	NA
		Which behaviour should agents show?	SD and SR diagrams	Sequence diagram
		Which information is given to the agents?	NA	Class diagrams
		Define model dynamics	SD and SR diagrams	Structural and Behavioural diagrams
		Define entities, state variables and scales	NA	Class, State-machine diagrams
Comprehensibility Appropriateness	Does it support graphical representation? - to help in communication	Representation of agent, topology and environment	Agent - actor and dependencies, topology and environments are NA	Structural diagrams for topology and environment and Behavioural diagrams for agent
		How does the information influence the agent's action in an environment?	Means-end links, Task decomposition	Activity diagrams
		What does the topology represent? Physical, geographical, social network	NA	Class diagrams
		Define number of topologies	NA	Class diagrams
		Define interaction between agents	Mean-end links	Use-case diagrams
		Define sets or subsets of attributes of agents	NA	Object diagrams
		Representation of different agents - homogeneity/heterogeneity, subgroups	NA	Object diagrams
		Define initial state of ABM	NA	State-machine diagram
		Design model concepts	SD diagrams	Structural diagrams
		Define entities, state variables and scales	Entities - actors, State variable and scales - NA	Object and Class diagrams
Technical Actor Interpretation Appropriateness	Formal semantics? — ensure that the model is not misunderstood	Define entities, state variables and scales	Entities - actors, State variable and scales - NA	Object and Class diagrams
		Representation of agent, topology and environment	Not so well defined	Well defined semantics
		Define interaction between agents	Possible ambiguities in definition	Well defined semantics in class and object diagrams
		Define sets or subsets of attributes of agents	Possible ambiguities in definition	Well defined semantics in class and object diagrams
Comprehensibility, Knowledge externalisability appropriateness	Well defined constructs	Representation of agent, topology and environment	NA	NA
		Define entities, state variables and scales	NA	Well defined constructs
Comprehensibility, Domain, Knowledge externalisability appropriateness	Expressivenes of power— relation between construct and views	Representation of agent, topology and environment	Only 1 view available - SD	One diagram to give an overview of the system - classdiagram
		Define interaction between agents	SD and SR diagrams, SR being detailed	More than one available to give differed perspectives of interaction

Fig. 2. Evaluation of *requirements to design agent-based models* and how the modelling languages meet these requirements

4.1   Requirements to Design Agent-Based Models and Solutions Offered by Modelling Languages

Although *SEQUAL* provides fundamental principles it is still abstract. An additional mapping to the principles which is detailed enough to evaluate the modelling languages is required. We adapted the mapped categories used by Matulevičius and Heymans [26], and compared i*Star and UML against only those categories that fit our *requirements for agent-based models* (see Fig. 2). Firstly, we found that the requirements that we have constructed for agent-based models satisfy four out of five principles of the *sequel framework*. The principle that we did not address is the *Participant knowledge appropriateness*, which adheres to our knowledge of using agent-based models, which as mentioned in the paper has improved with the usage. For the first two agent-based model requirements: *Identify the emergent aspect* and *a kind of dynamic*, we did not find a suitable diagram in both the languages, that fulfills the requirements. We added *NA* where we did not find a suitable language construct to meet the requirements.

4.2   Does the Chosen Modelling Language Offer a Real Benefit as a Basis for an Agent-Based Model?

Both modelling languages (i*Star and UML) offer certain benefits and fail at certain places in fulfilling the model requirements identified for agent-based models. Although i*Star is developed for designing agent-based models, the behavioural view is defined in the language, which is of concern as we require more well defined behavioural views for designing agent-based models. But, the i*Star language offers language constructs that are focused on goals, which also an important feature to have in mind while designing ABMs. On the other side, UML offers more than five different sub-languages for designing behaviour. Having more than one diagrams for designing a specific part of ABM would help in having more than one perspective of that aspect—which is also an important feature to have when designing ABMs. Secondly, i*Star does not offer well defined guidelines and methodologies, while UML has been standardised by the Object Management Group. Hence, the language ambiguities are taken care of.

From Fig. 2 **we discern that UML is more suitable for designing agent-based models** as it fits to be a more complete language offering different types of diagrams or sub-languages to design different parts of the agent-based model or different perspectives of an agent in the agent-based model. Although the i*Star language has its ambiguities, the i*Star language is more suitable for designing agent-based models when we want to know outcomes of the model like identifying the emergent aspects or testing if additional empirical data is required.

5   Conclusion

With this paper we evaluated different ways to design agent-based models. **We identified some leverages of using modeling languages to design agent-based models**. In contrast, we found that it takes longer time to design an agent-based model using a modelling language compared to designing it without. Still, when designing agent-based models, modellers should in general spend time in reconsidering, why the agent-based model is designed and whether it is designed to answer a research question of interest.

Although, we only reflected theoretically, whether modelling languages can help in designing agent-based models, this study can be used as a motivation for conducting and empirical analysis in this regard. Besides, we only focused on two modelling-languages, that we identified to be promising for creating agent-based models. **In the future, we would like to test our suggested approach to actually create agent-based models**. We plan to create agent-based models combining the use of the *ODD protocol* and the use of each modelling language we looked at in this study. In this way, we can evaluate better, whether it makes sense to include a modelling language in the design of agent-based models.

References

1. Grimm, V., et al.: "Supplementary file s1 to: Grimm, V., et al. (2020) 'the odd protocol for describing agent-based and other simulation models: a second update to improve clarity, replication, and structural realism". J. Artif. Soc. Soc. Simul. **23**(2) (2020)
2. Amouroux, E., Gaudou, B., Desvaux, S., Drogoul, A.: ODD: a promising but incomplete formalism for individual-based model specification. In: 2010 IEEE RIVF International Conference on Computing and Communication Technologies, Research, Innovation, and Vision for the Future (RIVF), Hanoi, pp. 1–4 (2010)
3. Martínez, C.P.A., et al.: A comparative analisys of i*-based agent-oriented modeling languages. In: Proceedings of the SEKE 2005, the 17th International Conference on Software Engineering & Knowledge Engineering: Technical Program, 14–16 July 2005, Taipei, Taiwan, Republic of China, pp. 43–50 (2005)
4. Bonabeau, E.: Agent-based modeling: methods and techniques for simulating human systems. Proc. Natl. Acad. Sci. USA **99**(Suppl 3), 7280–7287 (2002). https://doi.org/10.1073/pnas.082080899
5. Bruch, E., Atwell, J.: Agent-based models in empirical social research. Sociol. Methods Res. **44**(2), 186–221 (2015). https://doi.org/10.1177/0049124113506405. PMID: 25983351
6. Byrne, D.S.: Complexity Theory and the Social Sciences: An Introduction. Business and the World Economy. Routledge, London (1998). ISBN 9780415162968. https://books.google.de/books?id=NaVSZXVdc-0C
7. Castle, C.J., Crooks, A.T.: Principles and concepts of agent-based modelling for developing geospatial simulations (2006)
8. Conte, R., et al.: Manifesto of computational social science. Eur. Phys. J. Special Topics **2014**(1), 325–346 (2012). http://wrap.warwick.ac.uk/67839/
9. Curtis, B., Kellner, M.I., Over, J.: Process modeling. Commun. ACM **35**(9), 75–90 (1992)

10. Engels, G., Heckel, R., Sauer, S.: UML—a universal modeling language? In: Nielsen, M., Simpson, D. (eds.) ICATPN 2000. LNCS, vol. 1825, pp. 24–38. Springer, Heidelberg (2000). https://doi.org/10.1007/3-540-44988-4_3

11. Epstein, J.M.: Agent-based computational models and generative social science. Complexity **4**(5), 41–60 (1999). https://doi.org/10.1002/(SICI)1099-0526(199905/06)4:5⟨41::AID-CPLX9⟩3.0.CO;2-F(199905/06)4:5⟨41::AID-CPLX9⟩3.0.CO;2-F. ISSN 1076–2787

12. Epstein, J.M.: Generative Social Science: Studies in Agent-Based Computational Modeling (Princeton Studies in Complexity). Princeton University Press, Princeton (2007)

13. Fanelli, D.: Opinion: Is science really facing a reproducibility crisis, and do we need it to? Proc. Natl. Acad. Sci. USA **11**, 2628–2631 (2018)

14. Felderer, M., Herrmann, A.: Comprehensibility of system models during test design: a controlled experiment comparing UML activity diagrams and state machines. Softw. Qual. J. **27**(1), 125–147 (2019)

15. Franklin, S., Graesser, A.: Is it an agent, or just a program?: a taxonomy for autonomous agents. In: Müller, J.P., Wooldridge, M.J., Jennings, N.R. (eds.) ATAL 1996. LNCS, vol. 1193, pp. 21–35. Springer, Heidelberg (1997). https://doi.org/10.1007/BFb0013570

16. Grimm, V., et al.: A standard protocol for describing individual-based and agent-based models. Ecol. Model. **198**(1–2), 115–126 (2006). https://doi.org/10.1016/j.ecolmodel.2006.04.023. ISSN 0304–3800

17. Grimm, V., et al.: The odd protocol for describing agent-based and other simulation models: a second update to improve clarity, replication, and structural realism. J. Artif. Soc. Soc. Simul. **23**(2), 7 (2020). https://doi.org/10.18564/jasss.4259. ISSN 1460–7425. http://jasss.soc.surrey.ac.uk/23/2/7.html

18. Grimm, V., Berger, U., DeAngelis, D.L., Gary Polhill, J., Giske, J., Railsback, S.F.: The odd protocol: a review and first update. Ecol. Model. **221**(23), 2760–2768 (2010). https://doi.org/10.1016/j.ecolmodel.2010.08.019. ISSN 0304–3800. https://www.sciencedirect.com/science/article/pii/S030438001000414X

19. Hahn., C., A domain specific modeling language for multiagent systems. In: Proceedings of the 7th International Joint Conference on A"Utonomous Agents and Multiagent Systems, vol. 1, pp. 233–240. Citeseer (2008)

20. Helbing, D., Balietti, S.: How to do agent-based simulations in the future: from modeling social mechanisms to emergent phenomena and interactive systems design why develop and use agent-based models? Int. J. Res. Market., 1–55 (2011). https://doi.org/10.1007/978-3-642-24004-1. http://www.santafe.edu/media/workingpapers/11-06-024.pdf

21. Humphrey, W.S., Kellner, M.I.: Software process modeling: principles of entity process models. In: Proceedings of the 11th International Conference on Software Engineering, pp. 331–342 (1989)

22. Kavakli, E.: Goal-oriented requirements engineering: a unifying framework. Requirements Eng. **6**(4), 237–251 (2002)

23. Krogstie, J., Using a semiotic framework to evaluate UML for the development of models of high quality. In: Unified Modeling Language: Systems Analysis, Design and Development Issues, pp. 89–106. IGI Global (2001)

24. Macal, C.M., North, M.J.: Tutorial on agent-based modeling and simulation. In: Proceedings of the 2005 Winter Simulation Conference, pp. 2–15 (2005)

25. Matulevicius, R.: Improving the syntax and semantics of goal modelling languages. In: iStar, pp. 75–78 (2008)

26. Matulevičius, R., Heymans, P.: Comparing goal modelling languages: an experiment. In: Sawyer, P., Paech, B., Heymans, P. (eds.) REFSQ 2007. LNCS, vol. 4542, pp. 18–32. Springer, Heidelberg (2007). https://doi.org/10.1007/978-3-540-73031-6_2

27. Monks, T., Currie, C.S., Onggo, B.S., Robinson, S., Kunc, M., Taylor, S.J.E.: Strengthening the reporting of empirical simulation studies: introducing the stress guidelines. J. Simul. **1**(13), 55–67 (2019)

28. Peng, C., Guiot, J., Wu, H., Jiang, H., Luo, Y.: Integrating models with data in ecology and palaeoecology: advances towards a model-data fusion approach". Ecol. Lett. **14**(5), 522–536 (2011)

29. Polhill, J.G., Parker, D.C., Brown, D., Grimm, V.: Using the ODD protocol for describing three agent-based social simulation models of land-use change. J. Artif. Soc. Soc. Simul. **11**(2), 1–3 (2008)

30. Railsback, S.F.: Concepts from complex adaptive systems as a framework for individual-basedmodelling. Ecol. Model. **139**(1), 47–62 (2001)

31. Rand, W., Rust, R.T.: Agent-based modeling in marketing: guidelines for rigor. Int. J. Res. Market. **28**(3), 181–193 (2011). https://doi.org/10.1016/j.ijresmar.2011.04.002. ISSN 01678116

32. Retzlaff, C.-O., Ziefle, M., Calero Valdez, A.: The history of of agent-based modeling in the social sciences. In: Duffy, V.G., (ed.) HCII 2021, LNCS 12777, pp. 304–319. Springer, Cham (2021)

33. Schelling, T.C.: Models of segregation. Am. Econ. Assoc. **52**(2), 604–620 (2013)

34. Yu, E.S.-K.: Modelling strategic relationships for process reengineering. Ph.D. thesis, University of Toronto (1996)

35. Söderström, E., Andersson, B., Johannesson, P., Perjons, E., Wangler, B.: Towards a framework for comparing process modelling languages. In: Pidduck, A.B., Ozsu, M.T., Mylopoulos, J., Woo, C.C. (eds.) CAiSE 2002. LNCS, vol. 2348, pp. 600–611. Springer, Heidelberg (2002). https://doi.org/10.1007/3-540-47961-9_41

36. Calero Valdez, A., Ziefle, M.: Human factors in the age of algorithms. Understanding the human-in-the-loop using agent-based modeling. In: Meiselwitz, G. (ed.) SCSM 2018. LNCS, vol. 10914, pp. 357–371. Springer, Cham (2018). https://doi.org/10.1007/978-3-319-91485-5_27

37. Vincenot, C.E.: How new concepts become universal scientific approaches: insights from citation network analysis of agent-based complex systems science. In: Proceedings of the Royal Society B: Biological Sciences, vol. 285, p. 20172360 (2018)

38. Mitchell Waldrop, M.: Complexity: The Emerging Science at the Edge of Order and Chaos. Simon & Schuster, New York (1992). ISBN 0671767895

39. Wilensky, U., Rand, W.: An Introduction to Agent-Based Modeling: Modeling Natural, Social, and Engineered Complex Systems with NetLogo. The MIT Press (2015) ISBN 9780262731898. https://books.google.de/books?id=LQrhBwAAQBAJ

40. Wooldridge, M.: An Introduction to Multiagent Systems. Wiley, Hoboken (2009)

41. Wooldridge, M., Jennings, N.R.: Intelligent agents: theory and practice. Knowl. Eng. Rev. **10**, 115–152 (1995)

42. Wooldridge, M., Jennings, N.R.: Simulating sprawl: a dynamic entity-based approach to modelling North American suburban sprawl using cellular automata and multi-agent systems. Ph.D. Thesis (2004)

43. Zamli, K.Z., Lee, P.A.: Taxonomy of process modeling languages. In: Proceedings ACS/IEEE International Conference on Computer Systems and Applications, pp. 435–437. IEEE (2001)

The Role of Embodiment and Simulation in Evaluating HCI: Experiments and Evaluation

Nikhil Krishnaswamy[1]([envelope])[iD] and James Pustejovsky[2][iD]

[1] Colorado State University, Fort Collins, CO 80523, USA
nkrishna@colostate.edu
[2] Brandeis University, Waltham, MA 02453, USA
jamesp@brandeis.edu

Abstract. In this paper series, we argue for the role embodiment plays in the evaluation of systems developed for Human Computer Interaction. We use a simulation platform, VoxWorld, for building Embodied Human Computer Interactions (EHCI). VoxWorld enables multimodal dialogue systems that communicate through language, gesture, action, facial expressions, and gaze tracking, in the context of task-oriented interactions. A multimodal simulation is an embodied 3D virtual realization of both the situational environment and the co-situated agents, as well as the most salient content denoted by communicative acts in a discourse. It is built on the modeling language VoxML, which encodes objects with rich semantic typing and action affordances, and actions themselves as multimodal programs, enabling contextually salient inferences and decisions in the environment. Through simulation experiments in VoxWorld, we can begin to identify and then evaluate the diverse parameters involved in multimodal communication between agents. In this second part of this paper series, we discuss the consequences of embodiment and common ground, and how they help evaluate parameters of the interaction between humans and agents, and compare and contrast evaluation schemes enabled by different levels of embodied interaction.

Keywords: Embodiment · HCI · Common ground · Multimodal dialogue · VoxML

1 Introduction

In Part 1, we described the theory of computational common ground and its underlying semantics. We focused on the role of an agent's *embodiment* in cre-

This work was supported by Contract W911NF-15-C-0238 with the US Defense Advanced Research Projects Agency (DARPA) and the Army Research Office (ARO). Approved for Public Release, Distribution Unlimited. The views expressed herein are ours and do not reflect the official policy or position of the Department of Defense or the U.S. Government. We would like to thank Ken Lai, Bruce Draper, Ross Beveridge, and Francisco Ortega for their comments and suggestions.

V. G. Duffy (Ed.): HCII 2021, LNCS 12777, pp. 220–232, 2021.
https://doi.org/10.1007/978-3-030-77817-0_17

ating mechanisms through which to compute the parameter values that go into a common ground structure, such as the target of a pointing gesture.

This is crucial to evaluating human-computer interactions because it provides for bidirectional content: that is, each interlocutor has available all communicative modalities and can use them with reference to the current situation rather than having to communicate solely in abstractions, for lack of either a situated context or an ability to interact with it. Put simply, an agent needs to have at minimum the *notion* of a body and how it exists in an environment in order to reference said environment with any specificity. Figure 1 shows an example of this, with a human and an avatar making the smae gesture, that both of them can recognize and interpret.

Fig. 1. Bidirectional gesture recognition and generation.

Visual gesture recognition has long been a challenge [10,22]. Gesture recognition in our VoxWorld-based embodied HCI system is facilitated by Microsoft Kinect depth sensing [27] and ResNet-style deep convolutional neural networks (DCNNs) [7] implemented in TensorFlow [1]. As our goal in developing multimodal interactions is to achieve naturalistic communication, we must first examine what we mean by and desire of an interaction such as that illustrated in Sect. 2.

We take the view that a "meaningful" interaction with a computer system should model certain aspects of a similar interaction between two humans. Namely, it is one where each interlocutor has something "interesting" to say, and one that enables them to work together to achieve common goals and build off each other's contributions, thereby conveying the impression to the user that the computer system is experiencing the same events. We therefore build the evaluation scheme off of the following qualitative metrics:

1. Interaction has mechanisms to move the conversation forward [4,11]
2. System makes appropriate use of multiple modalities [2,3]
3. Each interlocutor can steer the course of the interaction [8]
4. Both parties can clearly reference items in the interaction based on their respective frames of reference [21,26,29]
5. Both parties can demonstrate knowledge of the changing situation [28]

In [18] we introduced a surface-level evaluation scheme that satisfies the above requirements. In this scheme, we took the view that a "meaningful" interaction with a computer system should model certain aspects of similar interactions between two humans, namely that each interlocutor should have something to contribute that enables them to work together toward common goals, building off each other's contributions. This is discussed in Sect. 2.1.

This multimodal evaluation scheme was an attempt to quantify qualitative metrics based on the body of work underlying "common ground" in communication and multimodality in human-computer interaction.

These metrics, or "hallmarks" of communication, come from a rubric initially developed by the MITRE Corporation to evaluate peer-to-peer communication with computers on collaborative tasks. It was recently published as a technical report [13]. The hallmarks are intended to evaluate collaborative computer systems engaged in tasks of various complexities where there is not a single ground truth or "right answer" to compare to.

The results of the surface-level evaluation made it clear that the single dimension of response time as a proxy for communicativity of the preceding utterances or actions was not exposing the deep semantics or information content of the multimodal utterance, even when conditioned on context. Therefore a finer-grained evaluation scheme was needed—one that took into fuller consideration the parameters of common ground. This will be discussed in Sect. 2.2. We will then conduct a novel comparison of the two scenarios and evaluation methods with regard to the parameters of the common ground, in Sect. 2.3.

2   Evaluation Schemes

We have conducted a variety of studies on multimodal interactions using *Diana*, an embodied agent capable of interpreting linguistic and gestural inputs. Diana is one of many kinds of agents that can be implemented within the VoxWorld platform; she is designed to communicate with a human in the context of collaborative tasks. VoxSim (discussed in Part 1) handles Diana's language interpretation using inputs from 3rd-party or custom speech recognition, while gestures are recognized using custom 11-layer deep convolution neural nets (DCNNs) trained over 2048-dimensional feature vectors extracted from RGBD video data.

Fig. 2. L: Diana c. 2018; R: Diana c. 2020.

Diana has undergone numerous updates over time, from taking gestural inputs only [15] to word-spotting to recognizing complete utterances [23], and from a turn-taking interaction to one that is more asynchronous [14]. It is this specific embodied interactive agent that we conducted our evaluations against, as we detail subsequently.

2.1 Time-Based Evaluation

In [25], Wang et al. conducted user studies of two humans engaged in a collaborative building task wherein a "builder" with a target pattern of blocks had to instruct a "signaler" on how to build that pattern out of a physical set of blocks. Users were placed in one of three conditions:

1. *Video only*, where the signaler and builder can see but not hear each other and must rely on gesture to communicate;
2. *Audio only*, where the signaler can see the builder but the builder can only hear the signaler—the two can use only language to communicate bidirectionally;
3. *Both audio and video*, where both gestural and spoken communication are available.

These elicitation studies gave rise to the gesture set used by the Diana system, and also showed an interesting conclusion: the subjects could complete the task in all conditions, but when both linguistic and gestural modalities were available, the users could complete the task in significantly less time. Figure 3 shows these differences in trial time based on modality.

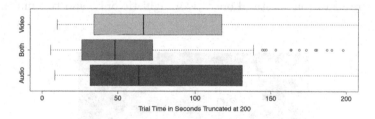

Fig. 3. In human-to-human collaborative studies, users complete tasks faster using both audio and visual channels. Figure credited to Dr. Jaime Ruiz of the University of Florida.

Therefore, in evaluating early versions of Diana, we adopted a similar assessment of communicative facility, where the time required to achieve a communicative goal was taken to be a surface-level indicator of the communicative content of the utterance, which was then assessed relative to the communicative modalities used.

This study was conducted using 20 graduate students placed in a live interaction with Diana (e.g., see Fig. 2L). They were tasked with building a 3-step staircase out of six blocks and were told that Diana could understand gesture and language but were not given a specific vocabulary to use. We collected no identifying audio or video directly from the user but logged all instructions the computer recognized from the user, and Diana's responses.

Details are given in [18], but among other findings, we discovered discrepancies in the communicative facility of the handedness of the pointing (right-handed pointing prompted quicker responses than left-handed pointing), affirmative vs. negative acknowledgments (affirmatives prompted *slower* responses than negatives, particularly when spoken instead of gestured), and "push" gestures vs. "carry" gestures (pushing prompted quicker responses than carrying). These and other particulars can be ascribed to a number of factors, including variance in the gesture recognition, complexity of the gesture being made, and the use of positive acknowledgment as an explicit requirement for the conversation to proceed vs. negative acknowledgment as a contentful way of redirecting the discourse (cf. [12]).

These conclusions were useful in making improvements to the Diana agent, but given the coarse granularity of this high-level evaluation, it is clear that multiple dimensions are being masked; the important discriminative factor(s) in the communicativity of an utterance by an embodied interlocutor in a multimodal discourse might not be the time to receive a response, but rather how much and what information is being introduced via the multimodal utterance.

2.2   Common Ground-Based Evaluation

In [19], we presented the EMRE (Embodied Multimodal Referring Expressions) dataset. This dataset contains 1,500 individual videos of Diana generating multimodal references to 6 different objects in 50 different configurations using 5 different strategies (one gestural only, two linguistic only, and two multimodal) (Fig. 4).

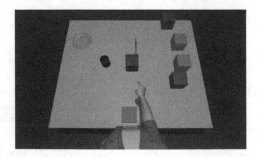

Fig. 4. Sample still from a video in the EMRE dataset. The accompanying utterance is "That red block on front of the knife". (Color figure online)

Each of these videos were then judged by 8 annotators on Amazon Mechanical Turk who indicated, on a Likert-type scale, how natural they thought the depicted referring expression was.

Initial analysis of the EMRE dataset provided similar surface-level conclusions to the time-based evaluation, and showed the evaluators preferred multimodal referring expressions and more descriptive language where language was used.

Following this, in [20], we conducted a further detailed evaluation of these object referencing strategies, using the common ground structure (CGS) as a feature generation strategy, and assessed how well individual classes of features predicted the Likert-type rating of the naturalness of a referring expression in the dataset. See Part 1 for an explanation of the CGS parameters that will be referenced below.

We extracted formal and propositional values as features from the EMRE data based on the information each feature introduces into the common ground. If the gesture ($\mathcal{G}$) or speech ($\mathcal{S}$) content in the referring expression demonstrates that either agent α (being either α_a the artificial agent or α_h the human) either *knows* or *perceives* some propositional content p that pertains to either the jointly perceived entities in **P** or the agents' beliefs **B** about what each other know or understand, this prompts an update to the common ground, and therefore new features for possible examination. This allows us to evaluate the behavior of annotators as a proxy for interlocutors, by examining what features are good predictors for naturalness judgments when interpreting referring expressions.

Details are given in [20]. We trained a multi-layer perceptron (MLP) classifier to predict the naturalness of a given referring strategy based on different combinations of input features. Possible input features included features taken directly from the EMRE dataset, sentence embedding features extracted from the linguistic portion of multimodal referring expressions, and features extracted from the CGS of each referring expression represented as individual one-hot vectors. For instance, if the communicative act $\mathcal{C}_a$ contains a speech component $\mathcal{S}$ that in turn contains the word *"other"* in conjunction with some attributive Att and an object type t, then this indicates that a knows 3 things: that there is more than one object of type t in the discourse, that they are distinct, and that Att predicates over both (or all) of them. Each of these knowledge elements $\mathcal{K}_a$ of the common ground is represented as a distinct one-hot vector.

This MLP classifier was then cross-validated on the EMRE data using 7 folds. We found that features that correlate formally with elements of the CGS improved the ability of the classifier to predict the annotator judgment on a referring expression by an average of 7–11%, when compared to the EMRE dataset features, with or without augmentation with sentence embeddings. When examining language-only referring expressions, addition of CGS-derived features improved classification accuracy by 5–16%, with using CGS-derived features *alone* providing the highest boost, bringing cross-validated classification accuracy up to ~80% from a baseline of ~64%.

CGS-derived features provided only a 1–5% boost in classifying ensemble (multimodal) referring expressions. However, we interpret this result as representing a redundancy in information communicated through the existence of a gesture as part of the referring expression, and the same content occurring in the common ground structure: $Point_g \rightarrow Obj$ occurs in the CGS and its use indicates that the agent α_a knows what a pointing gesture is intended to communicate, but that information is already contained in the EMRE dataset features, which tracks the modality used by each RE.

2.3   Comparing Time-Based and Common Ground-Based Evaluation

Let us now examine a specific sample from each of the two evaluation schemes where an agent makes a reference to an object in the scene, and look at how much and what kind of information the time-based and CGS-based metrics provide, respectively.

Figure 5 shows the log from the time-based evaluation. The first column is the index of the "move" in the interaction. The second column is a two-letter code representing the Avatar or the Human plus the modality (Gesture or Speech). The third column is the content of the move, which may be a utterance or gesture generated by the avatar, or a word recognized as being spoken by the human or a gesture recognized by the DCNN recognizer. For example, `right point low, X, Y` denotes a low-probability pointing gesture with the right hand at the 2D coordinates $<X, Y>$, which is then transformed in to 3D space. The fourth column is the timestamp (multiple moves can have the same timestamp).

```
81 AS "Which object do you want?"  34.3762
82 HG right point low,0.24,1.59    37.148
83 HG right point stop             38.7285
84 HG right point low,0.24,1.60    38.99577
85 HS PURPLE                       39.1167
86 AS "OK, go on."                 39.1167
87 AG reach(block7)                39.1167
```

Fig. 5. Sample of object referencing using time-based evaluation.

In this snippet, the avatar asked the human "Which object do you want?" (move 81) to which the human responded by starting to point (move 82). The tag `low` indicates that this gesture was not defind enough for the avatar to interpret. Eventually the human says "purple," (move 85) which the avatar is able to understand and respond to (move 86). From the point that the avatar requested input from the human to the point that the human supplied understandable input to the avatar, 4.7405 s elapsed. This number can thereafter be compared to similar blocks of moves where different gestures or different utterances are used to see how these sequence advances or slows the interaction. Examining this in isolation, we can also see that the most delay results from the difficulty the human has in pointing to a distinct, interpretable location (moves 82–84). The use of the linguistic modality is what allows the interaction to proceed here.

Figure 6 shows a still from a video in the EMRE dataset, with the corresponding common ground structure. The items in **P** are the non-agent items in

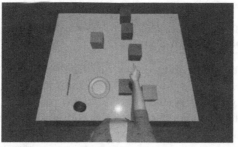

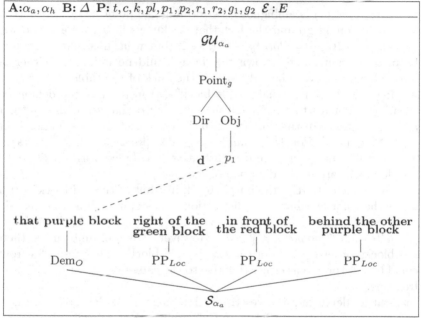

$$\lambda k_s \otimes k_g(\mathbf{that}(x)[\mathrm{block}(x) \wedge \mathrm{purple}(x) \wedge \mathrm{right}(x, g_1, v) \wedge \mathrm{in\_front}(x, r_1, v) \wedge$$
$$\mathrm{behind}(x, p_2, v)] \wedge k_s \otimes k_g(x)], \text{ where } v = \alpha_a$$

Fig. 6. Sample from the EMRE dataset, with accompanying utterance "that purple block right of the green block, in front of the red block, and behind the other purple block," and corresponding common ground structure. The semantics of the RE includes a *continuation* (in the abstract representation sense in computer science, cf. Van Eijck and Unger [24]) for each modality, k_s and k_g, which will apply over the object in subsequent moves in the dialogue. v denotes the viewer, i.e., frame of reference.

the scene, where the non-uniquely colored blocks are denoted by subscripts 1 and 2. **B** is the belief space Δ which is populated by elements of the common ground. Items in this belief space are extracted as one-hot vector features in the evaluation described in Sect. 2.2.

This referring expression was presented to the 8 annotators mentioned in the EMRE study, alongside 3 other choices to refer to the same object:

1. Pointing only;
2. "The purple block in front of the red block" (language only);
3. "That purple block" (with pointing).

Of the 8 annotators, 6 judged this referring expression to be most natural (5 on the 1–5 Likert-type scale), while the remaining 2 judged it to be a 4. The MLP classifier also predicted that this RE would receive a score of 5. Examining the individual features introduced into the common ground by each candidate RE illuminates why:

- Pointing alone (1) is ambiguous. Performing the pointing gesture introduces into the common ground the fact that α_a knows how to point and what it means: $C_a = (\mathcal{G} \mid \mathcal{G} = Point_g \rightarrow Obj \rightarrow \_)$, but what fills that slot is unclear. From the camera angle shown the deixis could be indicating either of the purple blocks or even the red block at the back of the table.
- Adding the utterance "that purple block" (3) introduces the demonstrative "that" (in contrast to "this") and suggests that α_a has some knowledge of the near/far distance distinction on which the demonstrative distinction is based: $C_a = (\mathcal{S}, \mathcal{G} \mid \mathcal{G} = Point_g \wedge '' that'' \in \mathcal{S}) \rightarrow \mathcal{K}_a[[near(sfc)]] \neq [[far(sfc)]]_{\mathcal{M}}$. This is still ambiguous; the demonstrative is coupled with deixis, but both purple blocks are in the direction of the gesture.
- The language-only RE "the purple block in front of the red block" (2) introduces the color attribute as a distinction α_a uses, as well as the spatial term "in front of": $C_a = (\mathcal{S} \mid ['' purple'', '' red'', b_{1_s}, b_{2_s}] \in \mathcal{S}) \rightarrow \mathcal{K}_a[['' purple''(b_1)]] \wedge [['' red''(b_2)]] \wedge [['' purple'']] \neq [['' red'']]$ However, it is still ambiguous; there are red blocks on either side of the two purple blocks. Therefore, "in front of" could be interpreted as either (relative to the camera) "closer to me" or "away from me."
- Integrating deixis and the descriptive language of the RE given in Fig. 6 singles out three relations relative to the target object as well as an interpretation of "other" relative to the attribute it scopes over (in this case, "purple"): $C_a = (\mathcal{S} \mid ['' other'', b_{1_s}, b_{2_s}] \in \mathcal{S} \wedge b_{1_s} = b_{2_s}) \rightarrow \mathcal{K}_a[[Att(b_1 \wedge b_2)]]_{\mathcal{M}} \wedge \mathcal{K}_a b_1 \neq b_2$, such that if $Att =$ "purple," α_a knows what that means, knows that it applies to both blocks b_1 and b_2, and knows that the two objects are distinct. Only one of these blocks is right of a green block, in front of a red block, in the direction of deixis, and far enough from the agent to use "that" as a demonstrative, and so resolve to the correct target object (see Fig. 7).

Compared to the time-based evaluation, using common ground structures as a data structure from which to extract evaluation-relevant features allows the examination of specific features relative to the information they introduce into the interaction. Many of the most informative features, such as what an agent α knows about distance and spatial relations between objects, are dependent upon how the agent is situated or embodied in the world.

Fig. 7. The target object of the RE depicted in Fig. 6, shown highlighted with a circle.

2.4   How Embodiment Enables Evaluation

By embedding the communicative interaction within an embodied simulation environment, we are able to vary the parameters involved in the interaction the human has with a computational agent, and thereby measure the consequences these changes have on the effectiveness of the specific components of the interaction. VoxML provides a dynamic, interpretable model of objects, events, and their properties. This allows us to create visualized simulations of events and scenarios that are rendered analogues to the "mental simulations" discussed in Part 1. VoxSim [16,17] serves as the event simulator within which these simulations are created and rendered in real time, serving as the computer's method of visually presenting its interpretation of a situation or event. Because modalities are modes of presentation, a multimodal simulation entails as many presentational modes as there are modalities being modeled. The visual modality of presentation (as in embodied gaming) necessitates "situatedness" of the agent, as do the other perceptual modalities. Therefore, when we speak of *multimodal simulations*, they are inherently situated. In a human-computer interaction using such a simulation, the simulation is a demonstration of the computational agent's "mind-reading" capabilities (an *agent simulation*). If the two are the same (where the agent is a proxy for the player or user, then the "mind-reading" is just a demonstration of the scenario) If, on the other hand, the two are separate (agent is *not* proxy for the user), then the simulation/demonstration communicates the agent's understanding of the user and the interaction. In this case, this demonstration entails the illustration of both epistemic and perceptual content of the agent.

We believe that simulation can play a crucial role in human-computer communication; it creates a shared epistemic model of the environment inhabited by a human and an artificial agent, and demonstrates the knowledge held by the agent publicly. Demonstrating knowledge is needed to ensure a shared understanding with its human interlocutor. If an agent is able to receive information from a human and interpret that relative to its current physical circumstances, it can create an epistemic representation of that same information. However, without a modality to express that representation independently, the human is unable to verify or query what the agent is perceiving or how that perception is being interpreted. In a simulation environment the human and computer share an epistemic space, and any modality of communication that can be expressed within that space (e.g., linguistic, visual, gestural) enriches the number of ways that a human and a computer can communicate within object and situation-based tasks, such as those investigated by Hsiao et al. [9], Dzifcak et al. [6], and Cangelosi [5], among others.

VoxWorld, and the accompanying simulation environment provided by VoxSim, includes the perceptual domain of objects, properties, and events. In addition, propositional content in the model is accessible to the simulation. Placing even a simple scenario, such as a blocks world setup, in a rendered 3D environment opens the search space to the all the variation allowed by an open world, as objects will almost never be perfectly aligned to each other or to a grid, with slight offsets in rotation caused by variations in interpolation, the frame rate, or effects of the platform's physics. Nevertheless, when the rendering is presented to a user, the user can use their native visual faculty to quickly arrive at an interpretation of what is being depicted.

3   Conclusion

In this paper series, we have brought together a number of definitions of "simulation" from the AI, cognitive science, and game development literature, into a single platform that creates both a formal and operational definition of "embodiment" in the content of Human-Computer Interaction. This framework provides both quantitative and qualitative outputs that can be used to produce, evaluate, and learn from datasets.

When combined with formal encodings of object and event semantics, at a level higher than treating objects as collections of geometries, or events as sequences of motions or object relations, 3D environments provide a powerful platform for exploring "computational embodied cognition". Recent developments in the AI field have shown that common-sense understanding in a general domain requires either orders of magnitude more training data than traditional deep learning models, or more easily decidable representations, involving context, differences in perspective, and grounded concepts, to name a few.

In Part 1, we introduced the underlying theory of computational common ground and its relation to the associated semantic literature. Included in this was the introduction of embodiment to our formulation and platform, as well as the formal notion of the common-ground structure, and how embodiment facilitates the populating thereof.

In Part 2, we presented and compared particular experiments done under versions of this framework using the embodied agent Diana. We hope to have demonstrated how the combination of formal semantics with the technologies provided by modern gaming engines lead to systems that afford gathering both traditional data for deep learning and representations of common sense, situated, or embodied understanding, thereby opening new doors for researchers to deploy and examine the role of embodiment in human-computer interaction both quantitatively and qualitatively.

References

1. Abadi, M., et al.: TensorFlow: a system for large-scale machine learning. In: Proceedings of the 12th USENIX Symposium on Operating Systems Design and Implementation (OSDI), Savannah, Georgia, USA (2016)
2. Arbib, M., Rizzolatti, G.: Neural expectations: a possible evolutionary path from manual skills to language. Commun. Cogn. **29**, 393–424 (1996)
3. Arbib, M.A.: From grasp to language: embodied concepts and the challenge of abstraction. J. Physiol. Paris **102**(1), 4–20 (2008)
4. Asher, N., Gillies, A.: Common ground, corrections, and coordination. Argumentation **17**(4), 481–512 (2003)
5. Cangelosi, A.: Grounding language in action and perception: from cognitive agents to humanoid robots. Phys. Life Rev. **7**(2), 139–151 (2010)
6. Dzifcak, J., Scheutz, M., Baral, C., Schermerhorn, P.: What to do and how to do it: translating natural language directives into temporal and dynamic logic representation for goal management and action execution. In: IEEE International Conference on Robotics and Automation, ICRA 2009, pp. 4163–4168. IEEE (2009)
7. He, K., Zhang, X., Ren, S., Sun, J.: Deep residual learning for image recognition. In: Proceedings of the IEEE Conference on Computer Vision and Pattern Recognition, pp. 770–778 (2016)
8. Hobbs, J.R., Evans, D.A.: Conversation as planned behavior. Cognit. Sci. **4**(4), 349–377 (1980)
9. Hsiao, K.Y., Tellex, S., Vosoughi, S., Kubat, R., Roy, D.: Object schemas for grounding language in a responsive robot. Connect. Sci. **20**(4), 253–276 (2008)
10. Jaimes, A., Sebe, N.: Multimodal human–computer interaction: a survey. Comput. Vis. Image Underst. **108**(1), 116–134 (2007)
11. Johnston, M.: Building multimodal applications with EMMA. In: Proceedings of the 2009 International Conference on Multimodal Interfaces, pp. 47–54. ACM (2009)
12. Koole, T.: Conversation analysis and education. In: The Encyclopedia of Applied Linguistics, pp. 977–982 (2013)
13. Kozierok, R., et al.: Hallmarks of human-machine collaboration: a framework for assessment in the darpa communicating with computers program. arXiv preprint arXiv:2102.04958 (2021)
14. Krishnaswamy, N., et al.: Diana's world: a situated multimodal interactive agent. In: AAAI Conference on Artificial Intelligence (AAAI): Demos Program. AAAI (2020)
15. Krishnaswamy, N., et al.: Communicating and acting: understanding gesture in simulation semantics. In: 12th International Workshop on Computational Semantics (2017)
16. Krishnaswamy, N., Pustejovsky, J.: Multimodal semantic simulations of linguistically underspecified motion events. In: Barkowsky, T., Burte, H., Hölscher, C., Schultheis, H. (eds.) Spatial Cognition/KogWis -2016. LNCS (LNAI), vol. 10523, pp. 177–197. Springer, Cham (2017). https://doi.org/10.1007/978-3-319-68189-4_11

17. Krishnaswamy, N., Pustejovsky, J.: VoxSim: a visual platform for modeling motion language. In: Proceedings of COLING 2016, the 26th International Conference on Computational Linguistics: Technical Papers. ACL (2016)
18. Krishnaswamy, N., Pustejovsky, J.: An evaluation framework for multimodal interaction. In: Proceedings of LREC (2018, forthcoming)
19. Krishnaswamy, N., Pustejovsky, J.: Generating a novel dataset of multimodal referring expressions. In: Proceedings of the 13th International Conference on Computational Semantics-Short Papers, pp. 44–51 (2019)
20. Krishnaswamy, N., Pustejovsky, J.: A formal analysis of multimodal referring strategies under common ground. In: Proceedings of The 12th Language Resources and Evaluation Conference, pp. 5919–5927 (2020)
21. Ligozat, G.F.: Qualitative triangulation for spatial reasoning. In: Frank, A.U., Campari, I. (eds.) COSIT 1993. LNCS, vol. 716, pp. 54–68. Springer, Heidelberg (1993). https://doi.org/10.1007/3-540-57207-4_5
22. Madeo, R.C.B., Peres, S.M., de Moraes Lima, C.A.: Gesture phase segmentation using support vector machines. Expert Syst. Appl. **56**, 100–115 (2016)
23. Narayana, P., et al.: Cooperating with avatars through gesture, language and action. In: Intelligent Systems Conference (IntelliSys) (2018, forthcoming)
24. Van Eijck, J., Unger, C.: Computational Semantics with Functional Programming. Cambridge University, Cambridge (2010)
25. Wang, I., et al.: EGGNOG: a continuous, multi-modal data set of naturally occurring gestures with ground truth labels. In: To appear in the Proceedings of the 12th IEEE International Conference on Automatic Face & Gesture Recognition (2017)
26. Wooldridge, M., Lomuscio, A.: Reasoning about visibility, perception, and knowledge. In: Jennings, N.R., Lespérance, Y. (eds.) ATAL 1999. LNCS (LNAI), vol. 1757, pp. 1–12. Springer, Heidelberg (2000). https://doi.org/10.1007/10719619_1
27. Zhang, Z.: Microsoft kinect sensor and its effect. IEEE MulitMedia **19**, 4–10 (2012)
28. Ziemke, T., Sharkey, N.E.: A stroll through the worlds of robots and animals: applying Jakob von Uexkull's theory of meaning to adaptive robots and artificial life. Semiotica-La Haye Then Berlin **134**(1/4), 701–746 (2001)
29. Zimmermann, K., Freksa, C.: Qualitative spatial reasoning using orientation, distance, and path knowledge. Appl. Intell. **6**(1), 49–58 (1996)

Tracking Discourse Topics in Co-speech Gesture

Schuyler Laparle[✉][iD]

University of California, Berkeley, Berkeley, CA 94704, USA
schuyler_laparle@berkeley.edu

Abstract. This paper argues for the integration of co-speech gesture into formal models of discourse structures. In particular, I use a variation of the Question Under Discussion (QUD) framework to show how features of co-speech gesture may be used to inform discourse analysis. To do this, I look at examples of three discourse relations: *clarification, citation* and *attitude expression*. All three of these involve a momentary digression from the main discourse topic, a phenomenon which I call 'micro-excursion'. I show that these micro-excursions correspond to particular and recurrent changes in co-speech gesture sequences. I provide micro-analyses of three discourse fragments taken from interviews on late night television. For each fragment, I look at speech-gesture alignment and then use this alignment to inform an analysis of the discourse's structure. In particular, I show the ways in which hand shape and orientation can be used to segment a discourse into different topics. By using features of co-speech gesture in this way, we are able to inform and justify a proposed discourse structure analyses in a principled and non-circular way. Furthermore, I show that this methodology can be straightforwardly integrated into existing models of discourse structure, despite them being designed for mono-modal discourses.

Keywords: Co-speech gesture · Discourse structure · Question under discussion

1 Introduction

Discourse is hierarchical, structured into topics and sub-topics which are used to complete communicative tasks, such as answering questions, providing instructions, and aligning interlocutors' beliefs as to how the world works. For each incoming utterance, interlocutors must make decisions as to its purpose, how it relates to previous utterances, and, ultimately, how it contributes to the discourse's overall

I would like to thank my advisors, Eve Sweetser and Line Mikkelsen, for their support in the evolution of this project. I would also like to thank my research assistants, Kahini Achrekar, Kat Huynh, Karsen Paul, Sarah Roberts, Sanjeev Vinodh and Irene Yi for their help in data collection, without which this project could not have been completed. Lastly, I would like to thank Andy Lücking for encouraging the development of my work.

V. G. Duffy (Ed.): HCII 2021, LNCS 12777, pp. 233–249, 2021.
https://doi.org/10.1007/978-3-030-77817-0_18

structure and goal. To do this, interlocutors have access to a variety of linguistic tools, including syntactic structures, discourse markers, prosody, and, I will argue, co-speech gesture.

Though there have been important recent developments in the incorporation of co-speech gesture into formal semantic models [1,19,20,33], the same cannot be said for models of discourse structure. In this paper, I seek to demonstrate the utility of integrating co-speech gesture into existing formal approaches to discourse structure, specifically the Question Under Discussion framework [31,32], henceforth QUD. This paper is exploratory. I do not seek to provide a completed framework for multimodal discourse analysis. Instead, I hope to show the systematic alignment of discourse structure and gesture sequences, and to argue that this alignment is able to provide us with insights into both the role of gesture in language and how naturally-occurring discourses are constructed.

The remainder of the paper is structured as follows: Sect. 2 reviews the use of co-speech gesture in discourse management from a functional perspective. In Sect. 3, I provide an outline of the QUD framework as used here and introduce ways in which gesture can be integrated into QUD analyses. In Sect. 4, I analyze the discourse structure and gesture alignment in three discourse fragments. Section 5 reviews the findings and concludes.

2   Co-speech in Discourse Management

There is an established literature on the use of co-speech gesture in discourse management, perhaps most notably in Bavelas et al.'s work on 'interactive gesture' [2] and Kendon's work on 'pragmatic gesture' [15,16]. Much of this work seeks to profile the function of individual gestures. For example, an upturned open hand held toward an interlocutor is frequently used when requesting and offering information [29]. In other work, so-called 'brushing aside' gestures, in which the hand moves in quick lateral movements away from the body, have been shown to correspond to expressions of negative assessment and dismissal of a discourse topic [5,6,34]. Studying form-meaning pairings of co-speech gesture in this way allows us to better understand the capacity of individual gestures to convey pragmatic meaning. However, this research tradition fails to provide significant insight into the overall alignment of discourse structure with sequences of gesture.

There is a more limited body of work that abstracts away from individual gestures to consider the ways in which gesture and discourse structure interact more generally. At the highest level of discourse structure, Kendon argues that gesture is used to establish and end participation in a discourse [17]. There is also significant evidence that hand gestures and gaze direction is used to regulate turns [3,4,9,10,12]. At more fine-grained levels of discourse organization, there is evidence that co-speech gesture may be used to delineate discourse units [13,14] and organize discourse referents [8,24,25,27]. For example, McNeill and colleagues found that discourse referents can be organized and referred to spatially by pointing to different regions of empty space when introducing and discussing different referents [25,27]. McClave found similar patterns in head movements, such that people frequently turn their head and direct their gaze in different directions when discussing different referents or topics [24]. Jannedy and colleagues have also shown that speakers are able to partition their gesture space in order to signal topic organization via the relative positioning of individual gestures [8]. Finally, and most relevantly, McNeill and colleagues also introduce the concept of *catchments*, which are used to refer to the recurrence of particular gesture features when discussing the same topic throughout a discourse [28]. However, none of these studies take the step of integrating these observations of gesture-discourse structure correspondence into formal approaches to discourse structure analysis.

The current work follows the latter research tradition in concerning itself with general gesture patterns rather than particular gesture forms. However, I will take an additional analytic step in order to show how repetition of gesture forms and switching between gesture forms reflect distinct discourse structural moves.

3   QUD - An Intuitive Approach to Discourse Structure

QUD is a hierarchical, goal-oriented approach to discourse, in which the ultimate goal is for interlocutors to reach an agreement and mutual understanding of the way the world is. Under this approach, a discourse is said to consist of a set of nested questions and sub-questions all of which contribute in part to answering an overall 'Big Question' – *what is the way things are?* Each discourse move, roughly each utterance, must contribute directly to the discourse goal by either answering a question or posing a new question that will help move the discourse forward. The goals for individual discourses are more specific, defined overtly or implicitly by situational factors and by the type of communicative task that is at hand. For example, the strategies a friend will use to tell you about their day will be very different from the strategies they will use to tell you their favorite cookie recipe. The first may permit digressions and commentary, and events may be described out of order, or not described at all. Communicating the recipe, on the other hand, will require strict adherence to chronology, will not permit omissions, and is unlikely to accommodate digressions.

When constructing a QUD-style analysis for a discourse or discourse fragment, there are three main tasks: discourse segmentation, segment organization, and implicit question identification. Discourse segmentation describes the process of dividing a string of utterances into question-answer pairs. Segment organization refers to the process of deciding where each segment "attaches" in the structure. Implicit question identification refers to the process of deducing the most immediate question under discussion based on contextual factors. The present paper will focus on the first two of these, and will only allude to how gesture may be used in implicit question identification.[1]

---

[1] For discussion of this final point, see work on prosodic cues [7] and discourse markers [30].

Because there is significant variation in the implementation of QUD, I will briefly outline my approach and the constraints I assume here. My goal is *not* to provide a full account of a multimodal QUD framework. My goal is only demonstrate the possibility and value of integrating multimodal data into a working QUD model.[2] My implementation of the QUD framework assumes the basic structure outlined in (1).

(1)   a. a question Q1 is posed (explicitly or implicitly)

　　　 b. an answer A1 is given

　　　 c. answer A1 is checked against the most immediately dominating question Q1:

　　　　　 i. if Q1 is sufficiently answered by A1, Q1 is closed. The discourse can either address a higher (more general) open question or begin a new topic by posing a new question Q2

　　　　　 ii. if Q1 is not sufficiently answered by A1, a sub-question Q1.1 is posed. Partial answer A1 is used to inform sub-question Q1.1

To demonstrate how these basic principles are used to build a discourse structure, I will use the classic toy example of a recipe.

Let us consider a scenario in which I would like to make cookies and have already found a recipe I would like to use. I know that the question I am trying to answer in this communicative task is *how do I make cookies?*. In hopes of answering this question, I begin to read the recipe. The first step in the recipe reads "gather flour, sugar, baking powder, vanilla extract, and an egg". According to the process in (1), this is an answer to the most immediately dominating question, which in this case is the overall discourse goal: *how do I make cookies.* This gives us the QUD structure in (2).

(2)   　　　　　　　　 *Q1: How do I make cookies?*

　　　　　　　　　　　　　　 |

A1: gather flour, sugar, baking powder, vanilla extract and an egg

I then check this answer against the immediately dominating question, and find that I do not yet know how to make cookies. But I do have *some* information that I didn't have before, and I use this information to ask the next question *what do I do with these ingredients?*. This then gives us the structure in (3).

(3)   　　　　　 *Q1: How do I make cookies?*

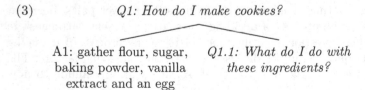

A1: gather flour, sugar,　　 *Q1.1: What do I do with*
baking powder, vanilla　　　 *these ingredients?*
extract and an egg

---

[2] I suspect that the arguments made here can be extended to other interpretations of the QUD framework, and reinterpreted in distinct models of discourse structure such as Discourse Representation Theory (DRT) [11] and Rhetorical Structure Theory (RST) [22].

The next line of the recipe reads "mix the flour, sugar an baking powder in a small bowl". This answer A1.1 is then checked against the immediately dominating open question Q1.1. Because this doesn't fully answer sub-question Q1.1, another sub-question Q1.2 is asked: *what do I do with the vanilla extract and egg?*. This gives us the structure in (4).

(4)

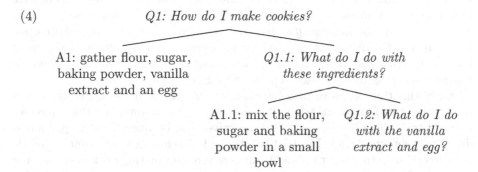

The next line of the recipe tells me to add the vanilla and egg to my previous mixture. I now check this answer against the most immediately dominating open question Q1.2 and see that it is fully answered – I have done something with the vanilla and egg – thus closing the question. I then check the next closest open question, Q1.1. Since I have now done something with all of the ingredients, this question is closed as well. Finally, I check the highest question only to find that I *still* don't know how to make cookies. At this point, I take all the information I've gained so far to inform my next strategy of inquiry. This stage of the discourse is represented in (5).

(5)

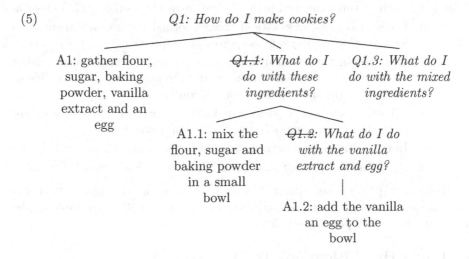

The discourse would continue until I reached the end of the recipe, with all the knowledge I need to make the cookies, and with all of the necessary strategies to get me from ingredients to baked goods reflected in the discourse's structure.

Of course, naturally occurring discourse is not so neatly organized. Discourse goals are rarely as clear, and can almost never be broken down into concretely achievable tasks. There are also matters of distraction, misunderstanding, and shifting goals which are all relatively avoidable in the context of a baking exercise. So, in order to account for naturalistic data, we will need clearer constraints on how an incoming utterance can attach to the extant discourse structure. For this, I assume that an incoming utterance can only attach to the discourse structure in three ways: (i) by answering or partially answering the most immediate open question, (ii) by answering or partially answering a sub-question of the most immediate open question, or (iii) by attaching to the most recently provided answer via a pragmatically accommodated ad hoc question.

Only this third form of attachment is controversial in the QUD literature. In allowing this form of attachment, I follow previous approaches that allow for answers to become 'feeders', which themselves can be questioned in particular discourse contexts [18,30]. I restrict this type of attachment to utterances that do not directly help to answer the most immediately dominating open question. For example, if I found that I didn't have any vanilla extract shortly after beginning a late evening baking venture, I may have to ask where I can get vanilla extract at eleven o'clock. This question would be embedded directly under answer A1 because A1 is the reason I have to ask about acquiring vanilla extract. However, the answer to where I can get vanilla extract does not add information about how to make cookies beyond the information I already have, i.e. that I need a particular set of ingredients to begin the cookie making process.

With our discourse analytic tools in order, we can now extend our framework to incorporate multimodal data. I propose the following principles to inform the integration of co-speech gesture into the above described QUD model.

(6)   i. Each gesture is aligned with a single answer to a single (sub-)question

   ii. Consecutive gestures with a shared formal feature are answers to sub-questions of the same superordinate question

   iii. A change in formal features during a gesture sequence reflects either (i) the closure of a main question and the beginning of a new line of inquiry, or (ii) the beginning of a secondary line of inquiry

   iv. All questions and answers are indexed for formal features of co-occurring gesture, namely hand shape and orientation

   v. Implicit questions inherit gesture features from their answers

   vi. By default, a question and its sub-questions share gesture features

These principles are not intended as an exhaustive list of gesture-QUD correspondences. However, it is these correspondences that will be explored in the three micro-analyses presented below.

4   Using Hand Shape to Track Topics

In this section, I analyze three discourse excerpts in which the speaker momentarily digresses from the immediate question under discussion. These digressions, which I call micro-excursions, are a common feature of naturally occurring discourse and, despite their frequency, pose significant problems for QUD-type analyses. These micro-excursions frequently add information that is related to an *answer* to a discourse question, rather than serving as an answer to an established open discourse question. In the previous section, I discussed how this can be resolved *formally* by allowing answers to serve as 'feeders' for new discourse topics. However, this allowance results in potential attachment ambiguities: how do we know when an utterance should be added to a secondary discourse topic embedded under a feeder, and how do we know when to return to the main line of inquiry? I will show that by indexing questions with gesture features, such ambiguities can be resolved systematically.

In all three examples analyzed, the speaker begins by discussing a topic using a single hand shape. The hand shape then changes for the duration of the micro-excursion, and is reestablished upon returning to the main discourse topic. For each example, I will also discuss the ways in which the changes in hand shape align with discourse structuring strategies in the verbal mode, such as the inclusion of discourse markers, or the partial repetition of an utterance. As stated in Sect. 2, I am not concerned with what the hand shapes actually are. I am only concerned with the preserving and changing of hand shapes, and how these two patterns correlate with elements of a discourse's structure.

4.1   Data

All of the data presented here are from interviews on the Late Show with Stephen Colbert. Data was collected using UCLA's Communication Studies Archive in collaboration with the Distributed Little Red Hen Lab. Initial data collection was conducted for a separate study looking at the recurrence of particular gesture forms with particular verbal discourse markers, including 'such as', 'actually', and 'which I'. A subset of this data set was analyzed in detail for surrounding discourse context and gesture sequences. The data discussed here has been taken from that subset.

For each discourse fragment, the speaker's gesture stream has been segmented into individual gestures. A gesture is defined as a *stroke* – a meaningful movement – that is optionally preceded by a preparation phase and pre-stroke hold, and optionally followed by a post-stroke hold and retraction [14, 26].

(7)   Gesture schema:

   [(preparation) (pre-stroke hold) **stroke** (post-stroke hold) (retraction)]

Movement that conveyed meaning and could be easily associated with some segment in the verbal mode was considered the stroke and constituted the core of each gesture. Movements that could not be easily associated with a meaning or function and that ended with the hands in a rest position were considered *retractions* from the preceding stroke. All other movements that could not be easily associated with a meaning or function were considered to be *preparations* for the proceeding stroke.

For each of the three micro-analyses, I provide a transcript, a set of corresponding screenshots, and a proposed discourse structure. Transcripts are segmented into gesture phrases using brackets, where each bracketed region corresponds to one gesture. Letter-number subscripts at the end of each bracketed region are co-indexed with particular frames in the corresponding set of screenshots. The letter of each subscript denotes hand shape; R = ring, F = flat, C = curled fingers, PD = palm down, PU = palm up. The number of each subscript denotes how many times the hand shape has been used. For example, PU2 would denote the second instance of a palm-up hand gesture in the given discourse fragment.

In the first two examples, one screenshot is given per gesture. In order to see the hand shape most clearly, each screenshot reflects the post-stroke hold of each gesture where present, and the stroke of the gesture only when there was no post-stroke hold. In the final example, I consider the potential of more fine-grained analyses by including the alignment of gesture *phases* rather than the gesture as a single unit [14]. For this example only, two screenshots are given for each gesture, the first corresponding to the stroke, and the second to the post-stroke hold.

4.2   Case Study 1: Clarification and Correction

The first example is an excerpt from an interview with Speaker of the House, Nancy Pelosi.[3] In this interview, Colbert and Pelosi are discussing the first impeachment trial of the former president Donald Trump and the Trump-Ukraine scandal. In the excerpt, Colbert wishes to comment on a leaked transcript of a phone call between the former president and the Ukrainian prime minister. Soon after beginning this discourse topic, Colbert performs a micro-excursion to clarify the nature of the evidence being discussed, which is then corrected by Pelosi. Colbert then acknowledges the correction, and returns to the topic of the phone call and his theory about why notes of the phone call were released.

In this clip, Colbert uses two distinct hand shapes while gesturing: a ring gesture (coded R), in which the fingers are curled into a fist and the thumb and index finger are pinched together to form a ring, and an upturned open palm (coded F for 'flat'). There is an additional third hand shape, coded here as C for 'curled fingers', which only appears when Colbert is not the speaker. This suggests that the curled hand shape occurs only as a retraction of flat palm hand shape, rather than as the dominate shape of an independent gesture.

(8)   COLBERT: [I have a theory]$_{R1}$ [that they released the transcript of the phone call,]$_{R2}$ [such as it is,]$_{F1}$ [because we're still learning]$_{F2}$ [that there's more transcript.]$_{F3}$ PELOSI: [It wasn't a transcript.]$_{C1}$ [It was notes.]$_{C2}$ COLBERT: [Notes.]$_{F5}$ [They released the notes]$_{R3}$ [because they couldn't see how it would play.]$_{R4}$ [They didn't perceive that action as corrupt as everyone would see it.]$_{R5}$

---

[3] File name: 2019-11-01_0635_US_KCBS_The_Late_Show_With_Stephen_Colbert.

Colbert introduces a topic for discussion by announcing that he has a theory. As he says this he holds his right hand up in a ring shape (R1). He then elaborates on his theory by stating what it is about, namely releasing a troublesome phone transcript (R2). During this elaboration, Colbert brings his hand down close to the desk and performs three beats at *released, transcript* and *phone*.[4] Colbert then stops elaborating on his theory in order to clarify his statement, at which point he changes hand shape (F1). As he clarifies that the transcript in question may not be the final transcript he performs a classic presentational gesture to elicit feedback from Pelosi [2]. Pelosi acts on this opportunity to correct Colbert's use of the word *transcript*. As Pelosi makes the correction, Colbert begins to

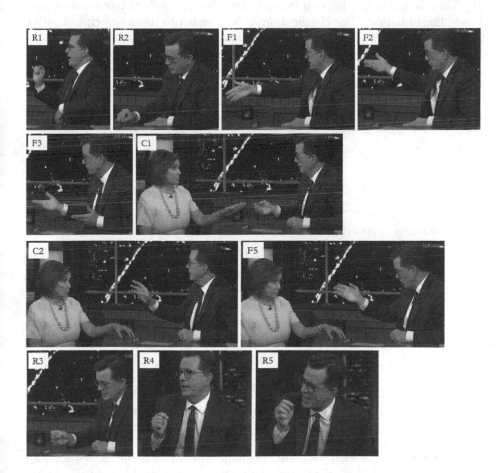

Fig. 1. Frames depicting the post-stroke hold of each gesture in the discourse in (8)

---

[4] I have chosen not to segment beats as separate gestures because they are predominantly used as a gestural parallel to prosodic stress [21,23]. This alignment may be used, as prosodic stress is, to identify implicit questions [7]. I will save further discussion for later work.

raise his hand toward Pelosi, and confirms his acceptance of her correction by repeating *notes* and performing another presentational gesture (F5). Colbert then signals a return to the main discourse topic by (i) partially repeating what his theory is about, using *notes* instead of *transcript*, and (ii) re-establishing the original ring gesture hand shape as he does so (R3). He then goes on to explain his actual theory in two statements, performing a vertical stroke at the two main verbs *see* (R4) and *perceive* (R5), and maintaining the same basic ring hand shape throughout (Fig. 1).

The proposed QUD structure for the primary line of inquiry-is given in (9). The statement *I have a theory* acts as a feeder and sets the QUD of the segment Q1. When he interrupts his own initial answer to Q1, Colbert introduces a secondary line of inquiry. The clarification as to whether to use *transcript* or *notes* does not directly contribute to answering the most immediate open question Q1, and so is embedded directly under A1'. This secondary line of inquiry is indexed by a distinct flat hand shape, primarily associated with Colbert's request for clarification. Once Q2 has been closed, that is once the correct term is agreed upon, the discourse returns to the main line of inquiry. Colbert repeats the initial answer, but with the correct term, *notes* rather than *transcript*.

(9)

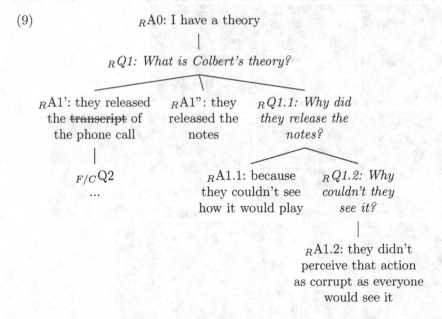

A1' and A1" tell us what his theory is about, but not what the theory actually is, so that when A1 is checked against Q1, a sub-question is posed. Colbert's next statement A1.1 potentially resolves the sub-question Q1.1. However, his subsequent statement provides more information as to why "they couldn't see how it would play" and why that resulted in the notes' release. Because this statement is directly informed by A1.1, I have analyzed it as the answer to a sub-question of Q1.1 triggered by A1.1 being an incomplete answer.

4.3   Case Study 2: Citation

The second discourse fragment comes from an interview with late show host Trevor Noah.[5] In this segment, Colbert has asked Noah about how he stays motivated while maintaining a busy lifestyle. Noah begins to answer the question, but realizes that his answer should be at least partially attributed to Colbert. After paying attribution to Colbert, both by addressing Colbert directly (using the pronoun 'you' to refer to Colbert) and by addressing the audience (using the pronoun 'he' to refer to Colbert). Noah then continues to answer the question by explaining what he loves about making his show.

In this clip, Noah uses three hand shapes: a firm one-finger point (coded P) when addressing Colbert directly, an open palm turned toward the audience (coded F) when telling the audience about what Colbert said, and loosely curled fingers (coded C) when actually answering the questions of what gives him energy and what he loves.

(10)   [You know I find I get my energy from doing things that I love.]$_{C1}$ [It's actually something I learned from you.]$_{P1}$ [I don't even know if you remember saying this.]$_{P2}$ [You said]$_{F1}$ [when creating the show, Stephen Colbert says,]$_{F2}$ [like he's not here,]$_{F3}$ [he said um he said that]$_{F4}$ [the joy of the show]$_{C2}$ [is not often times in performing it.]$_{C3}$ [The joy is derived from]$_{C4}$ [creating it]$_{C5}$

Noah begins answering the question posed to him by Colbert holding both hands up at chest level, fingers curled, and palms facing in as if to hold an object. His left hand remains still throughout the statement, while his right hand performs a series of small lateral beats at *from, doing* and *things*. It is interesting to note here that the beats only occur during the portion of utterance providing new information, whereas the hand shape is held throughout the restatement of the question (*I find I get my energy from*) *and* the new information (*doing the things that I love*). When Noah decides to attribute some of his thoughts to Colbert he turns, establishes mutual gaze with Colbert and points. The discourse marker *actually* signals a possible micro-excursion when it is used, as it is in this case, to qualify a point being made rather than to add additional information about the main discourse topic. After making the initial citation, pointing toward Colbert, Noah turns back toward the audience to tell them what Colbert said. As he continues to refer to Colbert he maintains a flat hand shape, and only fully returns to the initial curled hand shape when he begins to describe the joy of the show. As he says "the joy of the show", he holds both hands, fingers curled, out in front of his chest, just as he did in the beginning. When he says what the joy of the show is *not*, he maintains the curled hand shape with his left hand, but performs a flat-handed lateral flick with his right hand. He then returns to the two-handed hold to repeat "the joy of the show", and then performs a symmetrical outward movement as if shaping a large object.

If we only take speech indexed with the curled hand shape, we are able to construct the tree in (11) (Fig. 2).

---

[5] File name: 2017-06-15_0635_US_KCBS_The_Late_Show_With_Stephen_Colbert.

Fig. 2. Frames depicting either the post-stroke hold or stroke of each gesture in the discourse fragment given in 10.

(11)

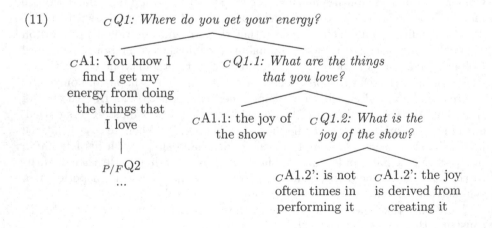

This QUD analysis seems to be an adequate surface representation of the information used in the discourse to directly address the main question under discussion, as posed by Colbert in an interview question. However, there are at least two segments worth further discussion. First, the shape of the gesture coded as F2 is actually somewhere *between* Noah's curled hand shape and the other instances of the flat hand shape. Like the other instances of the flat hand shape, his fingers are fully extended. *Unlike* the other instances of the flat hand shape, however, his fingers are spread, as they are in instances of the curled hand shape. This ambiguous gesture is aligned with the speech "when creating the show, Stephen Colbert says". This speech segment both adds to the main line of inquiry by introducing the thing Noah loves, *creating the show, and* continues the micro-excursion by citing Colbert again. The mixed hand shape directly correlates to the mixed contribution of the utterance it is aligned with. It is unclear how to best represent this in the QUD analysis.

Second, though there are two utterances after the micro-excursion, there are four gestures. Interestingly, the two utterances are split perfectly in gesture into repeated background information (*the joy of the show*), and new focused information (*performing* versus *creating*). Furthermore, the repetition of the background information is reflected in an almost perfect repetition of a two-handed holding gesture, whereas the two pieces of contrasting new information are aligned with distinct gestures. The QUD analysis provided in (11) fails to capture this distinction.

4.4   Case Study 3: Attitude Expression

The final discourse fragment is from an interview with actor Jennifer Lawrence.[6] In this segment, Lawrence is describing the steps that spies supposedly take to tell their children they are spies. Lawrence performs a micro-excursion, commenting on the second step, and then returns to the main line of inquiry to finish the list. In this discourse fragment, Lawrence uses two distinct gesture types, differentiated by *orientation* rather than *shape*; her palm is turned upward before and after the micro-excursion (coded PU for 'palm up'), but turned downward during the micro-excursion (coded PD for 'palm down').

(12)   So I was like, how do you tell your kids that you're spies? And what he told me [...] he basically said that, when they're at a certain age, [*they take them to* the museum, the spy museum,]$_{PU1}$ [*they show them* Spy Kids,]$_{PU2}$ [*which is* a great film,]$_{PD1}$ [*and* then]$_{PD2}$ [*they take them* through the spy museum,]$_{PU3}$ [*and then they're like* 'we're spies'.]$_{PU4}$

For each listed step, Lawrence performs a presentational gesture with her palm turned upward (PU1-PU2 and PU3-PU4). In all four iterations, the gesture structure is the same; during the preparation phase the arm is bent at the elbow and the hand is moved toward the body; during the stroke the hand moves away from the body and the arm partially straightens; following the stroke the hand is

---

[6] File name: 2018-04-03_0635_US_KCBS_The_Late_Show_With_Stephen_Colbert.

held away from the body until the end of the co-occurring utterance. When she comments on the second step, expressing her attitude about the film Spy Kids, she performs an almost identical gesture, but with her palm turned down. In order to show the similarity between the strokes of *all* the gestures, two frames are included for each gesture, one showing the stroke, and one showing the post-stroke hold. This is also reflected in the transcript in (12) where the periods of movement (strokes and preparations) are italicized, and post-stroke holds are underlined.

In addition to a change in hand orientation, the beginning of the micro-excursion is also marked by a distinct gaze shift. As she is discussing the main line of inquiry, *how spies tell their kids they're spies*, Lawrence is either looking down or directly at Colbert. It is only at the very start of the micro-excursion, as she says *which I*, that she momentarily turns her head and shifts her gaze to the audience (PD1) (Fig. 3).

Fig. 3. Frames depicting the stroke and post-stroke hold of each gesture in the discourse fragment in 12.

This discourse fragment is the most straightforward structurally of the three examples discussed. The main question under discussion is explicitly set in the immediately preceding discourse context, and two of the four partial answers are marked overtly with the discourse marker *and then*, signaling a sequence relation. Unlike the previous examples, the QUD structure is relatively flat, each step adds information directly to the main question of *how spies to their kids they're spies*.

(13)   *PU Q1: How do spies tell their kids that they're spies?*

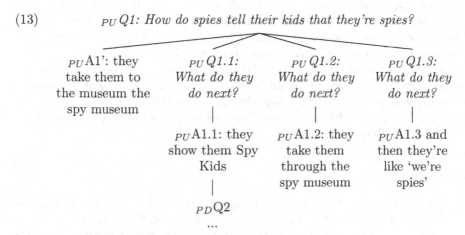

PU A1': they take them to the museum the spy museum	*PU Q1.1:* What do they do next?	*PU Q1.2:* What do they do next?	*PU Q1.3:* What do they do next?
	PU A1.1: they show them Spy Kids	*PU A1.2:* they take them through the spy museum	*PU A1.3* and then they're like 'we're spies'
	PD Q2 ...		

The correlation between a relatively flat and simple discourse structure and a lack of gestural variation is striking. In work on the palm-up open hand gesture, Müller observes that repeated presentational gestures often correspond to listed elements, including event sequences such as in this example [29]. However, I do not know of work that looks more generally at gesture-discourse relation repetition. This is a promising direction for future work.

5   Discussion

In this paper I have attempted to demonstrate the value of transitioning our monomodal models of discourse structure into multimodal frameworks. Within the Question Under Discussion framework, gesture information can be integrated into discourse analyses straightforwardly by indexing question-answer pairs with gesture features. In this work, I have only used a single feature as index, either hand shape (Sects. 4.2 and 4.3) or hand orientation (Sect. 4.4). Indexing question-answer pairs with even a single gesture feature was able to systematically differentiate utterances that contributed information to the main line of inquiry from those contributing to a secondary line of inquiry during micro-excursions from the discourse topic. However, we also saw that other features of the gesture sequences seemed to correlate to aspects of the discourse structure, including gaze direction, stroke repetition, and minor shape variations. In particular, we saw in the third example that the repetition of not only hand shape, but also of movement patterns reflected a repeated discourse relation, namely *sequence*. This suggests that using a *set* of gesture features such as *shape, position,* and *movement*, that can vary independently of each other may be able to inform a more detailed discourse structure.

Integrating gesture into existing models of discourse structure is not only relatively straightforward, it is also valuable to the development of theories in both discourse and gesture analysis. For example, using hand shape information helps to justify decisions about utterance attachment and the presence of sub-questions that may otherwise rely on ad hoc or even circular reasoning. For gesture studies, abstracting away from individual gestures to look at patterns of feature repetition and variation will allow us to make generalizations about gesture use that would otherwise escape our attention.

As we move away from written language biases in linguistic theory, and increasingly accept language as an inherently multimodal system, it becomes increasingly important to push our already developed theories toward multi-modality. This project has contributed to the early stages of this transformation in discourse analysis.

References

1. Alahverdzhieva, K., Lascarides, A., Flickinger, D.: Aligning speech and co-speech gesture in a constraint-based grammar. J. Lang. Model. **5**(3), 421–464 (2017)
2. Bavelas, J.B., Chovil, N., Lawrie, D.A., Wade, A.: Interactive gestures. Discourse Processes **15**(4), 469–489 (1992)
3. Bavelas, J.B., Coates, L., Johnson, T.: Listener responses as a collaborative process: the role of gaze. J. Commun. **52**(3), 566–580 (2002)
4. Bohle, U.: Gesture and conversational units. In: Body-Language-communication: An International Handbook on Multimodality in Human Interaction, vol. 2, pp. 1560–1567 (2014)
5. Bressem, J., Müller, C.: The family of away gestures: negation, refusal, and negative assessment. In: Body-Language-Communication: An International Handbook on Multimodality in Human Interaction, vol. 2, pp. 1592–1604 (2014)
6. Bressem, J., Müller, C.: The "negative-assessment-construction"-a multimodal pattern based on a recurrent gesture? Linguist. Vanguard **3**(s1), 1–9 (2017)
7. Büring, D.: On D-trees, beans, and accents. Linguist. Philos. **26**, 511–545 (2003)
8. Jannedy, S., Mendoza-Denton, N.: Structuring information through gesture and intonation. Interdiscip. Stud. Inf. Struct. **3**, 199–244 (2005)
9. Jokinen, K., Furukawa, H., Nishida, M., Yamamoto, S.: Gaze and turn-taking behavior in casual conversational interactions. ACM Trans. Interact. Intell. Syst. (TiiS) **3**(2), 1–30 (2013)
10. Jokinen, K., Nishida, M., Yamamoto, S.: Eye-gaze experiments for conversation monitoring. In: Proceedings of the 3rd International Universal Communication Symposium, pp. 303–308 (2009)
11. Kamp, H., Reyle, U.: From Discourse to Logic. Kluwer Academic Publishers, Dordrecht (1993)
12. Kendon, A.: Some functions of gaze-direction in social interaction. Acta psychologica **26**, 22–63 (1967)
13. Kendon, A.: Some relationships between body motion and speech. In: Siegman, A., Pope, B. (eds.) Studies in Dyadic Communication, pp. 177–210. Pergamon, Elmsford (1972)

14. Kendon, A.: Gesticulation and speech: two aspects of the process of utterance. Relat. Verbal Nonverbal Commun. **25**, 207–227 (1980)
15. Kendon, A.: Gestures as illocutionary and discourse structure markers in southern Italian conversation. J. Pragmat. **23**(3), 247–279 (1995)
16. Kendon, A.: Gesture: Visible Action as Utterance. Cambridge University Press, Cambridge (2004)
17. Kendon, A.: Spacing and orientation in co-present interaction. In: Esposito, A., Campbell, N., Vogel, C., Hussain, A., Nijholt, A. (eds.) Development of Multimodal Interfaces: Active Listening and Synchrony. LNCS, vol. 5967, pp. 1–15. Springer, Heidelberg (2010). https://doi.org/10.1007/978-3-642-12397-9_1
18. van Kuppevelt, J.: Discourse structure, topicality and questioning. J. Linguist., 109–147 (1995)
19. Lascarides, A., Stone, M.: Discourse coherence and gesture interpretation. Gesture **9**(2), 147–180 (2009)
20. Lascarides, A., Stone, M.: A formal semantic analysis of gesture. J. Semant. **26**(4), 393–449 (2009)
21. Leonard, T., Cummins, F.: The temporal relation between beat gestures and speech. Lang. Cogn. Processes **26**(10), 1457–1471 (2011)
22. Mann, W.C., Thompson, S.A.: Rhetorical structure theory: toward a functional theory of text organization. Text **8**(3), 243–281 (1988)
23. McClave, E.: Gestural beats: the rhythm hypothesis. J. Psycholinguist. Res. **23**(1), 45–66 (1994)
24. McClave, E.: Linguistic functions of head movements in the context of speech. J. Pragmat. **32**(7), 855–878 (2000)
25. McNeill, D.: Pointing and morality in Chicago. In: Pointing: Where Language, Culture, and Cognition Meet, pp. 293–306 (2003)
26. McNeill, D.: Gesture and Thought. University of Chicago Press, Chicago (2005)
27. McNeill, D., Cassell, J., Levy, E.T.: Abstract deixis. Semiotica **95**(1–2), 5–20 (1993)
28. McNeill, D., et al.: Catchments, prosody and discourse. Gesture **1**(1), 9–33 (2001)
29. Müller, C.: Forms and uses of the palm up open hand: a case of a gesture family. Semant. Pragmat. Everyday Gestures **9**, 233–256 (2004)
30. Riester, A.: Constructing QUD trees. In: Questions in Discourse, pp. 164–193. Brill (2019)
31. Roberts, C.: Information structure in discourse. In: Yoon, J., Kathol, A. (eds.) OSU Working Papers in Linguistics, vol. 49, pp. 91–136. Ohio State University (1996)
32. Roberts, C.: Information structure: towards an integrated formal theory of pragmatics. Semant. Pragmat. **5**, 1–69 (2012)
33. Schlenker, P.: Gestural grammar. Nat. Lang. Linguist. Theory **38**(3), 887–936 (2020)
34. Teßendorf, S.: Pragmatic and metaphoric-combining functional with cognitive approaches in the analysis of the "brushing aside gesture". In: Body-Language-Communication: An International Handbook on Multimodality in Human Interaction, vol. 2, pp. 1540–1557 (2014)

Patient-Provider Communication Training Models for Interactive Speech Devices

Patricia Ngantcha[1] , Muhammad Amith[2], Cui Tao[2(✉)], and Kirk Roberts[2]

[1] Texas Southern University, Houston, TX, USA
[2] School of Biomedical Informatics, University of Texas Health Science Center at Houston, Houston, TX, USA
{cui.tao,kirk.roberts}@uth.tmc.edu

Abstract. Patient-provider communication plays a major role in healthcare with its main goal being to improve the patient's health and build a trustworthy relationship between the patient and the doctor. Provider's efficiency and effectiveness in communication can be improved through training in order to meet the essential elements of communication that are relevant during medical encounters. We surmised that speech-enabled conversational agents could be used as a training tool. In this study, we propose designing an ontology-based interaction model that can direct software agents to train dental and medical students. We transformed sample scenario scripts into a formalized ontology training model that links utterances of the user and the machine that expresses patient-provider communication. We created two instance-based models from the ontology to test the operational execution of the model using a prototype software engine. The assessment revealed that the dialogue engine was able to handle about 62% of the dialogue links. Future direction of this work will focus on further enhancing and capturing the features of patient-provider communication, and eventual deployment for pilot testing.

Keywords: Ontology · Training · Dental education · Patient-provider communication · Conversational agent · Dialogue management

1 Introduction

Good patient-provider communication is an essential aspect of high-quality healthcare. It is a characteristic of clinical expertise that proves to be beneficial to both the provider and the patient. There is evidence that providers and patients do not communicate well and there is always a chance for possible misunderstandings [1]. Several misunderstandings that arise between providers and patients may be solved through a good rapport and communication. Inadequate provider-patient communication has been attributed to one of the root causes of increased violence in workplaces [2]. A rise in the lawsuits against doctors has been seen over the years and evidence has shown that poor communication between the provider and patient is an attributing factor [3, 4].

A good physician/dentist-patient communication greatly improves a patient's susceptibility to understand and follow the provider's instructions. This results in a reduction

© Springer Nature Switzerland AG 2021
V. G. Duffy (Ed.): HCII 2021, LNCS 12777, pp. 250–268, 2021.
https://doi.org/10.1007/978-3-030-77817-0_19

in patient anxiety, and an increase in patient satisfaction and adherence to healthy behaviors [5, 6], eventually leading to the desired treatment outcome. In a study done by Hall et al, they analyzed various outcomes of provider communication and found "adherence" to be a predictable outcome from good physician information delivery and more positive discussion [7]. Patient adherence is seen to be significantly related to provider-patient communication and that adherence, can be enhanced when a provider has undergone a training to be a better communicator [6]. The result of the analysis done by Zolnierek et al, showed that, "patients of physicians who communicate well have 19% higher adherence, and training physicians in communication skills improves patient adherence by 12%" [6]. *Therefore, communication proves to be an essential component of healthcare as shall be seen for both the dental and medical field.*

1.1 Training in Patient-Provider Communication

Effective communication is an essential element of medical care and should be a priority of medical education. According to Hausberg and colleagues, "[c]ommunication can be seen as the main ingredient in medical care" [8]. Professionalism being a fundamental aspect of good medical practice also demands not only knowledge and competence but also effective communication skill [9, 10]. As physicians progress from students to experts, their competence level has to expand as well from conducting generic communication task to successfully handling complex and demanding situations [11, 12] such as interacting with angry patients or families [13].

Medical students focus more on hands-on experiences to ameliorate their clinical skills and pay less attention to their communication skills. There is evidence that students' communication skills depreciate over time especially during their clinical years [14] and teaching these skill is neglected during those years [15]. Communication training is critical and may even be more important in residency training [16]. Medical students communication skills are indispensable when looking into their clinical competence [17], and "[c]ompetence in interpersonal skills should be demonstrated through sustained therapeutic patient relationships and in balancing the biotechnical and interpersonal aspects of care" [13]. Training medical students builds good communication skills during their formative years, and serves as an investment towards making good future practitioners [18]. These skills can be learned during training and perfected over the years.

1.2 Effect of Patient-Provider Communication

Patients need to have a good understanding of their disease, the associated risk and the benefit of consistent treatment in order to have improved healthcare outcomes. It is important to understand the "preferences", "beliefs" and "perspectives" [19] of patient during health evaluations so as to have a positive discussion and good information exchange. According to Epstein et al, physician-patient communication provides a means to manage the patient's uncertainty, address emotions, decision making [20] all contributing to a better understanding of the prognosis given [21]. Effective communication during patient consultation including history-taking and care planning has been positively correlated with emotional health, symptom management and pain control [22].

When there is a lack or poor communication between a provider and a patient, there is a higher chance of errors. Symptoms affecting patients may be missed or underestimated during consultations [23], which could potentially be attributed to lack of efficient communication between the physician and the patient. Experts estimate that approximately 98,000 people die in any given year from medical errors occurring in hospitals [24]. Before completing their education, physicians should demonstrate an ability to apply the essential skills of communication in a wide range of clinical situations. They should also be able to recognize and repair communication errors quickly [25].

Dental patient's satisfaction relies greatly on the relationship developed with their providers. A large portion of this relationship entails efficient communication and the quality of this communication is closely related to the overall patient satisfaction [26]. According to Bansal et al, quality of care depends on two major concepts which includes patient perspective and satisfaction [27]. Patients do not asses the medical competence of a provider; however, the experience they have during the process of care highlights their perception regarding the quality of the care they receive [28]. For a patient, what counts most in a provider-patient communication process is having a sense of partaking in the treatment process and a feeling of having their needs fully understood by the provider [29]. A good patient–provider communication should be able to give a patient that control they want over their illness [30] and treatment, while receiving comfort and support from the provider [31].

Dental providers differ from each other and patients are faced with a variety of providers to choose from. Every patient has preferences they take into consideration when selecting their ideal dental provider and these preferences are drawn by the dentist ability to "express empathy, manage pain and have good communication skill" [32]. Communication is mandatory in attaining patient satisfaction and has equal importance to a patient as the technical skill of the provider [33].

1.3 Ontology and Intelligent Agent Research

The canonical definition of ontologies is attributed to Gruber's, "an explicit specification of a conceptualization" through the use of binding concepts with expressive relationships for use by agents [34]. According to Feilmayr and Wöß, "[a]n ontology is a formal, explicit specification of a shared conceptualization that is characterized by high semantic expressiveness required for increased complexity" [35]. Ontologies are artifacts that represents domain knowledge using semantic web syntax languages expressed through OWL [36] and RDF [37, 38]. Using the syntax, we can encode high level concepts and logic, and then publish the artifact which can be shared and reused. Devices (i.e., agents) can read these artifacts and be able to conceptualize domain knowledge, thereby being able to perform reasoning capabilities and act upon that domain knowledge.

Some of the capabilities that are yielded through ontologies include facilitating exchange, sharing and standardization of data; providing support for natural language processing tools; represent complex information; and elicit machine reasoning using the "built-in" semantics of the artifacts.

The field of artificial intelligence (AI) research branches out to several categories – *knowledge representation, natural language understanding, learning, search, inference, planning and problem solving,* and *vision* [39]. Ontologies have wide-ranging impact on a few of the branches, most notability on *knowledge representation, inference*, and, within the context of the paper, *planning and problem solving. Knowledge representation* involves modeling physical and logical entities (e.g., using semantics and first order logic) and using these models to furnish meaning and understanding for agents. *Inference* involves producing missing or new information from available sources through logical reasoning. The machine reasoning from ontologies is capable of identifying categories of data, and analyzing logical consistency of the knowledge base. Agents that use the machine reasoning from ontologies are able to understand the meaning of concepts from the domain.

Planning and problem solving is another major topic in AI research. This topic involves a computational agent's use of deliberation to devise a plan for the agent to act on and then devising steps to perform the chosen act. This is accomplished through developing formal computational models for planning and reacting, and then developing technologies that support and implement the models. Overall goals of this area are to equip the computational agent with autonomous or automated behavior to preform intended tasks, and contribute to the ability to interact with a highly variable environment to account for scenarios unanticipated by the designers of the agent.

There exists some potential in utilizing ontologies for automated planning research [40–52]. Within a planning domain there exist *objects* (agents, non-agent things, etc.), *plans* and its *goals*, and the *actions* to enact those plans. As an artifact that represents the concepts in a domain, it can model and reason objects, actions, plans, and goals of a planning domain [40]. With the representational and inferencing ability, ontologies could potentially automate a specific interaction domain space between user and machine.

1.4 Utilizing Technology for Training Medical and Dental Students

In the last decades, there has been an unprecedented increase in the role of technology in healthcare at different levels. There are different aspects of technology that can train a medical student into becoming a well-rounded physician. These new teachings/ training technologies cover the vast spectrum of healthcare. For example; "virtual patient (VP) simulation training to support certain aspects of clinical education" [53], "devices for initial training of combat medics and first responders, devices for training surgical procedures, virtual reality systems for diagnosis and therapy, and team training systems for crisis or incident management" [54] which have being increasingly adopted.

In teaching communication skills in specific to prospective providers, virtual humans are frequently used during training, as they can provide a standardized experience for all students [55]. In the study done by Wiehagen, he proposed and focused on four categories of medical simulation devices for improving provider training. They included "PC-Based Interactive Systems, Digitally Enhanced Mannequins, Virtual Workbenches, and Total Immersion Virtual Reality" [54]. He further discussed on the limitations of these devices with some of them being the expensive and complex nature of the simulators. The findings in the study done by Yedidia suggest that medical schools that commit to incorporating communications training can expect improved student performance in regards to patient care [56]. Regardless of the prevalent acknowledgment of the importance of improved patient-provider communication, training in communications skills has not been thoroughly incorporated into most medical school curricula [57, 58] nor has it been subjected to evaluation across different schools [59].

Future providers should be able to communicate information, risk involved, and any uncertainty in ways that patients can understand and engage the patients when necessary in decisions taking [1]. Communication is a skill that can be taught in many different ways to future healthcare providers. For example, Stevens et al. developed a virtual standardized patient to teach students on developing their communication skills [60]. Also, actors are presently used to train University of Texas dental students at a cost greater than $100 per actor [61].

One takeaway based on our scoping review is the cost to deploy technology-based training. Another is the minimal initiative and research for standardizing the technology-based training for medical and dental students. Lastly, using technology to train these students (while not expansively used) has shown some promise in preparing the students for the challenges of patient-provider communication. To address some of these gaps we introduce the use of speech-based conversational agents (computational software that can automate discourse with consumers) that can be utilized to train dental and medical students to experience some aspects of patient-provider communication, and work towards ameliorating the communication skill of healthcare providers thereby building trust and overall satisfaction to both the patient and the provider; and provide a reusable and economical tool for medical training.

Noted earlier, the objectives of automated planning research are to develop computational models to implement self-directed deliberation and develop software and hardware to support the models. This project embarks on creating computational models through the use of ontologies to formalize patient-provider training and execute the models through a software agent engine using the ontology models. The impact of this work could lead us toward the deployment of our model-driven implementation that can improve communication efforts between patient and provider, reduce cost in training, and possibly standardize training to where the models can be shared and reused.

2   Methods and Tools

2.1   Ontology Framework for Health Communication

In our earlier work, we developed an ontology called *Patient Health Information Dialogue Ontology* (PHIDO) [62] that was conceived from data and dialogue flows from a Wizard of OZ study for patient-provider communication of vaccine counseling [63, 64]. The ontology provided a foundation to construct chains of utterances (*Speech Tasks*) and linking those chains to other chains to form network graph conversations. Figure 1 shows an explanation of the structure of the ontology model.

PHIDO's basic structure include a *Communication Goal*, which is a general goal for the machine to communicate. This class concept can be subclassed to specific communication goals for the agent to implement. For example, the Communication Goal can be subclassed to *Communicate Benefits of Yearly Check-ups* to encompass various speech tasks to fulfill the goal of communicating advantages of seeing one's dentist on a year basis.

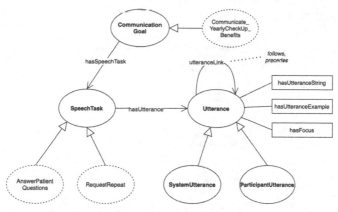

Fig. 1. Structure of Patient Health Information Dialogue Ontology. Dotted ellipses are example sub-classes.

The *CommunicationGoal* has speech tasks (*SpeechTasks*) connected through an object property of *hasSpeechTasks*. These *SpeechTasks* comprise of several sub-goals to fulfill their communication goal. Some of these tasks could be essential (answering patient questions, pleasantry interaction) or trivial tasks (repeating an utterance, requesting a repeat). Additionally, the *SpeechTasks* are comprised of linked utterances (*Utterance*) that are connected to *hasUtterance*. Each *Utterance* are linked with *utteranceLink* object property, which has sub-object properties of *follow* and *precedes* that are inverses of each other. The important utterances within the dialogue flow of this model are *ParticipantUtterance* (the utterance of the human user) and *SystemUtterance* (the utterance of the agent). Every Utterance is associated with *hasUtteranceString* (string text of what is to be evoked), *hasUtteranceExample* (sample utterances of that type of Utterance), and *hasFocus* (Boolean flag to indicate the position of the dialogue conversation). These links of *Utterances* models the network representation of the dialogue flow that we will discuss in the later sections. Overall, the PHIDO ontology model serves as a domain knowledge base for a specific type of health conversation with a consumer.

2.2 Ontology-Driven Software Engine for Conversational Agents

In a later study, we developed a software engine that uses the PHIDO model to reason and manage the health dialogue strategies [65]. This software engine is named *Conversational Ontology Operator (COO)*. The engine is a software wrapper that is composed of various software libraries – Stanford Core NLP [66], OWL-API [67], rdf4j [68], Hermit reasoner library [69], and some utility libraries. This engine aims to automate the dialogue interaction between a consumer and the agent. The automation of the dialogue is directed by the PHIDO model that maps out the potential sequences of utterances.

Figure 2 shows a brief description of the software engine's process of utilizing the *Utterance* classes and updating the position of the dialogue. The COO, the software engine, in tandem with the PHIDO model begins at an *Utterance* that has *hasFocus* flagged to true. The software engine determines what the next Utterance type is. If the Utterance type is a *SystemUtterance*, the next Utterance sends the *hasUtterance*

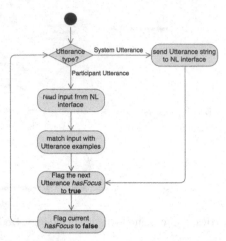

Fig. 2. Activity diagram showing the software engine loop's process of deciding the next steps in the dialogue interaction.

data string to the natural language interface, and then updates the *SystemUtterance* as the current *Utterance* by setting the *hasFocus* to true. If it is not, it captures input from the natural language interface and matches the input with two or more possible *ParticipantUtterances*. Once the engine finds the probable *ParticipantUtterance*, it flags the probable *Participant Utterance*'s *hasFocus* to true. This basic process loops through continuously. More detailed treatment of the process is provided in our previous work [65].

Compared to our previous efforts, the software engine initiates and directs the conversation mainly due to the ontology model representing a dialogue interaction as an expert in a health topic and the user as the passive consumer. In this effort, the software engine will be the passive actor in the interaction with the consumer, who is the domain expert (dental student). The system will be reliant on the dental student consumer to initiate and propel the conversation. To do this, we will create our PHIDO model to reflect this interaction, and the software engine will utilize the model to preform interaction decisions for dialogue.

2.3 Modeling Training Dialogue Interaction

In collaboration with the University of Texas Health Science Center's School of Dentistry, we were provided with sample training dialogue scenario scripts based on fictious personas representing a fictional archetype, essentially eight individual fictious patients. These eight training dialogue scripts were previously used in an experimental undergraduate project [61]. We drafted flow charts for each individual dialogue script using draw.io [70]. We qualitatively analyzed each of the drafted flow charts and attempted to find some common patterns that were shared in the charts. From our analysis, we derived and drafted a meta-level flow chart that captures the core interaction from the scripts. We also developed a list of *Utterance* types from our review of the script and assigned basic *Utterance* types to the meta-level flow chart. Table 1 shows the complete list of the *Utterances* classes specific to this domain, along with their association to the *ParticipantUtterance* and the *SystemUtterance* classes of PHIDO. Each specific *ParticipantUtterance* inquiries were paired with corresponding *SystemUtterances*. For example, an utterance that was *Oral_cancer_history_inquiry* (e.g., "Do you have a history of oral cancer in your family?") corresponds to an *Oral_cancer_history_information* response (e.g., "My father had oral cancer some years ago before he passed away ..").

In Fig. 3, we show the meta-level abstraction that models the basic dialogue interaction from our review of the dialogue scripts and charts. The dialogue interaction initiates with the *Participant Introduction Utterance* ("Hello, we will be completing your dental history today"). If the software engine does not capture the participant input, or if the input does not match any of the next *Utterances*, the PHIDO model will default to *Request Repeat Utterance* to ask for a repeat. Otherwise, the software engine will direct the conversation to the next *Utterance* of *Reciprocal System Introduction* ("Hi Doctor, okay! I am ready") and the *Chief Compliant inquiry*. Depending on the encoded utterance, the dialogue will segue to either the *Persona Appointment Agenda* where there is an utterance that expresses what the purpose of the patient visit is or go directly *Persona health information* that expresses a specific aspect of the patient issue. Afterwards, Fig. 3 outlines the dialogue interaction where there is a "drill down" inquiry by the student user probing for more information about the patient, and the patient responding with pieces of their personal health information ranging from cancer history, dental aesthetic information, prior appointments, etc.

Using Protégé 5.50 [71], we authored and represented the aforementioned dialogue interaction using the foundations provided through the PHIDO model as a new ontology artifact. Certain *Utterances*, like the *Participant Introduction Utterance*, were provided, but we added the *ParticipantUtterances* and *SystemUtterances* listed from Table 1 which are unique for this project. This ontology serves as a knowledge base to represent the training conversation in the scenarios that could be imported to COO, the aforementioned software engine that automate the dialogue interaction that specifically uses the PHIDO-based models. The ontology models created for the dialogue flow charts resulted in 142 Classes, 27 Object properties, and 6 Data properties.

2.4   Evaluation

To test the operationalization of the model, we developed two test data models based off of the two dialogue scenario scripts, representing two different patients, that had complex discourse. These test data models were published as two separate PHIDO-based ontologies with instance level data as linked utterances. Figure 4 shows the instances for one of the test ontologies.

We imported the test model ontologies into software engine which was executed through Eclipse IDE's command console. We interacted with the console in the role of dental student using the utterances from the test script and we recorded each successful and unsuccessful transition from one utterance to another on a spreadsheet. Later, we tallied the transition links accounting the number of successful and unsuccessful utterance links, and reviewed the test script models to assess the operational errors.

Table 1. Classification of the utterance pairs with sample descriptions. The colon(s) indicates depth of the class within the hierarchy.

ParticipantUtterance	SystemUtterance	Explanation/Example from script
Persona_health_inquiry	Persona_health_information	Patient's General care "Please tell me your height and weight", "patient's vital signs"
	:Confirmation_of_persona_health_information	Affirmative response to any inquiry. Applicable to any inquiry "Yes", "Ok"
	:Disconfirmation_of_persona_health_information	Dissenting response to any inquiry. Applicable to any inquiry. "No", "Sorry I don't …"
Persona_Dental_Health_inquiry	:Persona_Dental_Health_information	Questions specific to dental health "Tell me more about your toothache."
::Aesthetic_inquiry	::Aesthetic_information	Questions about appearance of teeth "Are you unhappy with the way your smile or how your teeth look or feel?", "Have you had your teeth Whitened before?"
::Anesthetic_inquiry	::Anesthetic_information	Questions about Anesthesia "Problems in past with local anesthetic?"
::Dental_Habit_inquiry	::Dental_Habit_information	Questions about Patient's involuntary dental habits. "Do you habitually clench or grind teeth during the day or night?"
::Oral_cancer_history_inquiry	::Oral_cancer_history_information	Patient's and family history of oral cancer "Do you have a history of oral cancer in your family?"
::Oral_Dental_Appliance_inquiry	::Oral_Dental_Appliance_information	Questions about present or past usage of oral appliance. "Yes, presently I am wearing my orthodontic retainers well…when I remember to wear them."
::Prior_Dental_Visit_inquiry	::Prior_Dental_Visit_information	Questions about past dental visits. "And do you remember what you had done the last time you saw a dentist?"

(continued)

Table 1. (*continued*)

ParticipantUtterance	SystemUtterance	Explanation/Example from script
Persona_General_Health_inquiry	::Persona_General_Health_information	Questions about patient's current status on health "Are you currently under the care of a physician?"
::Allergy_inquiry	::Allergy_information	Questions about patient's allergies. "Do you have any allergies (i.e., medications, foods, latex, cosmetics, and metals)?"
::Cancer_history_inquiry	::Cancer_history_information	Questions about previous or current cancer diagnosis. "What cancer were you diagnosed with?"
::Cardiovascular_inquiry	::Cardiovascular_information	Question relating to the heart "What treatment have you had for CAD (Coronary Artery Disease)?", "Do you have a pace maker?"
::Dermatological_inquiry	::Dermatological_information	Questions about skin conditions "Have you been diagnosed with any skin conditions?"
::Diabetic_History_inquiry	::Diabetic_History_information	Questions about diabetes "Do you have a first-degree relative with diabetes?"
::Endocrine_question	::Endocrine_information	Questions regarding the Endocrine system (glands) "Have you been diagnosed with any of the following conditions; Frequent thirst, Frequent urination?"
::Family_history_inquiry	::Family_history_information	Questions about diseases that run in patient's family "Do you have any diseases or medical problems that run in your family (i.e., arthritis, diabetes, cancer, cardiovascular disease)?"

(*continued*)

Table 1. (*continued*)

ParticipantUtterance	SystemUtterance	Explanation/Example from script
::HEENT_inquiry	::HEENT_information	Questions about Head, eyes, ears, nose, throat. "Have you been diagnosed with any of the following conditions? Head injury, Vision problems, Hearing, impairment, Allergic rhinitis, Chronic sinusitis"
::Hematological_Inquiry	::Hematological_information	Questions relating to blood disorders "Have you been diagnosed with any of the following conditions like Bleeding Disorders?"
::Immunological_inquiry	::Immunological_information	Questions regarding immune system. "Have you been diagnosed with an autoimmune disease?"
::Medication_inquiry	::Medication_information	Regarding patient's current medication status. "Are you currently taking any prescription medications?"
::Medication_dosage_inquiry	:::Medication_dosage_information	Questions about dosage of medication patient is currently taking. "Can you tell me the doses for each medication you're taking?"
::Musculoskeletal_inquiry	::Musculoskeletal_information	Question relating to the skeletal system "Have you been diagnosed with any of the following conditions? Arthritis, Osteoporosis, Gout, Other musculoskeletal disorders…"
::Neurological_and_Psychiatric_Inquiry	::Neurological_and_Psychiatric_information	Questions regarding to patient's mental state. "What form of depression have you been diagnosed with?"
::Obstetric_and_Gynecological_inquiry	::Obstetric_and_Gynecological_information	Questions regarding child bearing "Are you pregnant or think you might be pregnant?"

(*continued*)

Table 1. (*continued*)

ParticipantUtterance	SystemUtterance	Explanation/Example from script
::Physical_activity_and_Diet_inquiry	::Physical_activity_and_Diet_information	Question regarding patients physical activity and diet "What's your diet and physical activity like?"
::Previous_surgery_inquiry	::Previous_surgery_information	Past surgeries done. "I've had 3 surgeries for my melanoma, the first in January 1997…"
::Renal_and_Gastrointestinal_inquiry	::Renal_and_Gastrointestinal_information	Questions about kidneys/ relating to stomach and intestines "Have you been diagnosed with any of the following conditions? Renal failure or Insufficiency, Kidney stones/Stomach or duodenal ulcer, Crohn's disease",
::Respiratory_Inquiry	::Respiratory_information	Questions relating to respiratory system. "Do you presently suffer from any of the following? Chest pain exacerbated by deep breathing, Cough, Difficulty breathing, Sleep apnea/snoring, Wheezing"
::Sexually_transmitted_disease_inquiry	::Sexually_transmitted_disease_information	Questions about infectious diseases (STD) "Have you been diagnosed with any sexually transmitted disease such as Syphilis, HIV, or Herpes?"
::Social_Behavioral_inquiry	::Social_Behavioral_information	Questions regarding patient's leisure activities. "Do you smoke or consume tobacco?"

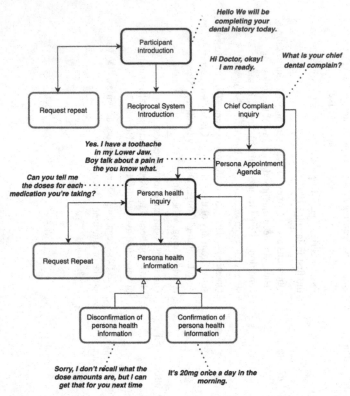

Fig. 3. Meta-level abstraction that represents the dialogue interaction for patient-provider training. Blue nodes are the *ParticipantUtterances* and the red nodes are the *SystemUtterances*.

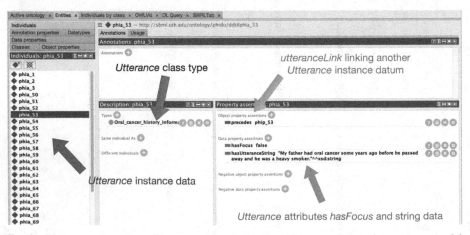

Fig. 4. Close-up screenshot of instances (utterance data) for one of the test ontology models viewed through Protégé.

3 Results

We created two test models from sample dialogues and performed an assessment with the test scripts through the dialogue software engine (that imported the knowledge base) to verify each dialogue chain in the script (235 dialogue chains in total). Figure 5 shows a sample demonstration from the command console prompt.

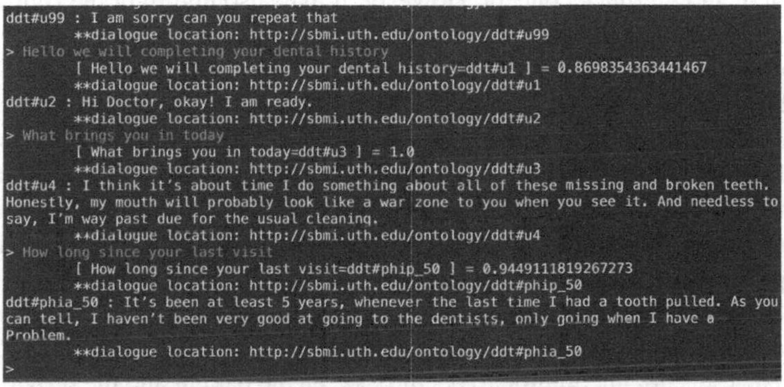

```
ddt#u99 : I am sorry can you repeat that
         **dialogue location: http://sbmi.uth.edu/ontology/ddt#u99
> Hello we will completing your dental history
         [ Hello we will completing your dental history=ddt#u1 ] = 0.8698354363441467
         **dialogue location: http://sbmi.uth.edu/ontology/ddt#u1
ddt#u2 : Hi Doctor, okay! I am ready.
         **dialogue location: http://sbmi.uth.edu/ontology/ddt#u2
> What brings you in today
         [ What brings you in today=ddt#u3 ] = 1.0
         **dialogue location: http://sbmi.uth.edu/ontology/ddt#u3
ddt#u4 : I think it's about time I do something about all of these missing and broken teeth.
Honestly, my mouth will probably look like a war zone to you when you see it. And needless to
say, I'm way past due for the usual cleaning.
         **dialogue location: http://sbmi.uth.edu/ontology/ddt#u4
> How long since your last visit
         [ How long since your last visit=ddt#phip_50 ] = 0.9449111819267273
         **dialogue location: http://sbmi.uth.edu/ontology/ddt#phip_50
ddt#phia_50 : It's been at least 5 years, whenever the last time I had a tooth pulled. As you
can tell, I haven't been very good at going to the dentists, only going when I have a
Problem.
         **dialogue location: http://sbmi.uth.edu/ontology/ddt#phia_50
>
```

Fig. 5. Sample execution of the dialogue model through the experimental software engine (COO) in debugging mode.

The total assessment from the two test models revealed that the dialogue engine was able to handle about 62% of the dialogue links (i.e., transition from one utterance to another). Most of the errors encountered were due to the link from *Persona health information* to *Persona health inquiry* (see Fig. 3), originating from the software engine's algorithm conflicting with a gap in ontology model. We deduced that a possible solution would be to add an utterance between *Persona health information* and *Persona health inquiry* to accommodate the error.

4 Discussion and Future Direction

This work adds to existing research on the utility of ontologies for automated planning and deliberation, specifically in the domain of dialogue management of patient- provider communication training. In addition, we exhibited possible extensions of our work with the PHIDO model and the COO engine for conversational agents beyond the vaccine education domain, and onto the domain of training dental students on patient-provider communication. Specifically, we demonstrated the flexibility of our previous works' approach by adapting the interaction to where the machine simulates the passive agent, taking on a non-expert role in the dialogue exchange with a human expert user.

In this study, we investigated the development of patient-provider training models to support training of prospective dental students to gain experience communicating with diverse patients. These training models were manifested as ontology artifacts that can be utilized by software and smart devices to automate the interaction of an individual patient from dialogue scripts that represented individual patient visits. We leveraged some of our previous work in an ontology-driven software engine for conversational agents for vaccine counseling but reorienting it to passive dental patient proxies. This arrangement places the conversational responsibility on the prospective dental student to initiate and engage the patient verbally.

While we were able to translate the dialogue scenario scripts to a formal model of dialogue interaction and execute it using our ontology-based method, we intend to refine the model to address the alluded the gap which we believe is easily rectifiable through the addition of an *Utterance* concept. However, it may also highlight the rigidity of the dialogue model, and we may encounter unanticipated challenges.

Bearing in mind we were given eight scripts/patients, the model we devised may be limited. In our previous work, we relied on using Wizard of Oz simulations as a way to gain authentic insight of how and what the dialogue interaction is executed. Through these simulations we were able to create the PHIDO-based model that mirror the authentic interactions of the simulation with live users. Our future direction may involve conducting simulations to gain an accurate insight, and also give us an avenue to pursue pilot testing with the automated deployment of the agent.

Another aspect for us to consider are some of the "trivial" social exchanges that sometimes occur between provider and patient. For example, small talk, or similar social emotional exchanges, is not uncommon to occur between the patient and the provider which has been cited to have some benefits in improving the relationship between them [72]. The dialogue scripts did contain minor small talk (e.g., parking issues by the patient), and our model did not include these types of interactions. However, a future research objective is to study social emotional exchanges in health care, and the underlying mechanism for us to represent it computationally.

There were also idiosyncrasies revealed in the different scripts that represented personality types through their utterances or choice words. One of our on-going, current focus involves the exploration of ontologies for personas that could link to the dialogue ontology model. These ontology-based personas could add a layer of interaction and possibly add more heterogeneous and individualized interaction of the agent.

5   Conclusion

Using scenarios provided by collaborators from UTHealth's School of Dentistry, we developed a standard computational model for patient-provider training using ontology-driven tools from our previous endeavors. Using sample utterances from the scenarios, we were able to automate the dialogue that mimics the fictionalized, individual patients from those scenario scripts. Our operational tests revealed some gaps that can be rectified through modification of the dialogue model. Future goals aim to further enhance the realism of the interaction by deploying or simulating the work with potential dental students and adding diverse, individualized dialogue discourse into the model.

Acknowledgements. Research was supported by the UTHealth Innovation for Cancer Prevention Research Training Program (Cancer Prevention and Research Institute of Texas grant # RP160015), the National Library of Medicine of the National Institutes of Health under Award Numbers R01LM011829 and R00LM012104, and the National Institute of Allergy and Infectious Diseases of the National Institutes of Health under Award Number R01AI130460 and R01AI130460-03S1.

References

1. Towle, A., Godolphin, W.: Framework for teaching and learning informed shared decision making. BMJ **319**, 766–771 (1999)
2. Khatri, R.: Client aggression towards health service providers in Nepal. Health Prospect. **14**, 22 (2015). https://doi.org/10.3126/hprospect.v14i2.14264
3. Virshup, B.B., Oppenberg, A.A., Coleman, M.M.: Strategic risk management: reducing malpractice claims through more effective patient-doctor communication. Am. J. Med. Qual. **14**, 153–159 (1999). https://doi.org/10.1177/106286069901400402
4. Ranjan, P., Kumari, A., Chakrawarty, A.: How can doctors improve their communication skills? J. Clin. Diagn. Res. **9**, JE01-04 (2015). https://doi.org/10.7860/JCDR/2015/12072. 5712
5. Anderson, R.: Patient expectations of emergency dental services: a qualitative interview study. Br. Dent. J. **197**, 331–334, discussion 323 (2004). https://doi.org/10.1038/sj.bdj.4811652
6. Haskard Zolnierek, K.B., DiMatteo, M.R.: Physician communication and patient adherence to treatment: a meta-analysis. Med. Care **47**, 826–834 (2009). https://doi.org/10.1097/MLR. 0b013e31819a5acc
7. Hall, J.A., Roter, D.L., Katz, N.R.: Meta-analysis of correlates of provider behavior in medical encounters. Med. Care **26**, 657–675 (1988). https://doi.org/10.1097/00005650-198807000-00002
8. Ong, L.M., de Haes, J.C., Hoos, A.M., Lammes, F.B.: Doctor-patient communication: a review of the literature. Soc. Sci. Med. **40**, 903–918 (1995). https://doi.org/10.1016/0277-9536(94)00155-m
9. Hausberg, M.C., Hergert, A., Kröger, C., Bullinger, M., Rose, M., Andreas, S.: Enhancing medical students' communication skills: development and evaluation of an undergraduate training program. BMC Med. Educ. **12**, 16 (2012). https://doi.org/10.1186/1472-6920-12-16
10. Modi, J.N., Anshu, Gupta, P., Singh, T.: Teaching and assessing professionalism in the Indian context. Indian Pediatr. **51**, 881–888 (2014). https://doi.org/10.1007/s13312-014-0521-x
11. Lipkin, M., Quill, T.E., Napodano, R.J.: The medical interview: a core curriculum for residencies in internal medicine. Ann. Inter. Med. **100**, 277–284 (1984). https://doi.org/10.7326/0003-4819-100-2-277
12. Smith, R.C., et al.: The effectiveness of intensive training for residents in interviewing. A randomized, controlled study. Ann. Inter. Med. **128**, 118–126 (1998). https://doi.org/10.7326/0003-4819-128-2-199801150-00008
13. Duffy, F.D., et al.: Assessing competence in communication and interpersonal skills: the Kalamazoo II Report. Acad. Med. **79**, 495–507 (2004)
14. Haidet, P., et al.: Medical student attitudes toward the doctor–patient relationship. Med. Educ. **36**, 568–574 (2002). https://doi.org/10.1046/j.1365-2923.2002.01233.x
15. Silverman, J.: Teaching clinical communication: a mainstream activity or just a minority sport? Patient Educ. Couns. **76**, 361–367 (2009). https://doi.org/10.1016/j.pec.2009.06.011
16. Rao, J.K., Anderson, L.A., Inui, T.S., Frankel, R.M.: Communication interventions make a difference in conversations between physicians and patients: a systematic review of the evidence. Med. Care **45**, 340–349 (2007). https://doi.org/10.1097/01.mlr.0000254516.049 61.d5
17. Chessman, A.W., Blue, A.V., Gilbert, G.E., Carey, M., Mainous, A.G.: Assessing students' communication and interpersonal skills across evaluation settings. Fam. Med. **35**, 643–648 (2003)
18. Choudhary, A., Gupta, V.: Teaching communications skills to medical students: introducing the fine art of medical practice. Int. J. Appl. Basic Med. Res. **5**, S41–S44 (2015). https://doi. org/10.4103/2229-516X.162273

19. Świątoniowska-Lonc, N., Polański, J., Tański, W., Jankowska-Polańska, B.: Impact of satisfaction with physician–patient communication on self-care and adherence in patients with hypertension: cross-sectional study. BMC Health Serv. Res. **20** (2020). https://doi.org/10. 1186/s12913-020-05912-0

20. Epstein, R.M., Fiscella, K., Lesser, C.S., Stange, K.C.: Why the nation needs a policy push on patient-centered health care. Health Aff. **29**, 1489–1495 (2010)

21. Ali, M.R.: Online virtual standardized patient for communication skills training. In: Proceedings of the 24th International Conference on Intelligent user Interfaces: Companion, pp. 155–156 (2019)

22. Skeels, M., Tan, D.S.: Identifying opportunities for inpatient-centric technology. In: Proceedings of the 1st ACM International Health Informatics Symposium, pp. 580–589. Association for Computing Machinery, New York (2010). https://doi.org/10.1145/1882992.1883087

23. Deandrea, S., Montanari, M., Moja, L., Apolone, G.: Prevalence of undertreatment in cancer pain. A review of published literature. Ann. Oncol. **19**, 1985–1991 (2008). https://doi.org/10. 1093/annonc/mdn419

24. Institute of Medicine (US) Committee on Quality of Health Care in America: To Err is Human: Building a Safer Health System. National Academies Press (US), Washington (DC) (2000)

25. Al-Busaidi, A.S.: Field guide to the difficult patient interview. Sultan Qaboos Univ. Med. J. **10**, 285–286 (2010)

26. Riley, J.L., Gordan, V.V., Hudak-Boss, S.E., Fellows, J.L., Rindal, D.B., Gilbert, G.H.: Concordance between patient satisfaction and the dentist's view: findings from The National Dental Practice-Based Research Network. J. Am. Dent. Assoc. **145**, 355–362 (2014). https:// doi.org/10.14219/jada.2013.32

27. Bansal, M., Gupta, N., Saini, G.K., Sharma, N.: Satisfaction level among patients visiting a rural dental institution toward rendered dental treatment in Haryana, North India. J. Educ. Health Promot. **7** (2018). https://doi.org/10.4103/jehp.jehp_20_18

28. Schoenfelder, T.: Patient satisfaction: a valid indicator for the quality of primary care? Primary Health Care **02** (2012). https://doi.org/10.4172/2167-1079.1000e106

29. Keating, N.L., Gandhi, T.K., Orav, E.J., Bates, D.W., Ayanian, J.Z.: Patient characteristics and experiences associated with trust in specialist physicians. Arch. Int. Med. **164**, 1015–1020 (2004). https://doi.org/10.1001/archinte.164.9.1015

30. Świątoniowska, N., Sarzyńska, K., Szymańska-Chabowska, A., Jankowska-Polańska, B.: The role of education in type 2 diabetes treatment. Diab. Res. Clin. Pract. **151**, 237–246 (2019). https://doi.org/10.1016/j.diabres.2019.04.004

31. Epstein, R.M., Hundert, E.M.: Defining and assessing professional competence. JAMA **287**, 226–235 (2002). https://doi.org/10.1001/jama.287.2.226

32. Gürler, G., Delilbaşı, Ç., Kaçar, İ.: Patients' perceptions and preferences of oral and maxillofacial surgeons in a university dental hospital. Eur. Oral Res. **52**, 137–142 (2018). https://doi. org/10.26650/eor.2018.483

33. Mitchell, S.T., et al.: Satisfaction with dental care among patients who receive invasive or non-invasive treatment for non-cavitated early dental caries: findings from one region of the National Dental PBRN. BMC Oral Health **17** (2017). https://doi.org/10.1186/s12903-017-0363-8

34. Gruber, T.: What is an Ontology? https://web.archive.org/web/20100716004426/http://www-ksl.stanford.edu/kst/what-is-an-ontology.html

35. Feilmayr, C., Wöß, W.: An analysis of ontologies and their success factors for application to business. Data Knowl. Eng. **101**, 1–23 (2016)

36. W3C Owl Working Group and others: OWL 2 Web Ontology Language Document Overview, 2nd edn. http://www.w3.org/TR/owl2-overview/. Accessed 09 July 2014

37. Brickley, D., Guha, R.V., McBride, B.: RDF Primer. https://www.w3.org/TR/rdf-schema/. Accessed 01 Jan 2021

38. Klyne, G., Carroll, J.J., McBride, B.: Resource Description Framework (RDF) 1.1 Concepts and Abstract Syntax. https://www.w3.org/TR/rdf11-concepts/. Accessed 01 Jan 2021
39. Barr, A.: The Handbook of Artificial Intelligence. William Kaufmann, Inc. (1981)
40. Gil, Y.: Description logics and planning. AI Mag. **26**, 73–73 (2005)
41. Giacomo, G.D., Iocchi, L., Nardi, D., Rosati, R.: Description logic-based framework for planning with sensing actions. In: Proceedings of the 1997 International Workshop on Description Logics (1997)
42. Sirin, E., Parsia, B., Wu, D., Hendler, J., Nau, D.: HTN planning for web service composition using SHOP2. J. Web Semant. **1**, 377–396 (2004)
43. Kuter, U., Sirin, E., Nau, D., Parsia, B., Hendler, J.: Information gathering during planning for web service composition. In: International Semantic Web Conference, pp. 335–349 (2004)
44. McIlraith, S., Son, T.C.: Adapting golog for composition of semantic web services. Kr **2**, 2 (2002)
45. Sohrabi, S., McIlraith, S.A.: Preference-based web service composition: a middle ground between execution and search. In: Patel-Schneider, P.F., et al. (eds.) ISWC 2010. LNCS, vol. 6496, pp. 713–729. Springer, Heidelberg (2010). https://doi.org/10.1007/978-3-642-17746-0_45
46. De Giacomo, G., Iocchi, L., Nardi, D., Rosati, R.: A theory and implementation of cognitive mobile robots. J. Logic Comput. **9**, 759–785 (1999)
47. Levesque, H.J., Reiter, R., Lespérance, Y., Lin, F., Scherl, R.B.: GOLOG: a logic programming language for dynamic domains. J. Logic Program. **31**, 59–83 (1997)
48. Lespérance, Y., Levesque, H.J., Lin, F., Marcu, D., Reiter, R., Scherl, R.B.: A logical approach to high-level robot programming–a progress report. In: Control of the Physical World by Intelligent Systems, Papers From the 1994 AAAI Fall Symposium, pp. 79–85 (1994)
49. Hartanto, R., Hertzberg, J.: Fusing DL reasoning with HTN planning. In: Dengel, A.R., Berns, K., Breuel, T.M., Bomarius, F., Roth-Berghofer, T.R. (eds.) KI 2008. LNCS (LNAI), vol. 5243, pp. 62–69. Springer, Heidelberg (2008). https://doi.org/10.1007/978-3-540-85845-4_8
50. Waibel, M., et al.: Roboearth. IEEE Rob. Autom. Mag. **18**, 69–82 (2011)
51. Tenorth, M., Beetz, M.: KnowRob: a knowledge processing infrastructure for cognition-enabled robots. Int. J. Rob. Res. **32**, 566–590 (2013)
52. Lemaignan, S., Ros, R., Mösenlechner, L., Alami, R., Beetz, M.: ORO, a knowledge management platform for cognitive architectures in robotics. In: 2010 IEEE/RSJ International Conference on Intelligent Robots and Systems, pp. 3548–3553 (2010)
53. Carnell, S., Halan, S., Crary, M., Madhavan, A., Lok, B.: Adapting virtual patient interviews for interviewing skills training of novice healthcare students. In: Brinkman, W.-P., Broekens, J., Heylen, D. (eds.) IVA 2015. LNCS (LNAI), vol. 9238, pp. 50–59. Springer, Cham (2015). https://doi.org/10.1007/978-3-319-21996-7_5
54. Wiehagen, G.B.: Medical simulation and training: breakthroughs and barriers. In: Proceedings of the 2008 Summer Computer Simulation Conference, pp. 1–7. Society for Modeling & Simulation International, Vista, CA (2008)
55. Carnell, S., Lok, B., James, M.T., Su, J.K.: Predicting student success in communication skills learning scenarios with virtual humans. In: Proceedings of the 9th International Conference on Learning Analytics & Knowledge, pp. 436–440. Association for Computing Machinery, New York (2019). https://doi.org/10.1145/3303772.3303828
56. Yedidia, M.J.: Effect of communications training on medical student performance. JAMA **290**, 1157 (2003). https://doi.org/10.1001/jama.290.9.1157
57. Makoul, G.: Essential elements of communication in medical encounters: The Kalamazoo consensus statement. Acad. Med. **76**, 390–393 (2001)
58. Novack, D.H., Volk, G., Drossman, D.A., Lipkin Jr., M.: Medical interviewing and interpersonal skills teaching in US medical schools: progress, problems, and promise. JAMA **269**, 2101–2105 (1993). https://doi.org/10.1001/jama.1993.03500160071034

59. Aspegren, K.: BEME Guide No. 2: teaching and learning communication skills in medicine-a review with quality grading of articles. Med. Teach. **21**, 563–570 (1999). https://doi.org/10.1080/01421599978979
60. Stevens, A., et al.: The use of virtual patients to teach medical students history taking and communication skills. Am. J. Surg. **191**, 806–811 (2006). https://doi.org/10.1016/j.amjsurg.2006.03.002
61. Lehman, L., Lu, C., Mathews, J., Tanwani, A.: Use of a Smart Speaker Device to Simulate Doctor-Patient Communication in Health Professions Education. Biomedical Engineering, Capstone Design., Cockrell School of Engineering - The University of Texas at Austin (2018)
62. Amith, M., Roberts, K., Tao, C.: Conceiving an application ontology to model patient human papillomavirus vaccine counseling for dialogue management. BMC Bioinform. **20**, 1–16 (2019)
63. Amith, M., et al.: Examining potential usability and health beliefs among young adults using a conversational agent for HPV vaccine counseling. AMIA Summits Transl. Sci. Proc. **2020**, 43 (2020)
64. Amith, M., et al.: Early usability assessment of a conversational agent for HPV vaccination. Stud. Health Technol. Inform., 17–23 (2019). https://doi.org/10.3233/978-1-61499-951-5-17
65. Amith, M., et al.: Conversational ontology operator: patient-centric vaccine dialogue management engine for spoken conversational agents. BMC Med. Inform. Decis. Mak. **20**, 259 (2020). https://doi.org/10.1186/s12911-020-01267-y
66. Manning, C.D., Surdeanu, M., Bauer, J., Finkel, J.R., Bethard, S., McClosky, D.: The stanford CoreNLP natural language processing toolkit. In: ACL (System Demonstrations), pp. 55–60 (2014)
67. Horridge, M., Bechhofer, S.: The OWL API: a Java API for OWL ontologies. Semant. Web **2**, 11–21 (2011)
68. Eclipse Foundation: Eclipse RDF4J (2019)
69. Glimm, B., Horrocks, I., Motik, B., Stoilos, G., Wang, Z.: HermiT: an OWL 2 reasoner. J. Autom. Reason. **53**, 245–269 (2014)
70. diagrams.net: draw.io. (2020)
71. Musen, M.A.: The protégé project: a look back and a look forward. AI Matters **1**, 4–12 (2015). https://doi.org/10.1145/2757001.2757003
72. Maupome, G., Holcomb, C., Schrader, S.: Clinician-patient small talk: comparing fourth-year dental students and practicing dentists in a standardized patient encounter. J. Dent. Educ. **80**, 1349–1356 (2016)

Semantically Related Gestures Move Alike: Towards a Distributional Semantics of Gesture Kinematics

Wim Pouw[1,2](✉) ⓘ, Jan de Wit[3] ⓘ, Sara Bögels[4] ⓘ, Marlou Rasenberg[2,5] ⓘ,
Branka Milivojevic[1] ⓘ, and Asli Ozyurek[1,2,5] ⓘ

[1] Donders Centre for Cognition, Brain, and Behaviour, Radboud University Nijmegen,
Nijmegen, The Netherlands
w.pouw@donders.ru.nl
[2] Max Planck Institute for Psycholinguistics, Nijmegen, The Netherlands
[3] Tilburg School of Humanities and Digital Sciences, Tilburg University, Tilburg,
The Netherlands
[4] Department of Communication and Cognition, Tilburg University, Tilburg, The Netherlands
[5] Center for Language Studies, Radboud University Nijmegen, Nijmegen, The Netherlands

Abstract. Most manual communicative gestures that humans produce cannot be looked up in a dictionary, as these manual gestures inherit their meaning in large part from the communicative context and are not conventionalized. However, it is understudied to what extent the communicative signal as such—bodily postures in movement, or kinematics—can inform about gesture semantics. Can we construct, in principle, a distribution-based semantics of gesture kinematics, similar to how word vectorization methods in NLP (Natural language Processing) are now widely used to study semantic properties in text and speech? For such a project to get off the ground, we need to know the extent to which semantically similar gestures are more likely to be kinematically similar. In study 1 we assess whether semantic word2vec distances between the conveyed concepts participants were *explicitly instructed* to convey in silent gestures, relate to the kinematic distances of these gestures as obtained from Dynamic Time Warping (DTW). In a second director-matcher dyadic study we assess kinematic similarity between *spontaneous* co-speech gestures produced between interacting participants. Participants were asked before and after they interacted how they would name the objects. The semantic distances between the resulting names were related to the gesture kinematic distances of gestures that were made in the context of conveying those objects in the interaction. We find that the gestures' semantic relatedness is reliably predictive of kinematic relatedness across these highly divergent studies, which suggests that the development of an NLP method of deriving semantic relatedness from kinematics is a promising avenue for future developments in automated multimodal recognition. Deeper implications for statistical learning processes in multimodal language are discussed.

Keywords: Manual gesture kinematics · NLP · Speech · Semantics · Time series comparison

V. G. Duffy (Ed.): HCII 2021, LNCS 12777, pp. 269–287, 2021.
https://doi.org/10.1007/978-3-030-77817-0_20

1 Introduction

Humans exploit a multitude of embodied means of communication, where each mode of communication has its own semiotic affordances. Manual and whole-body communicative movements, such as co-speech gestures or signs in a sign language, have been suggested to leverage iconicity to convey meaning [1–3]. Iconicity is a special type of referential act, as the form of the message can inform more directly about the content of the message as compared to arbitrary symbols, by establishing a spatio-temporal resemblance between form and referent; for example, by moving in a way that resembles brushing one's teeth (form), one can convey a meaning related to brushing one's teeth (content). What is particularly astonishing is that during spoken language manual iconic references are spontaneously constructed, in a way that does not necessarily need to be repeated later when the referent is mentioned again [4], nor does it need to be replicated exactly when gestured about it in a similar context by someone else [5]. Thus even when two gestures have a similar meaning and occur in a similar speech context, they do not need to be replicated in form. This "repetition without repetition" [6]—a good characterization of human movement in general—is one of the reasons why the iconic meaning of gestures is generally held to be unformalizable in a dictionary-like way [7, 8], with the exception of more conventionalized emblem gestures (e.g., "thumbs up"; e.g., [8, 9]). To complicate matters further, gestures' meaning is dependent on what is said in speech during gesturing, as well as the wider pragmatic context. All these considerations might temper expectations of whether information about the gesture's content can be derived from the gesture's form—bodily postures in motion, i.e., kinematics.

It is however an assumption that the kinematics of gestures are poorly informative of the meaning of a depicting or iconic gesture. Though it is undeniable there is a lot of variance in gestures' form to meaning mapping, at some level there is invariance that allows depicting gestures to depict, some kind of abstract structural similarity at a minimum [10]. It is also possible that gestures are semantically associated by the mode of representation [11, 12] they share (which is not the same as, but related to certain kinematic properties such as handshape). For example, it has been shown that gestures for manipulable objects are likely to be of the type "acting" (e.g., moving your hand as if you are brushing your teeth to depict toothbrush) compared to gestures depicting non-manipulable objects (which are more likely to be "drawn", e.g. tracing the shape of a house with the hands or index fingers) [3]. Gaining empirical insight in whether we can glean some semantic information from kinematics in a statistical fashion, is an important project as it would not only calibrate our deep theoretical convictions about how gesture kinematics convey meaning, but it would also pave the way for computer scientists to develop natural language processing (NLP) algorithms tailored for iconic gesture kinematics vis-à-vis semantics. Modern NLP procedures such as word embedding vectorization (word2vec) operate on the assumption of distributional semantics, holding simply that tokens that co-occur in similar contexts are likely semantically related. In the current study we will assess another assumption that could be powerfully leveraged by NLP procedures tailored to gesture semantics: Do gestures that semantically relate to one another move as one another?

If gestures do indeed show such statistical dependencies in form and meaning on the level of interrelationships, they offer a source of simplification of content that is similar in nature to statistical dependencies that characterize linguistic systems in general and are exploited by NLP [13]. Note though, that distributional semantics is something that simplifies the learning of a language for humans too, as for example an infant can leverage a language's syntactic, semantic, and phonological co-dependencies via statistical learning [14]. Similarly, the current investigation of potential statistical co-dependencies between semantic and kinematic relatedness in gestures are key for coming to an understanding of how humans really learn and use language, which is a sense-making process steeped in a rich multimodal context of different forms of expression [15].

1.1 Current Investigation

In two motion-tracking studies we assess whether the semantic (dis)similarity between concepts that are putatively conveyed by gestures, are related to the (dis)similarity of the gesture's kinematics. We computed word2vec distances between verbal labels of the concepts conveyed by gestures, and we computed kinematic distances using a well-known time-series comparison algorithm called Dynamic Time Warping (see e.g., [16–18]). By computing all possible distances between conveyed concepts, as well as gesture kinematics, we essentially map out a semantic and kinematic space that can be probed for covariances [13, 16, 19, 20].

For a large-scale charades-style study 1 with more than 400 participants, the concepts that were conveyed were defined from the outset, as participants were asked to convey in their own way a particular concept with a silent gesture (i.e., without speech) to a robot who was tasked to recognize the gesture [21]. Silent gestures are an idealized test case for us as they are designed to be maximally informative in that modality, and the structured nature of the interaction allows us to more definitively identify the semantic targets of the gestures.

However, silent gestures are not a common mode of expression in humans (note, signs in sign languages are not the same as silent gestures; for an introduction see [22]). Indeed, in most cases, gestures are generated spontaneously in the context of concurrent speech. There, speech often shares a communicative load with co-speech gestures, and verbally situates what is meant with a gesture [7]. Whatever semantic-kinematic scaling pattern we might find for highly communicatively exaggerated silent gestures, need thus not be replicated for co-speech gestures which perform their referential duties in a more speech-situated way.

In study 2, we opportunistically analyze dyadic interactions from a smaller lab study [23]. Dyads performed a director-matcher task, in which they took turns to describe and find images of novel 3D objects ('Fribbles' [24]). For each Fribble, we analyzed the gestural movements produced by both participants in the context of referring to that Fribble. Before and after the interaction, participants were individually asked to come up with a verbal label/name (henceforth "name") for each Fribble (1–3 words) that would enable their partner to identify the correct Fribble. This allows us, similarly to study 1, to relate gesture kinematic differences to possible semantic word2vec differences of the Fribble names before as well as after the interaction task. Importantly, with regards to study 1, we will analyze kinematic and semantic distances between individuals in a pair, such that we assess how gesture differences between Fribble i and j between participants in a pair relate to naming differences between participants for those Fribbles i and j. We thus analyze shared semantic and kinematic spaces, in search for covariances in their geometry.

2   General Approach

In both studies we computed the semantic ($\mathbf{D^s}$) and kinematic spaces ($\mathbf{D^g}$). Semantic spaces comprised semantic distances between concepts (study 1) or object names (study 2). Kinematic spaces comprised kinematic distances between the sets of gestures produced for two concepts (study 1) or two objects (study 2).

We used word2vec to compute semantic distances (1 - cosine similarity) between concepts that were (putatively) conveyed in gesture. To determine semantic dissimilarity between concepts we used SNAUT [25] to compute cosine similarity based on a Dutch model CoNLL17 [26][1].

For the kinematic distance computation, we use Dynamic Time Warping (DTW). DTW is a well-known time series comparison algorithm, and it measures the invariance of time series under variations in time shifts. It does this by finding a warping line between time series, by constructing a matrix containing all distances between time series' values. The warping line is a trajectory over adjacent cells of the matrix which seeks the lowest distances between the time series values (see for details, [17, 18]). Conceptually, this amounts to aligning the time series through warping and then calculating the distances (or error) still remaining. The distance score is then normalized for the lengths of the time series, so that the possible amount of accumulated error is similar for time series of different lengths. The time series can be multivariate (e.g., horizontal and vertical position of a body part through time) such that the DTW is performed in a multidimensional space (for a visual explanation see, [16]). In essence the distance scores that are computed provide a summary value of the differences between two time series. In our case a time series defined the kinematic x, y, and z trajectory of a body part. We used an unconstrained version of DTW [17] implemented in R-package 'dtw', whereby beginning and trailing ends were not force aligned, thereby circumventing issues of discrepant errors that can be produced when the start and end points of the meaningful part of an event in a time series are not well defined [27][2].

Given the exploratory nature of the current analysis, and given that we will be testing our hypothesis in two datasets, we will treat kinematic-semantic effects as statistically reliable at an Alpha of $<0.025(0.05/2)$.

Anonymized data and scripts supporting this report can be retrieved from our Open Science Framework page (https://osf.io/yu7kq/).

---

[1] The model used for word2vec can be downloaded here: http://vectors.nlpl.eu/repository/.

[2] For a visual example of how time series are compared by Dynamic Time Warping, see our supplemental figure https://osf.io/dz9vx/. This example from study 1, shows the vertical displacement of the left hand tip for three compared gestures that conveyed the concept "airplane".

2.1 Study 1

Study 1 utilizes the 'NEMO-Lowlands iconic gesture dataset' [21] for which 3D kine-matic data (Microsoft Kinect V2, sampling at 30 Hz) was collected for 3715 gestures performed by 433 participants (children and adults) conveying 35 different concepts (organized within 5 themes containing 7 concepts each: e.g., animals, musical instru-ments). Participants were tasked with conveying a concept to a robot with a silent gesture, much like playing charades. The robot was tasked with recognizing the gesture via a kinematic comparison with a stored lexicon. If it could not recognize the gesture, the participant was asked to perform the gesture again and such trials were also included in the final gesture dataset. Importantly, participants were not instructed how to gesture, and creatively produced a silent gesture for the requested concepts[3].

We computed the semantic distance for each pair of concepts using word2vec, rang-ing from a semantic dissimilarity or distance of 0 (minimum) to 1 (maximum). These semantic dissimilarity scores filled a symmetrical 35×35 semantic distance matrix $\mathbf{D^s}$ (without diagonal values) containing comparisons between each concept c_i and concept c_j:

$$D^s_{i,j} = 1 - cosine\_similarity(c_i, c_j), i \neq j$$

Gesture kinematic distance scores filled a similar 35×35 matrix, $\mathbf{D^g}$, with distances between all combinations of gestures belonging to concepts i and j, calculated using dynamic time warping:

$$D^g_{i,j} = ave \sum_{k_i, l_j}^{n_i, m_j} ave \sum_{o=1}^{p} dtw(t_{k_i o}, t_{l_j lo}), i \neq j$$

Kinematic distances ($D_{i,j}$) were computed between all combinations of gestures k_i for concept i, and gestures l_j for concept j, except not for when $i = j$ (i.e., no diagonal values were computed). The computations were performed for all combinations of gesture set n_i and gesture set m_j, and then averaged. A dynamic time warping algorithm ['dtw(query, referent)'] was used, where for each referent gesture k_i and each query gesture l_j a multivariate time series t was submitted, containing the x, y, and z trajectories for key point o (e.g., o = left wrist x, y, z). The computed distances were averaged over the total of $p = 5$ key points. We have previously observed that these body parts (as indexed by key points), left/right hand tip, left/right wrist, and head, are important for assessing the variance in silent gesture [22]. Note that each time series submitted to DTW was first z-scaled and centered, and time series were smoothed with a 3rd order Kolmogorov-Golai filter with a span of 2 frames (a type of Gaussian moving average filter).

Since we use an unconstrained version of DTW, computations can yield asymmetric results depending on which time series is set as the referent, so for each DTW distance calculation we computed the distance twice by interchanging the referent and query time series and then averaging, yielding a single distance score. Please see our OSF

---

[3] Due to time constraints, participants only performed gestures for five randomly selected concepts. The repetition rate due to the robot's failure to recognize the gesture was 79%.

page (https://osf.io/39ck2/) for the R code generating the kinematic matrix from the time series.

In sum, our analyses yielded a semantic distance matrix $\mathbf{D^s}$ and a similarly formatted kinematic distance matrix $\mathbf{D^g}$ containing information about semantic and kinematic (dis)similarity between each combination of 2 of the 35 concepts. This then allows us to assess whether semantic dissimilarity between concepts is related to the kinematic dissimilarity of the associated gestures. Figure 1 provides a geometric representation of the procedure's logic.

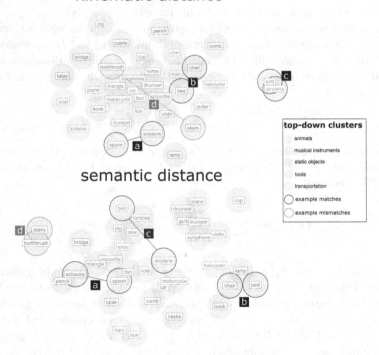

Fig. 1. Here the geometric/network representation is shown (using t-distributed stochastic neighbor embedding, for 2D projection through multidimensional scaling [28]) of the kinematic (above) and semantic distances between concepts conveyed by participants in the NEMO-Lowlands dataset. Examples of matches and a mismatch are highlighted, where matches (black boxes a–c) indicate that concepts that were kinematically alike were also semantically alike (e.g., spoon and scissors), and two red boxes (d) showing examples where concepts were kinematically dissimilar but semantically similar (e.g., stairs and toothbrush). Note that it could also be the other way around, such that there is high kinematic similarity but low semantic similarity (though we did not find this in the current dataset). (Color figure online)

2.2 Results Study 1

We performed mixed linear regression (see Fig. 2; analysis script: https://osf.io/kvmfc/) to assess whether semantic distances would scale with kinematic distances, with random intercepts for the concept that is used as reference (models with random slopes for the effect of semantic distance did not converge). Relative to a base model predicting the overall mean of kinematic distance, a model including semantic distance was reliably better in explaining variance, Chi-squared change $(1) = 16.23$, $p < .001$; Model coefficient semantic distance $b = 0.033$, $t(560) = 191.43$, $p < .001$, Cohen's $d = 0.34$.

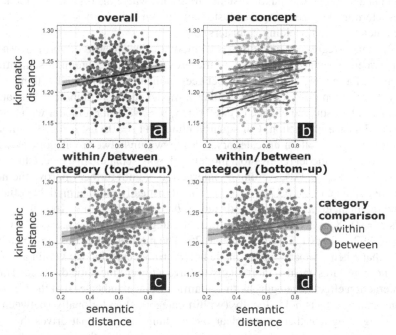

Fig. 2. Relations between semantic and kinematic distances are shown, overall slope and the simple correlation coefficient is given with colored points indicating the referent object (e.g., plane, bird) (panel a). Panel (b) shows separate slopes for each concept. Panel (c) shows different colors and slopes for the within top-down category (e.g., transportation-transportation) or between category comparisons (e.g., static object-transportation), and panel (d) shows different colors and slopes for within bottom-up category (e.g. cluster1-cluster1) and between category (e.g., cluster1-cluster2) comparisons. We can see that there is a positive relation between semantic and kinematic distance, which is globally sustained, such that within and between categories that positive relation persists. This indicates that gesture comparisons within a similar domain (either defined through some thematization by the researcher, or based on the structure of the data) are as likely to be related to semantic distance as when those comparisons are made across domains. Note further that it seems that semantic distances in panel (c) are lower for within category comparisons, suggesting that top-down categories are reflected in the semantic word2vec results (this aligns with Fig. 1 showing that categories tend to cluster in semantic space).

It is possible that this general weak but highly reliable relation between semantic vs. kinematic distance mainly relies on comparisons between concepts that are highly dissimilar, so that, say, the kinematic distance between two concepts that are within the same category (e.g., bus and train are in the category transportation) does not scale with semantic distance. To assess this, we compared the relation between kinematic vs. semantic distance for comparisons that are within a defined category versus between different categories. Firstly, we can use the top-down categories (e.g., transportation, musical instruments) that were used to group the stimulus set for the original study [21]. Secondly we used a bottom-up categorization approach, by performing k-means clustering analysis on the semantic distance matrices, where the optimal cluster amount was pre-determined by assessing the cluster amount with the highest average silhouette (i.e., silhouette method; yielding 2 clusters).

Further mixed regression modeling onto kinematic distance was performed by adding within/between category comparisons to the previous model containing semantic distances, as well as adding an interaction between semantic distance and within/between category. For the top-down category, neither a model adding within/between category as a predictor, Chi-squared change (1) = 0.0005, $p = .982$, nor a model with category x semantic distance interaction, Chi-squared change (1) = 0.113, $p = .737$, improved predictions. For the bottom-up category, adding within/between category as a main effect improved the model relative to a model with only semantic distance, Chi-squared change (1) = 8.50, $p = .004$. Adding an interaction did not further improve the model, Chi-squared change (1) = 0.17, $p = .674$. The statistically reliable model coefficients, indicated the main effect of semantic distance, $b = 0.020$, $t (559) = 166.29$, $p < .001$, Cohen's $d = 0.18$, as well as a main effect of category, $b_{\text{within vs. between}} = -0.006$, $t (559) = -2.92$, $p < .001$, Cohen's $d = -0.25$. The main effect of bottom-up category, indicates that when comparisons are made between concepts that are within a semantic cluster, those gestures are also more likely to have a lower kinematic distance. The lack of an interaction effect of category with semantic distance, indicates that the kinematic-semantic scaling effects holds locally (within categories) and globally (between categories), suggesting that there is no clear overarching category that drives the current effects. If this would be the case we would have found that the semantic-kinematic scaling relation would be absent for within category comparisons.

To conclude, we obtain evidence that silent gestures have a weak but reliable tendency to be more kinematically dissimilar if the concepts they are supposed to convey are also more semantically dissimilar.

3   Study 2

In study 2, there were 13 pairs, consisting of 26 participants (11 women and 15 men, $M_{\text{age}} = 22$ years, $Range_{\text{age}} = 18$–32 years). This is subset of the original data (20 pairs), as we only included data for which we also have some human gesture annotations for, which we could relate to our automatic processing. The participants were randomly grouped into 13 pairs (5 female dyads, 3 male dyads, and 5 mixed dyads) who performed a director-matcher task. The interlocutors took turns to describe and find images of novel 3D objects ('Fribbles' [24]). In each trial, a single Fribble was highlighted for the director, and participants worked together so that the matcher could identify this object among a set of 16 Fribbles on their screen (note that the order in which Fribbles were presented was not the same for the director and matcher). Matchers indicated their selection by saying the corresponding position label out loud, and used a button box to move to the next trial. There were six consecutive rounds, consisting of 16 trials each (one for each Fribble). Participants switched director-matcher roles every trial. Participants were instructed to communicate in any way they wanted (i.e., there was no explicit instruction to gesture). Figure 3 provides an overview of the 16 Fribbles used and the setup of the experiment.

Fig. 3. This participant was explaining how this Fribble (the one with a black rectangle around it on the right) has "on the right side sort of a square tower", producing a gesture that would be a member of the set of gestures she would produce for that Fribble.

During each trial we have information about which Fribble was the object to be communicated and thus all gestural kinematics that occurred in that trial are likely to be about that Fribble (henceforth target Fribble). Before and after the interaction, participants were individually asked to come up with a verbal label/name for each Fribble (1–3 words) that would enable their partner to identify the correct Fribble (henceforth 'naming task'). In order to enable word2vec processing for these names, spelling errors were corrected and compounds not available in the word2vec corpus were split up (see https://osf.io/x8bpq/ for further details on this cleaning procedure).

Similar to study 1, Kinect collected motion tracking data at 25 Hz, and traces were similarly smoothed with a Kolmogorov-Golai filter (span = 2, degree = 3).

Since we are now working with spontaneous, interactive data (where people move their body freely, though they are not constantly gesturing), we need an automatic way to detect potential gestures during the interactions. We used a custom-made automatic movement detection algorithm to identify potential iconic gestures, which was developed for this dataset (also see Fig. 4). This is a very simple rule-based approach, similar in nature to other gesture detectors [25], where we used the following rules:

1. A movement event is detected when the body part exceeds 15 cm per second speed (15 cm/s is a common movement start threshold, e.g., [26]).
2. If the movement event is next to another detected movement event within 250 ms, then they are merged as a single movement event. Note that for each gesture movement

two or multiple velocity peaks will often be observed: as the movement initiates, performs a stroke, potentially holds still, and detracts. The appropriate time interval for merging will treat these segments as a single event.

3. If a movement lasts less than 200 ms, it is ignored. This way very short movements were filtered out (but if there are many such short movements they will be merged as per rule 2 and treated as a relevant movement).

4. Gesture space is confined to movement above the person-specific -1 SD from the mean of vertical displacement. Participants in our study need to raise their hands to show their gestures to their interlocutor. This also prevents that button presses needed to move between trials were considered as gestures.

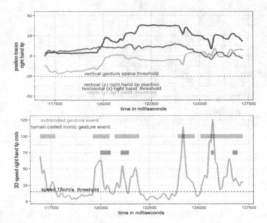

Fig. 4. Example automated gesture coding from time series. The upper panel shows for the right hand tip the three position traces (x = horizontal, y = depth, z = vertical), with the vertical axis representing the cm space (position traces are centered), and on the horizontal axis time in milliseconds. The vertical threshold line shows that whenever the z-trace is above this threshold, our autocoder will consider a movement as potentially relevant. In the lower panel, we have the 3D speed time series which are derived from the upper panel position traces. The vertical axis indicates speed in centimeters per second (cm/s). The autocoding event detections are shown in light red and the iconic gesture strokes as coded by a human annotator are shown in grey. The autocoder detects 5 gestures here, while the human coder detected 4 gesture strokes (note that they do not all overlap).

Note further, that for this current analysis we will only consider a subset of detected movements that were at least 500 ms in duration, as we ideally want to capture movements that are likely more complex and representational gestures, in contrast to gestures that are of a beat-like or very simple quality, which are known to take often less than 500 ms [29, 30]. Further we only consider right-handed movements, so as to ensure that differences in kinematics are not due to differences in hand used for gesturing, as well as for simplicity.

Note that the current automatic movement detection is a very crude and an imperfect way to identify communicative gestures, and rule-based approaches are known to have a relatively large number of false positives [31]. To verify the performance of our algorithm, we compared its output to human-coded iconic gestures for this data; we test against human-coded iconic gestures rather than all gestures, as iconic gestures are the gestures that are of interest for the current analysis (rather than e.g., beat-like gestures). Iconic gestures were coded for a subset of the current data (i.e., for 8 out of the 16 Fribbles in the first two rounds of the interaction). Only the stroke phase was annotated, for the left and right hand separately. We found that the number of iconic gestures detected per participant by the human coder was positively related to the number of auto-coded gestures, $r = .60, p < .001$. In terms of overlap in time of human-coded and auto-coded gesture events there was 65.2% accuracy (true positive $= 70\%$, false positive $= 86\%$, true negative $= 93\%$, false negative $= 1\%$).

The total number of auto-detected gestures (henceforth gestures) that were produced was 1429, M $(SD, min, max) = 208.84$ (75.35, 65, 306) gestures per participant (i.e., an average of 13 gestures per Fribble). The average time of a gesture was $M = 1368$ ms ($SD = 1558$ ms).

We used the same approach to construct semantic and kinematic matrices as in study 1, with some slight modifications. Semantic distances were computed for the names from the pre and post naming task separately, each matrix D^s_{pre} and D^s_{post} containing information about semantic distances between names of Fribble i to j (but not for identical Fribbles, i.e., $i \neq j$). There were 16 different Fribbles, yielding 16×16 distance matrices for each pair. These distance matrices were thus computed between participants in a dyad. See Fig. 5 for an explanation.

For the kinematics (see https://osf.io/u6vcq/ for script) we only submit right-hand related key points, with additional more fine-grained information about hand posture. Therefore, we selected x, y, z traces for key points of the hand tip and thumb, and the Euclidean distance over time between hand-tip and thumb. Again we z-normalized and centered the movement traces before submitting to DTW. The distance matrices for kinematics were also computed between participants in a dyad (as the semantic distance matrices). Further note, that when there were no gestures detected for a particular Fribble i, then no kinematic distance scores could be computed for any comparison that involved Fribble i, and the kinematic distance matrix would contain a missing value for that comparison.

Thus we will analyze the relation between the semantic distances and the kinematic distances between participants, both for naming in the pre as well as the post-test.

3.1 Results Study 2

We performed mixed regression analysis (analysis script: https://osf.io/a657t/), whereby we predict kinematic distances based on semantic distance of pre- and post-naming (in two different analyses). The names and kinematics were repeatedly generated per pair and between Fribbles, and therefore we added Pair nested in Fribble comparison (e.g., Fribble comparison 1:2) as random intercept. See Fig. 6 for the graphical results.

Between-participant kinematic distances were not better predicted by pre-interaction naming semantic distances, as compared to a base model predicting the overall mean, Chi-squared change (1) $= 0.06$, $p = .812$. However, post-interaction naming semantic distances as a predictor improved predictions as compared to a base model, Chi-squared change (1) $= 6.32$, $p = .012$. The resulting model showed that post-naming semantic

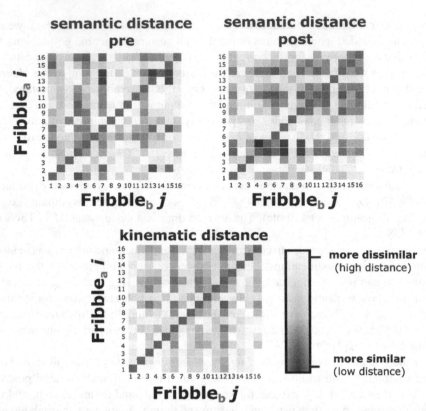

Fig. 5. Example of distance matrix data is shown as colored maps with lower distance scores in darker blue, with 16 rows and columns for each matrix, as there were 16 different Fribbles in total. Each comparison assesses for Fribble i for participant a (Fribble$_a$ i), versus Fribble j for participant b (Fribble$_b$ j) within a dyad the distances between the naming/kinematics between participants for each comparison between two Fribbles. This means that the upper and lower triangles of the matrix are asymmetrical and provide meaningful information regarding the distances in naming/kinematics between interlocutors within the dyad. For the analysis, similar to study 1, we only assess the relation between the off-diagonal cells of the pre and post naming distances with that of the off-diagonal of kinematic distances. Diagonals are in principle computable, and this would be measuring alignment between participants, but we are interested in the relation between gestures that convey different concepts and their semantic-kinematic relatedness.

distances reliably predicted kinematic distances between participants, $b = 0.045$, t (2583) $= 2.15$, $p = .012$, Cohen's $d = .10$. This means that Fribbles that had semantically more similar names produced after interaction by the interlocutors also were more likely to elicit gestures with similar gesture kinematics between interlocutors.

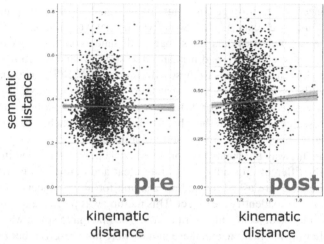

Fig. 6. Scatter plot for the relation between semantic distance between names of Fribble i versus j (pre- and post-interaction) and the kinematic distance between the set of gestures produced for Fribble i versus the set of gestures produced for Fribble j. This means that when a participant "a" showed a higher dissimilarity with "b" on the post naming for Fribble i_a versus j_b, then they also tended to have a more dissimilar set of gestures for Fribble i_a versus j_b. It can be seen that the pre-interaction names do not show any positive kinematic-semantic scaling relation, while the post-interaction names are related to the kinematic distances computed from gestures produced during the interaction.

4 Discussion

In this study we assessed whether gestures that are more similar in kinematics, are likely to convey more similar meanings. We provide evidence that there is indeed a weak statistical dependency between gestures' form (i.e., kinematics) and their (putative) meanings. We show this form-meaning relation in two studies, which were highly divergent in design. In a charades-style study 1, participants interacting with a robot were explicitly instructed to convey one of 35 concepts using silent gestures (i.e., without any speech). In a director-matcher style study 2, participants were interacting in dyads, producing spontaneous co-speech gestures when trying to refer to novel objects. Participants were asked to verbally name these novel objects before and after interacting with their partner. In both studies we obtain that the difference in the gestures' putative referential content (either the concepts to be conveyed, or the post-interaction naming of the objects) scales with the dissimilarity between the form of the gestures that certainly targeted (study 1) or were likely to target (study 2) that referential content. Thus in both silent gestures and gestures produced with speech, the kinematic space seems to co-vary with the putative semantic space.

There are some crucial caveats to the current report that need to be mentioned. Firstly, we should not confuse the semantics of a gesture with our measurement of the semantics, using word2vec distance calculations of the instructed (study 1) or post-interaction elicited (study 2) conceptualizations of the referential targets. Thus we should remind ourselves that when we say that two gestures' meanings are similar, we should actually say that the concepts that those gestures putatively signal show up in similar contexts in a corpus of Dutch webtexts (i.e., the word2vec model we used; [26]). Furthermore, there are also other measurements for semantic distance computations that possibly yield different results, e.g., [32], and it is an interesting avenue for future research to see how gesture kinematics relates to these different semantic distance quantifications [33]. This goes the other way too, such that there are different ways to compute the kinematic distances [e.g., 19, 34] for different gesture-relevant motion variables [e.g., 35] and more research is needed to benchmark different approaches for understanding semantic properties of communicative gesture kinematics.

Additionally, the way the putatively conveyed concept is determined in study 1 and 2 is dramatically different. In study 1 it is more clear and defined from the outset, but in study 2 participants are asked to produce a name for novel objects, such that their partner would be able to identify the object. This naming was performed before and after interacting about those objects with their partner. The kinematic space was only related to the names after the interaction, and these names were not pre-given but likely created through communicative interaction. Thus while we can say that in study 1 gestures that convey more similar concepts are also more likely to be more kinematically similar, for study 2 we must reiterate that kinematically similar gestures for two objects x and y produced by two interlocutors (in interaction), forges a context for those persons to name these two objects similarly. Thus it seems that gestures between participants can constrain—or are correlated to another process that constrains (e.g., speech)—the between-subject semantic space that is constructed through the interaction. We do not find this to be the case the other way around, as the semantic space verbally constructed before interaction (i.e., based on pre-interaction naming) did not relate to the kinematic space constructed gesturally.

It is clear that more research is needed to understand these effects vis-à-vis the semantic and kinematic relation of gestures in these highly different contexts of study 1 and 2. We plan more follow-up analyses taking into account semantic content of gestures' co-occurrent speech, as well as arguably more objective visual differences between the referential targets themselves (e.g., are Fribble objects that look alike also gestured about more similarly?). However, for the current report we simply need to appreciate the now promising possibility that gesture kinematic (dis-)similarity spaces are informative about their semantic relatedness. Implications are easily derivable from this finding alone.

For example, consider a humanoid whose job it is to recognize a gesture's meaning based on kinematics as to respond appropriately (as was the setup for study 1, [21]). The current results suggest that information about an undetermined gesture's meaning can be derived by comparing it to a stored lexicon of gesture kinematics of which the semantic content is determined. Though certainly no definitive meaning can be derived, the current statistical relation offers promise for acquiring some initial semantic gist of a semantically undefined gesture based on kinematic similarities computed against a library of representative set of gesture kinematics. The crucial importance of the current findings is that such a gesture kinematic lexicon does not need to contain a semantically similar or identical gesture to provide some minimal semantic gist about the semantically undefined gesture. It merely needs a computation of form similarity against its database of representative gesture kinematics. This also means that a humanoid without any such lexicon, with enough training, can at least derive some information about which gestures are more likely to be semantically related. A humanoid can build its kinematic space from the bottom up, by detecting gestures in interaction, construct a kinematic similarity space over time, and infer from the distance matrices which gestures are likely to be semantically related (given the assumption that kinematic space and semantic space tend to align). Moreover, the humanoid's own gesture generation process may be tailored such that there is some weak dependency between the kinematics of gestures that are related in content, thus optimizing its gesture behavior to cohere in a similar way as human gesture does [36–38]. The current findings thus provide an exciting proof-of-concept that continuous communicative bodily movements that co-vary in kinematic structure, also co-vary in meaning. This can be exploited by the field of machine learning which is known to productively leverage weak statistical dependencies to gauge semantic properties of communicative tokens (e.g., word2vec).

Note further that the principle of distributional semantics is said to provide an important bootstrapping mechanism for acquiring language in human infants (and language learners in general), as statistical dependencies yield some information about the possible meaning of an unknown word given its contextual or form vicinity to other words for which the meaning is more determined [26, 39]. Word learning is facilitated in this way, as language learners do not need explicit training on the meaning of each and every word, but can exploit statistical dependencies that structure the language [40, 41]. Here we show a statistical dependency that is similar in spirit, but for continuous communicative movements: the similarity between the putative semantic content of one gesture and that of another, can be predicted to some extent based on their movement similarity alone. It thereby offers a promising indication that gestures' contents too are to some extent more easily learnable based on their covariance in form. It opens up the possibility that gestures, similar to other forms of human communication, are not simply one-shot communicative patterns, but to some statistical extent constellated forms of expressions with language-like systematic properties amenable to geometric/network analysis performed on the level of interrelationships between communicative tokens [13, 29, 42].

Additionally, the potential of multimodal learning should be underlined here, as co-speech gesture kinematic interrelationships are informative about semantic space and therefore also likely co-informative about co-occurrent speech which you may not know the meaning of. Thus when learning a new language, gestures can come to reduce the potential meaning space of the entire communicative expression (i.e., including speech), reducing the complexity of word learning too. This mechanism can be related to another putative function of iconicity in gestures as a powerful starting point in acquiring language [43], as kinematics are informative about a referent given the kinematics structures by association through form-meaning resemblance (e.g., a digging movement may signal the referent of the word DIGGING in its close resemblance to the actual action of digging). However, this particular way of constraining semantics via iconicity necessitates some basic mapping on the part of the observer, so as to complete the iconic reference between form and meaning. The current kinematic-semantic scaling provides in potential a more indirect or bottom up statistical route to reduce the semantic space to likely meanings, namely by recognizing similarities of a gesture's form with other forms previously encountered, one can reduce the meaning space if the kinematic space and semantic space tend to be co-varying. Thus the current geometric relations between gesture kinematic and semantic space are a possible statistical route for constraining potential meanings from detecting covariances between form alone, at least in artificial agents, but potentially this is exploited by human infants and/or second-language learners too.

Though promising, the statistical dependency is currently underspecified in terms of how such dependencies emerge in the human ecology of gesture. It remains unclear which particular kinematic features tend to co-vary with semantic content. So we are not sure at what level of similarity or analogy gesture kinematics relate as they do semantically [44]. It is further not clear whether the semantic content co-varies with kinematics because the gestures are part of some kind of overarching movement type (e.g., static handshape, continuous movement, etc.) or mode of representation (acting, representing, drawing or personification; [11]) which may co-vary with semantic categories. Indeed, in previous research it has been shown that e.g., gestures representing manipulable objects are most likely to have 'acting' as mode of representation, while gestures depicting animals are more likely to recruit 'personification', as observed by human annotators [3]. We tried to assess in study 1 whether it is indeed the case that the reported effects might be due to local covariance of different gesture classes, leading to global kinematic-semantic differences between classes. Namely, if gestures are kinematically grouped by an overarching category, then within that class there should be no relation between gesture kinematic and semantic similarity. The results however, indicate that semantic-kinematic distance persisted both for comparisons within and between gesture classes, irrespective of whether we construct such classes based on human-defined themes, or empirically based kinematic cluster assignment. We hope the current contribution invites further network-topological study [13, 45] of the current geometrical scaling of gesture semantic and kinematic spaces so as to find the right level of granularity at which these spaces co-vary.

To conclude, the current results suggest a persistent scaling relation between gesture form and meaning distributions. We look forward to researching this more deeply from a cognitive science perspective, but we hope that the HCI as well as machine learning community could one day leverage covariances that we have identified between kinematic and semantic spaces, in the employment and development of an automatic detection of a gesture's meaning via principles of distributional semantics.

Acknowledgements. For study 2, we would like to thank Mark Dingemanse for his contributions in the CABB project to assess optimality of different word2vec models. For study 2, we would like to thank James Trujillo for his contributions to setting up the Kinect data collection. Study 2 came about in the context of a multidisciplinary research project within the Language in Interaction consortium, called Communicative Alignment in Brain and Behaviour (CABB). We wish to make explicit that the work has been shaped by contributions of CABB team members, especially (alphabetical order): Mark Blokpoel, Mark Dingemanse, Lotte Eijk, Iris van Rooij. The authors remain solely responsible for the contents of the paper. This work was supported by the Netherlands Organisation for Scientific Research (NWO) Gravitation Grant 024.001.006 to the Language in Interaction Consortium and is further supported by the Donders Fellowship awarded to Wim Pouw and Asli Ozyurek.

References

1. Motamedi, Y., Schouwstra, M., Smith, K., Culbertson, J., Kirby, S.: Evolving artificial sign languages in the lab: from improvised gesture to systematic sign. Cognition **192**, (2019). https://doi.org/10.1016/j.cognition.2019.05.001
2. Ortega, G., Özyürek, A.: Types of iconicity and combinatorial strategies distinguish semantic categories in silent gesture across cultures. Lan. Cogn. **12**, 84–113 (2020). https://doi.org/10.1017/langcog.2019.28
3. Ortega, G., Özyürek, A.: Systematic mappings between semantic categories and types of iconic representations in the manual modality: a normed database of silent gesture. Behav. Res. **52**, 51–67 (2020). https://doi.org/10.3758/s13428-019-01204-6
4. Gerwing, J., Bavelas, J.: Linguistic influences on gesture's form. Gesture **4**, 157–195 (2004). https://doi.org/10.1075/gest.4.2.04ger
5. Rasenberg, M., Özyürek, A., Dingemanse, M.: Alignment in multimodal interaction: an integrative framework. Cogn. Sci. **44**, (2020). https://doi.org/10.1111/cogs.12911
6. Bernstein, N.: The Co-ordination and Regulations of Movements. Pergamon Press, Oxford (1967)
7. McNeill, D.: Hand and Mind: What Gestures Reveal about Thought. University of Chicago Press, Chicago (1992)
8. Kendon, A.: Gesture: Visible Action as Utterance. Cambridge University Press, Cambridge (2004)
9. Kolorova, Z.: Lexikon der bulgarischen Alltagsgesten (2011)
10. Gentner, D., Brem, S.K.: Is snow really like a shovel? Distinguishing similarity from thematic relatedness. In: Hahn, M., Stoness, S.C. (eds.) Proceedings of the Twenty-first Annual Meeting of the Cognitive Science Society, pp. 179–184. Lawrence Erlbaum Associates, Mahwa (1999)
11. Müller, C.: Gestural modes of representation as techniques of depiction. In: Müller, C. (ed.) Body–Language–Communication: An International Handbook on Multimodality in Human Interaction, pp. 1687–1701. De Gruyter Mouton, Berlin (2013)
12. Streeck, J.: Depicting by gesture. Gesture **8**, 285–301 (2008). https://doi.org/10.1075/gest.8.3.02str
13. Karuza, E.A., Thompson-Schill, S.L., Bassett, D.S.: Local patterns to global architectures: influences of network topology on human learning. Trends Cogn. Sci. **20**, 629–640 (2016). https://doi.org/10.1016/j.tics.2016.06.003
14. Gleitman, L.R.: Verbs of a feather flock together II: the child's discovery of words and their meanings. In: Nevin, B.E. (ed.) The Legacy of Zellig Harris: Language and Information Into the 21st Century, pp. 209–229 (2002)
15. Fowler, C.A.: Embodied, embedded language use. Ecol. Psychol. **22**, 286 (2010). https://doi.org/10.1080/10407413.2010.517115
16. Pouw, W., Dixon, J.A.: Gesture networks: Introducing dynamic time warping and network analysis for the kinematic study of gesture ensembles. Discourse Processes **57**, 301–319 (2019). https://doi.org/10.1080/0163853X.2019.1678967
17. Giorgino, T.: Computing and visualizing dynamic time warping alignments in R: the dtw package. J. Stat. Softw. **31** (2009). https://doi.org/10.18637/jss.v031.i07
18. Muller, M.: Information Retrieval for Music and Motion. Springer, Heidelberg (2007). https://doi.org/10.1007/978-3-540-74048-3
19. Beecks, C., et al.: Efficient query processing in 3D motion capture gesture databases. Int. J. Semant. Comput. **10**, 5–25 (2016). https://doi.org/10.1142/S1793351X16400018
20. Pouw, W., Dingemanse, M., Motamedi, Y., Ozyurek, A.: A systematic investigation of gesture kinematics in evolving manual languages in the lab. OSF Preprints (2020). https://doi.org/10.31219/osf.io/heu24

21. de Wit, J., Krahmer, E., Vogt, P.: Introducing the NEMO-Lowlands iconic gesture dataset, collected through a gameful human–robot interaction. Behav. Res. (2020). https://doi.org/10.3758/s13428-020-01487-0
22. Müller, C.: Gesture and sign: cataclysmic break or dynamic relations? Front. Psychol. **9** (2018). https://doi.org/10.3389/fpsyg.2018.01651
23. Rasenberg, M., Dingemanse, M., Özyürek, A.: Lexical and gestural alignment in interaction and the emergence of novel shared symbols. In: Ravignani, A., et al. (eds.) Evolang13, pp. 356–358 (2020)
24. Barry, T.J., Griffith, J.W., De Rossi, S., Hermans, D.: Meet the Fribbles: novel stimuli for use within behavioural research. Front. Psychol. **5** (2014). https://doi.org/10.3389/fpsyg.2014.00103
25. Mandera, P., Keuleers, E., Brysbaert, M.: Explaining human performance in psycholinguistic tasks with models of semantic similarity based on prediction and counting: a review and empirical validation. J. Mem. Lan. **92**, 57–78 (2017). https://doi.org/10.1016/j.jml.2016.04.001
26. Zeman, D., et al.: CoNLL 2017 shared task: Multilingual parsing from raw text to universal dependencies. In: Proceedings of the CoNLL 2017 Shared Task: Multilingual Parsing from Raw Text to Universal Dependencies, Vancouver, Canada, pp. 1–19. Association for Computational Linguistics (2017). https://doi.org/10.18653/v1/K17-3001
27. Silva, D.F., Batista, G.A.E.P.A., Keogh, E.: On the effect of endpoints on dynamic time warping. Presented at the Proceedings of the 22nd ACM SIGKDD International Conference on Knowledge Discovery and Data Mining, San Francisco (2016)
28. Donaldson, J.: tsne: T-Distributed Stochastic Neighbor Embedding for R (t-SNE) (2016)
29. Pouw, W., Dixon, J.A.: Entrainment and modulation of gesture–speech synchrony under delayed auditory feedback. Cogn. Sci. **43**, (2019). https://doi.org/10.1111/cogs.12721
30. Pouw, W., Dixon, J.A.: Quantifying gesture-speech synchrony. In: Proceedings of the 6th meeting of Gesture and Speech in Interaction, pp. 68–74. Universitaetsbibliothek Paderborn, Paderborn (2019). https://doi.org/10.17619/UNIPB/1-812
31. Ripperda, J., Drijvers, L., Holler, J.: Speeding up the detection of non-iconic and iconic gestures (SPUDNIG): a toolkit for the automatic detection of hand movements and gestures in video data. Behav. Res. **52**, 1783–1794 (2020). https://doi.org/10.3758/s13428-020-01350-2
32. Kenett, Y.N., Levi, E., Anaki, D., Faust, M.: The semantic distance task: quantifying semantic distance with semantic network path length. J. Exp. Psychol. Learn. Mem. Cogn. **43**, 1470–1489 (2017). https://doi.org/10.1037/xlm0000391
33. Kumar, A.A., Balota, D.A., Steyvers, M.: Distant connectivity and multiple-step priming in large-scale semantic networks. J. Exp. Psychol. Learn. Mem. Cogn. **46**, 2261–2276 (2020). https://doi.org/10.1037/xlm0000793
34. Beecks, C., et al.: Spatiotemporal similarity search in 3D motion capture gesture streams. In: Claramunt, C., Schneider, M., Wong, R.C.-W., Xiong, L., Loh, W.-K., Shahabi, C., Li, K.-J. (eds.) SSTD 2015. LNCS, vol. 9239, pp. 355–372. Springer, Cham (2015). https://doi.org/10.1007/978-3-319-22363-6_19
35. Trujillo, J.P., Vaitonyte, J., Simanova, I., Özyürek, A.: Toward the markerless and automatic analysis of kinematic features: a toolkit for gesture and movement research. Behav Res. **51**, 769–777 (2019). https://doi.org/10.3758/s13428-018-1086-8
36. Hua, M., Shi, F., Nan, Y., Wang, K., Chen, H., Lian, S.: Towards more realistic human-robot conversation: a Seq2Seq-based body gesture interaction system. arXiv:1905.01641 [cs] (2019)

37. Alexanderson, S., Székely, É., Henter, G.E., Kucherenko, T., Beskow, J.: Generating coherent spontaneous speech and gesture from text. In: Proceedings of the 20th ACM International Conference on Intelligent Virtual Agents, pp. 1–3 (2020). https://doi.org/10.1145/3383652.3423874

38. Wu, B., Liu, C., Ishi, C.T., Ishiguro, H.: Modeling the conditional distribution of co-speech upper body gesture jointly using conditional-GAN and unrolled-GAN. Electronics **10**, 228 (2021). https://doi.org/10.3390/electronics10030228

39. Romberg, A.R., Saffran, J.R.: Statistical learning and language acquisition. WIREs Cogn. Sci. **1**, 906–914 (2010). https://doi.org/10.1002/wcs.78

40. Saffran, J.R., Aslin, R.N., Newport, E.L.: Statistical learning by 8-month-old infants. Science **274**, 1926–1928 (1996). https://doi.org/10.1126/science.274.5294.1926

41. Steyvers, M., Tenenbaum, J.B.: The large-scale structure of semantic networks: statistical analyses and a model of semantic growth. Cogn. Sci. **29**, 41–78 (2005). https://doi.org/10.1207/s15516709cog2901_3

42. Goldstein, R., Vitevitch, M.S.: The influence of clustering coefficient on word-learning: how groups of similar sounding words facilitate acquisition. Front. Psychol. **5** (2014). https://doi.org/10.3389/fpsyg.2014.01307

43. Nielsen, A.K., Dingemanse, M.: Iconicity in word learning and beyond: a critical review. Lang. Speech, 0023830920914339 (2020). https://doi.org/10.1177/0023830920914339

44. Forbus, K.D., Ferguson, R.W., Lovett, A., Gentner, D.: Extending SME to handle large-scale cognitive modeling. Cogn. Sci. **41**, 1152–1201 (2017). https://doi.org/10.1111/cogs.12377

45. Siew, C.S.Q., Wulff, D.U., Beckage, N.M., Kenett, Y.N.: Cognitive network science: a review of research on cognition through the lens of network representations, processes, and dynamics. https://www.hindawi.com/journals/complexity/2019/2108423/. https://doi.org/10.1155/2019/2108423. Accessed 29 Jan 2021

The Role of Embodiment and Simulation in Evaluating HCI: Theory and Framework

James Pustejovsky[1]([⊠]) [iD] and Nikhil Krishnaswamy[2] [iD]

[1] Brandeis University, Waltham, MA 02453, USA
jamesp@brandeis.edu
[2] Colorado State University, Fort Collins, CO 80523, USA
nkrishna@colostate.edu

Abstract. In this paper, we argue that embodiment can play an important role in the evaluation of systems developed for Human Computer Interaction. To this end, we describe a simulation platform for building Embodied Human Computer Interactions (EHCI). This system, VoxWorld, enables multimodal dialogue systems that communicate through language, gesture, action, facial expressions, and gaze tracking, in the context of task-oriented interactions. A multimodal simulation is an embodied 3D virtual realization of both the situational environment and the co-situated agents, as well as the most salient content denoted by communicative acts in a discourse. It is built on the modeling language VoxML, which encodes objects with rich semantic typing and action affordances, and actions themselves as multimodal programs, enabling contextually salient inferences and decisions in the environment. Through simulation experiments in VoxWorld, we can begin to identify and then evaluate the diverse parameters involved in multimodal communication between agents. VoxWorld enables an embodied HCI by situating both human and computational agents within the same virtual simulation environment, where they share perceptual and epistemic common ground. In this first part of this paper series, we discuss the consequences of embodiment and common ground, and how they help evaluate parameters of the interaction between humans and agents, and demonstrate different behaviors and types of interactions on different classes of agents.

Keywords: Embodiment · HCI · Common ground · Multimodal dialogue · VoxML

This work was supported by Contract W911NF-15-C-0238 with the US Defense Advanced Research Projects Agency (DARPA) and the Army Research Office (ARO). Approved for Public Release, Distribution Unlimited. The views expressed herein are ours and do not reflect the official policy or position of the Department of Defense or the U.S. Government. We would like to thank Ken Lai, Bruce Draper, Ross Beveridge, and Francisco Ortega for their comments and suggestions.

© Springer Nature Switzerland AG 2021
V. G. Duffy (Ed.): HCII 2021, LNCS 12777, pp. 288–303, 2021.
https://doi.org/10.1007/978-3-030-77817-0_21

1 Introduction

As multimodal interactive systems become both more common and more sophisticated, naive users come to use them with increasing expectations that their interactions will approximate aspects of typical interactions with another human. With this increased interest in multimodal interaction comes a need to evaluate the performance of a multimodal system on the various levels with which it engages the user. Thus, system evaluations and metrics should be able to account for the communicative ability of the various modalities in use, as well as how the modalities interact with each other to facilitate communication. Such evaluation metrics should be modality-agnostic and assess the communication between human and computer based on the semantics of objects, events, and actions situated within the shared context created by the human-computer interaction.

One way to facilitate this type of evaluation is to position the human and the computational agent within a shared conceptual space, where the agent is able to sufficiently interpret multimodal behavior and communicative commands from the human. This suggests an *embodied* presence within a *simulated* environment. Here we argue that a simulation platform provides just such an environment for modeling communicative interactions, what we call *Embodied Human Computer Interaction*, one facilitated by a formal model of object and event semantics that renders the continuous quantitative search space of an open-world, real-time environment tractable. We provide examples for how a semantically-informed AI system can exploit the precise, numerical information provided by a game engine to perform qualitative reasoning about objects and events, facilitate learning novel concepts from data, and communicate with a human to improve its models and demonstrate its understanding.

As a case in point, consider the two interactions in Fig. 1. On the left, we see a human-human interaction engaged in a joint task. On the right, the same task is being carried out between a human and an intelligent virtual agent (IVA), who is embodied in a simulation environment with the user.

Fig. 1. *Left:* Human-human collaborative interaction; *Right:* Human-avatar interaction.

The notion of embodiment has many diverse interpretations, depending on the discipline and field of study [1, 12, 42, 51, 67]. When discussing its role in HCI, we can identify (at least) three major factors of embodiment that contribute to how an artificial agent interacts effectively with its human partners:

- The artificial agent has some identifiable degree of *self-embodiment*: this is the "spatial presence" associated with the agent relative to the human partner, within the domain or space of the interaction (the embedding space). This might include a virtual presence on a screen, with face or even skeletal form; actual effectors for action and manipulation; and explicit sensors for audio and visual input.
- The agent is aware of the *human's embodiment*; that is, it has recognition of the human partner's linguistic and gestural expressions, facial expressions, and actions. The artificial agent continuously receives inputs through which it constructs and maintains a representation of its human partner's embodiment.
- The interaction enables *situated meaning* for the objects and actions in the environment; an elementary understanding of how objects behave relative to each other and as a consequence of the agent's actions (affordances, action dynamics, etc.). This also includes recognition of speaker intent and epistemic state.

While embodiment is a relatively recent theoretical development, the concept of simulation has played an important role in both AI and cognitive science for over 40 years. There are two distinct uses for the term *simulation*, particularly as used in computer science and AI. First, simulation can be used as a description for *testing a computational model*. That is, variables in a model are set and the model is run, such that the consequences of all possible computable configurations become known. Examples of such simulations include models of climate change, the tensile strength of materials, models of biological pathways, and so on. We refer to this as *computational simulation modeling*, where the goal is to arrive at the best model by using simulation techniques.

Simulation can also refer to an environment which allows a user to interact with objects in a "virtual or simulated world", where the agent is embodied as a dynamic point-of-view or avatar in a proxy situation. Such simulations are used for training humans in scripted scenarios, such as flight simulators, battle training, and of course, in video gaming: in these contexts, the software and gaming world assume an embodiment of the agent in the environment, either as a first-person restricted POV (such as a first-person shooter or RPG), or an omniscient movable embodied perspective (e.g., real-time or turn-based strategy). We refer to such approaches as *situated embodied simulations*. The goal is to simulate an agent within a situation.

Simulation has yet another meaning, however. Starting with Craik [17], we encounter the notion that agents carry a mental model of external reality in their heads. Johnson-Laird [39] develops his own theory of a mental model, which represents a situational possibility, capturing what is common to all the different ways in which the situation may occur [38]. This is used to drive inference and reasoning, both factual and counterfactual. Simulation Theory, as developed in philosophy of mind, has focused on the role that "mind reading" plays in modeling the mental representations of other agents and the content of their communicative acts [33–35,37]. Simulation semantics (as adopted within cognitive linguistics and practiced by Feldman [25], Narayanan [54], Bergen [7], and Evans [24]) argues that language comprehension is accomplished by means of such mind reading operations. Similarly, within psychology, there is an established body of work arguing for "mental simulations" of future or possible outcomes, as well as interpretations of perceptual input [6,36,73,74]. These simulation approaches can be referred to as *embodied theories of mind*. Their goal is to view the semantic interpretation of an expression by means of a simulation, which is either mental (a la Bergen and Evans) or interpreted graphs such as Petri Nets (a la Narayanan and Feldman).

We describe a simulation framework, VoxWorld, that integrates the functionality and the goals of all three approaches above. Namely, we situate an embodied agent in a multimodal simulation, with *mind-reading* interpretive capabilities, facilitated through assignment and evaluation of object and context parameters within the environment being modeled. This platform provides an environment for experimentation with multimodal interactions between humans and avatars or robots.

In [62], we discuss the challenges involved in creating an embodied agent for HCI and HRI. Two issues present themselves, to this end. First, it will be important to identify an operational definition of embodiment for this domain; and secondly, we should acknowledge that an agent cannot simply be embodied without also embodying the interaction within which the agent is acting.

2   Prior Work

There is a long and established tradition of multimodal interfaces that combine language and gesture, starting with [8], which anticipated some of the issues discussed herein, including the use of deixis to disambiguate references, and also inspired a community surrounding multimodal integration (e.g., [21,41,71]).

The psychological motivation for multimodal interfaces, as epitomized by [65], holds that speech and gesture are coexpressive and processed partially independently, and therefore complement each other. Using both modalities increases human working memory and decreases cognitive load [21], allowing people to retain more information and learn faster.

Visual information has been shown to be particularly useful in establishing common ground [14,15,19,22,23], or mutual understanding that enables further communication. Other research in HCI additionally emphasizes the importance of shared visual workspaces in computer-mediated communication [27–29,43], highlighting the usefulness of non-verbal communication in coordination between humans [10,11].

[9] shows that allowing for shared gaze increased performance in spatial tasks in paired collaborations. Multimodal systems of gaze and speech have also been studied in interaction with robots and virtual avatars [2,53,68]. However, few systems have centered the use of language and gesture in collaborative and communicative scenarios.

Communicating with computers becomes even more interesting in the context of shared physical tasks. When people work together, their conversation consists of more than just words. They gesture and they share a common workspace [13, 46, 48, 52]. Their shared perception of this workspace is the context for their conversation, and it is this shared space that gives many gestures, such as pointing, their meaning [44]. The dynamic computation of discourse [4], furthermore, becomes more complex when multiple modalities are at play. Fortunately, embodied actions (such as coverbal gestures) do not seem to violate coherence relations [47].

As shown in Part 2 of this paper series, we approach evaluation from a semantics-centered perspective, and use distinct semantic properties of specific elements in the interaction to determine what about the interaction enabled or hindered "shared understanding." This is typically referred to as the "common ground" in the literature, both in psychology and semantics [3, 14, 31, 59, 69, 70].

Within HCI and human device interaction (HDI) design, a related area involves the evaluation of gesture fields [40] for the expression of image schemas and how they map to interactions with the computer. The results in [49] on the FIGURE corpus are relevant for design decisions, raising evaluation criteria distinct from the hallmarks mentioned above. Similar concerns and suggestions are discussed in [66], for how gestures can improve the behavior of embodied conversational agents (ECAs).

3   Common Ground in VoxWorld

3.1   VoxML: Encoding Actions and Objects

In order to characterize the many dimensions of human-computer interactions, we will introduce an approach to evaluating interactions drawing on the most relevant parameters in a co-situated communicative interactions. By introducing a formal model of shared context, we are able to track the intentions and utterances, as well as the perceptions and actions of the agents involved in a dialogue. Our model, VoxWorld, integrates all three aspects of simulation discussed above into a situated embodied environment built on a game engine platform. The computer, either as an embodied agent distinct from the viewer, or as the totality of the rendered environment itself, presents an interpretation (*mind-reading*) of its internal model, down to specific parameter values, which are often assigned for the purposes of testing that model.

We assume that a simulation is a contextualized 3D virtual realization of both the situational environment and the co-situated agents, as well as the most salient content denoted by communicative acts in discourse between them. VoxWorld and VoxML [60], provide the following characteristics: object encoding with rich semantic typing and action affordances; action encoding as multimodal programs; it reveals the elements of the common ground in interaction between parties, be they humans or artificially intelligent agents. VoxWorld supports embodied HCI wherein artificial agents consume different sensor inputs for awareness of not only their own virtual space but also the surrounding physical space. It brings together the three definitions of simulation introduced above (Fig. 2).

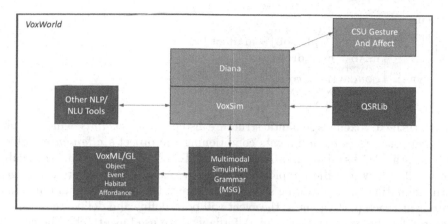

Fig. 2. VoxWorld architecture schematic.

Within the computational context of VoxWorld, common ground relies on implementations of the following aspects of the interaction:

1. *Co-situatedness* and *co-perception* of the agents, such that they can interpret the same situation from their respective frames of reference, such as a human and an avatar perceiving the same virtual scene from different perspectives;
2. *Co-attention* of a shared situated reference, which allows more expressiveness in referring to the environment (i.e., through language, gesture, visual presentation, etc.). The human and avatar might be able to refer to objects on the table in multiple modalities with a common model of differences in perspective-relative references;
3. *Co-intent* of a common goal, such that adversarial relationships between agents reflect a breakdown in the common ground. Here, human and agent are collaborating to achieve a common goal, each sharing their knowledge with the other.

VoxML (Visual Object Concept Markup Language) is the representation language used to encode knowledge about objects, events, attributes, and functions by linking lexemes to their visual instantiations, termed the "visual object concept" or *voxeme*. In parallel to a lexicon, a collection of voxemes is termed a *voxicon*. There is no requirement on a voxicon to have a one-to-one correspondence between its voxemes and the lexemes in the associated lexicon, which often results in a many-to-many correspondence. That is, the lexeme *plate* may be visualized as a [[SQUARE PLATE]], a [[ROUND PLATE]], or other voxemes, and those voxemes in turn may be linked to other lexemes such as *dish* or *saucer*.

Each voxeme is linked to either an object geometry, a program in a dynamic semantics, an attribute set, or a transformation algorithm, which are all structures easily exploitable in a rendered simulation platform. For example, a *cup* can be typed as a cylindroid with concavity, as shown below:

$$\begin{bmatrix} \textbf{cup} \\ \text{LEXICAL} = \begin{bmatrix} \text{PREDICATE} = \textbf{cup} \\ \text{TYPE} = \textbf{physobj} \bullet \textbf{artifact} \end{bmatrix} \\ \text{TYPE} = \begin{bmatrix} \text{HEAD} = \textbf{cylindroid}[1] \\ \text{COMPONENTS} = \textbf{surface, interior} \\ \text{CONCAVITY} = \textbf{concave} \\ \text{ROTATIONAL\_SYMMETRY} = \{Y\} \\ \text{REFLECTION\_SYMETRY} = \{XY, YZ\} \end{bmatrix} \end{bmatrix}$$

An OBJECT voxeme's semantic structure also provides *habitats*, which are situational contexts or environments conditioning the object's *affordances*, which may be either "Gibsonian" affordances [30] or "Telic" affordances [56,57]. A habitat specifies how an object typically occupies a space. When we are challenged with computing the embedding space for an event, the individual habitats associated with each participant in the event will both define and delineate the space required for the event to transpire. Affordances are used as attached behaviors, which the object either facilitates by its geometry (Gibsonian) or purposes for which it is intended to be used (Telic). For example, a Gibsonian affordance for [[CUP]] is "grasp," while a Telic affordance is "drink from." This allows procedural reasoning to be associated with habitats and affordances, executed in real time in the simulation, inferring the complete set of spatial relations between objects at each frame and tracking changes in the shared context between human and computer (Fig. 3).

Fig. 3. Cup in different habitats. Both allow **holding**, while the left allows **sliding** and the right allows **rolling**.

$$\begin{bmatrix} \textbf{cup} \\ \text{LEXICAL} = \begin{bmatrix} \text{PREDICATE} = \textbf{cup} \\ \text{TYPE} = \textbf{physobj} \bullet \textbf{artifact} \end{bmatrix} \\ \text{TYPE} = \begin{bmatrix} \text{HEAD} = \textbf{cylindroid}[1] \\ \text{COMPONENTS} = \textbf{surface, interior} \\ \text{CONCAVITY} = \textbf{concave} \\ \text{ROTATIONAL\_SYMMETRY} = \{Y\} \\ \text{REFLECTION\_SYMETRY} = \{XY, YZ\} \end{bmatrix} \\ \text{HABITAT} = \begin{bmatrix} \text{INTRINSIC} = [2] \begin{bmatrix} \text{CONSTR} = \{Y > X, Y > Z\} \\ \text{UP} = align(Y, \mathcal{E}_Y) \\ \text{TOP} = top(::Y) \end{bmatrix} \\ \text{EXTRINSIC} = [3] \begin{bmatrix} \text{UP} = align(Y, \mathcal{E}_{\perp Y}) \end{bmatrix} \end{bmatrix} \\ \text{AFF\_STR} = \begin{bmatrix} A_1 = H_{[2]} \rightarrow [put(x, on([1]))] \, support([1], x) \\ A_2 = H_{[2]} \rightarrow [put(x, in([1]))] \, contain([1], x) \\ A_3 = H_{[2]} \rightarrow [grasp(x, [1])] \, hold(x, [1]) \\ A_4 = H_{[3]} \rightarrow [roll(x, [1])] \, \mathcal{R} \end{bmatrix} \\ \text{EMBOD} = \begin{bmatrix} \text{SCALE} = \textbf{<agent} \\ \text{MOVABLE} = \textbf{true} \end{bmatrix} \end{bmatrix}$$

Activities and events are interpreted in VoxML as programs, π, in terms of a dynamic event semantics, Dynamic Interval Temporal Logic (DITL) [64]. The advantage of adopting a dynamic interpretation of events is that linguistic expressions map directly into simulations through an operational semantics. A formula is interpreted as a propositional expression, with assignment of a truth value in a specific state in the model. For our purposes, a state is a set of propositions with assignments to variables at a specific time index. Atomic programs are relations from states to states, and hence interpreted over an input/output state-state pairing (cf. also [26,55]).

The structure in (a) below represents a **state**, e^i, at time i, with the propositional content, φ. The event structure in (c) illustrates how program α takes the world from e^i with content φ, to the adjacent state, $e_2^{i::1}$, where the propositional content has been negated, $\neg\varphi$. This corresponds directly to **achievements**. From these two types, the other two Vendlerian classes can be generated. **Processes** can be modeled as an iteration of simple transitions, where two conditions hold: the transition is a change in the value of an identifiable attribute of the object; every iterated transition shares the same attribute being changed. This is illustrated in (b) below. Finally, **accomplishments** are built up by taking an underlying process event, e:P, denoting some change in an object's attribute, and synchronizing it with an achievement (simple transition): that is, e:P is unfolding while ψ is true, until one last step of the program α makes it the case that $\neg\psi$ is now true.

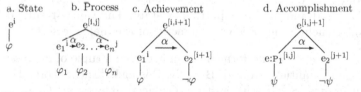

To illustrate the dynamic encoding of state and action information in VoxML, consider the voxeme for the accomplishment verb *put*, shown below.

$$
\begin{bmatrix}
\textbf{put} & & \\
\text{LEX} = & \begin{bmatrix} \text{PRED} = \textbf{put} \\ \text{TYPE} = \textbf{transition\_event} \end{bmatrix} & \\
\text{TYPE} = & \begin{bmatrix} \text{HEAD} = \textbf{transition} \\ \text{ARGS} = \begin{bmatrix} A_1 = \textbf{x:agent} \\ A_2 = \textbf{y:physobj} \\ A_3 = \textbf{z:location} \end{bmatrix} \\ \text{BODY} = \begin{bmatrix} E_1 = grasp(x,y) \\ E_2 = [while(hold(x,y), move(x,y))] \\ E_3 = [at(y,z) \rightarrow ungrasp(x,y)] \end{bmatrix} \end{bmatrix}
\end{bmatrix}
$$

In this way, simulation becomes a way of tracing the consequences of linguistic spatial cues through the narrative structure of an event and presenting the computer system's understanding of it.

VoxWorld also allows the system to reason about objects and actions independently. When simulating the objects alone, the simulation presents how the objects change in the world. By removing the objects and presenting only the actions that the viewer would interpret as *causing* the intended object motion (i.e., a pantomime of an embodied agent moving an object without the object itself), the system can present a "decoupled" interpretation of the action, for example, as an animated gesture that traces the intended path of motion. By composing the two, it demonstrates that particular instantiation of the complete event. This allows an embodied situated simulation approach to easily compose objects with actions by directly interpreting at runtime how the two interact.

3.2   Multimodal Semantics for Common Ground

In the previous section, we illustrated how the objects in the embedding space shared by participants in an interaction are encoded as VoxML multimodal representation. In this section, we describe the module within VoxWorld that is responsible for encoding and tracking the shared situational elements in a dialogue. Given the emphasis on evaluation of multimodal communication, we will pay particular attention to the semantics of integrated multimodal expressions in the context of task oriented dialogues. This will include the co-situated space the conversational agents share, beliefs about and perception of the objects in the environment, and the goals and intentions associated with both the task and the users, respectively, but also affordances associated with the objects present in the environment.

Following [58,61], we model this *common ground structure* (CGS), the information associated with a state in a dialogue, as a state monad, $M\alpha = State \rightarrow (\alpha \times State)$ [72]. We adopt a continuation-based semantics for both communicative acts in discourse, as outlined in [5,18]. The dialogue monad corresponds to computations that read and modify a particular state. The values returned by querying the monad include the following elements of the dialogue state:

- The communicative act, C_a, performed by an agent, a: a tuple of expressions from the diverse modalities involved. Broadly, this includes the modalities of a linguistic utterance, S (speech), gesture, G, facial expression, F, gaze, Z, and an explicit action, A: $C_a = \langle S, G, F, Z, A \rangle$.
- **A**: The agents engaged in communication;
- **B**: The salient shared belief space;
- **P**: The objects and relations that are jointly perceived in the environment;
- $\mathcal{E}$: The embedding space that both agents occupy in the communication.

Here we focus on a speech-gesture multimodal interaction, to illustrate how the common ground is computed. We first initialize the common ground based on shared beliefs and dynamic perceptual content for each of the agents. This can be represented graphically as below, where an agent, a_i, makes a communicative act either through gesture, $\mathcal{G}$ in (3.2a), or linguistically, as in (3.2b.)[1]

(1) a.
$$\frac{\textbf{A:}a_1, a_2 \quad \textbf{B:}\Delta \quad \textbf{P:}b \quad \mathcal{E}:E}{\mathcal{G}_{a_1}}$$
b.
$$\boxed{\begin{array}{l} \textbf{A:}a_1, a_2 \quad \textbf{B:}\Delta \quad \textbf{P:}b \quad \mathcal{E}:E \\ \mathcal{S}_{a_1} = \text{"You}_{a_2} \text{ see it}_b\text{"} \end{array}}$$

---

[1] This is similar in many respects to the representations introduced in [16,32] and [20] for modeling action and control with robots.

In order to see how embodiment and common ground structures contribute to the interpretation of multimodal expressions, let us review our assumptions regarding our model. Typically, a linguistic expression, S, is computed relative to a model, $\mathcal{M}$, and the relevant assignment functions, e.g., g: $[[\, S\,]]^{\mathcal{M},g}$. For every expression made in the dialogue, the information state (our monad) is updated through continuation-passing, as in [5]. For example, given the current discourse, D, and the new utterance, S, S integrates into D as follows:

(2) $[[\, \overline{(\mathbf{D.S})}\,]]^{M,cg} = \lambda i \lambda k.\ [[\, \overline{\mathbf{D}}\,]]i(\lambda i'.\ [[\, \overline{\mathbf{S}}\,]]i'k)$

This states that the current discourse has two arguments, its left context i (where we are), and what is expected later in the discourse, k.

When we move into multimodal dialogues, however, this model is not expressive enough, since it does not capture the interpretation of other modalities in the communication that convey denotative information (such as gesture), nor does it provide a situated grounding for the expressions within the dialogue state of the current context.

In order to enable reference to other modalities and their situational denotations, we introduce a *simulation* within which communicative expressions are interpreted. A simulation, $\mathcal{S}$, is defined as a triple, $\langle \mathcal{M}, \mathcal{E}, \mathcal{CG} \rangle$, consisting of a conventional model, $\mathcal{M}$, an embedding space, $\mathcal{E}$, together with a common ground structure, $\mathcal{CG}$. This definition brings together the three types of simulation discussed above. Now we can refer to an interpretation of an expression, α, within a simulation, as $[[\, \alpha\,]]^{\mathcal{S}}$.

Given a model within which we can potentially interpret additional modalities, let us briefly outline how one modality, gesture, can be modeled compositionally, and interpreted within a simulation, alone and when used in aligned co-gestural speech acts. We assume a dynamic interpretation for gesture that references the common ground structure in discourse. Extending the approach taken in [40] and [48], a gesture's **Stroke** will denote a range of primitive action types, $\mathcal{ACT}$, e.g., *grasp, pick up, move, throw, pull, push, separate,* and *put together*. In a multimodal dialogue, these gestures have two features; (a) the action's object is an embodied reference in the common ground; and (b) the gesture sequence must be interpreted dynamically, to correctly compute the end state of the event. Hence, we model two kinds of gestures in our dialogues: (a) establishing a reference; and (b) depicting an action-object pair.

(3) a. **Deixis:** $D_{obj} \rightarrow Dir\ Obj$
     b. **Action:** $G_{Af} \rightarrow Act\ Obj$

A gesture is directly interpretable by the agents in the context if and only if the value is clearly evident in the common ground, most likely through visual inspection. Directional or orientational information conveyed in a gesture identifies a distinct object or area of the embedding space, E, by directing attention to the End of the designated pointing ray (or cone) trace [48,50,58].

(4) $[[\, \mathbf{D}_{obj}\,]]^{\mathcal{S}} = End([[\, ray\,]]^{\mathcal{S}}([[\, \mathbf{d}\,]]^{\mathcal{S}}))$

In multimodal dialogue, language and gesture work together in a number of ways, where gesture might enhance an expression emotionally, or pick out a reference in context, or depict an action through iconic representation. For example, deictic gesture acts like a demonstrative in a referring expression, and embodied gesture, when enacted, becomes part of the embedding space. The embodied artificial agent can interpret and generate expressions like "this/that block," accompanied by deixis, and can do the same when referring to the embodiment of its interlocutor (e.g., "my/your arm"). While agents in the interaction are considered separately from objects in the model, the typing of embodied agents show they have properties of physical objects (e.g., a convex hull, an interaction with the physics of the world, etc.), and so can be discussed in similar terms.

In our theory, a multimodal communicative act, C, consists of a sequence of gesture-language ensembles, (g_i, s_i), where an ensemble is temporally aligned in the common ground. Let us assume that a linguistic subexpression, s, is either a word or full phrase in the utterance, while a gesture, g, comports with the gesture grammar described above.

(5) **Co-gestural Speech Ensemble:**
$$\begin{bmatrix} \mathcal{G} & g_1 \cdots g_i \cdots g_n \\ \mathcal{S} & s_1 \cdots s_i \cdots s_n \end{bmatrix}$$

We assume an aligned language-gesture syntactic structure, for which we have provided a continuized semantic interpretation [45,63]. Both of these are contained in the common ground state monad introduced above. For each temporally indexed and aligned gesture-speech pair, (g, s), we have a continuized interpretation, as shown below. Each modal expresssion carries a continuation, k_g or k_s, and we denote the alignment of these two continuations as $k_s \otimes k_g$, seen in (3.2).

(6) $\lambda k_s.k_s(\llbracket \mathbf{s} \rrbracket)$
   $\lambda k_g.k_g(\llbracket \mathbf{g} \rrbracket)$
   $\lambda k_s \otimes k_g.k_s \otimes k_g(\llbracket \mathbf{(s,g)} \rrbracket)$

Each of these modalities will contribute information if it is present. We bind co-gestural speech to specific gestures in the communicative act, within a common ground, CGS. A dashed line in an ensemble expression indicates that a co-gestural speech element, $\mathcal{S}$, is aligned with a particular gesture, $\mathcal{G}$. For example, the CG structure for the expression in Fig. 4 illustrates the alignment of the spoken demonstrative *that* with the denotation of the deictic gesture, following the computation in (3.2). This then takes the continuized right context of the gesture sequence, and binds this referent into the parameter structure for *grab*, resulting in the interpretation below.

(7) $Grab(a_2, b_1)$

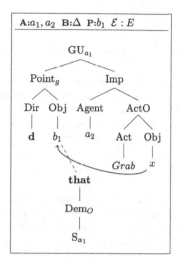

Fig. 4. Common-ground structure for "that" (ensemble) + "grab" (speech).

4   Conclusion

Across different fields and in the existing AI, cognition, and game development literature, there exist many different definitions of "simulation." Nonetheless, we believe the common thread between them is that simulations as a framework facilitate both qualitative and quantitative reasoning by providing quantitative data (for example, exact coordinates or rotations) that can be easily converted into qualitative representations. This makes simulation an effective platform for both producing and learning from datasets.

When combined with formal encodings of object and event semantics, at a level higher than treating objects as collections of geometries, or events as sequences of motions or object relations, 3D environments provide a powerful platform for exploring "computational embodied cognition." Recent developments in the AI field have shown that common-sense understanding in a general domain requires either orders of magnitude more training data than traditional deep learning models, or more easily decidable representations, involving context, differences in perspective, and grounded concepts, to name a few.

Technologies in use in the gaming industry are proving to be effective platforms on which to develop systems that afford gathering both traditional data for deep learning and representations of common sense, situated, or embodied understanding. In addition, game engines perform a lot of "heavy lifting," providing APIs for UI and physics, among others, which allows researchers to focus on implementing truly novel functionality and develop tools to deploy and examine the role of embodiment in human-computer interaction both quantitatively and qualitatively. In Part 2, we will describe such a system and experimental evaluations on it.

References

1. Anderson, M.L.: Embodied cognition: a field guide. Artif. Intell. **149**(1), 91–130 (2003)
2. Andrist, S., Gleicher, M., Mutlu, B.: Looking coordinated: bidirectional gaze mechanisms for collaborative interaction with virtual characters. In: Proceedings of the 2017 CHI Conference on Human Factors in Computing Systems CHI 2017, pp. 2571–2582. ACM, New York (2017). https://doi.org/10.1145/3025453.3026033, http://doi.acm.org/10.1145/3025453.3026033
3. Asher, N.: Common ground, corrections and coordination. J. Semant. (1998)
4. Asher, N., Lascarides, A.: Logics of Conversation. Cambridge University Press, Cambridge (2003)
5. Asher, N., Pogodalla, S.: SDRT and continuation semantics. In: Onada, T., Bekki, D., McCready, E. (eds.) JSAI-isAI 2010. LNCS (LNAI), vol. 6797, pp. 3–15. Springer, Heidelberg (2011). https://doi.org/10.1007/978-3-642-25655-4_2
6. Barsalou, L.W.: Perceptions of perceptual symbols. Behav. Brain Sci. **22**(4), 637–660 (1999)
7. Bergen, B.K.: Louder than Words: The New Science of How the Mind Makes Meaning. Basic Books, New York (2012)
8. Bolt, R.A.: "Put-that-there": voice and gesture at the graphics interface, vol. 14. ACM (1980)
9. Brennan, S.E., Chen, X., Dickinson, C.A., Neider, M.B., Zelinsky, G.J.: Coordinating cognition: the costs and benefits of shared gaze during collaborative search. Cognition **106**(3), 1465–1477 (2008). https://doi.org/10.1016/j.cognition.2007.05.012. http://www.sciencedirect.com/science/article/pii/S0010027707001448
10. Cassell, J.: Embodied Conversational Agents. MIT Press, Cambridge (2000)
11. Cassell, J., Stone, M., Yan, H.: Coordination and context-dependence in the generation of embodied conversation. In: Proceedings of the First International Conference on Natural Language Generation, vol. 14, pp. 171–178. Association for Computational Linguistics (2000)
12. Chrisley, R.: Embodied artificial intelligence. Artif. Intell. **149**(1), 131–150 (2003)
13. Clair, A.S., Mead, R., Matarić, M.J., et al.: Monitoring and guiding user attention and intention in human-robot interaction. In: ICRA-ICAIR Workshop, Anchorage, AK, USA, vol. 1025 (2010)
14. Clark, H.H., Brennan, S.E.: Grounding in communication. In: Resnick, L.B., Levine, J.M., Teasley, S.D. (eds.) Perspectives on Socially Shared Cognition, vol. 13, pp. 127–149. American Psychological Association, Washington DC (1991)
15. Clark, H.H., Wilkes-Gibbs, D.: Referring as a collaborative process. Cognition **22**(1), 1–39 (1986). https://doi.org/10.1016/0010-0277(86)90010-7. http://www.sciencedirect.com/science/article/pii/0010027786900107
16. Cooper, R., Ginzburg, J.: Type theory with records for natural language semantics. In: Lappin, S., Fox, C. (eds.) The Handbook of Contemporary Semantic Theory, p. 375. Wiley, Hoboken (2015)
17. Craik, K.J.W.: The Nature of Explanation. Cambridge University, Cambridge (1943)
18. De Groote, P.: Type raising, continuations, and classical logic. In: Proceedings of the Thirteenth Amsterdam Colloquium, pp. 97–101 (2001)
19. Dillenbourg, P., Traum, D.: Sharing solutions: persistence and grounding in multimodal collaborative problem solving. J. Learn. Sci. **15**(1), 121–151 (2006)

20. Dobnik, S., Cooper, R., Larsson, S.: Modelling language, action, and perception in type theory with records. In: Duchier, D., Parmentier, Y. (eds.) CSLP 2012. LNCS, vol. 8114, pp. 70–91. Springer, Heidelberg (2013). https://doi.org/10.1007/978-3-642-41578-4_5
21. Dumas, B., Lalanne, D., Oviatt, S.: Multimodal interfaces: a survey of principles, models and frameworks. In: Lalanne, D., Kohlas, J. (eds.) Human Machine Interaction. LNCS, vol. 5440, pp. 3–26. Springer, Heidelberg (2009). https://doi.org/10.1007/978-3-642-00437-7_1
22. Eisenstein, J., Barzilay, R., Davis, R.: Discourse topic and gestural form. In: AAAI, pp. 836–841 (2008)
23. Eisenstein, J., Barzilay, R., Davis, R.: Gesture salience as a hidden variable for coreference resolution and keyframe extraction. J. Artif. Intell. Res. 31, 353–398 (2008)
24. Evans, V.: Language and Time: a Cognitive Linguistics Approach. Cambridge University Press, Cambridge (2013)
25. Feldman, J.: Embodied language, best-fit analysis, and formal compositionality. Phys. Life Rev. 7(4), 385–410 (2010)
26. Fernando, T.: Situations in LTL as strings. Inf. Comput. 207(10), 980–999 (2009)
27. Fussell, S.R., Kraut, R.E., Siegel, J.: Coordination of communication: effects of shared visual context on collaborative work. In: Proceedings of the 2000 ACM Conference on Computer Supported Cooperative Work CSCW 2000, pp. 21–30. ACM, New York (2000). https://doi.org/10.1145/358916.358947, http://doi.acm.org/10.1145/358916.358947
28. Fussell, S.R., Setlock, L.D., Yang, J., Ou, J., Mauer, E., Kramer, A.D.I.: Gestures over video streams to support remote collaboration on physical tasks. Hum. Comput. Interact. 19(3), 273–309 (2004). https://doi.org/10.1207/s15327051hci1903_3
29. Gergle, D., Kraut, R.E., Fussell, S.R.: Action as language in a shared visual space. In: Proceedings of the 2004 ACM Conference on Computer Supported Cooperative Work CSCW 2004, pp. 487–496. ACM, New York (2004). https://doi.org/10.1145/1031607.1031687, http://doi.acm.org/10.1145/1031607.1031687
30. Gibson, J.J., Reed, E.S., Jones, R.: Reasons for Realism: Selected Essays of James J. Gibson. Lawrence Erlbaum Associates, Mahwah (1982)
31. Gilbert, M.: On Social Facts. Princeton University Press, Princeton (1992)
32. Ginzburg, J., Fernández, R.: Computational models of dialogue. In: Clark, A., Fox, C., Lappin, S. (eds.) The Handbook of Computational Linguistics and Natural Language Processing, vol. 57, p. 1. Wiley, Hoboken (2010)
33. Goldman, A.I.: Interpretation psychologized*. Mind Lang. 4(3), 161–185 (1989)
34. Goldman, A.I.: Simulating Minds: The Philosophy, Psychology, and Neuroscience of Mindreading. Oxford University Press, Oxford (2006)
35. Gordon, R.M.: Folk psychology as simulation. Mind Lang. 1(2), 158–171 (1986)
36. Graesser, A.C., Singer, M., Trabasso, T.: Constructing inferences during narrative text comprehension. Psychol. Rev. 101(3), 371 (1994)
37. Heal, J.: Simulation, theory, and content. In: Carruthers, P., Smith, P.K. (eds.) Theories of Theories of Mind, pp. 75–89. Cambridge University Press, Cambridge (1996)
38. Johnson-Laird, P.N., Byrne, R.M.: Conditionals: a theory of meaning, pragmatics, and inference. Psychol. Rev. 109(4), 646 (2002)
39. Johnson-Laird, P.: How could consciousness arise from the computations of the brain. In: Mindwaves, pp. 247–257 Basil Blackwell, Oxford (1987)
40. Kendon, A.: Gesture: Visible Action as Utterance. Cambridge University Press, Cambridge (2004)

41. Kennington, C., Kousidis, S., Schlangen, D.: Interpreting situated dialogue utterances: an update model that uses speech, gaze, and gesture information. In: Proceedings of SigDial 2013 (2013)
42. Kiela, D., Bulat, L., Vero, A.L., Clark, S.: Virtual embodiment: a scalable long-term strategy for artificial intelligence research. arXiv preprint arXiv:1610.07432 (2016)
43. Kraut, R.E., Fussell, S.R., Siegel, J.: Visual information as a conversational resource in collaborative physical tasks. Hum. Comput. Interact. 18(1), 13–49 (2003). https://doi.org/10.1207/S15327051HCI1812_2
44. Krishnaswamy, N., Pustejovsky, J.: Multimodal semantic simulations of linguistically underspecified motion events. In: Barkowsky, T., Burte, H., Hölscher, C., Schultheis, H. (eds.) Spatial Cognition/KogWis -2016. LNCS (LNAI), vol. 10523, pp. 177–197. Springer, Cham (2017). https://doi.org/10.1007/978-3-319-68189-4_11
45. Krishnaswamy, N., Pustejovsky, J.: Multimodal continuation-style architectures for human-robot interaction. arXiv preprint arXiv:1909.08161 (2019)
46. Lascarides, A., Stone, M.: Formal semantics for iconic gesture. In: Proceedings of the 10th Workshop on the Semantics and Pragmatics of Dialogue (BRANDIAL), pp. 64–71 (2006)
47. Lascarides, A., Stone, M.: Discourse coherence and gesture interpretation. Gesture 9(2), 147–180 (2009). https://doi.org/10.1075/gest.9.2.01las. http://www.jbe-platform.com/content/journals/10.1075/gest.9.2.01las
48. Lascarides, A., Stone, M.: A formal semantic analysis of gesture. J. Semant. 26, 393–449 (2009)
49. Lücking, A., Mehler, A., Walther, D., Mauri, M., Kurfürst, D.: Finding recurrent features of image schema gestures: the figure corpus. In: Proceedings of the Tenth International Conference on Language Resources and Evaluation (LREC 2016), pp. 1426–1431 (2016)
50. Lücking, A., Pfeiffer, T., Rieser, H.: Pointing and reference reconsidered. J. Pragmat. 77, 56–79 (2015)
51. Marshall, P., Hornecker, E.: Theories of embodiment in HCI. In: Price, S., Jewitt, C., Brown, B. (eds.) The SAGE Handbook of Digital Technology Research, vol. 1, pp. 144–158. Sage, Thousand Oaks (2013)
52. Matuszek, C., Bo, L., Zettlemoyer, L., Fox, D.: Learning from unscripted deictic gesture and language for human-robot interactions. In: AAAI, pp. 2556–2563 (2014)
53. Mehlmann, G., Häring, M., Janowski, K., Baur, T., Gebhard, P., André, E.: Exploring a model of gaze for grounding in multimodal HRI. In: Proceedings of the 16th International Conference on Multimodal Interaction ICMI 2014, pp. 247–254. ACM, New York (2014). https://doi.org/10.1145/2663204.2663275, http://doi.acm.org/10.1145/2663204.2663275
54. Narayanan, S.: Mind changes: a simulation semantics account of counterfactuals. Cogn. Sci. (2010)
55. Naumann, R.: Aspects of changes: a dynamic event semantics. J. Semant. 18, 27–81 (2001)
56. Pustejovsky, J.: The Generative Lexicon. MIT Press, Cambridge (1995)
57. Pustejovsky, J.: Dynamic event structure and habitat theory. In: Proceedings of the 6th International Conference on Generative Approaches to the Lexicon (GL2013), pp. 1–10. ACL (2013)
58. Pustejovsky, J.: From actions to events: communicating through language and gesture. Interact. Stud. 19(1–2), 289–317 (2018)

59. Pustejovsky, J.: From experiencing events in the action-perception cycle to representing events in language. Interact. Stud. **19** (2018)
60. Pustejovsky, J., Krishnaswamy, N.: VoxML: A visualization modeling language. In: Chair, N.C.C., et al. (eds.) Proceedings of the Tenth International Conference on Language Resources and Evaluation (LREC 2016). European Language Resources Association (ELRA), Paris, France, May 2016
61. Pustejovsky, J., Krishnaswamy, N.: Embodied human-computer interactions through situated grounding. In: Proceedings of the 20th ACM International Conference on Intelligent Virtual Agents, pp. 1–3 (2020)
62. Pustejovsky, J., Krishnaswamy, N.: Embodied human computer interaction. Künstliche Intelligenz (2021)
63. Pustejovsky, J., Krishnaswamy, N.: Situated meaning in multimodal dialogue: Human-robot and human-computer interactions. Traitement Automatique des Langues **62**(1) (2021)
64. Pustejovsky, J., Moszkowicz, J.: The qualitative spatial dynamics of motion. J. Spatial Cognit. Comput. **11**, 15–44 (2011)
65. Quek, F., et al.: Multimodal human discourse: gesture and speech. ACM Trans. Comput.-Hum. Interact. (TOCHI) **9**(3), 171–193 (2002)
66. Ravenet, B., Pelachaud, C., Clavel, C., Marsella, S.: Automating the production of communicative gestures in embodied characters. Front. Psychol. **9**, 1144 (2018)
67. Shapiro, L.: The Routledge Handbook of Embodied Cognition. Routledge, New York (2014)
68. Skantze, G., Hjalmarsson, A., Oertel, C.: Turn-taking, feedback and joint attention in situated human-robot interaction. Speech Commun. **65**, 50–66 (2014). https://doi.org/10.1016/j.specom.2014.05.005. http://www.sciencedirect.com/science/article/pii/S016763931400051X
69. Stalnaker, R.: Common ground. Linguist. Philos. **25**(5–6), 701–721 (2002)
70. Tomasello, M., Carpenter, M.: Shared intentionality. Dev. Sci. **10**(1), 121–125 (2007)
71. Turk, M.: Multimodal interaction: a review. Pattern Recogn. Lett. **36**, 189–195 (2014)
72. Unger, C.: Dynamic semantics as monadic computation. In: Okumura, M., Bekki, D., Satoh, K. (eds.) JSAI-isAI 2011. LNCS (LNAI), vol. 7258, pp. 68–81. Springer, Heidelberg (2012). https://doi.org/10.1007/978-3-642-32090-3_7
73. Zwaan, R.A., Pecher, D.: Revisiting mental simulation in language comprehension: six replication attempts. PLoS ONE **7**(12), e51382 (2012)
74. Zwaan, R.A., Radvansky, G.A.: Situation models in language comprehension and memory. Psychol. Bull. **123**(2), 162 (1998)

The History of Agent-Based Modeling in the Social Sciences

Carl Orge Retzlaff[ID], Martina Ziefle[ID], and André Calero Valdez[✉][ID]

Human-Computer Interaction Center, RWTH Aachen University,
Campus-Boulevard 57, 52076 Aachen, Germany
`carl.orge.retzlaff@rwth-aachen.de`,
`{ziefle,calero-valdez}@comm.rwth-aachen.de`

Abstract. Agent-based modeling is a powerful technique that allows modeling social phenomena ab-initio or from first principles. In this paper, we review the history of agent-based models and their role in the social sciences. We review 62 papers and create a timeline of developments starting from 1759 and Adam Smith into the recent past of 2020 and efforts to model the Covid-19 pandemic. We reflect on model validation, different levels of model complexity, multi-scale models, and cognitive architectures. We identify key trends for the future use of agent-based modeling in the socials sciences.

Keywords: Literature review · Agent-based models · System Dynamics · Complex systems · Disease modeling · Model evaluation

1 Introduction

Agent-based modeling (ABM) is an increasingly popular modeling type that allows researchers to let virtual agents interact with each other. By defining a set of simple rules on the micro-scale, complex behavior at the macro-scale can emerge. The ant hive for example is a highly complex building with a faceted hierarchy and interaction, which emerges from the interaction of the very basic instincts of individual ants.

The agents-based approach is inherently bottom-up, facilitating understanding of how complex phenomena emerge from seemingly simple interactions at the micro-level. ABM is a relatively young modeling technique from the 1970s and deeply connected to the social sciences. ABM focuses, much like the social sciences, on how individual behavior produces larger patterns. This explains why some of the most important contributions to ABM are tied to social phenomena like the neighborhood segregation (Axelrod 1980) or the spread of opinions (Hegselmann and Krause 2002).

Current applications of ABM can be found in biology and infection modeling, finance and market models, robotics, and cargo routing. With the growth of the Artificial Intelligence field, especially with Machine and Deep Learning approaches, the capabilities of cognitive architectures for individual agents changes, and further applications like generating training data are being investigated.

© Springer Nature Switzerland AG 2021
V. G. Duffy (Ed.): HCII 2021, LNCS 12777, pp. 304–319, 2021.
https://doi.org/10.1007/978-3-030-77817-0_22

2   Research Methods and Result Structure

This paper is focused on explaining the history of ABM models and its major influences. As main body of this paper, the most significant authors and their contributions to the field of ABM are detailed. The choice of the selected contributions is influenced by the number of citations on Google Scholar as well as the scope of influence on other contributions. To exemplify the application of ABM in different fields, fewer cited papers are also taken into account.

In overall, 62 contributions are included in this paper to create a comprehensive overview. Four main epochs of ABM were identified, ranging from 1970 to 2021 and described. A central result of this paper is Fig. 1, which provides an overview of the different epochs of Agent-Based Modeling, its predecessors and main contributors.

3   History of ABM and Social Sciences

As Engbert et al. (2020) stated, one of the drawbacks of conventional disease-modeling techniques such as SIR is their assumption of homogeneous population mixing, which does not reflect the behaviour of individuals in the real world. A technique that allows to incorporate this kind of behaviour is Agent-Based modeling. The concept of ABM is the simulation of multiple individual agents whose behavior is described by simple rules. By describing the autonomous behavior and properties of the discrete agents on micro-scale, complex behavior at the macro-scale (in the following also referred to as macro-behavior) can be modeled (Rand and Rust 2011). An ABM usually is set in a given space, which is then used to simulate and track the movement of individuals alone and between social groups. This allows to further investigate the spatial aspect of the transmission of diseases, which was a limitation of classic differential equation based models (Perez and Dragicevic 2009).

Railsback and Grimm (2011) name other examples that show the benefits of ABM, such as in the modeling of biological systems (Railsback et al. 2013), the finance market or cargo routing. Buchanan (2009) states that disasters such as the financial crisis from 2008 are partially due to untested political measures that set off unforeseen consequences, and recommends testing the impact of those measures on the market using ABM before deploying them.

Heath (2010) traces the history of the ABMs back for hundreds of years, when complex phenomena, applied to vastly different systems, were captured with mechanisms at micro-scale by ground-laying works of the like of Adam Smith, Donald Hebbs and Richard Dawkins.

In Adam Smiths Invisible Hand of 1759, individual agents take self-interested actions, which result in mutual advantage an unintended social benefits for the community (Smith 2002). The phenomena of the Invisible Hand is the central justification for neoliberal theories of free markets (Binkley 2002).

Donald Hebbs theory of Cell Assembly of 1949 states that the complex phenomenon of memory is created by the comparatively simple interaction of individual neurons in certain hierarchy patterns (Attneave et al. 1950), and is often summarized as "Neurons wire together if they fire together" (Löwel and Singer 1992).

Dawkins coins the term "memes" in 1976 as a self-replicating, cultural unit, that is subject to the pressures of evolution as observed in biological systems, and results in the complex cultural patterns that can be seen in the real world (Dawkins 2014).

What all of these works have in common is the idea of simple, individual agents that, by interacting with each other, generate some observed pattern, just as the Agent-Based Models aim to. But an important intermediate step between the underlying concept of emerging patterns and the computer-based ABMs we see today, is the Cellular Automata (CA).

3.1 Roots of ABM

The concept of a CA is based on Von Neumannm, who constructed the theory of a self-reproducing machine in 1950. This theoretical machine carries a blueprint and tools to reproduce itself, and also allows its offspring to again be able to reproduce even further. This machine was very complex, resulting in 29 different logical states of the machines components to reproduce itself successfully (Langton 1984). Von Neumann was convinced that complex patterns required complex mechanisms, and adhered to the top-down approach of understanding the global system before investigating the constituents of it.

Von Neumanns colleague Ulam added the idea of a cellular automaton (CA) to the self-replicating machine, which is composed of individual cells on a checkerboard field that interact with each other. This idea also introduced parallelism to the automaton, which allowed to model global behaviour based on the interaction of single agents, and represents a change from the top-down to bottom-up approach. It also accounted for the parallelism often observed in nature (Heath 2010).

Scientists began to use CAs when investigating the complexity of nature and observed patterns. One of the most famous uses of CA was introduced by Conways "Game of Life", which was using very simple rules to generate a virtual world (Gardner 1970). From these simple rules, patterns such as "gliders" can emerge, and eventually even patterns were found that allow the self-replication of objects, alluding to complex life forms that are composed of simple atoms joined together (Aaron 2010). What separates CA from ABM is that in cellular automata, agents are stationary, whereas agents can move freely (according to their programmed behaviour) across their given space in ABM, which allows to represent and model a much wider variety of phenomenons (Wilensky and Rand 2015).

Another important factor in the development of ABMs were Complex Adaptive Systems (CAS). CAS are rooted in biological systems and take factors like diversity (i.e., different reactions to the same stimulus) and information flow between agents into account. They are, for example, used to gain insights into the formation of complex behaviour and the creation of biological systems as a whole, and were an important base for the design of ABM (Macal and North 2006).

Another important influence was the System Dynamics approach by Forrester which models the nonlinear behaviour of a system with feedback loops, signal delays, and other complex behaviour. It is for example known for its application in the "Limits to Growth" model from the Club of Rome where the exponential growth of economy and population and linear growth of available resources is simulated (Turner 2008).

In the previous paragraphs the deterministic and stochastic modeling techniques were compared. Adding to this comparison, the System Dynamics approach allows the precise study of a complex system, but requires that the rules are stated at macro-level, which is not always feasible (Rand and Rust 2011).

3.2 Evolution of ABMs and the Influence of Social Sciences

What the hereinafter discussed models have in common is that they aim to generate some of the emerging behaviours observed in complex systems from a simple set of rules. This makes it possible to observe and understand the behaviours of complex systems without knowledge of the entire system and with limited computing resources (Heath 2010). While Multi-Agents Systems (MAS) are more often applied with a focus on solving a specific scientific problem (Abdallah and Lesser 2007), ABMs are used to examine and understand systems and patterns from the bottom up. Helbing and Balietti (2011) names heterogeneity (individual behaviour can vary between agents) and stochasticity (the system can exhibit random variations) as two important properties of ABMs. Figure 1 was created to provide an overview of the evolution of ABMs with a timeline of important contributions to ABM and its influences.

One of the first ABMs was the Segregation model, presented by Schelling in 1971. Schelling shows how in a shared space, agents with individual preferences for neighbours of the same type can generate segregated neighbourhoods, much like those that can be observed in the real world. The first versions of this model were paper-based, but still embodied the agent-based approach of individual agents on a shared space, creating a complex outcome based on the agents behaviour and preferences (Schelling 2013).

In the 1970s and 1980s, many other ABMs were developed, such as the Prisoners Dilemma Tournament and Culture Dissemination model from Axelrod. Both show how the application of ABMs became more common, facilitated by advanced computing powers and software. The Prisoners Dilemma model was intended as a tournament, where different strategies for the famous prisoners dilemma were used to investigate which behaviour would prove most beneficial to an individual agent. Surprisingly, the winning strategy was the simplest strategy, "Tit for That", which mimicked the last action of the opposing player, and showed how altruistic behaviour (termed "niceness") can be in the long run favourable for an individual (Axelrod 1980).

The model of Culture Dissemination is based on the tendency of individuals to exhibit some kind of cultural convergence, that is to adapt the traits (be it beliefs, attitudes, or behaviour) of neighbours. Axelrod (1997) aims to model the social influence of others and the emerging patterns such as a global differences despite local convergence. An important feature is that the exchange of traits is not sequential but parallel, allowing interaction between different traits, which is also an important aspect in real-life behaviour (Axelrod 1997).

The next steps towards modern ABMs were facilitated by the development of different modeling software in the 1990s, which enabled easier creation and configuration of ABMs. Software such as Ascape enabled SugarScape, a multi-purpose ABM from Epstein and Axtell which inspired many generative social science models and was used to investigate and model different social phenomena (Wilensky and Rand 2015). Axtell and Epstein also provided several implementations of the SugarScape model and showed how collective behavior like cultural transmission, exchange of goods, and fighting between agents emerges from simple rules and behaviors (Epstein and Axtell 1998). Other widely used software was NetLogo (1999), Swarm (1997), Repast (2000) and MASON (2003), as reviewed by Railsback et al. (2006).

Of course, most of these tools have their own focus on a certain field. Whereas Repast focuses on large-scale simulation and social science aspects, Swarm was specialized on the simulation of biology. Together, these different tools allowed ABM to be applied in vastly different contexts, such as the study of social systems, ecology, economics or geography (Samuelson and Macal 2006).

(Jackson et al. 2017) find that ABM is especially useful to study the emergence of phenomena, which is a subject often studied in social psychology. The idea that aggregation of small-scale individual behavior leads to different collective behaviors is often reflected in real-world phenomenons like traffic jams and human consciousness. The authors furthermore point out that often, the magnitude of emergence furthers the impact the ABM—that is, to explain a lot of complexity with simple rules.

The advantages of ABM, especially for the application to social sciences, are a large statistical power since experiments can be scaled up easily and be well controlled, opposed to real-world experiments. Also, nonlinear dynamics can be introduced and mechanisms isolated, which poses a significant problem in conventional experiments.

As (Calero Valdez and Ziefle 2018) points out, these advantages could be applied to many modern problems where human interaction with technology leads to the emergence of a variety of extremely nonlinear phenomena. In the field of social simulation, the effect of social bots, fake news and filter bubbles could be explored since ABMs could account for the complexity of interaction as well as provide the controlled environment for such experiments.

An example application in the field of social science is the model of Opinion Dynamics of Hegselmann and Krause (2002). It investigated the formation of opinions in interacting groups and whether consensus, polarization or fragmentation emerged from this interaction. In this non-spatial model, bounded confidence emerges as the most important parameter, which describes the phenomenon that the opinion of an agent can not be influenced by a source when he disagreed strongly with it. The factor of opinion distance describes this difference, and if the difference becomes too great, opinion change does not occur.

Other recent contributions to the social sciences and the modeling of epidemics were made by Epstein, such as the technique of growing phenomena of interest in a society of agents (Epstein 2012), introducing fear and flight as important factors in agent behaviour during an epidemic (Epstein et al. 2008) and refining agent behaviour by endowing them with modules for emotional, cognitive and social reasoning (Epstein 2014).

Another example for the application of ABM in recent times is the finance sector. As Franke and Westerhoff (2012) find, ABMs are better suited to explain the stochastic volatility on the pricing dynamics of assets. Fagiolo and Roventini (2017) evaluate that ABMs have become a valid alternative to conventional Dynamic Stochastic General Equilibrium models in macroeconomic policies. After the financial crisis of 2008, many present models that predicted an general equilibrium in the financial sector were reevaluated since they failed to predict the significant crisis that occurred. Since ABMs can provide an alternative to the present model, many models have emerged that studied the impact of regulations on the financial market or warning signals of future crises (Buchanan 2009).

An interesting project at the intersection of financial and social model is the EURACE model, an European project that attempts to generate an ABM of the European economy. The model is devised as massively parallel ABM, containing a large agent population and a complex economic environment. It is based on the philosophy of the research on Generative Social Science from Epstein and Axtell (1998) and one of the first successful attempts to build an ABM of a complete economy, integrating mechanisms of the economy and its most important markets into it (Cincotti et al. 2010).

To support such a complex model, the Flexible Large-scale Agent modeling Environment (FLAME) was developed, which allowed performant parallel computation and the big scale of agents (Deissenberg et al. 2008). From computational experiments with the model, many publications about macro-economic effects resulted, such as about the importance of the lending activity of regulating banks (Raberto et al. 2019), the relevance of credit (Cincotti et al. 2010) or housing market bubbles (Erlingsson et al. 2014).

In the highly influential work of (Bonabeau 2002), Bonabeu names four main areas where ABMs can be applied to business processes in the real world: diffusion, market, organizational, and flow simulation. He emphasises the importance of social aspects of these models and their use as learning tool, which can help better understand marketplaces and customers.

ABMs provide a new approach to the presented methods (deterministic, stochastic, cellular automata, system dynamics, multi-agent system). Agents can behave deterministic or random, based on their programmed behavior, since they allow the modeler to select which behavior to employ. Random behavior can be a good choice when not all aspects of the model have to be specified for reasons of complexity, and still achieve a passable approximation of real world concepts (Wilensky and Rand 2015).

ABMs can provide a micro-level view of the disease spread instead of the population-level view of the SIR model, which allows to better explore behavior at the individual-level and the resulting large-scale patterns. To construct an equation-based model, knowledge of the global behaviour is required so that the model can be verified against the real-world phenomenon, which is not always the case. Oftentimes, insight into the global behavior is even the goal one wants to achieve with the model, which makes ABM a valid candidate for disease spread simulation (Wilensky and Rand 2015).

This approach however also introduces three difficulties as stated by Keeling and Danon (2009): understanding the individual behavior with regard to disease spread, required data at individual rather than global level, and finally complexity and computational requirements.

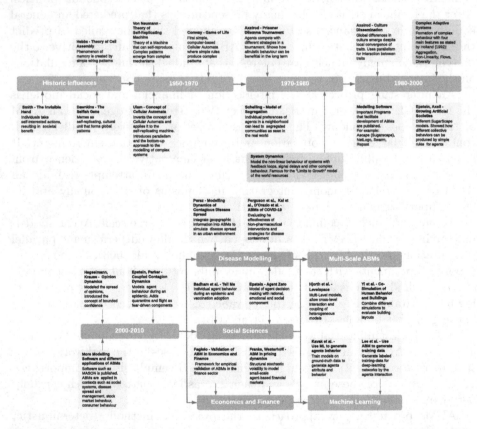

Fig. 1. Timeline of the evolution of ABM and its influences. ABM started in the 1950s and is now applied to fields like disease modeling, social sciences and economics. ABM was influenced by approaches like Complex Adaptive Systems and System Dynamics. For a larger version of this figure, got to https://osf.io/8jk9h/

3.3   Current Topics in ABM

Two major and ongoing research topics in the field of ABM are model-validation and verification and the modeling and realistic replication of human behavior (Kennedy 2011). A third noteworthy topic is the lack of influence of ABM, especially with regard to the Social Sciences. Regarding the validation of ABMs, Windrum et al. (2007) identified four major issues: a lack of a core set of modeling frameworks, issues in regard to the comparability of ABMs, no unified standard procedures for the construction of ABMs, and a difficult empirical validation. This leads to the first of the two most recent trends: model validation.

The validity of a model shows whether the model output is consistent with the results seen in the real world and if the developed, conceptual model represents the modeled system adequately. Through the process of calibration, the model parameters are adjusted with the aim to increase the model accuracy (Xiang et al. 2005). The conventional method for validation is the result validation approach, which simply compares the results of the ABM simulation with data from the real-world system. This validation method motivates the requirement for accurate data of the real-world system, which might not be always available or otherwise infeasible to obtain (Olsen and Kaunak 2016). Windrum et al. (2007) published an influential study about development approaches and the empirical validation of ABMs for economic models which highlighted the need for empirical model validation techniques for the reasons mentioned above. The study compared empirical validation procedures and found the "Indirect Calibration Approach" to be the most popular.

In 2019, Fagiolo et al. (2017) did a renewed survey of validation methods based on the review of Windrum et al. and evaluated the Indirect Calibration Approach as still most widely adopted approach. It consists of four steps (Fagiolo et al. 2017, pp. 3–5):

1. Identification of real-world stylized facts
2. Specification of model behavior
3. Validation and hypothesis testing
4. Application of the model for policy analysis

These steps provide a comprehensive guide for the validation of an ABM and will be taken into account in the model validation of this paper.

The second major development in ABMs was the progress in the development agent behaviour, based on abstractions of real cognitive processes. As Caillou et al. (2017) state, the biggest obstacles for cognitive architectures in ABM are limited processing power and the added complexity of modeling the behaviour.

Kennedy (2011) categorizes three different cognitive approaches for modeling human behavior in ABMs: mathematical, conceptual and cognitive. The mathematical approach generates the agent behavior by mathematical simplifications, for example by comparing a threshold against an input value. The conceptual approach takes concepts like the emotional state and intentions of the agent into account, but is still just a conceptual framework that abstracts cognitive functioning. The cognitive approach aims to model the cognitive function of the target agent, the basic cognitive system of the agent does not change during the model execution.

The mathematical approach was the first architecture that was used in ABM and can be seen in examples such as Schellings segregation model (Schelling 2013) or Axelrods model of culture dissemination (Axelrod 1997). These models have in common that the behavior of the agent is represented by a very simplified reasoning captured in an intuitive mathematical model. The conceptual approach to ABM introduces more complex agent reasoning process with concepts such as beliefs, desires, or emotional states, which was facilitated by advancing computational resources that allowed to simulate this behaviour. An example is the introduction of the Beliefs Desire Intentions or BDI architecture to the modeling language GAML (Caillou et al. 2017), or the architecture of the Agent Zero agent with an emotional, rational, and social component (Epstein 2014). These models provide a middle ground between the simple rules of the mathematical models and the complexity of a model of human cognition of the cognitive approach. They allow for a more realistic, complex agent behaviour while keeping computational costs and model complexity so far in check as to allow sizeable models.

The cognitive approach uses cognitive architectures that model human behaviour. Since human behavior is not fully understood by now, different architectures implement different mechanisms to partially or fully replicate human behavior in different aspects (Ritter et al. 2019). As of now, cognitive models are mainly employed in controlled environments, since they can be unnecessary complex for tasks where simpler agent models could lead to a similar behaviour fit with less complex cognitive models (Reitter and Lebiere 2010). The drawback of high complexity manifests in a lower number of active agents for simulations with complex cognitive architectures, so that with the application of SOAR of Naveh and Sun (2006) no more than ten cognitive agents are active at a time, while the work of Bhattacharya et al. (2019) with a simpler cognitive architecture employs up to three million simultaneous agents. These agent numbers are not objectively compared, but rather serve to exemplify the magnitude of difference.

This performance drawback was reduced over time with advancements in computational power and the steady development of high-performance cognitive models such as ACT-UP (Reitter and Lebiere 2010) or Matrix (Bhattacharya et al. 2019), which aim to make these models more accessible, easier to develop and faster to compute. Especially ACT-R and SOAR are well-established and have an active community (Kennedy 2011). Examples of the application of cognitive architecture are the implementation of Naveh and Sun, which implement the CLARION model to simulate academic science and publications (Naveh and Sun 2006).

Reitter and Lebiere (2010) demonstrated up to 1000 active agents in their model ACT-UP, in the Matrix model up to three million agents were simulated on computing nodes with 30+ cores (Bhattacharya et al. 2019). Salvucci (2009) modeled the dangers of using a telephone while driving a car, based on the cognitive model ACT-R with a vision and motor system connected to a driving simulator, while the same cognitive agent was instructed to go through the steps of dialing a telephone. However, the overall evolution of cognitive models still proves challenging. Modern AI has made a lot of improvements in this direction, but the long-promised unified theory of cognition is, more than 30 years after its conception, still just within reach Ritter et al. (2019).

A third current non-topic is the lack of major impact on mainstream social science research of ABMs (Bruch and Atwell 2015). The most influential examples, the neighborhood segregation and prisoners dilemma models, were mentioned in the history of ABM. The lack of communication between experts in social science research and the ABM modeling community is identified as central reason for the discrepancy between the advantages stated earlier and the lack of significant works. However, this gap is closing with the growing accessibility of ABM and general prevalence of software in all aspects of our lives, and ABMs have found more use in recent times.

More recent examples of the application of ABMs can be found in the Social Epidemiology. Cerdá et al. (2018) investigate the influence of interventions on development of violence in urban neighborhoods. An explanation of group formation in homogeneous populations, where in-group cooperation is observed even though no clear-cut definition of in- and out-members and self-evident group identity, is presented by Gray et al. (2014).

A significant recent application is found at the intersection of disease and social modeling with the COVID-19 epidemic. Since 2020, 1300 articles were published according to Google Scholar, indicating great interest in the topic. Since Non-Pharmaceutical Interventions form a central aspect of every COVID-control strategy and rely on the acceptance of the population, modeling the uptake and upkeep of such measures is of great interest (Hoertel et al. 2021). Furthermore, modeling the social networks itself is of importance since these form an essential part of disease transmission Hinch et al. (2020). These aspects could be much improved when applying the expertise of social scientist familiar with the intricacies and mechanisms of risk perception and reaction to it.

3.4   Future Trends

On a model level scale, the adaptation of multi-scale models is a noteworthy trend. The level-space extension of Hjorth et al. (2020) adapts the concept of multi-level agent based models. This approach allows to connect and integrate multiple models and levels, allowing cross-level interaction, adapting the level of detail dynamically and generally coupling heterogeneous models to simulating interacting systems. This ultimately allows researchers to investigate causality across different levels and complex phenomena. Though not explicitly stated, the approach of Yi (2020) also uses a similar approach by combining different simulations with each other, integrating human behavior with thermodynamic building properties.

A trend that at first sight lends itself for strong consideration with respect to cognitive models lies in cooperation with the broad field of Machine Learning. Most recent AI research has been in the field of Machine Learning, especially, much so that it is often used synonymously. In general however, Deep Learning approaches have not been widely adopted due to the inherent lack of explainability, which often constitutes the most important research goal. This explains the tendency for application in industries, where Deep Learning models are treated as black-boxes that "just work", which is of course no option for research. In contrast, rule-based approaches are often better understandable. Furthermore, the computational effort is often significant and provides a hindrance for model development and testing. However, computational advances and modeling breakthroughs have removed some of these barriers and facilitated recent applications.

Kavak et al. (2018) propose an integration of Machine Learning and ABMs by training models on ground-truth data and applying these models at individual-level to the agents to generate attributes and behavior, ultimately developing better empirical ABMs.

A second approach is proposed by Lee et al. (2020), which generate the labeled training-data for their deep-learning network, resulting in accurate predictions of emerging spatial patterns and proving the applicability to complex interactions. Other authors recommend the combined application of ABMs and ML models to economic problems and policy analysis by emulating micro-scale behavior of economic agents or data-generation with full-scale ABMs (van der Hoog 2017).

The paper of Yi (2020) adapts a ML approach by using a Gaussian Process Classifier, a ML classification approach, to find optimal spatial positions for their agents in a building, enabling designers to receive direct feedback on the predicted usage of a building. This shows how cognitive architectures will receive more and more input from ML approaches, presumably shifting away from the manual expert-systems of SOAR and ACT-R. Thanks to the development of ML libraries such as SciKit Lean and PyTorch, these processes become more and more accessible and therefore find their way into more publications.

However, the use of one or the other does not have to be exclusive. (Johora et al. 2020) recommend the combination of expert-systems (another approach for AI by making complex, manually generated rule-sets) and Deep Learning approaches into a single ABM predicting the interaction of mixed road traffic.

4   Conclusion

The journey of ABM has been a long one as there is no end in sight, yet. The bottom-up approach of ABM gains more and more traction, focusing on the explainability of phenomena and facilitating insights into complex problems. Impactful works of Axelrod (1980, 1997) and Epstein et al. (2008) show how simple rules can produce the emergence of complex phenomena and generate insights into the workings of societies.

Several applications in the areas of social sciences, finance, infection modeling and robots show how the concept of ABM can be transferred to other disciplines and help with understanding emerging behavior. However, there is still a lack of mainstream research (especially in the social sciences) with ABMs, mainly as product of a lack of communication between the ABM modeling and social sciences community.

This communication gap seems to be closing, helped by the growing prevalence and acceptance of software in the researchers' everyday life and the growing evidence of successful applications. Also, the current trend of improved model validation helps building trust in ABMs. The development of cognitive models is also progressing, allowing researchers to build agents with more detailed and realistic behavior patterns.

In the future, multi-scale models enable ABMs to simulate even more elaborate models, connecting different scales of detail and phenomena. The combination with Machine Learning approaches enables researchers to generate the ever-needed data sets for training ML models and integrate smarter, self-learning cognitive architectures and agents, ultimately facilitating research in a variety of fields and understanding of complex phenomena.

Acknowledgements. This research was supported by the Digital Society research program funded by the Ministry of Culture and Science of the German State of North Rhine-Westphalia.

References

Aaron, J.: Life simulation spawns its first replicator. New Sci. **206**(2765), 6–7 (2010). https://doi.org/10.1016/s0262-4079(10)61461-3. ISSN 02624079

Abdallah, S., Lesser, V.: Multiagent reinforcement learning and self-organization in a network of agents. In: Proceedings of the International Conference on Autonomous Agents (2007). https://doi.org/10.1145/1329125.1329172. ISBN 9788190426275

Fred Attneave, M.B., Hebb, D.O.: The organization of behavior; a neuropsychological theory. Am. J. Psychol. (1950). https://doi.org/10.2307/1418888. ISSN 00029556

Axelrod, R.: Effective choice in the prisoner's dilemma. J. Confl. Resolut. **24**(1), 3–25 (1980). https://doi.org/10.1177/002200278002400101. ISSN 15528766

Axelrod, R.: The dissemination of culture: a model with local convergence and global polarization. J. Confl. Resolut. **41**(2), 203–226 (1997). https://doi.org/10.1177/0022002797041002001. ISSN 00220027

Bhattacharya, P., Kuhlman, C.J., Lebiere, C., Morrison, D., Wilson, M.L., Orr, M.G.: The matrix : an agent-based modeling framework for data intensive simulations. (Aamas), pp. 1635–1643 (2019)

Binkley, S.: Market Society: Markets and Modern Social Theory, by Don Slater and Fran Tonkiss. Polity Press, Cambridge (2002). ISSN 07352751

Bonabeau, E.: Agent-based modeling: methods and techniques for simulating human systems. Proc. Natl. Acad. Sci. USA (2002). https://doi.org/10.1073/pnas.082080899. ISSN 00278424

Bruch, E., Atwell, J.: Agent-based models in empirical social research. Sociol. Methods Res. (2015). https://doi.org/10.1177/0049124113506405. ISSN 15528294

Buchanan, M.: Economics: meltdown modelling. Nature **460**(7256), 680–682 (2009). https://doi.org/10.1038/460680a. ISSN 00280836

Caillou, P., Gaudou, B., Grignard, A., Truong, C.Q., Taillandier, P.: A simple-to-use BDI architecture for agent-based modeling and simulation. In: Jager, W., Verbrugge, R., Flache, A., de Roo, G., Hoogduin, L., Hemelrijk, C. (eds.) Advances in Social Simulation 2015. AISC, vol. 528, pp. 15–28. Springer, Cham (2017). https://doi.org/10.1007/978-3-319-47253-9_2

Calero Valdez, A., Ziefle, M.: Human factors in the age of algorithms. Understanding the human-in-the-loop using agent-based modeling. In: Meiselwitz, G. (ed.) SCSM 2018. LNCS, vol. 10914, pp. 357–371. Springer, Cham (2018). https://doi.org/10.1007/978-3-319-91485-5_27

Cerdá, M., Tracy, M., Keyes, K.M.: Reducing urban violence: a contrast of public health and criminal justice approaches. Epidemiology (2018). https://doi.org/10.1097/EDE.0000000000000756. ISSN 15315487

Cincotti, S., Raberto, M., Teglio, A.: Credit money and macroeconomic instability in the agent-based model and simulator eurace. Econ.: Open-Access Open-Assess. E-J. 4(2010–26), 1 (2010). https://doi.org/10.5018/economics-ejournal.ja.2010-26. ISSN 1864–6042

Dawkins, R.: The Selfish Gene. Essays and Reviews, pp. 1959–2002 (2014). https://doi.org/10.1016/0047-2484(79)90117-9. ISBN 9781400848393

Deissenberg, C., van der Hoog, S., Dawid, H.: EURACE: a massively parallel agent-based model of the European economy. Appl. Math. Comput. 204(2), 541–552 (2008). https://doi.org/10.1016/j.amc.2008.05.116. ISSN 00963003

Engbert, R., Rabe, M.M., Kliegl, R., Reich, S.: Sequential data assimilation of the stochastic SEIR epidemic model for regional COVID-19 dynamics. medRxiv (2020). https://doi.org/10.1101/2020.04.13.20063768. http://medrxiv.org/content/early/2020/04/17/2020.04.13.20063768.abstract

Epstein, J.M.: Generative Social Science : Studies in Agent-Based Computational Modeling (2012). https://doi.org/10.5038/2162-4593.11.1.8. ISBN 0691125473

Epstein, J.M.: Agent_Zero. Toward Neurocognitive Foundations for Generative Social Science (2014). https://doi.org/10.23943/princeton/9780691158884.001.0001. ISBN 9781400848256

Epstein, J.M., Axtell, R.: Growing artificial societies: social science from the bottom up. Southern Econ. J. (1998). https://doi.org/10.2307/1060800. ISSN 00384038

Epstein, J.M., Parker, J., Cummings, D., Hammond, R.A.: Coupled contagion dynamics of fear and disease: mathematical and computational explorations. PLoS ONE 3(12) (2008). https://doi.org/10.1371/journal.pone.0003955. ISSN 19326203

Erlingsson, E.J., Teglio, A., Cincotti, S., Stefansson, H., Sturluson, J.T., Raberto, M.: Housing market bubbles and business cycles in an agent-based credit economy. Economics 8(1) (2014). https://doi.org/10.5018/economics-ejournal.ja.2014-8. ISSN 18646042

Fagiolo, G., Roventini, A.: Macroeconomic policy in DSGE and agent-based models redux: new developments and challenges ahead. JASSS (2017). https://doi.org/10.18564/jasss.3280. ISSN 14607425

Fagiolo, G., Guerini, M., Lamperti, F., Moneta, A., Roventini, A.: Validation of agent-based models in economics and finance. In: Beisbart, C., Saam, N.J. (eds.) Computer Simulation Validation. SFMA, pp. 763–787. Springer, Cham (2019). https://doi.org/10.1007/978-3-319-70766-2_31

Franke, R., Westerhoff, F.: Structural stochastic volatility in asset pricing dynamics: estimation and model contest. J. Econ. Dyn. Control (2012). https://doi.org/10.1016/j.jedc.2011.10.004. ISSN 01651889

Gardner, M.: Mathematical Games - the fantastic combinations of John Conway's new solitaire game "life". Sci. Am. 223, 120–123 (1970)

Gray, K., Rand, D.G., Ert, E., Lewis, K., Hershman, S., Norton, M.I.: The emergence of "Us and Them" in 80 lines of code: modeling group genesis in homogeneous populations. Psychol. Sci. (2014). https://doi.org/10.1177/0956797614521816. ISSN 14679280

Heath, B.L.: The History, Philosophy, and practice of agent-based modeling and the development of the conceptual model for simulation diagram. A Dissertation submitted in partial fulfillment of the requirements for the degree By Brain L. Health. Practice (2010)

Hegselmann, R., Krause, U.: Opinion dynamics and bounded confidence: models, analysis and simulation. JASSS **5**, 1–2 (2002). ISSN 14607425

Helbing, D., Balietti, S.: How to do agent-based simulations in the future: from modeling social mechanisms to emergent phenomena and interactive systems design. Why develop and use agent-based models? Number 11-06-024 (2011). ISBN 978-3-642-24003-4. https://doi.org/10.1007/978-3-642-24004-1. http://www.santafe.edu/media/workingpapers/11-06-024.pdf

Hinch, R., et al.: OpenABM-Covid19 - an agent-based model for non-pharmaceutical interventions against COVID-19 including contact tracing (2020)

Hjorth, A., Head, B., Head, B., Wilensky, U.: Levelspace: a netlogo extension for multi-level agent-based modeling. JASSS (2020). https://doi.org/10.18564/jasss.4130. ISSN 14607425

Hoertel, N., et al.: Optimizing SARS-CoV-2 vaccination strategies in France results from a stochastic agent-based model. medRxiv (2021). https://medrxiv.org/cgi/content/short/2021.01.17.21249970

Jackson, J.C., Rand, D., Lewis, K., Norton, M.I., Gray, K.: Agent-based modeling: a guide for social psychologists. Soc. Psychol. Pers. Sci. (2017). https://doi.org/10.1177/1948550617691100. ISSN 19485514

Johora, F.T., Cheng, H., Müller, J.P., Sester, M.: An agent-based model for trajectory modelling in shared spaces: a combination of expert-based and deep learning approaches. In: Proceedings of the International Joint Conference on Autonomous Agents and Multiagent Systems, AAMAS (2020). ISBN 9781450375184

Kavak, H., Padilla, J.J., Lynch, C.J., Diallo, S.Y.: Big data, agents, and machine learning: towards a data-driven agent-based modeling approach. In: Simulation Series (2018). https://doi.org/10.22360/springsim.2018.anss.021

Keeling, M., Danon, L.: Mathematical modelling of infectious diseases. Br. Med. Bull. **92**(1), 33–42 (2009). https://doi.org/10.1093/bmb/ldp038. ISSN 00071420

Kennedy, W.G.: Modelling human behaviour in agent-based models. In: Heppenstall, A., Crooks, A., See, L., Batty, M. (eds.) Agent-Based Models of Geographical Systems. Springer, Dordrecht (2012). https://doi.org/10.1007/978-90-481-8927-4_9

Langton, C.G.: Self-reproduction in cellular automata. Phys. D: Nonlinear Phenom. (1984). https://doi.org/10.1016/0167-2789(84)90256-2. ISSN 01672789

Lee, J.Y., et al.: Deep learning predicts microbial interactions from self-organized spatiotemporal patterns. Comput. Struct. Biotechnol. J. (2020). https://doi.org/10.1016/j.csbj.2020.05.023. ISSN 20010370

Löwel, S., Singer, W.: Selection of intrinsic horizontal connections in the visual cortex by correlated neuronal activity. Science (1992). https://doi.org/10.1126/science.1372754. ISSN 00368075

Macal, C., North, M.: Tutorial on agent-based modeling and simulation part 2: how to model with agents. In: Proceedings of the 2006 Winter Simulation Conference, pp. 73–83. IEEE, December 2006. https://doi.org/10.1109/WSC.2006.323040. http://ieeexplore.ieee.org/document/4117593/. ISBN 1-4244-0501-7

Naveh, I., Sun, R.: A cognitively based simulation of academic science. Comput. Math. Organ. Theory **12**(4), 313–337 (2006). https://doi.org/10.1007/s10588-006-8872-z. ISSN 1381298X

Olsen, M., Kaunak, M.: Metamorphic validation for agent-based simulation models. Simul. Ser. **48**(9), 234–241 (2016). https://doi.org/10.22360/summersim.2016.scsc. 041. ISSN 07359276

Perez, L., Dragicevic, S.: An agent-based approach for modeling dynamics of contagious disease spread. Int. J. Health Geograph. **8**(1), 1–17 (2009). https://doi.org/10.1186/1476-072X-8-50. ISSN 1476072X

Raberto, M., Ozel, B., Ponta, L., Teglio, A., Cincotti, S.: From financial instability to green finance: the role of banking and credit market regulation in the Eurace model. J. Evol. Econ. **29**, 429–465 (2019)

Railsback, S.F., Grimm, V.: Agent-Based and Individual-Based Modeling: A Practical Introduction (2011). https://books.google.de/books?hl=en&lr=&id=Zrh2DwAA QBAJ&oi=fnd&pg=PP1&dq=agent+based+modeling&ots=OAUK98sb0k&sig=5x UvW9WGentqE_1Q3ORK-sPOEws#v=onepage&q=agentbasedmodeling&f=false. ISBN 9780691136738

Railsback, S.F., Lytinen, S.L., Jackson, S.K.: Agent-based simulation platforms: review and development recommendations. SIMULATION **82**(9), 609–623 (2006). https://doi.org/10.1177/0037549706073695. ISSN 00375497

Railsback, S.F., Gard, M., Harvey, B.C., White, J.L., Zimmerman, J.K.H.: Contrast of degraded and restored stream habitat using an individual-based salmon model. North Am. J. Fish. Manag. **33**(2), 384–399 (2013). https://doi.org/10.1080/02755947.2013.765527. ISSN 02755947

Rand, W., Rust, R.T.: Agent-based modeling in marketing: guidelines for rigor. Int. J. Res. Market. **28**(3), 181–193 (2011). https://doi.org/10.1016/j.ijresmar.2011.04.002. ISSN 01678116. https://linkinghub.elsevier.com/retrieve/pii/S0167811611000504

Reitter, D., Lebiere, C.: Accountable modeling in ACT-UP, a scalable, rapid-prototyping ACT-R implementation. In: Proceedings of the 10th International Conference on Cognitive Modeling, ICCM 2010 (2010)

Ritter, F.E., Tehranchi, F., Oury, J.D.: ACT-R: a cognitive architecture for modeling cognition. Wiley Interdiscip. Rev.: Cogn. Sci. **10**(3), 1–19 (2019). https://doi.org/10.1002/wcs.1488. ISSN 19395086

Salvucci, D.D.: Rapid prototyping and evaluation of in-vehicle interfaces. ACM Trans. Comput.-Hum. Interact. (2009). https://doi.org/10.1145/1534903.1534906. ISSN 10730516

Samuelson, D., Macal, C.: Agent-based simulation comes of age. OR MS TODAY **33**(4), 34 (2006). https://www.informs.org/ORMS-Today/Archived-Issues/2006/orms-8-06/Agent-Based-Simulation-Comes-of-Age

Schelling, T.C.: Models of Segregation. Am. Econ. Assoc. **52**(2), 604–620 (2013)

Smith, A.: Adam Smith: The Theory of Moral Sentiments (2002). https://doi.org/10.1017/cbo9780511800153

Turner, G.M.: A comparison of The Limits to Growth with 30 years of reality. Global Environ. Change **18**(3), 397–411 (2008). https://doi.org/10.1016/j.gloenvcha.2008.05.001. ISSN 09593780

van der Hoog, S.: Deep learning in (and of) agent-based models: a prospectus* (2017). ISSN 23318422

Wilensky, U., Rand, W.: An Introduction to Agent-Based Modeling: Modeling Natural, Social, and Engineered Complex Systems with NetLogo. The MIT Press, Cambridge (2015). ISBN 9780262731898. https://books.google.de/books?id=LQrhBwAAQBAJ

Windrum, P., Fagiolo, G., Moneta, A.: Empirical validation of agent-based models: alternatives and prospects. JASSS (2007). http://jasss.soc.surrey.ac.uk/10/2/8.html. ISSN 14607425

Xiang, X., Kennedy, R., Madey, G.: Verification and validation of agent-based scientific simulation models. In: Agent-Directed Simulation Conference, pp. 47–55 (2005). http://www.nd.edu/~nom/Papers/ADS019_Xiang.pdf

Yi, H.: Visualized co-simulation of adaptive human behavior and dynamic building performance: an agent-based model (ABM) and artificial intelligence (AI) approach for smart architectural design. Sustainability (Switzerland) **12**(16) (2020). https://doi.org/10.3390/su12166672. ISSN 20711050

Medical-Based Pictogram: Comprehension of Visual Language with Semiotic Theory

Yuxiao Wang[✉]

Tsien Hsue-Shen College, Nanjing University of Science and Technology,
200, Xiaolingwei Street, Nanjing 210094, Jiangsu, People's Republic of China
roy_zoe@sina.com

Abstract. In this increasingly technical world, pictograms have become a significant part of our daily lives through their use in public areas, such as public transit system, warning signs and pharmaceutical pictograms. Compared with icons, which are simple, concrete, and self-explanatory of the text or meaning they represent, pictograms seems to be more abstract, they use analogy or symbolic representation for conveying messages (Michael 2013). However, it turns out that not all pictograms could reach this goal, understanding could vary between different groups of people (Mara 2018), many pictograms are not understood as intended. The interpretation of medical-based pictograms could result in violation of medical advice, and symptoms can range from gain less treatment benefit to get ill.

Despite the function of communication is significant in pictograms, there is few principles to guide and suggest pictograms design. This research aims to use the theory of semiotic to disassemble the meaning of pictograms into three parts: Semantics, Syntactics and Pragmatics, these three branches of semiotic include the interpretation in different angles, and each construction of signs in the pictogram would influence perception of interpretation, it turns out that misunderstanding of visual messages in pictograms has multiple causes, and proved that semiotic theory could developed to interpret visual messages. This study may help to further elucidate the visual grammar of medical-based pictograms that are universally understood and reduce the risk of ambiguous medicine labels and instruction.

Keywords: Pharmaceutical pictogram · Symbol · Semiotic · Visual message

1 Introduction

People use different words to describe different uses of images, such as symbols, signs, or pictograms. According to Zender (2013), a symbol is an image that refers to something else; a sign is a non-representational symbol that viewers need to learn its specific referent; an icon is an image that represents a common group objects and does not need viewers to learn the categorical referent; a pictogram is a combination of symbols and icons that communicates a narrative, story, or data set. Pictograms attempt to create comprehension and recall of an object's meaning and were historically a communication system for people with different cultural backgrounds or low linguistic abilities.

© Springer Nature Switzerland AG 2021
V. G. Duffy (Ed.): HCII 2021, LNCS 12777, pp. 320–342, 2021.
https://doi.org/10.1007/978-3-030-77817-0_23

According to Montagne (2013), studies have found pictograms positively influence people's ability to locate and enhance comprehension and recall of health and medical information, especially when used in combination with text information which about professional medical instruction. Houts' (2006) research shows that pictures could increase patient attention, comprehension, recall, and adherence during treatment, especially among patients with lower linguistics skills. Erdinc's (2010) research emphasised that warning symbols could contribute to effectiveness of flight manual warnings. Kools (2006)'s research emphasizes the point that pictures are conducive to text instruction. Dowse and Ehlers (2004) experiment in South Africa found that pictograms based on the local culture could enhance people' comprehension of written medicine instruction, overcoming the low literacy barrier.

Some researchers have proved that not all the medical pictograms are optimally understood. For instance, one experiment showed that age could influence understanding of pictogram meaning (Beaufils et al. 2014); Dowse and Ehlers (2001) experiment in Eastern Cape proved that interpretation of pharmaceutical pictograms could be affected by education level. Different cultural backgrounds could also result in the misunderstanding of pictograms (Kassam 2004). These findings emphasise that although medical pictograms could help to improve the usability of drug leaflets by making information easier to understand and recall (Van Beusekom et al. 2018), pictograms could also be misunderstood for a variety of reasons.

Although communication is significant in pictograms, there are few principles to guide pictograms design. According to Dowse and Ehlers (2001), pictogram can communicate information to an international population, but constant exposure to this type of visual language is required for the population to become accustomed to it. Pictograms are two-dimensional, and their interpretation depends on people learning the conventions of representing three-dimensional reality on a two-dimensional surface (Mangan 1978). Without this learning process, the visual messages that are effectively communicated to one person could be meaningless to another.

Without this learning process, people are likely to misunderstand medical pictograms. This could obstruct the proper use of drugs and cause damage to people's bodies. Recent studies primarily focus on how different group of people read pictograms and the elements that influence people's perspectives of the images. Unfortunately, there is not much research into the visual language of medical pictograms and the principles of image-based communication. To address this problem, this paper analyses what factors contribute to the understanding or misunderstanding of pictograms using semiotic theory.

Semiotics is a sub discipline of linguistics that studies sign construction and the rules that govern how signs are perceived and developed (Chandler 1994). Signs and symbols are significant to this study. Different from linguistics, semiotics has also been used to study non-linguistic sign systems. Semiotics analyses how text, layout, and illustration are interpreted by members of society (Korenevsky 2013). Charles William Morris, an American semiotician and philosopher, in his 1938 book, Foundations of the Theory of Signs, described semiotics as having three branches: semantics, syntactics, and pragmatics. Semantics is the relationship between signs and the things to which they refer. Syntactics explores the construction of signs and the relationships between each part. Pragmatics is about how people read and interpret signs.

A pictogram, as a combination of symbols, signs, and icons, uses analogy or symbolic representation to convey messages (Montagne 2013). I hypothesised that analysing the meaning of medical pictograms using Morris's three branches could reveal the reasons why people misunderstand pictograms. The objectives of this study were to (1) conclude the feature of pictograms through the developing processof visual message; (2) identify the elements of pictograms that cause misapprehension using semantics, syntactics and pragmatics; (3) develop suggestions for future pictogram design on the basis of semiotics theory; and (4) design better-understood medical pictograms to reduce the risk of patient harm or confusion due to misunderstanding pictograms.

This research uses semiotic theory to interpret the meaning of pictograms. Each part of a pictogram can influence a viewer's perception and interpretation. This study finds that there are multiple reasons why pictograms might be misunderstood and that semiotic theory could be developed to help interpret visual messages. This study may further elucidate the visual grammar of medical pictograms that are universally understood and reduce the risk of ambiguous medicine labels and instruction.

Fig. 1. Evolution of chinese characters by Wu and Cheng (2002)

2   Chapter 1

Since ancient times, images have been used for communication. The word "icon" can be traced back to the ancient Greek word, "eikon," which means "likeness" or "image." Biblical Greek translates eikon as image in Colossians 1:15, in which Jesus is described as "the image of invisible god." Image implies not only physical resemblance but also the concept of a visual signifier (Zender 2013). Hieroglyphic symbols in Egyptian tombs describe the lifetime the owner. Ancient Chinese character evolved from hieroglyphic images. The word "日" (which means sun), for instance, is based on the image of the sun: a circle (Fig. 1).

Throughout history, images have been used to communicate in language environments. Images are still used today in international venues and to create a universal language. Pictograms are a significant part of this language because of their use in public areas (such as public transit systems), on warning signs, and pharmaceutical products. The United State Pharmacopeia created a system of standardised pharmaceutical pictograms, offering 81 pictograms to help convey medication instructions and warnings to patients, especially those with limited literacy and non-native English speakers (Unite

State Pharmacopeia 1997). In 2013, based on the usage of the pictorial blood loss assessment chart (PBAC), a new menstrual pictogram was developed for modern feminine products (Magnay et al. 2013). Atthe 1964 Tokyo Olympic Games, pictograms were shown to be a universally understood visual method of communication, establishing a shared international visual language inspired by the principles of the pictogram design (Traganou 2011). This series of pictograms (Fig. 2) were seen as the biggest achievement of its designer, Yamashita Yoshiro, because as an international visual language, it not an abstractly conceived modernity. It kept the Japanese visual in heritage, and combine Japan culture and modern symbol together.

Fig. 2. Tokyo 1964: A universal language by Yoshiro Yamashita (1964)

Compared with icons—which are simple, concrete, and self-explanatory of the text or meaning they represent—pictograms are more abstract. They use analogy or symbolic representation to convey messages (Montagne 2013). Pictograms have two parts: an image and a referent. The image is the direct visual perception of the object, which is also known as a signifier; a referent is what the image represents or its function, which is also known as a signified. In general, a referent does not represent a particular instance. It comes to represent a concept or category through a process of abstraction, limiting features so as to share general features of a class of objects (Dondis 1973).

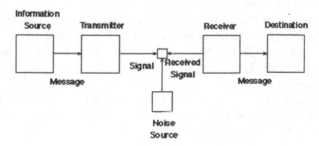

Fig. 3. Shannon and Weaver type communication model by Shannon and Weaver (1948)

To better understand the process that viewers receive visual message, Shannon and Weaver's communication model (Fig. 3) has been used to determine who or what the participants are in the process of reading pictograms. According to Kress and Leeuwen (2006, p. 46), the boxes in Fig. 3 represent participants, and the arrows represent the processes that relate them. There are two kinds of participants in the communication process: interactive participants and represented participants. Interactive participants are in the act of communication; they send the message. Represented participants are the subjects of the communication; they receive the message.

During the process of communicating messages, visual messages require an emitter and a receiver participant. They are encoded by the emitter and decoded by the receiver (Ashwin 1984). As Fig. 4 shows, the original pictogram is initially read as an information source. It then turns to a destination, encoded by a transmitter and decoded by a receiver. For example, according to Fig. 4 a USP pharmaceutical pictogram, the signifier is the needle in the middle of the picture; the signified is to what the injector refers: injection.

Injection

Fig. 4. USP Pictograms by Unite State Pharmacopeia (1997)

As pictograms tend to have a definite intended meaning of referent, they have been used in venues that require specific interpretation of multistep instructions. Pictograms are considered the visual message which can convey complicated information using limited resources, such as shape, colour, and size. The method of reading pictograms is the key to interpreting visual instruction; it requires learning a visual language and the principles of image grammar. This language should not only be easy to learn but also able to represent numerous concepts. As mentioned earlier, pictograms are more abstract and use specific objects to represent a concept, which could result in a lack of obvious representation (Rosa 2015).

Unlike text messages, visual messages require people to be able to perceive and understand. When people read a text message, it gives very accurate and specific instruction using linguistics. People can distinguish instruction, conditional instruction, and conditional action through the grammar of a sentence. Developing visual literacy requires the ability to create and use visual symbols for communicating and thinking. While these skills are not taught formally, they are normally acquired through exposure to pictorial material and mass media (Dowse and Ehlers 2004). People who do not have professional visual literacy have trouble reading images.

Fig. 5. Tire pressure monitoring systems light by Schrader (2010).

Reading visual messages requires not only understanding of image construction, but also recognition of what each specific part refers to. For instance, in 2009, Schrader, a company that makes tyre pressure monitoring systems, reported that their TPMS (tire pressure monitoring systems) icon was not recognised by most of their customers (Fig. 5). This icon illuminates when tyre pressure is 25% below the manufacturer's recommended amount. However, one-third of the drivers do not understand what this icon means, creating a potential safety hazard (Schrader 2010). According to a study by Insurance.com, most motorists find the signals on the instrument cluster confusing and unintelligible. The design of the shape of signals does not help them (Szczesny 2013). Although people could easily read the text message "tyre pressure is too low," they cannot understand the abstract image without explanation. Whether or not pictogram will be effective depends on various characteristics of the situation, the person, as well as the pictogram itself (Lesch 2003).

Medical pictograms contain professional instructions and require accurate descriptions because they concern people's health. Incorrect interpretation of label instructions could lead to a loss of drug potency or a change in the rate of absorption of the medication, causing patients to become ill or gain less treatment benefit (Webb et al. 2008). The International Organization for Standardization (ISO) and the American National Standards Institute (ANSI) recommend that pictorial symbols reach at least 85% correct comprehension on an accuracy test. However, not all medical pictograms can reach this criterion as understanding varies between different groups of people (Van Beusekom et al. 2018). That's because the communication between health professionals and patients is inherently problematic. Professionals use technical terminology to make the communicate clearly and accurately, but patients can't understand it even they have high education level. And they focus on symptoms, it makes them upset and hard to concentrate (Houts et al. 2003). This current situation gives more meaning to analyze how people read pictograms and which elements should be developed to make it easy to understand.

According to Storkerson (2010), semiotic theory has been as a theory of signification, it might connect design, and moves to the meanings they communicate. It's not the first time that the theory of semiotic is used to analyze images, on the basis of Sifaki and Papadopoulou (2015)'s research, "Concepts and terminology from different semiotic schools of thought are applied in order to unravel the logonomic system that shapes the messages' production and reception."

Charles William Morris classified three areas of semiotics: semantics, syntactics, and pragmatics. According to *A functional model of language theory*, a text is divided into topics or subject matter, who is involved, and how the text is structured (Forrest

2017). Based on this theory, every sign is formed by three parts: a sign vehicle, which is the construction of sign; referent, which is the object or concept to which the sign refers; and the interpreter, which is the person who uses the sign and follows its instruction. The relationship between these three parts forms the semiotic meanings: compositional meaning, representational meaning, and interactional meaning. These three meanings are the three thinking model that offered by reading images, which is based on a Hallidayan social semiotic approach to language (Thuy 2006).This model is used not only for language but for all modes of representation, including images (Kress and van Leeuwen, p. 20). This model proves that interpreting the meaning of pictograms involves analysing these three meanings. These three meanings of pictograms represent the relationship between a symbol and other symbols in the same system, a symbol and its referent, and a pictogram and its user. They include the whole meaning of the sign.

Although theories are based on different studies, they provide a reference that can be used to interpret the meaning of pictograms: the construction of images, the meaning to which the image refers, and the user's influence on the reading of the image.

3   Chapter 2. Case Study: Communi-Card

According to Morris's theory, syntactics is defined as the relationship between signs in formal structures. "Signs" refers to text signs as well as visual signs. Syntactics is the construction between a sign and other signs in the same system (Morris 1946). Every sign exists as a part of a language system rather than independently. This explains why every sign is connected to other signs. This connection develop a meaning, which based on the position among every signs, is called compositional meaning. Composition is the way in which the representational and interactive elements are made to related to each other, the way they are integrated into a meaningful whole (Kress and van Leeuwen, pp. 181).

A project could be used as an instance of compositional meaning in pictograms. Visual communication tools enable rapid and effective communication between the staff and patients (Van Beusekom et al. 2018). One such tool is Communi-Card (Fig. 6), designed by Richard Poulin and developed in cooperation with the Patient Representative Department of Mount Sinai Medical Center. Communi-Card is a series of cards that illustrate symptoms, medical, physical, and emotional needs. It can also indicate specific healthcare professionals for patients who have trouble describing their symptoms.

Both language and images can represent theconstruction of culture and its meaning within one society, which caused that there is a considerable degree of congruence between language and images. According to Halliday and Matthiessen's (2004) functional model of language theory, language choices are determined by the immediate context of the situation. This theory has been applied to visual images (Van Beusekom et al. 2018). Kress and van Leeuwen considered that, "What in language is realised by locative prepositions, is realised in pictures by the formal characteristics the relations that can be realised in language can also be realised in picture, or vice versa, that all the relations that can be realised in pictures can also be realised in language" (p. 44).These provides the reason that the analysis of pictogram can related to linguistic theory.

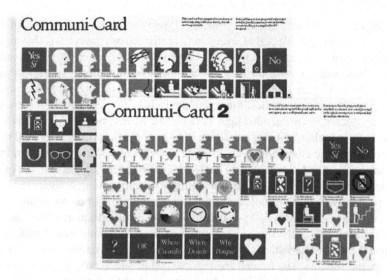

Fig. 6. CommuniCard 1 and 2 by Poulin (2017)

Compositional meaning refers to the message from intralinguistic relations that exist between words. It relates the representational and interactive meanings of the picture to each other through three interrelated systems: information value, the placement elements gives them with the specific informational values; salience, the elements used to attack viewers' attention to different degrees; framing, which disconnect of connect elements of pictograms, distinguish if they belong or not belong to each other. (Kress and van Leeuwen, pp. 183).

Authors use the feature of the word in grammar or vocabulary to achieve a particular rhetorical effect. When applied to visual communication, compositional meaning refers to the new message that is established when the information of two or more symbols in a pictogram is combined. A noun changes its meaning by adding a verb or adjective. The interpretation of both words and images should consider the context. As shown in Fig. 7, adding a cross and a six-pointed star to the man icon suggests Christian and Judaism. The combination of the man icon and religion icons represents "clergy."

Fig. 7. CommuniCard 1 by Poulin (2017)

Perceptual psychologist Rudolf Arnheim (1969) confirmed the function of context. During the general cognitive period, everything is affected by context. It is also modulated by that context at an elementary level of comprehension. Zender (2013) presented the concept of immediate context: the local space formed by a specific boundary in which all the elements of an image interact with one another to form an integrated message. If we read pictograms using syntactics, the relationship between symbols in the pictograms must be concerned. "An intended spot is detached from a non intended environment by means of a boundary" (Arnheim 1969), it's the earliest condition of visual thinking. As a form of graphic containment, immediate context creates an environment in which images are not read individual objects but as associated ones (Zender 2013). And that is the environment which compositional meaning produced, among associcated symbols. Therefore, the scope that symbols build relationships is the immediate context.

In Communi-Card, all the images are restricted to coloured squares. The same colour represents the objects of the same group: red represents the symptoms of patients, green represents the medical assistance the patients need, and blue represents normal requirement from the patients. The frames create a context in which only symbols in the same square can interact with one another. As colour is used to distinguish function, users can realise that all the pictograms in red squares are used to describe symptoms just by reading one of them. The colour system creates a context that simplifies the process of classification, shortening the interpretation process. From the view of construction, elements organised in one type of square are in the same system, and they construct meaning. In the red squares, the human profile symbols are used in combination with other symbols to suggest different meanings.

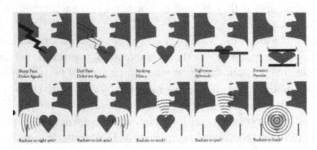

Fig. 8. CommuniCard 1 by Poulin (2017)

Most of the red squares on Fig. 8 use the image of a human body and a red heart, indicating these cards describe heart issues. Different black lines represent different symptoms of heart disease. The action is suggested by the combination of visual nouns. The black lines represent an action without any particular action icon. Reading each pictogram as a sentence, the human body image could be considered the subject (the object performing the action), and the black lines the predicate, which complete the idea about the subject.

The purpose of this project is to prove why Communi-Card could be conceived and realised to ease patient and staff anxiety in a hospital setting (Poulin 2017): it establishes a simple and easily identifiable visual system. Patients can infer the meaning of each pictogram using syntactics rules and compositional meaning. Presently, Communi-Card is used in more than 150 hospitals and healthcare facilities throughout the United States and Canada (Poulin+Morris Inc. 2017).

There is no doubt Communi-Card is a successful communication tool for patients and staff. The construction of these pictograms follows the principles of syntactics and builds a clear relationship between symbols in pictograms. This provides an understandable interpretation for users. Syntactics can be used to read pictograms by analysing the construction of symbols in a pictogram and the immediate context which restricted to the scope of the symbols' combination. The object and action of the image can be distinguished by the layout, size, colour, medium, and arrangement of symbols. It proves that the misunderstanding of pictograms is enabling to analysed throughout syntactics theories. When reading medical pictograms, analysing the construction of symbols is the first step in the user's cognitive process. The misunderstanding of compositional meaning would result in the misconception of pictogram from the initial reading.

4   Chapter 3. Case Study: A Set of Healthcare Icons Developed by a Five-School Consortium

According to Carnap, in an investigation of a language, if designatum but not speakers are referred to, this language issue belongs to semantics (Sayward 2018). Semantics focuses on the relationship between the symbol and its referent. The meaning of this relationship is called representational meaning. For instance, in linguistics, the word "table" could refer to a piece of furniture. The referent is not always a specific object; it could also represent a behaviour, process, abstract concept, or an entire environment.

A research project was designed to analyse the semantics of pictograms by adding or changing one of the individual symbols within a pictogram. In 2009, undergraduate design students from the five-school consortium (which is organised by The Society for Experiential Graphic Design and Hablamos Juntos and devoted to improving healthcare environments) designed candidate healthcare icons to replace a previously developed set of healthcare icons. A tested group of candidate symbols were finally developed by designer Mies Hora. In this project, undergraduate design students redesigned medical icons by replacing one or more symbols in an icon and evaluating if it affected their comprehension. For instance, the top scoring candidate icon, representing a medical library, consisted of an image of a person holding a book and a line at the person's waist representing a desk. In the upper right there is a line representing a bookshelf and a book with a medical cross indicating medical journals. Mies simplified the icon by deleting the images of desk and bookshelf.

Fig. 9. Medical library test icon by Zender and MeJÍA (2017).

There were thirtysubjects been invited to participate in this research. They were asked to image they were in a healthcare facility and to describe the meaning of each icon. Their comprehension was evaluated using the ANSI open-ended comprehension test method, which is currently the most valid instrument for the evaluation of icon comprehension (Zender 2013). According to the quantitative analysis and visual analysis, the icon with the bookshelf and desk symbols is easier to understand (Fig. 9). Analysis of the subjects' written answers for this icon shows that most of the correct answers used the words "read" or "reading". This shows that the image of a person holding a book suggests the concept of reading. In semantics theory, this image not only represents a reader but also refers to the idea of reading.

Comparing these two pictograms, the main difference is the object that the designer chooses to represent "library". The image of a man holding a book could refer to the action of "reading". However, to create the atmosphere of a library, the desk symbol and bookshelf symbol are much more specific than the cross symbol. Researchers designed a second study to test which part is the primary carrier of meaning. They divided the medical library pictogram into individual parts and tested the accuracy of comprehension (Fig. 10). The results showed that adding a bookshelf symbol enhanced comprehension, and the concept of a man sitting behind a desk is more relevant to "library" than the image of a man sitting on a sofa. The later creates a relaxed and comfortable reading state, which is more suitable for the word "rest" or "resting." This image was more likely to be identified as "lounge".

Fig. 10. Role of bookshelf symbol in Medical Library icon by Zender and MeJÍA (2017)

Comprehension of these pictograms is influenced by the representation of interactions and the conceptual relations between the people, places, and things depicted in images. In a pictogram, the representational meaning—which is the relationship that semantics focus on—is about a symbol and to what it refers. It is the distinctive feature of the object; hence, its representation of a class of things rather than a specific object.

As it mentioned in Sect. 2, an image involves the representative participants and interactive participants. According to Kress and Leeuwen (p. 119), interactive participants are real people who produce and make sense of images in the context of social institutions which regulate what may be said in images, and how it should be said, and how it should be interpreted. Sometimes the interaction of reading an image is not immediate because the image producer is absent. The producers and viewers of medical pictograms, for instance, do not know each other. When viewers read these pictograms in the hospital or at home, they do not participate in face-to-face interaction. When there is a disjunction between the context of production and the context of reception, the producer is not physically present; the viewer is alone with the image and cannot reciprocate the proper action that the producer expect (p.120). A similar situation occurs in writing. Writers and readers, like producers and viewers, are alone with the written word and cannot interact with each other. This similarity makes the method of analysing pictograms through linguistics and semiotics more authentic.

According to Kress and Leeuwen (p.120), although there is a disjunction between the context of production and the context of reception, they do have elements in common: the image itself, a knowledge of the communicative resources that allow its articulation and understanding, and a knowledge of the way social interactions and relations can be encoded in images. In the above-mentioned study of healthcare icons, there is another pictogram that illustrates how knowledge difference is the primary cause of semantic misunderstanding. In this study, another group of pictograms was compared. According to Fig. 11, the original pictogram means "inpatient cares". The new design replaced the crescent moon symbol with a clock symbol. However, the study found that the clock symbol hurt comprehension because it has less connection with the meaning "night" or "stay the night" compared to the moon symbol.

Fig. 11. Inpatient care icon by Zender and MeJÍA (2017)

In general, most peoples' mental image of inpatient care relates to an overnight stay (Zender 2013). Compared to the clock symbol, which could represent any time in a day, moon symbol closer in meaning to "night". Overnight is a more specific idea than time, but can be inferred from the concept of "night". In this study, the producer of the pictogram chose the clock symbol to represent time passing. It was based on his existing understanding that the image represented inpatient care, but the viewers did not share this understanding. The producer, who understands what message will be sent, has active knowledge, allowing the sending as well as the receiving of messages. The viewers' knowledge is passive; they can only receive information from producers. Fundamentally, producers and viewers faced an unfair interaction with unequal knowledge. That is why their comprehension of symbols and referents is different, causing viewers to misunderstand the representational meaning of pictograms.

To avoid the misunderstanding of pictograms, Dowse and Ehlers (1998) suggested that collaboration with the target population is "essential to gain insight into the knowledge, beliefs, and concerns of the target population about the problem to be addressed." To achieve equal knowledge and comprehension between producers and viewers, designers are required to shorten the distance between the object and to the referent. This means the elements chosen to represent a class of objects should be commonly observed by the target population. Every symbol in the pictogram should have a single meaning and be as simply as possible to ensure maximum recognition and comprehension.

Fig. 12. Medical pictogram in Jinling Hospital, Nanjing, China.

For instance, Fig. 12 was taken in Jinling Hospital, Nanjing, China. The text beside this pictogram shows that this is the place for the cashier and registration. However, without the text, few people can interpret its meaning correctly. To prove this, I conducted interviews with two graphic design tutors, one illustration tutor, and one design tutor from the University of Edinburgh, Art College. The participants were asked to describe this pictogram without text. None was able to distinguish to what the image referred. Participants all recognised the hat with a cross mark symbol as representing a nurse's cap. However, none of the participants could interpret the square symbol in the nurse's hand. To the producers of this pictogram, this square symbol refers to cash and cash machines because of its shape and the action of the nurse holding it. However, viewers who are not familiar with the hospital cashier (those in the United Kingdom, for instance, who do not have to pay for the medical treatment in governmental hospitals), have unequal knowledge. According to the participants, this image would be much more understandable if a pound sign appeared on this pictogram. To simplify an image does not means remove useful details. Medical pictograms should communicate the most significant and essential messages to patients, but removing detail could also reduce comprehension (Dowse and Ehlers 1998).

5   Chapter 4. Case Study: The Evaluation of Pharmaceutical Pictograms in a Low-Literate South African Population

Pragmatics studies how context contributes to meaning. The immediate context, which is related to semantics, has been discussed in the previous chapter. The context for pragmatics refers to environmental context. Environmental context is a concept proposed by Zender (2006). He defined it as the environment in which images function. For instance, an airplane sign at an airport could create a context that promotes the reading of the sign as "departing flights". This sign could also represent an exhibition of historic aircraft if it appeared in the museum. To some extent, this theory suggests the importance of environmental context to establishing the meaning; however, it is clearly suggested in the definition of pragmatics that this study not only focuses on structural and linguistic knowledge of the speaker and listener but also on the pre-existing knowledge and inferred intent of the speaker (Shaozhong 2009). If pictograms are interpreted using the pragmatics method, the context is not only the physical environment but also the features of viewers and users.

A research study was designed to prove that the ability to reading pictograms correctly is related to the user and the environment. In 2000, Dowse and Ehlers evaluated 23 pictograms from the USP-DI and a corresponding set of 23 locally developed, culturally sensitive pictograms. These pictograms were evaluated using 46 Xhosa participants who had a maximum of 7 years education. During the study, participants were required to interpret the USP-DI pictograms without any hints. After that, each local pictogram and the corresponding USP pictogram were shown to the participants, and the correct explanations were provided. Participants were required to pick between the USP-DI pictograms and the local pictograms. After three weeks, the participants were required to interpret these 46 pictograms again to test their memorability. At the follow-up interview, 20 of the local pictograms and 11 of USP-DI pictograms were understandable, which complied with the ANSI criterion of ≥85% comprehension. Participants expressed an obvious preference for pictograms connected with the local culture and environment.

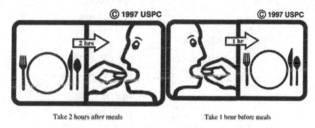

Take 2 hours after meals   Take 1 hour before meals

Fig. 13. USP Pictograms by Unite State Pharmacopeia (1997)

When reading pictograms using the pragmatics method, there are two factors which could influence comprehension: the viewers themselves and the environment around the pictograms. In this study, the level of education correlated significantly with the comprehension of the pictogram. This proved that the features of viewers could affect their interpretation. In this study, only three out of the 46 participants revealed that education influenced the initial interpretation of individual pictograms. In thistwo pictograms of Fig. 13, only participants with more than five years of education could understand that these two images conveyed the passage of time (a very abstract concept). Although in this research project, the influence of education level is not obvious and convictive, there is still other similar test could prove this speculate. In a test the effect of aging and educational level (Beaufils et al. 2014), the subjects included 63 young adults and 19 older adults, among these 63 young adults, 43 had high education level and 20 had low educational level. All the subjects were asked to interpreted 20 pictograms and test their ability of abstraction and logic. The data analysis showed that there were significant differences of comprehend between the high education level young adults and low education level young adults, people has high education is able to understand visual message better. And age can influence the understanding of pictograms. Pictograms combined several symbols that people must interpret, this requires logic and abstraction skills that are dependent on education level (Beaufils et al. 2014).

To further explore the concept of reading pictograms with pragmatics and interactional meaning, A questionnaire was developed for data collection. The demographic characteristics of the 523 participants are presented in Table 1. The questionnaire provided 8 UPS-DI pictograms, participants were asked to pick the most appropriate interpretation among four supplied options.

Table 1. Demographic characteristics (n = 523)

Demographic characteristics	Participants n (%)
Age (yr)	
<18	6 (1.15%)
18–30	192 (36.71%)
30–50	109 (20.84)
>50	216 (41.3%)
Degree (Education level)	
Bellow Bachelor degree	135 (25.81%)
Bachelor degree	272 (52.01%)
Master degree	96 (18.36%)
Doctor degree or above	20 (3.82%)

In order to prove that age and education level can influence the interpretation of pictograms, Table 2 and Table 3 recorded the correct answer in each group. In Table 2 it can be seen that except "insert into vagina" icon and "this medicine may make you drowsy", most old participants (older than 50) can't understand these pictograms well, the highest accuracy focus on the group of young and middle ages, which are the people from 18 to 50. Table 3 divided participants into different education level according to their degrees. The data analysis is not as obvious as Table 2, but it still can be seen that high education level brings high rate of correct answer, especially in pictograms 1, 2, 3, 4, 7 (Fig. 14).

The environment could also affect comprehension in this research. People in South Africa have trouble recognise the medicine bottle symbol because the medicine that patients received from public sector clinics is commonly dispensed in resealable plastic bags. A study that compared the understanding of 54 universal medical icons in rural Tanzania and the United States shows that cultural environment affects the comprehension of pictograms (Zender 2013). For instance, the icon of the combined cross and cartoon bear, which represents paediatrics, was misunderstood in Tanzania; there are no bears in Tanzania and stuffed bears are not common children's toys. These errors could be prevented if designers considered the environmental context of people (Fig. 15).

Table 2. Number (%) of participants correctly locating and understanding information of pictogram, in their own age group (n = 523)

pictogram	<18	18-30	30-50	>50
If you have questions, call this number 1	1(16.67%)	99(51.56%)	56(51.38%)	79(36.57%)
Take 2 times a day with meals 2	5(83.33%)	148(77.08%)	60(55.05%)	101(46.76%)
Do not take with meals 3	4(66.67%)	152(79.17%)	75(68.81%)	112(51.85%)
Insert into vagina 4	3(50%)	112(58.33%)	77(70.64)	132(61.11%)
This medicine may make you drowsy 5	1(16.67%)	96(50%)	65(59.63%)	154(71.30%)
Do not share your medicine with others 6	1(16.67%)	102(53.13%)	42(38.53%)	39(18.06%)

(continued)

Table 2. (*continued*)

pictogram	<18	18-30	30-50	>50
© 1997 USPC Avoid too much sun or use of sunlamp 7	4(66.67%)	125(65.1%)	77(70.64%)	134(62.04%)
© 1997 USPC Read the label 8	0(0%)	46(23.96%)	33(30.28%)	65(30.09%)

Environment was also been proved by the questionnaire. For the pictogram for "Do not take drugs with meals," only 65.58% of participants recognise the plate with fork image as representing a meal. Participants over 50 years old are more used to traditional Asian cultural concepts, relating meals to rice, bowls, and chopsticks. Young age group is more familiar with the symbol of knife and fork and what they represent. For young age group, they acquire the ability of interpret the pictograms without intent or awareness, they suppose that pictogram is a universal language for communication. However, these researches proved pictograms are heavily laden with culture-bound conventions, they need to be learnt if they are to be understood (Levie 1987, cited by Houts et al. 2003). Differences do exist between specific pictograms depending on an individual's country of residence, education level, and age. Pictograms could be interpreted differently depending on the individual (Richler et al. 2012) (Table 4).

During the follow-up interviews after answering the questionnaire, Zhonghe Song, anMFA2 illustration student from Korea, expressed that the "meal" symbol should be consistent with cultural background. "It's really necessary to have discussion with ordinary people who really need hospital or medical treatment, for example, children, or the elderly," she said. "The pictograms with too much details and cultural diversities can rarely access to them. These images should serve for people who don't have general information, instead of training people to read them."

In the angle of pragmatics, features of viewers and environment context affect the way that viewers read pictograms. As the most significant connection between sending messages and reacting, viewers' features should be a central issue. Analysing the features of target viewers, cultural background, and environmental context can establish the appropriate link between pictograms and individuals to enhance comprehension.

Table 3. Number (%) of participants correctly locating and understanding information of pictogram, in their own education level group (n = 523).

pictogram	Bellow Bachelor degree	Bachelor degree	Master degree	Doctor degree or above
If you have questions, call this number 1	56(41.48%)	124(45.59%)	45(46.88%)	10(50%)
Take 2 times a day with meals 2	74(54.81%)	158(58.09%)	70(72.92%)	12(60%)
Do not take with meals 3	73(54.07%)	183(67.28%)	72(75.00%)	15(75%)
Insert into vagina 4	67(49.63%)	171(62.87%)	67(69.79%)	19(97%)
This medicine may make you drowsy 5	81(60%)	167(61.4%)	51(53.13%)	17(85%)
Do not share your medicine with others 6	35(25.93%)	103(37.87%)	38(39.58%)	7(35%)

(*continued*)

Table 3. (*continued*)

pictogram	Bellow Bachelor degree	Bachelor degree	Master degree	Doctor degree or above
© 1997 USPC Avoid too much sun or use of sunlamp 7	89(65.93%)	174(63.97%)	62(64.58%)	15(75%)
© 1997 USPC Read the label 8	35(25.93%)	79(29.04%)	26(27.08%)	4(20%)

Fig. 14. Local pictograms compared with USP pictograms by Dowse and Ehlers (2001).

Fig. 15. Pediatrics icon by Zender and Cassedy (2014).

Table 4. The answer of pictogram "do not take with meals".

pictogram © 1997 USPC Do not take with meals	Age(yr)			
	<18	18-30	30-50	>50
	4(66.67%)	152(79.17%)	75(68.81%)	112(51.85%)
	The rate of each answers			
	Don't take with empty stomach	Don't take with meals (correct answer)	Don't take this pill as meals	Don't use your knife and fork cut up the pill
	122(23.33%)	343(65.58%)	50(9.56%)	8(1.53%)

6 Conclusion

Reading pictograms requires the ability of perception and comprehension. Pictograms cannot be understood unless people can infer the same intended meaning of a pictogram. Only understandable pictograms can certify the superiority of visual communication. The interpretation of pictograms is based on comparing the meaning and the elements which influence how the message is conveyed. This research falls under semiotics, the linguistic study of how signs are composed and perceived (Korenevsky et al. 2013).

It is evident that medical pictograms can be misinterpreted because pictograms comprise three different relationships between symbols, referents, and viewers. These three theories help interpret the compositional meaning, representational meaning, and interactional meaning, of pictograms and distinguish what part of the design causes misunderstanding. To build a clear interpretation system, this article proved that three branches of semiotics could be used to analyse the construction and meaning of pictograms: semantics, syntactics and pragmatics. Semantics discusses the relationship between signs and their referents. Syntactics analyses the construction of each individual part of a pictogram. Pragmatics is how viewers and environment context influence the interpretation of pictograms.

Medical pictograms should explain professional medical information as an adjunct to counselling. The most important determinants of their success are their appropriate use by the healthcare provider (Dowse et al. 2001). Semiotics can be used as a principle to design pictograms that create a universal communication system for medical treatment and pharmaceutical instruction and help patients correctly interpret visual instructions to avoid the danger of medication errors. Future research should focus on how semiotic theories could be used to improve the comprehension of medical pictograms, and build a User-Centered Design universal visual language system.

References

1. Ashwin, C.: Drawing, design and semiotics. Des. Issues 1(2), 42 (1984). https://doi.org/10.2307/1511498

2. Barros, I., Alcantara, T., Mesquita, A., Bispo, M., Rocha, C., Moreira, V., Lyra, D.: Understanding of pictograms from the United States Pharmacopeia Dispensing Information (USP-DI) among elderly Brazilians. In: Patient Preference and Adherence, 2014, vol. 8, pp. 1493–1501 (2014)
3. Beaufils, E., et al.: The effect of age and educational level on the cognitive processes used to comprehend the meaning of pictograms. Aging Clinical Exp. Res. **26**(1), 61–65 (2014)
4. Chandler, D.: Semiotics for Beginners. s3.amazonaws (1994). http://s3.amazonaws.com/szm anuals/bb72b1382e20b6b75c87d297342dabd7
5. Cornish, K., Goodman-Deane, J., Kai Ruggeri, P., Clarkson, J.: Visual accessibility in graphic design: a client–designer communication failure. Des. Stud. **40**, 176–195 (2015). https://doi.org/10.1016/j.destud.2015.07.003
6. Dondis, D.A.: A Primer of Visual Literacy. MIT Press, Cambridge, Mass, London, pp. 71–72 (1974)
7. Dowse, R., Ehlers, M.S.: Pictograms in pharmacy. Int. J. Pharm. Pract. **6**(2), 109–118 (1998). https://doi.org/10.1111/j.2042-7174.1998.tb00924.x
8. Dowse, R., Ehlers, M.: The evaluation of pharmaceutical pictograms in a low-literate South African population. Patient Educ. Couns. **45**(2), 87–99 (2001). https://doi.org/10.1016/S0738-3991(00)00197-X
9. Dowse, R., Ehlers, M.: Pictograms for conveying medicine instructions: comprehension in various South African language groups. South African J. Sci. **100**(11), 687–693 (2004)
10. Dowse, R., Ehlers, M.: The influence of education on the interpretation of pharmaceutical pictograms for communicating medicine instructions. Int. J. Pharm. Pract. **11**(1), 11–18 (2013)
11. Erdinc, O.: Comprehension and hazard communication of three pictorial symbols designed for flight manual warnings. Saf. Sci. **48**(4), 478–481 (2010)
12. Fierro, I., Gómez-Talegón, T., Alvarez, F.: The Spanish pictogram on medicines and driving: the population's comprehension of and attitudes towards its use on medication packaging. Accid. Anal. Prev. **50**, 1056–1061 (2013)
13. Forrest, S.: How does it make me feel?: using visual grammar to interact with picturebooks. Literacy Learn. Middle Years **25**(1), 41–52 (2017)
14. Houts, P., Doak, C., Doak, L., Loscalzo, M.: The role of pictures in improving health communication: a review of research on attention, comprehension, recall, and adherence. Patient Educ. Couns. **61**(2), 173–190 (2006)
15. Kassam, R., Vaillancourt, L., Collins, J.: Pictographic instructions for medications: do different cultures interpret them accurately? Int. J. Pharm. Pract. **12**(4), 199–209 (2004)
16. Knapp, P., Raynor, D., Jebar, A., Price, S.: Interpretation of medication pictograms by adults in the UK. Ann. Pharm. **39**(7–8), 1227–1233 (2005)
17. Kools, M., van de Wiel, M., Ruiter, R., Kok, G.: Pictures and text in instructions for medical devices: effects on recall and actual performance. Patient Educ. Counsel. **64**(1), 104–111 (2006)
18. Korenevsky, A., et al. (2013). How many words does a picture really tell? Cross-sectional descriptive study of pictogram evaluation by youth. Can. J. Hosp. Pharm. **66**(4), 219–26
19. Kress, G., Leeuwen, T.: Reading Images: The Grammar of Visual Design, pp. 20–183. Routledge, London, New York (1996)
20. Lakhan, K., Sensen, X., Afonso, C.: Assessing the understanding of pharmaceutical pictograms among cultural minorities: the example of hindu individuals communicating in European Portuguese. Pharmacy **6**(1), 22 (2018)
21. Lesch, M.: Comprehension and memory for warning symbols: age-related differences and impact of training. J. Saf. Res. **34**(5), 495–505 (2003)
22. Magnay, J., Nevatte, T., Seitz, C., O'Brien, S.: A new menstrual pictogram for use with feminine products that contain superabsorbent polymers. Shaughn Fertil. Steril. **100**(6), 1715–1721 (2013)

23. Mangan, J.: Cultural conventions of pictorial representation: iconic literacy and education. ECTJ **26**(3), 245–267 (1978)
24. Mayer, D., Laughery, K.: Identifiability and Effectiveness of Graphic Symbols used in Warning Messages. ProQuest Dissertations Publishing (1990)
25. McDonald, L.: A Literature Companion for Teachers. Primary English Teaching Association Australia, Newtown, NSW (2013)
26. Montagne, M.: Pharmaceutical pictograms: a model for development and testing for comprehension and utility. Res. Soc. Adm. Pharm. **9**(5), 609–620 (2013)
27. Moris, C.: Signs, Language and Behaviour. Braziler, New York (1946)
28. Ng, A., Chan, A., Ho, V.: Comprehension by older people of medication information with or without supplementary pharmaceutical pictograms. Appl. Ergon. **58**, 167–175 (2017)
29. Poulin, R.: CommuniCard 1 and 2. Poulinmorris (2017). http://www.poulinmorris.com/pro jects/print/CommuniCard.html
30. Richler, M., Vaillancourt, R., Celetti, S., Besançon, L., Arun, K., Sebastien, F.: The use of pictograms to convey health information regarding side effects and/or indications of medications. J. Commun. Healthcare **5**(4), 220–226 (2012)
31. Roberts, L.: Can Graphic Design Save Your Life? pp. 89–91. GraphicDesign, London (2017)
32. Rosa, C.: Design processes in pictogram design: form and harmony through modularity. Procedia Manuf. **3**, 5731–5738 (2015)
33. Arnheim, R.: Visual Thinking (1969)
34. Sayward, C.: The received distinction between pragmatics, semantics and syntax. Found. Lang. **11**(1), 97–104 (2018)
35. Schrader: One third of drivers can't recognize this idiot light. Mazdas247 (2010). https:// www.mazdas247.com/forum/showthread.php?123782984-One-third-of-drivers-can-t rec ognize-this-idiot-light
36. Shaozhong, L.: "What is pragmatics?" Archived from the original on 7 March 2009. Accessed 18 Mar 2009
37. Sharif, S., Abdulla, M., Yousif, A., Mohamed, D.: Interpretation of pharmaceutical pictograms by pharmacy and non-pharmacy university students. Pharmacol. Pharm. **05**(08), 821–827 (2014)
38. Sifaki, E., Papadopoulou, M., Sifaki, E.: Advertising modern art: a semiotic analysis of posters used to communicate about the Turner Prize award. Vis. Commun. **14**(4), 457–484 (2015)
39. Soares, M.: Legibility of USP pictograms by clients of community pharmacies in Portugal. Int. J. Clin. Pharm. **35**(1), 22–29 (2013)
40. Storkerson, P., Storkerson, P.: Antinomies of semiotics in graphic DESIGN. Visible Lang. **44**(1), 5–37 (2010)
41. Szczesny, J.: Drivers Struggle to Recognize Dashboard Warning Lights. Thedetroitbureau (2013). http://www.thedetroitbureau.com/2013/12/drivers-struggle-to-recognize-dashboard-warning-lights/
42. Thuy, T.: Reading Images - The Grammar of Visual Design, Routledge, pp. 164–168. ISBN-13 (2006)
43. Traganou, J.: Tokyo's 1964 Olympic design as a 'realm of design memory'. Sport Soc. **14**(4), 466–481 (2011)
44. Van Beusekom, M., Kerkhoven, A., Bos, M., Guchelaar, H., Van Den Broek, J.: The extent and effects of patient involvement in pictogram design for written drug information: a short systematic review. Drug Dis. Today **23**(6), 1312–1318 (2018)
45. Webb, J., Davis, T., Bernadella, P., Clayman, M., Parker, R., Adler, D., Wolf, M.: Patient-centered approach for improving prescription drug warning labels. Patient Educ. Couns. **72**(3), 443–449 (2008)
46. Zender, M.: Advancing icon design for global non verbal communication: or what does the word bow mean? Visible Lang. **40**(2), 177–206 (2006)

47. Zender, M.: Improving icon design: through focus on the role of individual symbols in the construction of meaning. Visible Lang. **47**(1), 66–89 (2013)
48. Zender, M., Cassedy, A.: (Mis)understanding : icon comprehension in different cultural contexts. Visible Lang. **48**(1), 69–95 (2014)
49. Schrader: tire pressure monitoring systems light. https://www.mazdas247.com/forum/showthread.php?123782984-One-third-of-drivers-can-t-recognize-this-idiot-light (2006). Accessed 24 Aug 2010
50. Shannon and Weaver: Shannon and Weaver Type Communication Model. https://www.researchgate.net/publication/220517623_Our_little_help_machines_and_their_invisibilities (1948). Accessed Nov 2001
51. Unite State Pharmacopeia: USP Pictograms. http://www.usp.org/health-quality-safety/usp-pictograms (1997). Accessed 1997
52. Wu, W., Cheng, H.Y.: Evolution of Chinese Characters. https://www.ocf.berkeley.edu/~wwu/chinese/handout.html (2002). Accessed 20 Feb 2002
53. Yamashita, Y.: Tokyo 1964: A Universal Language (1964). https://www.olympic.org/tokyo-1964
54. Zender, M., Mejía, M.: Improving icon design: through focus on the role of individual symbols in the construction of meaning. http://visiblelanguagejournal.com/issue/156 (2017). Accessed July 2013

Data Mining in Systematic Reviews: A Bibliometric Analysis of Game-Based Learning and Distance Learning

Jingjing Xu[1], Brendan M. Duffy[2,3]([✉]), and Vincent G. Duffy[4]

[1] School of Electrical and Computer Engineering, Purdue University, West Lafayette, IN 47906, USA
[2] Purdue University, West Lafayette, IN 47906, USA
duffy@purdue.edu
[3] West Lafayette High School, West Lafayette, USA
[4] School of Industrial Engineering, Purdue University, West Lafayette, IN 47906, USA

Abstract. This paper used bibliometric analysis tools to analyze bibliometric data in the field of game-based learning combined with distance learning. This study utilized the analysis tools MAXQDA, Harzing, VosViewer, Mendeley, CiteSpace, and AuthorMapper. The results illustrate an emerging area in game-based learning with distance learning, based on analyses of the keywords, trends, and co-citation data. The data mining methods of this study yielded the background information, central concepts, and theoretical foundations of the field of game-based learning and distance learning. The bibliometric analysis of this study offers a form of preliminary statistical and content analysis from a vast number of publications in academic databases. Based on the findings, we can trace the developing path of the literature and obtain valuable and educational information for the direction of future research.

Keywords: Game-based learning · Distance learning · Bibliometric analysis · Harzing · VosViewer · MAXQDA · CiteSpace · AuthorMapper · Self-determination theory · Constructivist theory

1 Introduction

With the rapid development of technology, games exhibited more and more functions other than entertainment. Though games were created for amusement, plenty of research explored their educational potential. Researchers have indicated that educational games can be a practical approach to providing a more exciting learning environment for students to acquire knowledge (Erhel and Jamet 2013). In recent years, various issues of educational games have been widely discussed because of the rapid development of computer and multimedia technologies (Erhel and Jamet 2013). Digital game-based learning is a novel approach for lifelong learning, and gaming is becoming a novel form of interactive content, worthy of exploration (Prensky 2003; Kiili 2005; Van Eck 2006;

© Springer Nature Switzerland AG 2021
V. G. Duffy (Ed.): HCII 2021, LNCS 12777, pp. 343–354, 2021.
https://doi.org/10.1007/978-3-030-77817-0_24

Pivec 2007; Burgos et al. 2007; Ebner & Holzinger 2007; Charles et al. 2011; Plass et al. 2015; Cozar-Gutierrez & Saez-Lopez 2016; Hamari et al 2016; Ronimus et al. 2019).

There are four arguments for game-based learning. Motivation has shown the capability of engaging people for a longer time. Player Engagement, one reason for applying digital game-based learning, can be designed based on different purposes and settings to achieve a wide range of learners. Adaptivity, related to different cognitive abilities and current levels of knowledge, can reflect the specific situation of each learner. Graceful Failure is arranged under expectation and is even necessary for the education process (Kapur and Kinzer 2009).

2 Background

2.1 Distance Learning

Rapid developments in information technology (IT) have generated potential changes in teaching and learning. In particular, technology-mediated distance learning-a new method of distance education-is currently in use (Webster and Hackley 1997). Students who enroll in distance learning courses do so for convenience. They are either time-bound due to work or travel schedules or location-bound due to geographic or family responsibilities (Galusha 1997). Over two decades, development in the network and mobile technology promoted the application of online learning. Mainly, distance learning uses online resources, including audio, video, or real-time online teaching. Getting resources online is now one of the typical approaches. Other than obtaining information, traditional education in distance learning for students has become common. Due to the nature of distance learning, there are perceived challenges in attaining an equivalent effectiveness.

2.2 Self-determination Theory

Self-Determination Theory (SDT) evolved from studies comparing the intrinsic and extrinsic motives. It addresses both intrinsic and extrinsic motivation (Gagne & Deci 2005). SDT identifies three innate needs that, if satisfied, allow optimal function and growth for individuals. They are Competence, Relatedness, and Autonomy. According to SDT, intrinsic motivation is a crucial type related to games. Many people do not appreciate the rewards from games, but they enjoy playing them. Autonomy, seen as the wellness of doing an activity, can be diminished when one feels controlled or put off while doing work. Thus, diminished autonomy can impair intrinsic motivation (Deci and Ryan 2012).

Competence, the second need, can be provided for individuals by playing games. People perceive a sense of accomplishment or satisfaction from paying. The experience meets people in getting positive feedback and stimulates people interested in it (Ryan et al. 2006). Relatedness, the other concept discussed in SDT, is a willingness for individuals to interact or communicate with others. Games provide players a virtual situation where people can be connected with other players. Applying self-determination theory (SDT) to education has been exhibited to be a productive undertaking (Reeve 2002).

Purdue colleagues have incorporated this into a program called IMPACT (Instruction Matters: Purdue Academic Course Transformation) (Hsu et al. 2019). Video games offer players virtual settings where opportunities for action are manifold. The growth of participation in these settings suggests that they can be highly motivating (Ryan et al. 2006).

2.3 Constructivist Theory

Constructivism, a concept in epistemology, is related to the theory of learning (Harasim 2018). It is a term in education that refers to the idea that learners construct knowledge for themselves as he or she learns (Hein 1991). Some main guiding principles are that people obtain information from outside and give them meaning, and the process is active. The process of making information meaningful is the process of learning. From this process, individuals can take care of learning methods. Constructing happens in the mind. Therefore, activities in the mind are also as necessary as physical experience (Hein 1991). This process involves the relations between functions of activities or games with students in learning new things and improving the learning effectiveness. Since games were shown to have educational potential in improving the effectiveness and time in learning, the significance of constructivism was gradually understood and accepted.

3 Purpose of Study

The purpose of this study is to conduct a systematic literature review and a bibliometric analysis of articles on game-based learning fields applied to distance learning. Other examples that illustrate the bibliometric analysis methodology with similar approach are shown in the literature (Fahimnia et al. 2015; Duffy and Duffy 2020). Bibliometric analysis, including scientific methodologies, provides a systematic and overall analysis in showing developing paths over two decades on game-based learning. Bibliometric analysis methods including MAXQDA, VOS Viewer, Publish or Perish-Harzing, Mendeley, Author Mapper were used in this study for data collection, content analysis, trend analysis, and co-citation analysis. Results and conclusions can be drawn based on these bibliometric data analyses.

4 Methodology

4.1 Data Collection

Initial metadata was collected using software tool Harzing (Harzing's Publish or Perish n.d.) with "Game-based Learning" keywords search. In this study, Publish or Perish provides a search based on publication year with data from Google Scholar database with a maximum of 1000 papers. Illustrating the high number of publications over two decades, it took 5 min for every five years on a search conducted with keywords "Game-based Learning". The result in Fig. 1 shows the increasing number of publications in this area in recent years. The potential of games for educational purposes is gaining more and more attention from scholars worldwide.

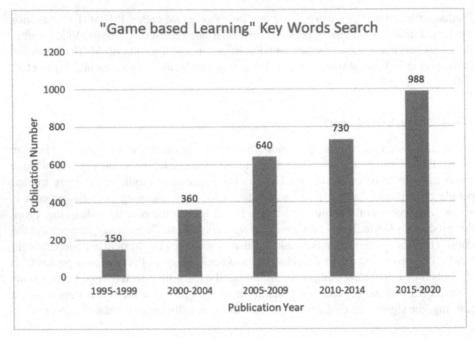

Fig. 1. Keyword search on Harzing (Harzing's Publish or Perish n.d.)

4.2 Trend Analysis

Keywords generated by the word cloud from the previous step have shown that the word "Digital" has a high appearance frequency, and it is one of the important focuses in this field. For better analyzing the developing path of game-based learning and distance learning, Harzing's software provides lots of information for trend analysis based on the keyword search from various databases including Google Scholar, Web of Science, Scopus and Microsoft Academic.

Publication data for every five years from the year 1995 to the year 2020 have been collected from Harzing while it accessed Google Scholar. Five minutes for each search time were provided. Shown below is the number of publications with "distance learning" as keyword in search shown in blue and with "digital game-based learning" search shown in orange are increasing. The data collected showed these two fields are gaining increasing attention from researchers and scholars (Fig. 2).

In addition to Harzing, metadata are obtained from Mendeley (Mendeley n.d.) and AuthorMapper. AuthorMapper (AuthorMapper n.d.), provides more detailed information for trend analysis including an author map and institution information especially from Springer publications. Publication numbers for Keyword search with Game-based Learning and Game-based Distance Learning results are shown in the figure below. The data shows that the interdisciplinary area is growing and maturing over two decades.

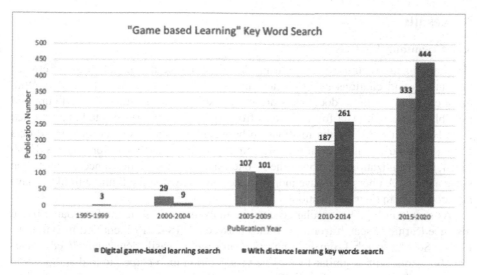

Fig. 2. Key word search on with distance learning and digital game-based learning

To observe the developing trend for game-based distance learning, data was collected from AuthorMapper to generate the static graph below. Figure 3 shows the publication number per year all over the world. From the graph, positive correlations can be identified. Games used in distance education are obtaining increasing attention.

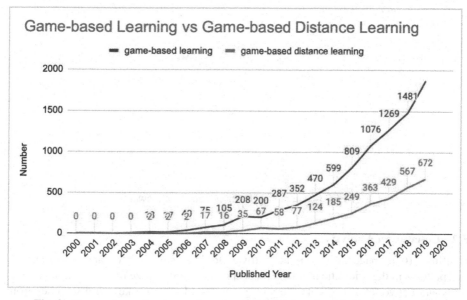

Fig. 3. Keyword search on game-based and distance learning (AuthorMapper n.d.)

5   Results

5.1   Co-author Analysis

Co-citation and co-author analysis using VosViewer give a connection map between the authors and citations using cluster analysis. The clusters are color coded. With more co-citations, these documents are more likely to be included in the figure and possibly connected. Data for 40 articles from 2018 to 2019 are selected and reported from Harzing to observe the relationship between publications. Web of science data format is stored as output from Harzing and imported to VosViewer for analysis. From Fig. 4, the visualization map shows the co-citations result and tight connections between some authors. Authors who have more connections shown in the figure will likely have a shared focus in their publications.

As shown in Fig. 4, a similar co-citation analysis was also made for "Game-based distance learning" search from 40 articles between 2018–2019 identified in Harzing's Google Scholar search. From the connection map, we can easily detect the related articles or publications with a similar focus. The visualization map helped to find authors who focus on a similar target interdisciplinary area (Fig. 5).

Fig. 4. Co-citation visualization map (VOSviewer n.d.)

5.2   Co-citation Analysis

CiteSpace (CiteSpace n.d.) is another software tool that can visualize and analyze trends and patterns in the scientific literature and especially to visualize the co-citation connections and network map. A data file with game-based learning keyword searches from the Web of Science, and 2000 publication's information, including cited references, is imported to CiteSpace. The generated graph shows a keyword cluster. The result shows digital games are a major proportion of games (Fig. 6).

Fig. 5. Co-author visualization map for game-based distance learning (VOSviewer n.d.)

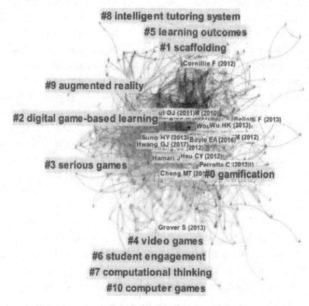

Fig. 6. Co-citation cluster visualization map (CiteSpace n.d.)

Another approach of searching subjects and references between related areas is the use of citation bursts. The strength shown in the figure can refer to the guiding information in the literature review on targeted topics. References with stronger citation bursts might include concepts or theories as foundations for the chosen area. Besides, analyzing the focuses or topics for articles with compelling citation bursts can give us a possible future research direction or prior research emphasis. References with more substantial citation bursts in both fields can guide interested researchers to more resources in both areas. This analysis in CiteSpace can be an effective way of identifying research and results in interdisciplinary fields (Fig. 7).

Top 25 References with the Strongest Citation Bursts

References	Year	Strength	Begin	End	2016 - 2020
Przybylski AK, 2010, REV GEN PSYCHOL, V14, P154, DOI	2010	2.2587	2016	2017	
Huizenga J, 2009, J COMPUT ASSIST LEAR, V25, P332	2009	4.758	2016	2017	
Wilson KA, 2009, SIMULAT GAMING, V40, P217, DOI	2009	2.712	2016	2017	
Tuzun H, 2009, COMPUT EDUC, V52, P68, DOI	2009	4.0748	2016	2017	
Miller LM, 2011, COMPUT EDUC, V57, P1425, DOI	2011	2.2587	2016	2017	
Crookall D, 2010, SIMULAT GAMING, V41, P898, DOI	2010	3.3928	2016	2017	
Klopfer E, 2009, MOVING LEARNING GAME, V0, P0	2009	3.1658	2016	2017	
Deshpande AA, 2011, COMPUT APPL ENG EDUC, V19, P399, DOI	2011	1.806	2016	2017	
Fu FL, 2009, COMPUT EDUC, V52, P101, DOI	2009	3.1658	2016	2017	
Lester JC, 2014, INFORM SCIENCES, V264, P4, DOI	2014	2.712	2016	2017	
Kebritchi M, 2010, COMPUT EDUC, V55, P427, DOI	2010	2.1115	2016	2017	
Jackson GT, 2013, J EDUC PSYCHOL, V105, P1036, DOI	2013	2.0323	2016	2017	
Kim B, 2009, COMPUT EDUC, V52, P800, DOI	2009	2.9388	2016	2017	
Ke F, 2009, HDB RES EFFECTIVE EL, VI, P1, DOI	2009	3.62	2016	2017	
Bourgonjon J, 2010, COMPUT EDUC, V54, P1145, DOI	2010	3.62	2016	2017	
Papastergiou M, 2009, COMPUT EDUC, V52, P1, DOI	2009	15.38	2016	2017	
Hainey T, 2011, COMPUT EDUC, V56, P21, DOI	2011	1.806	2016	2017	
Yang YTC, 2013, COMPUT EDUC, V68, P334, DOI	2013	1.867	2017	2018	
Plass JL, 2013, J EDUC PSYCHOL, V105, P1050, DOI	2013	1.867	2017	2018	
Ke FF, 2016, ETR&D-EDUC TECH RES, V64, P219, DOI	2016	3.6802	2018	2020	
Bressler DM, 2013, J COMPUT ASSIST LEAR, V29, P505, DOI	2013	1.9589	2018	2020	
Grover S, 2013, EDUC RESEARCHER, V42, P38, DOI	2013	3.4338	2018	2020	
Reinders H, 2015, RECALL, V27, P38, DOI	2015	2.2043	2018	2020	
Sandberg J, 2014, COMPUT EDUC, V76, P119, DOI	2014	2.2043	2018	2020	
OFlaherty J, 2015, INTERNET HIGH EDUC, V25, P85, DOI	2015	1.9589	2018	2020	

Fig. 7. Co-citation analysis with citation bursts (CiteSpace n.d.)

5.3 Content Analysis

In addition to keywords, cluster maps, and citation bursts, word clouds from the software MAXQDA are an effective method to review content and keywords. The software creates a word cloud from a folder of article.pdfs, which quantifies the size of keywords and scales the significance of each based on its frequency. MAXQDA can identify and extract all of the text from the literature that the user wants to analyze. Once compiled, the user must filter out non-content words (de-select) from the data set to omit useless results. Then the software can generate the word cloud. For this study, 13 core articles about "game-based distance learning" were selected and imported, then filtered to create the word cloud in Fig. 8.

Fig. 8. Word cloud generated fromMAXQDA considering key articles that contained overlapping subjects game-based learning and distance learning (MAXQDA n.d.)

Data collected and analyzed from software tools have shown the increasing development of game-based applications in the distance learning area. More content analysis is necessary for observing the focuses and subjects within the area. AuthorMapper provides advanced filter search including author, countries, and subject. Subject or classifications were exported for an advanced keyword search from data obtained from 2015–2020. The pivot table and chart were generated from that metadata. The minimum threshold for terms to appear in the table was 30 (frequency of occurrence). Figures 9 and 10 represent the frequency of subject appearance for publications. Some keywords, including "network, technology, mobile, AI," are also the keywords in the distance learning area. The spring semester of the 2020 academic year required that the world transition rapidly to distance learning, and at the same time, publications in Mobile Teaching and learning started to climb before 2015. With this data, it is clear that game-based learning is an emerging field in distance learning as educators and researchers race to find active online teaching methodologies.

Subjects	Number of Publications
Immersive Learning Research Network	30
Encyclopedia of Computer Graphics and Games	31
International Journal of Artificial Intelligence in Education	31
Smart Learning Environments	34
Journal of NeuroEngineering and Rehabilitation	36
Entertainment Computing and Serious Games	36
Wireless Personal Communications	39
Journal of Science Education and Technology	40
Wireless Networks	41
Technology, Knowledge and Learning	42
TechTrends	42
Second Handbook of Information Technology in Primary and Secondary Education	46
Journal of Computers in Education	48
Universal Access in the Information Society	50
Handbook of Mobile Teaching and Learning	50
Artificial Intelligence in Education	59
Serious Games	63
Educational Technology Research and Development	95
Multimedia Tools and Applications	110
Education and Information Technologies	123
Games and Learning Alliance	171
Grand Total	**1217**

Fig. 9. Keywords search with subject classification table (AuthorMapper n.d.)

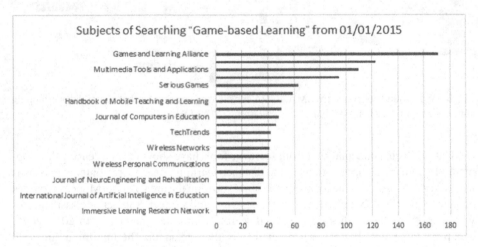

Fig. 10. Keywords search with subject classification graph (AuthorMapper n.d.)

6   Conclusion

The bibliometric analysis demonstrates relationships, trends, content analysis, co-citation, and co-author analysis from a vast database. When dealing with a new topic or area, these software tools provide a direct and thorough way to examine the overall picture in this field. MAXQDA generates the keywords word cloud, showing integral words in this area. VosViewer analyzes the data from Harzing and other network resources to generate a cluster map, providing a visualized connection for bibliometrics. Citespace deals with the Web of Science data with references and generates clusters and citation burst figures. Overall, in addition to understanding the background and fundamental theories for chosen fields, the bibliometric analysis also yields data to observe the developmental stages of a thematic area and informs decisions about a potential direction for future work.

Data trend analysis, game-based learning, and distance learning are growing and maturing. According to the trends displayed in this study, game-based learning in distance education has become more prevalent in literature throughout the past five years. The development of Self-Determination Theory and Constructivism promotes the application of games in the education environment. As digital and mobile technology develops, mobile games play a more significant role in our lives, promoting distance learning and our need for effective virtual learning practices. The educational function of games led to their increasing utilization in distance learning areas.

7 Future Work

Game-based distance learning is becoming a trend since people are hoping to save time and energy for learning. However, without regular supervision from teachers or instructors, keeping students focused is a difficult problem. Games, which stimulate and motivate players, could become the most effective learning method applied in distance learning. Also, distance learning provides people an educational approach when in specific hard times, such as the Covid-19 period when students over the US use distance learning instead of onsite learning. Thus, applying games in distance learning and improving learning effectiveness would be appropriate for future work.

References

AuthorMapper: (n.d.). https://www.authormapper.com/. Accessed 04 May 2020

Burgos, D., van Nimwegen, C., van Oostendorp, H., Koper, R.: Game-based learning and the role of feedback: a case study. Adv. Technol. Learn. **4**(4) (2007)

Charles, D., Charles, T., McNeill, M., Bustard, D., Black, M.: Game-based feedback for educational multi-user virtual environments. Br. J. Edu. Technol. **42**(4), 638–654 (2011). https://doi.org/10.1111/j.1467-8535.2010.01068.x

CiteSpace: (n.d). http://cluster.cis.drexel.edu/~cchen/citespace/. Accessed 07 May 2020

Cózar-Gutiérrez, R., Sáez-López, J.M.: Game-based learning and gamification in initial teacher training in the social sciences: an experiment with MinecraftEdu. Int. J. Edu. Technol. Higher Edu. **13**(1), 1–11 (2016)

Deci, E.L., Ryan, R.M.: Self-determination theory. In: Van Lange, P.A.M., Kruglanski, A.W., Higgins, E.T. (eds.) Handbook of Theories of Social Psychology, pp. 416–436. Sage Publications Ltd. (2012)

Duffy, B.M., Duffy, V.G.: Data mining methodology in support of a systematic review of human aspects of cybersecurity. In: Duffy, V.G. (ed.) HCII 2020. LNCS, vol. 12199, pp. 242–253. Springer, Cham (2020). https://doi.org/10.1007/978-3-030-49907-5_17

Ebner, M., Holzinger, A.: Successful implementation of user-centered game based learning in higher education: an example from civil engineering. Comput. Educ. **49**(3), 873–890 (2007). https://doi.org/10.1016/j.compedu.2005.11.026

Erhel, S., Jamet, E.: Digital game-based learning: Impact of instructions and feedback on motivation and learning effectiveness. Comput. Educ. **67**, 156–167 (2013)

Fahimnia, B., Sarkis, J., Davarzani, H.: Green supply chain management: a review and bibliometric analysis. Int. J. Prod. Econ. **162**, 101–114 (2015)

Gagné, M., Deci, E.L.: Self-determination theory and work motivation. J. Organ. Behav. **26**(4), 331–362 (2005). https://doi.org/10.1002/job.322

Galusha, J.: Barriers to learning in distance education. Interpersonal Comput. Technol. **5**, 6–14 (1997)

Hamari, J., Shernoff, D.J., Rowe, E., Coller, B., Asbell-Clarke, J., Edwards, T.: Challenging games help students learn: an empirical study on engagement, flow and immersion in game-based learning. Comput. Hum. Behav. **54**, 170–179 (2016). https://doi.org/10.1016/j.chb.2015.07.045

Harasim, L.: Constructivist learning theory. In: Learning Theory and Online Technologies, pp. 61–79 (2018). https://doi.org/10.4324/9781315716831-5

Harzing' s Publish or Perish (n.d.). https://harzing.com/resources/publishor-perish. Accessed 04 May 2020

Hein, G.E: Constructivist learning theory. Institute for Inquiry (1991). http://www.exploratorium.edu/ifi/resources/constructivistlearning

Hsu, H.-C., Wang, C.V., Levesque-Bristol, C.: Reexamining the impact of self-determination theory on learning outcomes in the online learning environment. Educ. Inf. Technol. **24**(3), 2159–2174 (2019). https://doi.org/10.1007/s10639-019-09863-w

Kapur, M., Kinzer, C.: Productive failure in CSCL groups. Int. J. Comput.-Support. Collaborative Learn. (ijCSCL) **4**(1), 21–46 (2009)

Kiili, K.: Digital game-based learning: towards an experiential gaming model. Internet Higher Edu. **8**(1), 13–24 (2005). https://doi.org/10.1016/j.iheduc.2004.12.001

MAXQDA: (n.d.). https://www.maxqda.com/. Accessed 04 May 2020

Mendeley: (n.d.). https://www.mendeley.com/?interaction_required=true. Accessed 04 May 2020

Pivec, M.: Editorial: play and learn: potentials of game-based learning. Br. J. Edu. Technol. **38**(3), 387–393 (2007)

Plass, J.L., Homer, B.D., Kinzer, C.K.: Foundations of game-based learning. Edu. Psychol. **50**(4), 258–283 (2015). https://doi.org/10.1080/00461520.2015.1122533

Prensky, M.: Digital game-based learning. ACM Comput. Entertainment **1**(1), 1–4 (2003)

Reeve, J.: Self-determination theory applied to educational settings. In: Deci, E.L., Ryan, R.M. (eds.) Handbook of Self-determination Research, pp. 183–203. University of Rochester Press (2002)

Ronimus, M., Eklund, K., Pesu, L., Lyytinen, H.: Supporting struggling readers with digital game-based learning. Edu. Tech. Res. Dev. **67**(3), 639–663 (2019). https://doi.org/10.1007/s11423-019-09658-3

Ryan, R.M., Rigby, C.S., Przybylski, A.: The motivational pull of video games: a self-determination theory approach. Motiv. Emot. **30**(4), 347–363 (2006). https://doi.org/10.1007/s11031-006-9051-8

Van Eck, R.: Digital game-based learning: it's not just the digital natives who are restless. Educause Rev. **41**(2), 1–16 (2006). https://doi.org/10.1145/950566.950596

VOSviewer: (n.d.). https://www.vosviewer.com/. Accessed 14 Feb 2020

Webster, J., Hackley, P.: Teaching effectiveness in technology-mediated distance learning. Acad. Manage. J. **40**(6), 1282–1309 (1997)

Sequence-to-Sequence Predictive Model: From Prosody to Communicative Gestures

Fajrian Yunus[1], Chloé Clavel[2], and Catherine Pelachaud[1,3](✉)

[1] Sorbonne University, Paris, France
{fajrian.yunus,catherine.pelachaud}@upmc.fr
[2] Télécom ParisTech, Institut Polytechnique de Paris, Paris, France
chloe.clavel@telecom-paris.fr
[3] CNRS, Paris, France

Abstract. Communicative gestures and speech acoustic are tightly linked. Our objective is to predict the timing of gestures according to the acoustic. That is, we want to predict when a certain gesture occurs. We develop a model based on a recurrent neural network with attention mechanism. The model is trained on a corpus of natural dyadic interaction where the speech acoustic and the gesture phases and types have been annotated. The input of the model is a sequence of speech acoustic and the output is a sequence of gesture classes. The classes we are using for the model output is based on a combination of gesture phases and gesture types. We use a sequence comparison technique to evaluate the model performance. We find that the model can predict better certain gesture classes than others. We also perform ablation studies which reveal that fundamental frequency is a relevant feature for gesture prediction task. In another sub-experiment, we find that including eyebrow movements as acting as beat gesture improves the performance. Besides, we also find that a model trained on the data of one given speaker also works for the other speaker of the same conversation. We also perform a subjective experiment to measure how respondents judge the naturalness, the time consistency, and the semantic consistency of the generated gesture timing of a virtual agent. Our respondents rate the output of our model favorably.

Keywords: Machine learning · Communicative gesture · Prosody

1 Introduction

Human naturally performs gestures while speaking [25]. There are different types of communicative gestures which vary based on the types of information they convey [36] such as iconic (e.g., linked to the description of an object), metaphoric (e.g. conveying abstract idea), deictic (indicating a point in space) or beat (marking speech rhythm). Gesture helps the locutor to form what he or she wants to

© Springer Nature Switzerland AG 2021
V. G. Duffy (Ed.): HCII 2021, LNCS 12777, pp. 355–374, 2021.
https://doi.org/10.1007/978-3-030-77817-0_25

convey and also helps the listener to comprehend the speech [13]. Thus, it is desirable for a virtual agent which interacts with humans to show natural-looking gesturing behaviour. Because of that, researchers have been working on automatic gesture generation in the context of human-computer interaction [9, 30]. The techniques behind these generators are based on the principle that gestures and speech are related [36]. Most of the prior gesture generators simplify the problem by focusing and generating only one type of gesture (e.g. beat inly or iconic only). There is also a recent work [31] which tries to infer the gesture from both the speech acoustic and the text, which in principle enables the model to learn both the beat gestures and the semantic gestures. However, there is also a benefit of separating the learning of the gesture timing (when does it occur in relation to speech) from the learning of the gesture shape (the hands shape, wrist position, palm orientation, etc.). By learning them separately, it would enable different models to be plugged in. On the other hand, if a model which does everything happens to not perform well on a certain task (e.g. generating the shape of semantic gestures), then fixing that weakness would require modifying the whole model. In our current work, we first attempt to compute when a virtual-agent should perform a certain type of gesture. That is, we compute the gesture timing. We also simplify the problem by considering two categories of gesture: beat and other gesture types.

We compute the gesture class based on the speech acoustic. We learn their relationship by using a recurrent neural network with an attention mechanism [2]. The input is the sequence of speech prosody and the output is the sequence of gesture classes. Our input features are the fundamental frequency (F_0), the F_0 direction score, and intensity. These features have been found to be highly correlated with gesture production. We also experiment with using other acoustic features that consider human perception of speech, namely the Mel-Frequency Cepstral Coefficients (MFCC) as the input features because they have been successfully used to generate body movements [21, 30]. It should be noted that the model we are developing uses only the acoustic features as the input; the semantic feature is not considered yet. Our model aims to predict where gestures occur; more precisely the type of gestures (beat or ideational) and the timing of occurrence of gesture phases (stroke and other phases). We are not yet dealing with the problem of predicting the form of the gestures nor which hand is used for the gesture. We will deal with this topic in a next step.

In Sect. 2 (Background), we explain the background concepts. In Sect. 3, we explain the relevant prior works about gesture and gesture generation techniques. In Sect. 4, we explain the dataset we use for our experiments. We explain the raw content and the various annotations provided in the dataset. In Sect. 5, we explain about how we extract usable data from the raw dataset. In Sect. 6, we explain the model which we use and how it is implemented. In Sect. 7, we present the way we measure the performance of the model. In Sect. 8, we describe our objective experiments. In Sect. 9I, we describe our subjective experiment. In Sect. 10, we discuss our results and we draw the conclusions. Finally, we explain our future direction in Sect. 11.

2   Background

Gestures and speech are related. In most cases, communicative gestures only occur during speech [36]. They are also co-expressive, which means that gestures and speech express the same or related meanings [36]. They are also temporally aligned, that is gesture strokes happen at almost the same time as the equivalent speech segment [36]. Gesture strokes themselves are known to occur slightly before or at the same time as the pitch accent [27]. McNeill [36] splits gestures into four classes, namely metaphorical, deictic, iconic, and beat. This classification is based on the information conveyed by the gesture. Metaphorical gestures are used to convey an abstract concept. Deictic gestures are used to point at an object or a location. Iconic gestures are used to describe a concrete object by its physical properties. Lastly, beat gesture does not convey any specific meaning, but it marks the speech rhythm.

The semantic gestures (communicative gestures other than beat, also called "ideational gesture" [7]) are characterized by temporal phases, namely preparation, pre-stroke-hold, stroke, post-stroke-hold, hold and retraction [27]. The stroke phase carries the meaningful segment of a gesture; it is obligatory while the other phases are optional. Successive gestures may co-articulate one from the others. That is, when multiple gestures are performed consecutively, the gesture phases can be chained together. On the other hand, beat gestures do not have a phase [36]. They are often produced with a soft open hand gestures and mark the speech rhythm.

Beat gestures can also be performed by facial and head movements [29]. Specifically, it is noted that eyebrow movements can be related to beat gestures [29]. It was observed that eyebrow movements tend to accompany prosodically prominent words [43]. It was also observed that pitch accents are accompanied by eyebrow movements [17,43,46].

3   Related Work

Embodied Conversational Agents (ECAs) are virtual agents endowed with the capacity to communicate verbally and non-verbally [9]. We present existing works that aim to compute communicative gestures ECAs should display while speaking. Many researchers agree that gestures and speech are generated from a common process [27,36]. Most prior computational models simplify this relationship into that gestures can be inferred from speech. The earliest gesture generators for ECAs are rule-based [9,32]. However, the relationship between speech and gestures is complex. Lately, to deal with the lack of precise knowledge, researchers develop machine-learning based gesture generators.

A common approach among the machine-learning based generators is generating a sequence of the gestures based on the acoustic. These techniques have a similar formulation: they express the problem as a time series prediction problem where the input is the acoustic and the output is the gesture motion. Hasegawa et al. use Bi-Directional LSTM [21] with MFCC as their input.

Kucherenko et al. extend the work of Hasegawa et al. by compacting the representation of the motion by using Denoising Autoencoder [30]. Kucherenko et al. also experiment with other prosodic features, namely the energy of the speech signal, the fundamental frequency contour logarithm, and its derivative. Kucherenko et al. report their technique yields a more natural movement. Ginosar et al. [19] use UNet and use MFCC as their input. They also add an adversarial learning component to enable mapping an input to multiple possible outputs. Ferst et al. [16] expand the use of adversarial learning further. They use multiple discriminators to evaluate the generated motion according to several qualities: phase structure, motion realism, intra-batch consistency, and displacement. They use fundamental frequency (F_0) and MFCC as their input. Interestingly, embedded within their model architecture, there is a phase classifier. The classifier takes the three-dimensional velocities of the joints and the F_0 as input and yield the phase (preparation, hold, stroke, and other). The purpose of the phase classifier is to enforce of a realistic phase structure. For example, a preparation cannot be immediately followed by a retraction.

Among the machine-learning based generators, there are also text-based generators. Their aim is to generate ideational gestures. These gestures are related to the semantics, which are inferred from the text. Bergmann et al. [6] use Bayesian Decision Network to generate iconic gestures, by using the referent features and the pre-extracted discourse context. Ishii et al. [24] use Conditional Random Field to generate a whole body pose. This technique does not model temporal dependency: the technique works at the level of phrase and the dependency between consecutive phrases is not modeled. Ahuja and Morency [1] use a joint-embedding of text and body pose. The text is processed by using Word2Vec [38]. The technique generates whole body pose including arm movement.

There are also approaches which learns gesture statically. Nihei et al. [39] use neural network to statically learn iconic gestures from a set of images. They use various images of similar objects, feed them into a pre-trained image-recognition neural network, and then extract the simplified shapes from the network. These simplified shapes can be reproduced as iconic gestures. Lücking et al. [35] attempt to statically gather the typical metaphoric gesture for each image schema by running a human experiment. Image schema itself is a recurring pattern of reasoning to map one entity to another [26].

There is also an approach which use both the acoustic and the text. Kucherenko et al. [31] build a neural network model which takes both the text and the acoustic as the input to generate body movements. The text is represented as BERT embedding and the acoustic is represented by log-power mel-spectrogram. Because this technique takes both the text and acoustic as the input, in principle it can generate both the beat gestures and the ideational gestures. Interestingly, in their subjective study, they find that their respondents have a low agreement on which segments of the gestures represent the semantic.

Some interesting developments we observe in the recent work are the shift toward neural network [1,16,19,21,23,30,31,39], the use of adversarial learning [16,19], and the use of word embedding [1,23,31]. Neural network has been successful in recent years, which therefore makes it into a reasonable choice for machine learning problems. Adversarial learning enables one input to be correctly mapped to multiple different outputs. Effectively, it allows the same acoustic input to be mapped into different body movements. Word embedding is a representation of word as a vector. Two similar words will have their corresponding vectors also close to each other. Therefore, given 2 similar text inputs, the outputs would also be similar.

Our work is a bridge between the acoustic-based generators and the text-based generators. We attempt to tell when a virtual agent should perform a certain type of gesture. We distinguish beat gestures from ideational. First of all, the ideational gestures convey a specific meaning, beat gestures mark the speech rhythm. Moreover, beat gestures tend to appear during the theme while ideational gestures tend to appear [9] during the rheme that carry the new information [20]. Additionally, we also distinguish the stroke phase from the other phases because the stroke phase is known to usually be near the pitch accent [27]. Although it can be argued that a technique which learns the body movements from both the text and the acoustic also implicitly learns the timing, there is also a benefit from separating the learning of the timing and the shape. By learning them separately, it would enable different models to be plugged in. For example, as Kucherenko et al. [31] find in their subjective study, the respondents have a low agreement on which segments are actually the semantic gestures. It suggests that the semantic gestures they generate probably happen to be not so prominent. However, because they have only one model, attempts to make the semantic gestures more prominent might change something else. Our usage of gesture phases as the classes is similar to [16]. However, their phases do not differentiate between beat and ideational gestures. Besides that, their phase classifier takes both acoustic and body movements as input while we do not have any body movement data. We evaluate our results by using a sequence comparison technique which tolerates shift and dilation. The spirit is similar to adversarial learning: for each input, there can be multiple correct output.

4 Dataset

We use the Gest-IS English corpus [41]. The corpus consists of 9 dialogues of a dyad, a man and a woman, discussing various topics in English face to face. The total duration is around 50 min. In those dialogues, the speakers are talking about physical description of some places, physical description of some people, scenes of two-person interactions, and instructions to assemble a wooden toy.

The corpus has been annotated along different layers [41]: gesture phases (preparation, pre-stroke hold, stroke, post-stroke hold, partial retraction, retraction, and recoil), gesture types (iconic, metaphoric, concrete deixis, abstract deixis, nomination deixis, beat, and emblems), chunk boundaries, classification annotations on whether the gesture is communicative (i.e. contributing to the dialogue discourse) or non-communicative (e.g. rubbing the eyes or scratching nose), the transcription with timestamps. The gesture annotations only consider

Fig. 1. Both speakers during a dialogue

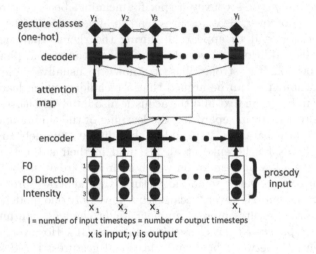

Fig. 2. The neural network model

gestures which are performed by at least one hand. The transcription timestamps include the starting timestamps and the ending timestamps of each word.

We divide the communicative gestures into beats and ideational gestures (i.e. iconic, metaphoric, etc.). As explained above beat gestures appear often during the theme while the other gesture types during the rheme. Theme and rheme are marked by different prosodic features [20,22]. We also divide the gesture phases into strokes and non-strokes. Strokes are often temporally aligned with pitch accent. Therefore, we classify the gestures into four classes:

- "NoGesture": when no gesture is done
- "Beat": when beat gesture is done
- "IdeationalOther": when a non-stroke phase (e.g. preparation, retraction) of an ideational gesture is done
- "IdeationalStroke": when the stroke phase of an ideational gesture is done

5 Feature Extraction

We decompose the speech into utterances where an utterance is defined by sequence of words surrounded by pauses. One utterance is one sample. To define the utterance boundaries, we use the concept of Inter-Pausal Unit (IPU) [33]: two consecutive utterances are separated by a silence of at least 200 ms long [40].

We use OpenSmile [15] to extract the audio features with 100 ms time-step. We choose 3 prosody features, fundamental frequency/F_0, F_0 direction score, and intensity, for their temporal relation with gestures [11,34]. We also extract the Mel-frequency cepstral coefficients (MFCC), which is represented as a 13-dimensional vector. MFCC has been successfully used to generate body movements [21,30].

We also extract eyebrow movements by using OpenFace [4]. There are 3 relevant action units (AU): AU1 (inner brow raiser), AU2 (outer brow raiser), and AU4 (brow lowerer). AU 1 and 2 represent rising eyebrow while AU 4 represents lowering eyebrow.

After we obtain the raw AU values, we filter out those whose confidence value is below 0.85 or the AU is absent. Then, we group them into consecutive blocks and we eliminate those whose average value is less than 1. This is done to eliminate noisy data.

The samples are natural utterances that have different lengths. Thus, we pad the sequences to make them have the same length. We pad the inputs with 0-vectors and we pad the outputs with the "suffix" auxiliary class. In our full dataset, we have 4161 time-steps of "NoGesture"s (6.14%), 1106 time-steps of "Beat"s (1.63%), 4208 time-steps of "IdeationalOther"s (6.20%), 2739 time-steps of "IdeationalStroke"s (4.04%), and 55616 time-steps of the auxiliary "suffix"s (81.99%). In total, we have 798 samples.

6 Model

We use recurrent neural network with attention mechanism [2] to perform the prediction. We use the model which we propose in our previous work [47].

6.1 Problem Statement

Let X be the input and Y be the output. Both X and Y are sequences with the same length. Onward, we will refer to their length as l. X is a sequence of vector. Let X_i be the vector at timestep i, X_i is a 3-dimension vector of real numbers containing the three speech prosody features, namely the fundamental frequency (F_0), the F_0 direction score, and the intensity. Y is a sequence of gesture class (Formulae 3 and 2).

$$X_i = (F_0, F_0\ direction\ score, intensity) \in \mathbb{R}^3, \tag{1}$$

$$CLASSES = \{NoGesture, Beat, IdeationalOther, IdeationalStroke, Suffix\} \tag{2}$$

$$Y_i \in CLASSES \tag{3}$$

6.2   Model Overview and Implementation

The recurrent neural network with attention mechanism is an extension of the encoder-decoder model. The standard encoder-decoder model compresses the entire information from the input sequence into the last encoder node. The attention mechanism adds an attention map between the encoder and the decoder. The map itself is a neuron matrix of the size l^2. If w_{ij} is the weight in the attention map at position $\langle i, j \rangle$, then w_{ij} represents the weight of the input at timestep i on the output at timestep j. This neuron matrix enables focusing the "attention" toward some specific input timesteps. Because this is a multi-class classification problem, we use a one-hot encoding to encode Y_i. The model schema is in Fig. 2.

We implement the code by using the Zafarali[1]'s code as the template. The code is written in Keras[2]. We replace the input of the original code [3] by the input we describe in Subsect. 6.1. We use categorical cross-entropy as the loss function and Adam as the optimization method. To deal with the class imbalance, we assign weights inversely proportional to the class frequency.

7   Evaluation Measure

The prior works which also use encoder-decoder model like us use domain specific measurements to evaluate their model. Sutskever et al. [42] use BiLingual Evaluation Understudy (BLEU) to evaluate their language translator. Chorowski et al. [10] use phoneme error rate (PER) to evaluate their speech recognizer. Meanwhile, Bahdanau et al. [3] use Character Error Rate (CER) and Word Error Rate (WER) to evaluate their speech recognizer.

There is not always a gesture on every pitch accent. Moreover gesture stroke may precede the speech prominence. Thus, our evaluation technique should tolerate shifts and dilations to a certain extent. It means that the technique must tolerate that the matching blocks can start at different times and can have different lengths to a certain extent. For example, in Fig. 3a, the predicted "IdeationalStroke" starts 100 ms earlier and is 200 ms longer.

Dynamic Time Warping [5] is a sequence comparator which tolerate shifts and dilations. However, this technique does not have a continuity constraint. That is, two consecutive elements which belong to the same class in a sequence might be matched against 2 non-consecutive elements. Without the continuity constraint, we might end up with a match like in Fig. 3b. In that figure, we can see that the "NoGesture"s in the middle of the ground truth are matched with the "NoGesture"s in the prediction before and after the "IdeationalStroke". However, a continuous "NoGesture" is different from a "IdeationalStroke" preceded and followed by "NoGesture".

---

[1] https://github.com/datalogue/keras-attention.

[2] https://keras.io/.

[3] Originally for date format translation (e.g. the input is "Saturday 9 May 2018" string and the output is "2018-05-09" string).

Thus, we propose a sequence comparison technique to quantify the similarity between the ground truth and the prediction where a block of consecutive elements with the same class is matched against a block of consecutive elements of that class. We use this technique to evaluate our result.

Our measurement uses the sequence comparison algorithm proposed by Dermouche and Pelachaud [12]. It measures the city-block distance between a block in the ground truth and a block in the prediction. This distance metric tolerates shift and dilation up to a certain threshold. If the distance between the 2 blocks is below the threshold, then they are aligned. We define b_{ps} and b_{pe} respectively as the start and the end of the prediction block. Correspondingly, we define b_{ts} and b_{te} respectively as the start and the end of the ground truth block. We also define T as the distance threshold. We define the alignment condition between the prediction block and ground truth block in Formula 4.

$$ALIGNED \iff |b_{ps} - b_{ts}| + |b_{pe} - b_{te}| \leq T \tag{4}$$

We measure the alignment based on how many blocks are aligned and we normalize it against the lengths of those blocks and the frequency of that particular class. Basically, we try to find out for how many time-steps the prediction is aligned to the ground truth, subject to the condition that consecutive time-steps in the ground truth which share the same class must be matched to consecutive or the same time-steps in the prediction which belong to that class as well. This is then normalized against the frequency of that class.

We also introduce the concept of "insertion" and "deletion". A block which exists in the prediction but has no match in the ground truth is considered to be "inserted". This is conceptually similar to *false positive*. The block exists in the prediction but it does not exist in the ground truth. Similarly, a block which exists in the ground truth but has no match in the prediction is considered to be "deleted". This is similar to *false negative*. For example, in Fig. 3c, we observe an "inserted" "NoGesture" block and a "deleted" "IdeationalOther" block. The precise definition of alignment, insertion, and deletion score are at Formulae 5. In the Formulae, n stands for the number of samples in the dataset, t_c is the timestep count of class c in the dataset, p_c is proportion of class c in the dataset, l is sample length (which is the same for all samples), $b.d$ stands for deleted block, d_c is the deletion score of class c, $b.i$ stands for inserted block, $b.p$ stands for predicted block, $b.t$ stands for ground truth block, and a_c is the class c's alignment score. The ideal alignment score is 1 while the ideal deletion and insertion score are 0. It means everything is aligned and there is neither deleted nor inserted block. The insertion score of class c can exceed 1 if we predict class c more frequently than it actually occurs. On the other hand, the deletion score is always between 0 and 1. The deletion score of class c is 1 when we fail to predict any of the block of that class. For the alignment score, if the predictor is accurate but slightly overestimates the length of the block, then the alignment score will be slightly higher than 1. On the other hand, if the predictor is accurate but often slightly underestimates the length of the block, then the alignment score will be slightly lower than 1.

$$p_c = \frac{t_c}{n \times l}$$

$$d_c = \frac{\Sigma_{b.d} length(b.d)}{n \times l \times p}$$

$$i_c = \frac{\Sigma_{b.i} length(b.i)}{n \times l \times p}$$

$$a_c = \frac{\Sigma_{(b.p, b.t).aligned}(length(b.p) + length(b.t))}{2 \times n \times l \times p}$$

(5)

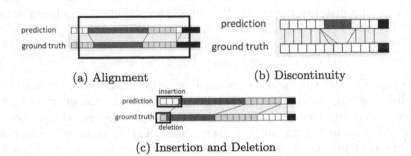

(a) Alignment   (b) Discontinuity

(c) Insertion and Deletion

Fig. 3. Each cell is 100 ms long. White: "NoGesture", Yellow: "IdeationalOther", Blue: "IdeationalStroke". (Colour figure online)

8   Objective Experiments

In **Experiment 1 (random output)**, we generate random outputs only according to the probability distribution of the gesture classes. Specifically, we measure two sets of probabilities, namely the probabilities that a sample is started by a particular class and the probabilities that a class follows another (or the same) class. This is done because our data consist of sequences, where each element affects the next element. We match this result against the output from our ground truth. We do this 55 times and we measure the average of their performances. This can be seen as an extremely simple predictor and thus can be seen as the baseline result.

In **Experiment 2 (using neural network with the entire dataset)**, we build a neural network model and then we train it. Besides that, We also check whether the validation performance is a reliable proxy of the performance on the testing performance. In a regular machine learning work, we train the model several times, validate each of them, and choose the model with a good performance in the validation. This is based on the assumption that the validation performance is a reliable proxy of the testing performance. We run each of the trained models on both the validation and the testing data set. For each gesture class, we measure the correlation between the alignment scores in the 2 data sets.

In **Experiment 3 (ablation study)**, we want to observe how different prosody features affect the model performance. We use the model from Experiment 2, but we replace some or all input features (intensity, fundamental frequency/F_0, and F_0 direction score) with random values. Thus, we render those features useless and we force the model to rely only on the remaining features.

In **Experiment 4 (inclusion of eyebrow movements)**, we want to find out whether inclusion of eyebrow movements helps on predicting beat class. Eyebrow movements often mark speech prosody and are aligned with pitch accent [8,14]. We include the eyebrow movements in the "Beat" class. We compare the model performance when the data includes only hand movements, when the data considers hand movements and upward eyebrow movements (Action Unit/AU 1 or 2), and when the data considers hand movements and both upward and downward eyebrow movements (AU 1, 2, or 4). We measure the alignment, insertion, and deletion scores of the "Beat" class and we also measure the validation reliability.

In **Experiment 5 (MFCC as input)**, we use the MFCC instead of prosody as the input features for our neural network. We measure the performance and the validation reliability.

In **Experiment 6 (both MFCC and prosody as input)**, we use both the MFCC and the prosody as the input features for our neural network. We measure the performance and the validation reliability.

In **Experiment 7 (trained with one speaker, tested on the other speaker)**, we train the model with one speaker of the dyad in our corpus and test it on the second speaker, and then we do the reverse. It should be noted that one speaker is a man and the other one is a woman.

In Experiments 1, 2, 3, 4, 5, and 6, we partition the full data set into training, validation, and testing data sets identically. We mix all samples from all videos from both speakers and then we randomly split our data with the proportion of 64%, 16%, and 20% for training, validation, and testing data. This is chosen according to the common 80/20 rule. Experiment 7, by its nature, requires us to partition the dataset according to the speaker. We use 80% of a speaker's data for training, the remaining 20% for validation, and 100% of the data of the other speaker for testing.

To make the results comparable, we expend equivalent "effort" to train the neural network models. We randomly vary the encoder and decoder dimensions from 1 up to the number of features: 3 with prosody, 13 with MFCC, 16 with both prosody and MFCC. We run 25 trainings with 500 epochs, 25 trainings with 1000 epochs, and 5 training with 2000 epochs. Therefore, we have 55 models for each problem. To choose the best model during the validation, we use the weighted average of "Beat Alignment", "IdeationalStroke Alignment", "IdeationalOther Alignment", and "NoGesture Alignment" scores, subject to the constraint that each of them must be at least 0.05. The weights are based on the frequency of those classes in the data set. A challenge we face is that the loss function used in the training concerns only the matches at the same timestep, therefore ignoring the possibilities of shifts or dilations, which means that the network is not completely optimized for our objective. Therefore, we have to rely on the stochasticity of the neural network. This situation triggers a question on whether the performance we see with the validation data set is a reliable proxy of what we will see when we use the testing data set.

Table 1. Subjective experiment questions and results

Naturalness		
How natural are the gestures?		
How smooth are the gestures?		
How appropriate are the gestures?		
Random output score	Model output score	p-value
8.565	9.796	$\mathbf{1.040 \times 10^{-5}}$
Time consistency		
How well does the gesture timing match the speech?		
How well does the gesture speed match the speech?		
How well does the gesture pace match the speech?		
Random output score	Model output score	p-value
8.565	10.409	$\mathbf{7.271 \times 10^{-9}}$
Semantic consistency		
How well do the gestures match the speech content?		
How well do the gestures describe the speech content?		
How much do the gestures help you understanding the speech content?		
Random output score	Model output score	p-value
7.855	9.457	$\mathbf{4.487 \times 10^{-6}}$

9   Subjective Experiment

In the subjective experiment, 31 respondents watched 12 videos online of a virtual agent speaking and performing communicative gestures. Among them, 17 (55%) are male, 13 (42%) are female, and 1 (3%) refuses to disclose the gender. On the age breakdown, 6 (19%) are 18–20 years old, 20 (65%) are 21–30 years old, 2 (6%) are 31–40 years old, and 3 (10%) are 41–50 years old.

The 12 videos consist of 6 pairs. We extract 6 segments from the Gest-it corpus (3 segments with a man, 3 segments with a woman). We replicate the real human gestures on the virtual agent. We match the human gender to the agent gender. Each pair of videos consists of the baseline and the gesture generation model's output. The gesture timing of the baseline videos is decided by randomly shuffling the timing from the ground truth. In both baseline and model output videos, we retain the ground truth's gesture shapes. In both videos, the agents

Table 2. Alignment: Exists in both prediction and ground truth Insertion: Exists in the prediction only Deletion: Exists in the ground truth only

Exp 1: Random output result			
	Alignment	Insertion	Deletion
Beat	**0.009**	0.936	0.990
IdeationalStroke	0.084	0.485	0.904
IdeationalOther	0.109	0.563	0.882
NoGesture	**0.533**	0.940	0.453

Exp 2: Using neural network with the entire dataset			
	Alignment	Insertion	Deletion
Beat	**0.194**	3.127	0.802
IdeationalStroke	**0.507**	0.485	0.582
IdeationalOther	**0.304**	0.226	0.671
NoGesture	0.567	0.554	0.398

Exp 4: inclusion of eyebrow movements			
	Alignment	Insertion	Deletion
Hand Only	**0.194**	3.127	0.802
With Upward Eyebrow Movement	0.136	1.038	0.829
With Upward & Downward Eyebrow Movement	**0.222**	0.280	0.774

Exp 5: MFCC as input			
	Alignment	Insertion	Deletion
Beat	0.171	2.619	0.849
IdeationalStroke	**0.166**	0.977	0.855
IdeationalOther	0.362	0.538	0.652
NoGesture	0.440	0.789	0.551

Exp 6: MFCC and prosody as input			
	Alignment	Insertion	Deletion
Beat	0.000	2.429	1.000
IdeationalStroke	0.388	0.790	0.640
IdeationalOther	0.362	0.584	0.613
NoGesture	0.441	0.891	0.563

Exp 7: trained with one speaker tested on the other			
Trained on speaker 1, tested on speaker 2			
	Alignment	Insertion	Deletion
Beat	0.015	1.049	0.982
IdeationalStroke	**0.506**	1.142	0.559
IdeationalOther	0.367	0.359	0.575
NoGesture	0.517	0.441	0.459
Trained on speaker 2, tested on speaker 1			
	Alignment	Insertion	Deletion
Beat	0.132	3.679	0.856
IdeationalStroke	**0.396**	0.846	0.650
IdeationalOther	0.217	0.221	0.746
NoGesture	0.538	0.589	0.424

Exp 3: Ablation study			
All features are randomized			
	Alignment	Insertion	Deletion
Beat	0.040	0.643	0.929
IdeationalStroke	0.038	0.072	0.952
IdeationalOther	0.025	0.027	0.960
NoGesture	0.347	0.275	0.641
Using intensity only			
	Alignment	Insertion	Deletion
Beat	0.0	0.786	1.000
IdeationalStroke	0.077	0.063	0.922
IdeationalOther	0.039	0.040	0.936
NoGesture	0.376	0.298	0.589
Using F_0 and the F_0 direction score only			
	Alignment	Insertion	Deletion
Beat	**0.175**	2.444	0.802
IdeationalStroke	**0.481**	0.503	0.563
IdeationalOther	**0.313**	0.179	0.637
NoGesture	**0.596**	0.555	0.379
Using F_0 only			
	Alignment	Insertion	Deletion
Beat	**0.179**	2.540	0.802
IdeationalStroke	**0.521**	0.515	0.553
IdeationalOther	**0.273**	0.155	0.664
NoGesture	**0.577**	0.570	0.393
Using F_0 direction score only			
	Alignment	Insertion	Deletion
Beat	0.044	0.548	0.929
IdeationalStroke	0.024	0.083	0.965
IdeationalOther	0.019	0.013	0.969
NoGesture	0.379	0.311	0.630

Table 3. Validation reliability

Exp 2: Using neural network with the entire dataset			
Alignment score of	Mean at validation data	Mean at testing data	Correlation
Beat	**0.202**	**0.244**	**-0.037**
IdeationalStroke	0.317	0.361	0.875
IdeationalOther	0.202	0.274	0.809
NoGesture	0.537	0.546	0.679
Exp 4: inclusion of eyebrow movements, "Beat" alignment score			
Alignment score of	Mean at validation data	Mean at testing data	Correlation
Hand only	0.202	0.2444	-0.037
With upward Eyebrow movement	0.078	0.102	**0.414**
With upward/downward Eyebrow movement	0.226	0.219	**0.925**
Exp 5: MFCC as input			
Alignment score of	Mean at validation data	Mean at testing data	Correlation
Beat	0.060	0.084	**-0.056**
IdeationalStroke	0.248	0.256	0.405
IdeationalOther	0.283	0.340	0.502
NoGesture	0.452	0.467	0.204
Exp 6: both MFCC and prosody as input			
Alignment score of	Mean at validation data	Mean at testing data	Correlation
Beat	0.080	0.0745	**0.025**
IdeationalStroke	0.272	0.265	0.472
IdeationalOther	0.302	0.351	0.622
NoGesture	0.425	0.465	0.386

have the same appearance and say the same sentence. We also use the original voice from the corpus. Thus, the differences in the video pairs are only in the gesture timings. The agent animation contains only the arm gestures. There is no other animation (no head motion, gaze, posture shift, etc.). Moreover, we blur the face of the agent because its still blank face could have distracted the respondents. The sequence of the 12 videos is shuffled so that a pair will not be shown consecutively.

Our objective is to compare the respondent's perception differences between the videos based on the model output and the baseline videos. We compare the naturalness, the time consistency, and the semantic consistency of the videos. For each of those dimensions, we measure it by asking the respondents to answer 3 questions. Each question asks the user to give a rating in likert scale from 1 to 5. We sum the respondent's scores on the three questions to get the score of that dimension. We adapt the questions from the subjective study of Kucherenko et al. [30]. We find that in all the 3 dimensions, the videos created based on the model output have higher average score. We also check the significances by using one-way ANOVA test. The questions and results are in Table 1.

10   Discussion

We observe in "Exp 1: Random output result" (Table 2), different classes have different complexities. For example, "Beat" classifier (alignment score = 0.009) needs a higher Vapnik-Chervonenkis (VC) dimension than the classifiers of another classes do. VC dimension is an abstract measure of how complex a classifier function can be. Meanwhile, the "NoGesture" class, with (alignment score = 0.533), can work with a lower VC-dimensioned classifier, despite the fact that we select our samples only when the person is speaking.

Experiment 1 result might be caused by the data imbalance. The "NoGesture" class is almost 300% larger than the "Beat" class. The "Beat" rarity might cause the prediction to have a lower performance. Besides that, our corpus is small (798 samples), which makes the training hard.

When we run our network ("Exp 2: Using neural network with the entire dataset", Table 2), we observe that the alignment scores outperform the random output on all classes. It suggests that the 3 prosody features (F_0, F_0 direction score, and intensity) enable prediction of the gesture classes with a certain degree of reliability. However, the "Beat" class result is not reliable. As we observe in "Exp 2: Using neural network with the entire dataset, Validation reliability" (Table 3), the correlation between the validation performance and the testing performance is almost zero. It means that in respect to the "Beat" class, validation is useless, thus the testing result can be attributed to chance. However, the mean alignment scores of the "Beat" class is still higher than the random output ("Exp 1: Random output result", Table 2), which suggests that the neural network still learns some pattern. However, as we have noted earlier, "Beat" is rare in our corpus.

Therefore, we wonder if we can predict "Beat" better should we have more data. Besides that, "Beat" gestures can also be performed by head or facial movements [8,14,28]. Indeed, in Experiment 4 we find the "Beat" class alignment score is slightly higher when we include both the upward and downward eyebrow movements ("Exp 4: inclusion of eyebrow movements", Table 2). More importantly, the validation reliability markedly improves ("Exp 4: inclusion of eyebrow movements", Table 3). These results shows that beat gestures can indeed be performed by eyebrow movements. Therefore, including eyebrow movements increases the amount of "Beat" data and, thus, enhances our model's reliability.

On the "IdeationalStroke" class, our predictor surpasses the random output generator. This class encompasses the stroke of all communicative gestures except beat gestures. The model can predict where a gesture stroke is aligned with the acoustic features. This phase is well-studied in gesture literature as it carries the gesture meaning. This phase usually happens around or slightly before the pitch accent [44]. In our case, we have the intensity, F_0, and F_0 direction score as our input. They participate to the characterization of the pitch accent. We also find that our result is reliable, because the alignment scores at the validation data set and at the testing data set show a positive correlation.

On the "IdeationalOther" class the model yields an alignment score higher than the random output, but the alignment score is still low. As a recall, this class contains all the gesture phases (e.g., preparation, hold, retraction) except the stroke phase for all ideational gestures. We can notice that, in all our experiments, we never obtain a good alignment on this class. This class is made of different gesture phases that may not correspond to the same prosodic profile. Their alignment may obey to different synchronisation needs [44]. However, we still find that our validation result is reliable.

In the ablation study (Experiment 3), we replace some features with random values to observe how it affects the model performance. We start by replacing the entire input with random values and use it on the trained model ("Exp 3: Ablation study, All features are randomized", Table 2), we observe that all the alignment scores are lower than in the random output result, except for "Beat" which is 0.040, which only marginally outperforms the random output. Subsequently, when we use the intensity alone ("Exp 3: Ablation study, Using intensity only", Table 2), we find again that the model's alignment scores fail to outperform the random output result. This result does not prove either that it is impossible to learn the gesture timing from the intensity. Our model simply happens to largely ignore the intensity feature, yet it still can predict some classes (as shown in Experiment 2 results). Finally, in the sub-experiment where we only use fundamental frequency "Exp 3: Ablation study, Using F_0 only", Table 2), the alignment scores are similar to what we get when we use all prosody features ("Exp 2: Using neural network with the entire dataset", Table 2). This result suggests that F_0 is tied and is very pertinent to the gesture timing.

In Experiment 5 where we use MFCC instead of the prosody features ("Exp 5: MFCC as input", Table 2), we find that the alignment scores of "Beat", "IdeationalStroke", and "IdeationalOther" outperform the random output. However, the "IdeationalStroke" alignment score is considerably lower than when we use prosody features ("Exp 2: Using neural network with the entire dataset", Table 2). A possible reason is because the MFCC are represented as a 13-dimensional vector while the prosody features are represented as a 3-dimensional vector. The higher dimension makes the search space much larger, and thus making the training slower. Another possible reason is that the MFCC is indeed less informative about stroke timing. Indeed, it has been reported in several studies that F_0/pitch are related to gesture stroke timing [35, 44]. On the validation reliability, we also find that the correlation between the validation alignment scores and on the testing alignment scores of the "Beat" class is close to zero ("Exp 5: MFCC as input", Table 3). This is similar to we when use prosody features ("Exp 2: Using neural network with the entire dataset, Validation reliability", Table 3).

In Experiment 6 where we use both the prosody features and MFCC ("Exp 6: both MFCC and prosody as input", Table 2), the alignment score of the "Beat" falls to 0.000 while the alignment score of "IdeationalOther" increases to 0.362. The alignment score of "Beat", like in Experiments 2 and 5, can be attributed to chance as shown by the almost zero correlation in the validation reliability test ("Exp 6: both MFCC and prosody as input", Table 3). The alignment score of "IdeationalOther", which is still lower than what we get when we use prosody features only, can likely be contributed to the presence of the prosody features, especially the F_0 which we have shown to be pertinent to gesture timing. Although having more features enables the neural network to learn more information, it also makes the search space larger, which in turn makes the search slower.

In Experiment 7 where we train the with one speaker and test it on the other speaker of the same interaction ("Exp 7: trained with one speaker tested on the other", Table 2), we find that the models' alignment scores outperform the random output, which suggests that some generalizability exists even-though people have different gesturing styles. These results may also be due as both speakers are part of the same interaction and conversation participants tend to automatically align to each other, at different levels, such as phonology, syntax and semantics [37], as well as gesture types [45]. These different alignments make the conversation itself successful [18].

In our subjective experiment, we measure the naturalness, time consistency, and semantic consistency of the gestures and speech. We compare the perception by human participants of the animation of the virtual agent where we manipulated the timing of the gestures. It allows measurement of the impact of the timing generated by the neural network against random timing along the 3 qualities: naturalness of the agent gesturing, time consistency of the gesture production and of the speech prosody, and the semantic alignment of both. The random timing acts as the baseline. The idea is similar to what we do in our objective evaluations (Experiments 1 and 2). We find that the timing from the model outperforms the baseline in all measured qualities, and the differences are significant ($p - value < 0.05$). It shows that overall the generated result is perceived better by the human respondents along the 3 qualities. It also shows that gesture timing is important to how well-perceived the gestures are by humans. We keep the gesture shapes from the ground truth in both the output of our model and the baseline, we act only on the timing of the gestures, yet the output of our model is perceived more favourably.

11   Conclusion and Future Work

In this paper we have presented a model to predict where to place gestures based only on the acoustic features. We limit the scope of the problem to only the gesture timing. We use 3 prosodic features as the input, namely the fundamental frequency (F_0), F_0) direction score, and intensity. We also experiment with using Mel-frequency cepstral coefficients (MFCC) as the input. We consider 2 classes of communicative gestures (beats and ideational gestures) and 2 classes of gesture phases (stroke and others). In an experiment we also add eyebrow movements that can have communicative functions, such as being prosodic markers. We conduct several objective studies to evaluate the model as well as a subjective study. Our results show the pertinence of the F_0 to determine gesture timing. We also find that considering eyebrow movements as beat gestures increases the beat prediction accuracy.

However, gesture generation is also tightly linked to what is being said. In the future, our aim is to consider not only the prosody but also the semantics of the speech. The question of representing the semantics arises. We are planning to rely on a higher representation level such as image schema that can be linked to metaphoric gestures [26]. Combining both of semantics and the prosody is a challenge by itself. A big part of the challenge is that aligning meaning, prosody and gestures is far from being a trivial problem. In the future, we intend to go into this direction.

Acknowledgement. This project has received funding from the European Union's Horizon 2020 research and innovation programme under grant agreement No 769553. This result only reflects the authors' views and the European Commission is not responsible for any use that may be made of the information it contains. We thank Katya Saint-Amand for providing the Gest-IS corpus [41].

References

1. Ahuja, C., Morency, L.P.: Language2Pose: natural language grounded pose forecasting. In: 2019 3DV. IEEE (2019)
2. Bahdanau, D., Cho, K., Bengio, Y.: Neural machine translation by jointly learning to align and translate (2014). arXiv preprint: arXiv:1409.0473
3. Bahdanau, D., Chorowski, J., Serdyuk, D., Brakel, P., Bengio, Y.: End-to-end attention-based large vocabulary speech recognition. In: 2016 IEEE ICASSP. IEEE (2016)
4. Baltrusaitis, T., Zadeh, A., Lim, Y.C., Morency, L.P.: Openface 2.0: facial behavior analysis toolkit. In: 2018 13th IEEE FG 2018. IEEE (2018)
5. Bellman, R., Kalaba, R.: On adaptive control processes. IRE Trans. Autom. Control **4**(2), 1–9 (1959)
6. Bergmann, K., Kopp, S.: GNetIc – using bayesian decision networks for iconic gesture generation. In: Ruttkay, Z., Kipp, M., Nijholt, A., Vilhjálmsson, H.H. (eds.) IVA 2009. LNCS (LNAI), vol. 5773, pp. 76–89. Springer, Heidelberg (2009). https://doi.org/10.1007/978-3-642-04380-2_12
7. Biancardi, B., Cafaro, A., Pelachaud, C.: Analyzing first impressions of warmth and competence from observable nonverbal cues in expert-novice interactions. In: Proceedings of the 19th ACM ICMI (2017)
8. Bolinger, D.: Intonation and its Uses. Stanford University Press, Palo Alto (1989)
9. Cassell, J., Vilhjálmsson, H., Bickmore, T.: BEAT: the behavior expression animation toolkit. In: Computer Graphics Proceedings, Annual Conference Series. ACM SIGGRAPH (2001)
10. Chorowski, J.K., Bahdanau, D., Serdyuk, D., Cho, K., Bengio, Y.: Attention-based models for speech recognition. In: Advances in NIPS (2015)
11. Cravotta, A., Busà, M.G., Prieto, P.: Effects of encouraging the use of gestures on speech. J. Speech Lang. Hearing Res. **62**(9), 3204–3219 (2019)
12. Dermouche, S., Pelachaud, C.: Sequence-based multimodal behavior modeling for social agents. In: Proceedings of the 18th ACM ICMI. ACM (2016)
13. Driskell, J.E., Radtke, P.H.: The effect of gesture on speech production and comprehension. Hum. Factors **45**(3), 445–454 (2003)

14. Ekman, P.: About brows: emotional and conversational signals. In: von Cranach, M., Foppa, K., Lepenies, W., Ploog, D. (eds.) Human Ethology: Claims and Limits of A New Discipline: Contributions to The Colloquium, pp. 169–248. Cambridge Uni Press, Cambridge, England; New-York (1979)
15. Eyben, F., Wöllmer, M., Schuller, B.: Opensmile: the Munich versatile and fast open-source audio feature extractor. In: Proceedings of the 18th ACM MM. ACM (2010)
16. Ferstl, Y., Neff, M., McDonnell, R.: Multi-objective adversarial gesture generation. In: Motion, Interaction and Games, pp. 1–10 (2019)
17. Flecha-García, M.L.: Non-verbal communication in dialogue: alignment between eyebrow raises and pitch accents in English. In: Proceedings of the CogSci, vol. 29 (2007)
18. Garrod, S., Pickering, M.J.: Joint action, interactive alignment, and dialog. Topics Cogn. Sci. 1(2), 292–304 (2009)
19. Ginosar, S., Bar, A., Kohavi, G., Chan, C., Owens, A., Malik, J.: Learning individual styles of conversational gesture. In: Proceedings of the IEEE CVPR (2019)
20. Halliday, M.A.K.: Explorations in the Functions of Language. Edward Arnold, London (1973)
21. Hasegawa, D., Kaneko, N., Shirakawa, S., Sakuta, H., Sumi, K.: Evaluation of speech-to-gesture generation using bi-directional LSTM network. In: Proceedings of the 18th ACM IVA. ACM (2018)
22. Hirschberg, J., Pierrehumbert, J.: The intonational structuring of discourse. In: 24th ACL, New-York (1986)
23. Ishii, R., Ahuja, C., Nakano, Y.I., Morency, L.P.: Impact of personality on nonverbal behavior generation. In: Proceedings of the 20th ACM IVA (2020)
24. Ishii, R., Katayama, T., Higashinaka, R., Tomita, J.: Generating body motions using spoken language in dialogue. In: Proceedings of the 18th ACM IVA. ACM (2018)
25. Iverson, J.M., Goldin-Meadow, S.: Why people gesture when they speak. Nature 396(6708), 228 (1998)
26. Johnson, M.: The Body in The Mind: The Bodily Basis of Meaning, Imagination, and Reason. University of Chicago Press, Chicago (2013)
27. Kendon, A.: Gesticulation and speech: two aspects of the. In: The Relationship of Verbal and Nonverbal Communication, vol. 25, p. 207(1980)
28. Krahmer, E., Swerts, M.: More about brows. In: Ruttkay, Z., Pelachaud, C. (eds.) From Brows till Trust: Evaluating Embodied Conversational Agents. Kluwer (2004)
29. Krahmer, E., Swerts, M.: The effects of visual beats on prosodic prominence: acoustic analyses, auditory perception and visual perception. J. Mem. Lang. 57(3), 396–414 (2007)
30. Kucherenko, T., Hasegawa, D., Henter, G.E., Kaneko, N., Kjellström, H.: Analyzing input and output representations for speech-driven gesture generation. In: Proceedings of the 19th ACM IVA (2019)
31. Kucherenko, T., et al.: Gesticulator: a framework for semantically-aware speech-driven gesture generation. In: Proceedings of the 2020 ICMI (2020)
32. Lee, J., Marsella, S.: Nonverbal behavior generator for embodied conversational agents. In: Gratch, J., Young, M., Aylett, R., Ballin, D., Olivier, P. (eds.) IVA 2006. LNCS (LNAI), vol. 4133, pp. 243–255. Springer, Heidelberg (2006). https://doi.org/10.1007/11821830_20
33. Levitan, R., Hirschberg, J.: Measuring acoustic-prosodic entrainment with respect to multiple levels and dimensions. In: 12th Annual Conference of the ISCA (2011)

34. Loehr, D.P.: Temporal, structural, and pragmatic synchrony between intonation and gesture. Lab. Phonol. **3**(1), 71–89 (2012)
35. Lücking, A., Mehler, A., Walther, D., Mauri, M., Kurfürst, D.: Finding recurrent features of image schema gestures: the figure corpus. In: Proceedings of the Tenth LREC (2016)
36. McNeill, D.: Hand and Mind: What Gestures Reveal About Thought. University of Chicago press, Chicago (1992)
37. Menenti, L., Garrod, S., Pickering, M.: Toward a neural basis of interactive alignment in conversation. Front. Hum. Neurosci. **6**, 185 (2012)
38. Mikolov, T., Sutskever, I., Chen, K., Corrado, G.S., Dean, J.: Distributed representations of words and phrases and their compositionality. In: Advances in NIPS (2013)
39. Nihei, F., Nakano, Y., Higashinaka, R., Ishii, R.: Determining iconic gesture forms based on entity image representation. In: 2019 ICMI (2019)
40. Peshkov, K., Prévot, L., Bertrand, R.: Prosodic phrasing evaluation: measures and tools. In: Proceedings of TRASP 2013 (2013)
41. Saint-Amand, K.: Gest-is: multi-lingual corpus of gesture and information structure (2018). (Unpublished Report)
42. Sutskever, I., Vinyals, O., Le, Q.V.: Sequence to sequence learning with neural networks. In: Advances in NIPS (2014)
43. Swerts, M., Krahmer, E.: Visual prosody of newsreaders: effects of information structure, emotional content and intended audience on facial expressions. J. Phon. **38**(2), 197–206 (2010)
44. Wagner, P., Malisz, Z., Kopp, S.: Gesture and speech in interaction: an overview. Speech Commun. **57**, 209–232 (2014)
45. Wessler, J., Hansen, J.: Temporal closeness promotes imitation of meaningful gestures in face-to-face communication. J. Nonverbal Behav. **41**(4), 415–431 (2017)
46. Yasinnik, Y., Renwick, M., Shattuck-Hufnagel, S.: The timing of speech-accompanying gestures with respect to prosody. In: Proceedings of the International Conference: From Sound to Sense, vol. 50. Citeseer (2004)
47. Yunus, F., Clavel, C., Pelachaud, C.: Gesture class prediction by recurrent neural network and attention mechanism. In: Proceedings of the 19th ACM IVA (2019)

Author Index

Printed in the United States
by Baker & Taylor Publisher Services

Printed in the United States
by Baker & Taylor Publisher Services